BLACK WOMEN'S BLUES

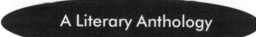

A Literary Anthology

1934–1988

BLACK WOMEN'S BLUES

A Literary Anthology

1934–1988

Rita B. Dandridge

G.K. HALL & CO.
New York

MAXWELL MACMILLAN CANADA
Toronto

MAXWELL MACMILLAN INTERNATIONAL
New York Oxford Singapore Sydney

G. K. Hall & Co.
Simon & Schuster Macmillan
1633 Broadway
New York, NY 10019-6785

Library of Congress Catalog Card Number: 92-19728

Printed in the United States of America

printing number
   2   3   4   5   6   7   8   9   10

Library of Congress Cataloging-in-Publication Data

Dandridge, Rita B.
   Black women's blues : a literary anthology, 1934-1988 / Rita B.
Dandridge.
      p.   cm.
   ISBN 0-8161-9084-4
   1. American literature—Afro-American authors.   2. American
literature—Women authors.   3. American literature—19th century.
4. Afro-American women—Literary collections.   I. Title.
PS508.N3D25   1992
810.8'0352042—dc20   92-19728
                                                      CIP

The paper used in this publication meets the minimum requirements of American National Standard for Information Sciences—Permanence of Paper for Printed Library Materials. ANSI Z39.48-1984. ⊚™

Contents

Contents

Contents

PART 3

BLACK WOMEN AND THE BLACK FEMINIST MOVEMENT   233

Contents

Acknowledgments

To friends who aided me in this endeavor, I wish to extend a hearty thanks: Michele Wallace, who provided me with a network for tracking down little-known contributors; James L. Hill, who shared his blues materials on black women blues singers; Ann Allen Shockley, who found information on Marian Minus and who recommended me for this project to her editor at G.K. Hall.

I also offer thanks to Henry L. Albritton, Odessa Baker, Nell Barnes, Cheryl Clarke, William Cloud, Arthenia J. Bates Millican, Ruth A. Perry, Sonia Sanchez, and Barbara Smith, who offered words of kindness and encouragement; Hazel Blunt, who promptly filled my numerous interlibrary loan requests at Norfolk State University; and Esme E. Bhan, who steered me to the Works Progress Administration (WPA) Collection in the Moorland-Spingarn Research Center at Howard University.

In addition, I thank Leslie V. Ripley, a former G.K. Hall editor, who initiated this project; Elizabeth Holthaus, who became my editor and kept this project alive; and Henriette Campagne, editor, and India Koopman, development editor, who helped to dispel my blues.

Acknowledgments

Daisy Bates, "The Volcano of Hate Erupts," from *The Long Shadow of Little Rock*, Copyright © 1962 by Daisy Bates. Reprinted by permission of David McKay Co., a division of Random House.

Frances Beal, "Double Jeopardy: To Be Black and Female," Copyright © 1969 by Frances Beal. Reprinted from *Sisterhood Is Powerful: An Anthology of Writings from the Women's Liberation Movement*, ed. Robin Morgan (1970), by permission of Random House.

Marita Bonner, "Patch Quilt," *The Crisis* 47 (March 1940). Reprinted by permission of *The Crisis*.

Gwendolyn Brooks, "If You're Light and Have Long Hair," from *Maud Martha*, copyright 1953 by Gwendolyn Brooks, Copyright © renewed 1987 by Gwendolyn Brooks, reprinted in Brooks, *Blacks* (Chicago: David Co., 1987); reprinted by permission of the author. "To Those of My Sisters Who Kept Their Naturals," Copyright © 1987 by Gwendolyn Brooks, reprinted in Brooks, *Blacks*. Reprinted by permission of the author.

Shirley Chisholm, "Facing the Abortion Question," from *Unbought and Unbossed*, Copyright © 1970 by Shirley Chisholm (Boston: Houghton Mifflin). Reprinted by permission of the author.

Angela Davis, excerpt from part 4, from *Angela Davis: An Autobiography*. Copyright © 1974, 1988 (New York: Random House, 1974). Reprinted by permission of Angela Y. Davis.

Porter Grainger and Everett Robbins, "'Tain't Nobody's Biz-ness If I Do," words and music by Porter Grainger and Everett Robbins, Copyright 1922 by MCA Music Publishing, a division of MCA, Inc.; Copyright renewed and assigned to MCA Music Publishing, a division of MCA, Inc., Copyright 1950 by MCA Music Publishing, a division of MCA, 1755 Broadway, New York, N.Y. 10019. Reprinted with permission from MCA Music Publishing, a division of MCA, Inc. All rights reserved.

Jacquelyn Grant, "Black Theology and the Black Woman," from *Black Theology: A Documentary History 1966–1979*, ed. Gayraud S. Wilmore and James H. Cone, Copyright © 1979 by Jacquelyn Grant. Reprinted by permission of Orbis Books, Maryknoll, N.Y.

Bell Hooks, "Sisterhood: Political Solidarity between Women," from *Feminist Theory from Margin to Center*, Copyright © 1984 by Bell Hooks. Reprinted with permission of South End Press, 116 St. Botolph Street, Boston, Mass. 02115.

Zora Neale Hurston, chapter 6 from *Their Eyes Were Watching God*, Copyright 1937 by J. B. Lippincott Co.; Copyright © renewed 1965 by John C. Hurston and Joel Hurston. Reprinted by permission of Harper & Row, Publishers, Inc.

Audre Lorde, "I Am Your Sister: Black Women Organizing across Sexualities," from *A Burst of Light*, Copyright © 1988 by Audre Lorde. Reprinted by permission of Firebrand Books, Ithaca, N.Y.

Deborah E. McDowell, "New Directions for Black Feminist Criticism," from *Black American Literature Forum* 14 (Winter 1980), Copyright © 1980 by Indiana State University. Reprinted with permission of the author and *Black American Literature Forum.*

Arthenia J. Bates Millican, "chapter 51," from *The Deity Nodded,* Copyright © 1973 by Arthenia Bates (Detroit: Harlo). Reprinted by permission of the author.

Marian Minus, "Girl, Colored," *The Crisis* 47 (September 1940). Reprinted by permission of *The Crisis.*

Anne Moody, chapter 2 from *Coming of Age in Mississippi,* Copyright © 1969 by Anne Moody. Reprinted by permission of Doubleday, a division of Bantam Doubleday Dell Publishing Group, Inc.

Toni Morrison, excerpt from "Winter" from *The Bluest Eye,* Copyright © 1970 by Toni Morrison. Reprinted by permission of Henry Holt and Company.

Gloria Naylor, "Kiswana Browne," from *The Women of Brewster Place,* Copyright © 1983 by Gloria Naylor. All rights reserved. Reprinted by permission of Viking Penguin, a division of Penguin Books USA, Inc. and Hodder & Stoughton Limited.

Ann Petry, excerpt from chapter 18, from *The Street,* Copyright 1946 by Ann Petry. Reprinted by permission of Houghton Mifflin Co.

Crystal V. Rhodes, *The Trip,* Copyright © 1981 by Crystal V. Rhodes. Reprinted with permission of author.

Faith Ringgold, excerpt from "Being My Own Woman," Copyright © 1983 by Faith Ringgold. Reprinted with permission of author.

Carolyn Rodgers, "I Have Been Hungry," from *How I Got Ovah,* Copyright © 1975 by Carolyn Rodgers. Reprinted by permission of Doubleday, a division of Bantam Doubleday Dell Publishing Group, Inc.

Sonia Sanchez, *Uh, Uh; But How Do It Free Us?,* Copyright © 1974 by Sonia Sanchez. Reprinted by permission of the author.

Ann Allen Shockley, "Is She Relevant?" *Black World* 2 (January 1971), Copyright © 1971 by Ann Allen Shockley; reprinted by permission of the author. "To Be a Man," *Negro Digest* 18 (July 1969), Copyright © 1969 by Ann Allen Shockley; reprinted by permission of the author.

Bessie Smith, "In the House Blues," Copyright 1931 by Bessie Smith; Copyright © renewed 1958 by Jack Gee.

Alice Walker, "Battle Fatigue," from *Meridian,* Copyright © 1976 by Alice Walker; reprinted by permission of Harcourt Brace Jovanovich, Inc. and the Wendy Weil Agency, Inc. "The Revenge of Hannah Kemhuff," from *In Love and Trouble; Stories of Black Women,* Copyright © 1973 by Alice Walker; reprinted by permission of Harcourt Brace Jovanovich, Inc. and the Wendy Weil Agency, Inc.

Margaret Walker, "On Being Female, Black and Free," Copyright © 1980 by Margaret Walker, from *The Writer and Her Work,* ed. Janet Sternburg. Reprinted by permission of W. W. Norton and Company, Inc. and W.B. Agency.

Michele Wallace, "Anger in Isolation: A Black Feminist's Search for Sisterhood," *Village Voice* (28 July 1975), Copyright © 1975 by Michele Wallace. Reprinted with permission of *Village Voice.*

Acknowledgments

Dorothy West, "Mammy," *Opportunity* 18 (October 1940). Reprinted with permission of *Opportunity*.

J. M. Williams and Ida Cox, "Oh! The Blues Ain't Nothin' Else But," Copyright 1924 by Chicago Music Publishing Co.

Works Progress Administration Collection. WPA Box 119–6, folders 87–91. Letters reprinted with permission of Manuscript Division, Moorland-Spingarn Research Center, Howard University, Washington, D.C.

Introduction

Elizabeth Fox-Genovese has observed that "the autobiographies of black women, each necessarily personal and unique," at the same time "constitute a running commentary on the collective experience of black women in the United States. They are inescapably grounded in slavery and the literary tradition of slave narratives."[1] Although only a few of the works presented here are autobiographies in the strictest sense, all of them are autobiographical in that they speak directly from and to the life experiences of black American women, giving testament to a history that is uniquely theirs. As such they belong to the "running commentary" Fox-Genovese describes.

The book is organized chronologically around those twentieth-century events whose effect on black American women has been most pronounced—the Depression, the civil rights and black power movements, and the black feminist movement; part 1 focuses on the 1930s and 1940s, part 2 on the 1950s, 1960s, and early 1970s, and part 3 on the 1970s and early 1980s. Because my intent is to convey something of the quality of life of black women rather than to track the literary development of black women writers, the selections have been arranged by the time periods they concern themselves with, not the time in which they were written. The excerpt from Toni Morrison's 1970 novel *The Bluest Eye,* for instance, is presented in part 1 as a Depression piece because the story takes place during the 1930s.

The selections are further organized around several themes dominant in the lives of black women during each time period. These themes are quite broad and fairly simple. During the Depression and war years black women encountered racism, sexism, and intraracial prejudice. From the 1950s through the early 1970s they fought against racism and sexism; in addition, black mothers and daughters were often in conflict during these pivotal years. In the 1970s and early 1980s black women searched for sisterhood and self-definition, and they demanded accountability from the prevailing culture. Focusing on these themes enables us to trace not only the problems that have been black women's social, psychological, and political heritage but the patterns of their responses to those problems.

Mary Helen Washington, editor of the anthology *Black-Eyed Susans, Midnight Birds: Stories by and about Black Women* (1990), has identified in African-American literature written by women three interrelated psychological cycles that reflect "the experiences of black women as a series of movements from a woman totally victimized by society and by men to a growing, developing woman whose consciousness allows her to have some control over her life." Black women who are products of the nineteenth century and the early decades of this century have often not progressed beyond the first cycle, *suspension*. Victimized by racial and sexual oppression, they have limited choices in life and are often defeated by social and historical circumstance. The second cycle, *assimilation*, characterizes women who came of age in the 1940s, 1950s, and early 1960s. Washington describes them as having had "greater potential for shaping their lives," but they are "still thwarted because they feel themselves coming to life before the necessary changes have been made in their political environment." The third cycle, *emergence*, is available to women affected by the political climate of the 1960s and the various changes stemming from the civil rights, black power, and feminist movements. These women are "coming just to the edge of a new awareness and making the first tentative steps into an uncharted region." They create new options for themselves by researching their cultural roots and traditions and by "re-examining their relationship to the black community."[2] I have adapted these cycles to serve as a paradigm for this anthology.

Many of the women depicted in part 1 are in Washington's state of suspension, victims not only of racism and sexism but of the general impoverishment of the times. Their lives are characterized by frustration, immobility, a sense of entrapment, and seemingly insoluble problems. Black women of the Depression era were only a generation removed from slavery; no longer slaves by law, they often remained slaves to circumstance. In Chicago some were "so desperate for employment that they actually offered their services at the so-called 'slave markets'— street corners where Negro women congregated to await housewives who came daily to take their pick and bid wages down."[3] In the years before World War II a full 70 percent of working black women were employed as domestics.[4] The readings in part 1 illustrate the pain black women suffered in being denied both work and government assistance because of their color, being exploited and abused because of their sex, and being psychically wounded by the general view that light skin was superior to dark, that a fair-skinned African-American woman was more desirable and attractive than a woman of deep brown color. These women experience fear, desperation, shame, rage; in large part they struggle not to express these emotions but to contain them. Many of the women in part 1 are noticeably silent; their fear of the consequences of expression is overpowering and certainly not unfounded. When some of them do unleash their feelings, as in Ann Petry's *The Street* (1946), Marita Bonner's "Patch Quilt" (1940), and Alice Walker's "The Revenge of Hannah Kemhuff" (1973), it is usually after a long period of interior struggle. Even then the result is not deliverance but worse trouble, or retribution come too late to make positive difference in their lives.

This is not the case with the women in part 2. In the charged political climate of the civil rights and black power movements the struggle changed from containing emotion to expressing it, acting on it, learning to confront—in Mary Helen Washington's term, assimilating, assuming one's rightful place in society. Promoting nonviolence to achieve racial harmony, the civil rights movement emphasized the dismantling of the barriers of racial segregation. Black women made great strides in education, housing, and employment as they tried to overcome a history of social deprivation and enter an era of racial progress. Despite the assimilationist nature of their efforts, however, society was not always ready for black women's assertiveness. Many were physically attacked by white racists. Neither was society ready for the women who championed the black power movement, which called for greater self-government in the black community, celebrated an African heritage, and emphasized race pride and black unity. Black women encountered sexism from black men and overprotectiveness from their mothers. The readings in part 2 depict black women's participation in the fight against racism by sitting at segregated lunch counters, driving children to segregated schools, and rallying blacks to peaceful protests, their struggle against sexism in the civil rights and black power movements, and the conflict between a generation of young black women eager for change and their resistant mothers.

In part 3 the nature of the struggle shifts again: black women emerged—again using Washington's term—from the fight for their right to a place in the world to a realization that they needed to define that place. In the 1970s and early 1980s the black feminist movement encouraged self-examination, attempted to stabilize the black community in the face of ongoing racism, and gave black women a greater voice in the issues that concerned them as women. Black feminists examined their relationships with themselves, with other black women, and with black men, and tackled certain preeminent issues: self-determination, abortion rights, the role of women in the black church, and heterosexuality. The selections in part 3 explore the nature and value of female friendship and political solidarity, articulate the search for individual identity and for the identity of the black feminist movement, and address the social and political issues pertinent to black women. The black women in these readings deal with the problems they have inherited by virtue of their race and sex with a tremendous mindfulness of their position as *black women*. Mae Gwendolyn Henderson describes Janie Crawford, the heroine of Zora Neale Hurston's classic *Their Eyes Were Watching God* (1937), as having progressed "from voicelessness to voice, from silence to tongues."[5] This description can be aptly applied to the various women in this volume.

Covering a wide range of expression and experience, the selections are drawn from many genres—letters, short stories, poems, drama, essays, novels and autobiographies. (I have chosen novel excerpts with extreme care so as not to violate the integrity of the work.) Represented are both acclaimed writers and women for whom composing a letter was a difficult task. In part 1 powerfully eloquent letters written by destitute black women to government officials appear alongside a story by the celebrated writer Alice Walker. In part 3 a poem by Gwendolyn Brooks celebrates the black woman establishing her own definition of beauty, and an essay by Deborah McDowell explores the ongoing struggle of black feminist critics to articulate their own "aesthetic," to define the literary territory of the African-American writer. All the readings have been selected and positioned in this manner so as to play off and complement one another, each contributing to a fuller, more considered portrait of black women's collective experience in the twentieth century. The writings coalesce to form what might be called black women's blues, representing, as do the blues, both the pain of the struggle and the need to tell of it.

NOTES

1. Elizabeth Fox-Genovese, "My Statue, My Self: Autobiographical Writings of Afro-American Women," in *Reading Black, Reading Feminist: A Critical Anthology,* ed. Henry Louis Gates, Jr. (New York: Meridian, 1990), 178–79.

2. Mary Helen Washington, "Teaching *Black-Eyed Susans:* An Approach to the Study of Black Women Writers," *Black American Literature Forum* 11 (Spring 1977): 22–24.

3. St. Clair Drake, *Black Metropolis: A Study of Life in a Northern City* (New York: Harcourt, Brace, 1945), 246.

4. William Henry Chafe, *The American Woman: Her Changing Social, Economic, and Political Roles, 1920–1970* (New York: Oxford University Press, 1972), 142.

5. Mae Gwendolyn Henderson, "Speaking in Tongues: Dialogics, Dialectics, and the Black Woman Writer's Literary Tradition," in Gates, *Reading Black, Reading Feminist*, 124.

PART 1

Black Women, the Depression,
and the 1940s

Oh Papa, Papa, Papa, Mama's done gone mad;
Oh Papa, Papa, Papa, Mama's done gone mad;
Oh, the blues ain't nothin' but a good woman feelin' bad.
                    —J. M. Williams and Ida Cox
                        Oh! The Blues Ain't Nothin'
                        Else But

Black Women and Racism

• • • • •

"By the time Mom and I had got together and found us a place of our own in Harlem," recalled Billie Holiday, "the Depression was on. A depression was nothing new to us, we'd always had it. The only thing new about it was the bread lines. And they were about the only thing we missed."[1]

The precarious economic position of the many black women like Billie Holiday already suffering hard times during the Depression years and those that followed—the 1930s and 1940s—was a vestige of slavery. As slaves, black women had been regarded by their owners as "profitable labor units."[2] Joel Kovel captures the slave master's thoughts about the African-American woman:

> Your body shall serve me in many ways: by work on my capitalist plantations to extract the most that can be taken from the land in the cheapest and therefore most rational manner; as a means to my bodily pleasure—both as nurse to my children and as female body for sexual use (for my own women are somehow deficient in this regard); and as a medium of exchange, salable like any other commodity of exchange along with or separate from the bodies of your family.[3]

Slave owners made every effort to get the best "return" on their "investment." They made sure that the "breeders" bore children "as often as biologically possible,"[4] and that these women returned to the fields soon after the birth of their children. Girls were sent to the fields as

3

well, and children too young for such work were made to help out elsewhere. At four, Elizabeth Keckley was told to babysit her mistress's baby and was then severely flogged when she accidentally overturned the cradle.[5] Female slaves worked in coal mines and iron foundries, where they were used as beasts of burden to pull trams. And they worked alongside men as lumberjacks and ditchdiggers.[6]

After slavery was abolished a small percentage of black women managed to enter various professions, primarily teaching, but most continued to labor at menial tasks. Their generally poor position in the labor force during the 1930s and 1940s perpetuated the assumptions of the slave system that black women's bodies should be used to benefit whites economically, and that blacks in general were "unsuited for all branches of industry which require the slightest care, forethought, or dexterity."[7] Nowhere are the consequences of these assumptions more painfully exposed than in the letters of ex-slave women to government officials during the 1930s. Having worked as menials all of their lives, they had no means of support in their old age. In 1935 a 100-year-old ex-slave wrote Pres. Franklin Delano Roosevelt that she "was turned a lose [from slavery] with nothin.'"[8] She begged him for help; she was too old to work, and her only provider, a daughter, had had a stroke. In 1936 another ex-slave wrote to Eleanor Roosevelt, "I can't get anything to eat. I am almost starved to death."[9]

Although most black women who worked during the Depression were domestics, these jobs were not easy to come by, and the work involved could be equated to slave labor. White women expected their hired help "to scrub floors on her bended knees, to hang precariously from window sills, cleaning window after window, or to strain and sweat over steaming tubs of heavy blankets, spreads, and furniture covers. The slavelike bond between many black domestics and white employers was formed from the very beginning of their association; accounts indicate that it was not unusual to see black women gathered on street corners in the Bronx to await white women who came "to buy their strength and energy for an hour, two hours, or even a day at the munificent rate of fifteen, twenty, twenty-five, or if luck be with them, thirty cents an hour."[10] That they could be had so cheaply can be attributed in part to the government's laissez-faire attitude toward black women's work and to the legacy of slavery. The 1935 Social Security Act did not make provisions for domestic workers, who were also excluded from other social legislation on minimum wages and health and employment benefits.

In addition to the hard work, low pay, and lack of benefits, black women were often mistreated by white women. Bettina Aptheker comments on the dynamic between them:

The ornamental role of upper- and middle-class white women reduced them, in fact, to a nonhuman existence. Regarded as mere objects of male pleasure and a demonstration of male wealth, they frequently treated their servants with cruel and capricious contempt in a pathetic effort to reclaim some semblance of their own dignity and worth. In this way, their upper-class bias and racist bigotry were combined with their actual degradation, to pit woman against woman in a vicious cycle of subjugation that left Black women battered and impoverished.[11]

Black women's fiction depicts this destructive relationship between black and white women. Marian Minus's "Girl, Colored" reveals the contempt of a white woman for the young black woman she coerces into accepting a job as a maid for little pay and practically no time off. In Alice Walker's "The Revenge of Hannah Kemhuff," a white government relief agent abuses her power over a starving black mother and her family by denying them food stamps because they are neatly dressed in white folks' cast-off clothes.

Such discrimination in the distribution of assistance was common in President Roosevelt's New Deal programs, which were instituted from 1933 until 1939 to produce immediate economic relief and various reforms in industry, agriculture, labor, and housing. The Works Progress Administration (WPA) and the Civilian Conservation Corps (CCC) were created to give emergency governmental aid and provide employment in the construction of buildings, bridges, and public roads, and tasks for youth in the conservation and development of national resources. The National Recovery Administration (NRA) formulated industrial codes that governed employees' wages and hours, child labor, and collective bargaining. The Public Works Administration (PWS) provided public jobs for the needy, and the Civil Works Administration (CWA), a temporary relief program, hired approximately four million people for emergency projects. Social security measures were enacted in 1935 and 1939 to provide unemployment compensation, disability insurance, and benefits to widows and the aged.

In May 1935, 3 million of the 18 million Americans on relief were blacks. President Roosevelt, according to historian Benjamin Quarles, "did not design his program with the Negro in mind (the New Deal actually had no fixed policy toward the Negro), but he was opposed to any racial discrimination implementing it."[12] Nevertheless, many of the local officials who dispersed the aid practiced discrimination openly. According to black women's letters to the federal government, local officials coerced them into accepting menial jobs that paid less than government-regulated allocations; assigned poorly clad black women to outdoor work in inclement weather, thus making them susceptible to tuberculosis and bronchitis; deliberately kept black women off the relief rolls to provide more aid to white women; assigned work to black women but none to their unemployed husbands; encouraged elderly black women to give up their few possessions and work on county farms; and forced black women with as many as eight dependents to accept jobs that netted only $13 a month after paying for lunch and carfare.[13]

World War II brought economic relief to some black women who went to work in war factories. But the war and the 1940s brought additional problems with food shortages, rationing, and breadlines. The benefits of President Roosevelt's 1941 proclamation ordering equal employment opportunities were counterbalanced by the dismantling of the WPA in 1943, cutting off the support it had lent to the black aged and infirmed. Black women workers continued to receive wages below those of their white female counterparts and endured segregation in the workplace, schools, theaters, churches, recreational centers, restaurants, and public conveyances. And after death, they continued to be buried in segregated cemeteries.

NOTES

1. Billie Holiday with William Duffy, *Lady Sings the Blues* (1956; reprint, New York: Penguin, 1984), 32.
2. Angela Davis, *Women, Race, and Class* (New York: Random House, 1981), 5.
3. Joel Kovel, *White Racism: A Psychohistory* (New York: Pantheon, 1970), 18–19.
4. Davis, *Women, Race, and Class*, 8.
5. Elizabeth Keckley, *Behind the Scenes: Thirty Years a Slave and Four Years in the White House* (1868; reprint, Salem, N.H.: Ayer, 1985), 19–20.
6. Robert S. Starobin, *Industrial Slavery in the Old South* (New York: Oxford University Press, 1970), 165–66.
7. John E. Cairnes, *The Slave Power: Its Character, Career, and Probable Designs,* 2d ed. (New York: Augustus M. Kelley, 1968), 46.
8. Mariah Wood, letter to Franklin Delano Roosevelt, 9 June 1935, Works Progress Administration Collection, Moorland-Spingarn Research Center, Howard University, Washington, D.C.; reprinted in this volume.
9. Eliza Washington, letter to Mrs. Franklin Delano Roosevelt, 3 February 1936, WPA Collection.
10. Ella Baker and Marvel Cooke, "The Bronx Slave Market," *The Crisis* 42 (November 1935): 330–31.
11. Bettina Aptheker, *Woman's Legacy* (Amherst: University of Massachusetts Press, 1982), 116.
12. Benjamin Quarles, *The Negro in the Making of America* (New York: Macmillan, 1969), 209.
13. See WPA Collection.

• • • • •

Letters of the Depression

From the Works Progress Administration Collection, Howard University

These letters written to Pres. Franklin D. Roosevelt, his wife Eleanor, and federal relief administrators tell firsthand of the plight of black women who struggled with old age, ill health, poverty, and racism during the Depression era. Of the 626 letters in Howard University's collection, 80 percent were written by black women. Some wrote to Washington for help several times. In searching the WPA files in Washington, D.C., I found no evidence that those letters were answered.

15 December 1934

Dear Administrator:

I write to you all again for help. I wrote to the Tower building[1] like you told me and they answered my letter and told me that they cant put me on the relief. They sent my Administrator and he told me that they could not put me on relief, they was to lay them off what they got on it and told me they was fixing a place on the County farm for all of them they got on the relief. So I told him I would not like to go to the County farm and asked him what I do with my things. He told me to sell them.

So I am asking you cant you all do something for me? I have redish in [registered for] every thing and they have taken my name in everything, in the PWA, CWA, NRA, and havn't give me anything. If it is anybody needs help it is me. As long as I have been trying to get on I think you all orter give me something one time any way. I would thank you all for it. If I did not need it I wouldn't ask for it. Xmas is near and I aint got nothing. Aint got everyday clothes either shoes.

Mary Ramsey
Near the Sylum on the
Canton Road
Route 3, Box 17
Jackson, Mississippi

ca. May 1935

Dear Mrs. Roosevelt:

I guess you will be surprise to hear from some one that you don't know anything about, but I have come to you begging for help if it is nothing but some old clothes. I lost one of my sons, was sick for a year and he died with tuberculosis. I had to burn most of my bedding. I have seven in the family, no clothes, trying to farm and nothing to farm with. Big Doctor bill and funeral bill to pay. I am a widow and this child I lost was one of my only help. I went to the *relief* for help, but they said that they couldn't help no one but them that they gave work. I have no one to work. I have a note due on my mule thirty dollars. I am looking for them to come and take her any time, if they can be anything done for me. I would thank you so many times. I will be waiting for a reply. From an unknown woman (colored)

Mrs. Lillie Brenton
Route 1, Box 165
Groveland, Georgia

2 May 1935

Honorable Franklin D. Roosevelt
President of United States
Washington, D.C.

Dear Mr. President:

We understand from the radio speech delivered by you on Sunday night, April 28, 1935 concerning the Relief Administration that if anything is done to the people unfairly to write to you about it.

We, the colored women workers here in New Orleans, feel that we are not being treated fairly. Most of us are working in our husbands' places, having him and our children to support, pay house rent, feed and clothe the children, and pay other bills. The most a woman worker can earn a month, the way the work is planned for us here, is twenty dollars and forty cents ($20.40) without any help from the visitors [officials from FERA, the Federal Emergency Relief Administration]. After carfare and lunch money have been taken out there is left only about thirteen dollars ($13.00) to run a home with a husband and five or six children.

Mr. President, you know that no family of five or six or seven or even two can live on an income of seventy-five cents a day, and the worker probably not making the whole month.

Instead of the executive trying to help the poor poverty-stricken women, they are seemingly trying to starve them out. We have been cut twice, and the poor workers have had one riot and are threatening another because they are being driven to their work like oxen. At some times the women are not allowed to remain in the comfort stations without being disturbed by the floor walkers [supervisors]. We are sure if some step is not taken to better the conditions of the colored women down here, much blood will be shed as they have become desperate in some instances. We are asking you to please look into this matter.

Most of the women would prefer to do private work or work for private business houses rather than get relief. But the trouble is that the work is not open for the women to get jobs.

You will notice, Mr. President, that this letter is not signed with individual names. That is because we do not wish to be fired. In one instance, when a worker made a complaint against a group here in the city, the floor walker stated that if she knew who had made it, she would fire that person. And since we have no other means of support other than what we get from FERA, we would not care to have this happen. However, all the facts are authentic.

Hoping that you will give this matter your careful attention. We remain,

> Respectfully yours,
> The FERA Colored Women Workers
> New Orleans, Louisiana

3 May 1935

Mrs. President and Mr. President:

I am riting to you, first, as I am sick and need a doctor's treatment. I went to the relief office, and they say that there was nothing they could do for they did not have no money to get no doctor for me; that I was not able to work. All they give me is weekly orders for commodities, and that is only canned stuff and part of the time they say they don't have that when I go after it, and some weeks give me. They will give me a $1.35, and some weeks $1.00 and some weeks nothin, and I about naked, and I can't get them to give me nothin, not even every day dresses, and I can stand around, the commodity store, and the white lady get from two to three dresses at a time, first I am black and 56 years too, and I think they think I can go naked. And I beg the relief for a matress and they want give me a comfort or matress, only that I can stuff so I wish you would please give me some aid at once, as I am greatly in need. I don't hardly have bread and nothin to pay house rent. So if you can help, I would be glad. . . . I would be glad to get old age pension for I don't have no help at all so please answer at once.

Ella Capell
Jasper, Alabama

9 June 1935

Dear President
Dear Sir:

To you and the Government, few instructions to you to advise me. I learn that you was helping all old ages of peoples. So I am one who are in a needy help. My age is 100, I was hire in the civil war doing all the slave time, and I was serve through slave, and I was turned a lose with nothing. I have give my age in to many people, but I don't know how they have been turn in to the order of yours, as the begiving. So you find my record any where, Our Lumbrge Country and many other country where I have been, serve. So I have no income at all, is near to my recommending. My husband been dead some 40 or 45 years. I am old, I can't kept it remember. I give it to you near as I can. I am with my baby child, and she are in bad health now. She have been in bad health for some 3 years. . . . Please if you can help me in my old age, if it is so I will preciate it great honor. I am old, and can't not work any at all. Can't do anything to make a living. I staying with my baby child which is a girl, she been looking after me all of her life, she is the only one have stuck to me. Please sir, advise me if any good you can do for me. I am colored.

From *Mariah Wood (Mrs.)*
Route 4, Box 32
Keysville, Virginia

12 February 1936

Washington, D.C.
Mr. F. D. Roosevelt

Dear Mr. President:

I am writing to you for help and to tell you how we are treated down here in Corinth, Mississippi they are doing every thing they can to keep from giving us Negroes anything at all, the money you send down here for the relief, we dont get it, if you please send some one down here and see how they are doing us. They have taken the women out on landscaping in this cold weather we cannot stand this outside work like men. They let all the white women stay inside the sewing room put us Negroes out with shovels to dig like men because we dont go in the snow they have taken our card and tell us we are cut off from the relief and wont give us nothing to eat nothing wear no coal to burn.

They promise to give us twenty two dollars a month $22.00. I have not worked since November. That when they put us out in the cold the last of November and I am not able to use a big shovel and out in cold like they try to make us do. They drive us Negroes about like we are cows and horses You will learn for yourself, Mr. President if you just send some one down here and see. They wont pay me all what they owe me they just give $11.00 and wont give the other $11.00 and wont let me work at the sewing room out of the cold till it get worm. they know we cant get anything unless they give it to us. Most all the white women get everything [they] want and got some one to help them along but we cannot ask them any thing if we do they [ask] us to stay away from them. My case No. is 3390-R please answer soon.

Elizabeth Mitchell
P. O. Box 185
Corinth, Mississippi

15 September 1936

Mr. President
Dear Sir:

My name is Eulalia Foster, am colored and am 52 yrs. and 8 mos. old. I were working on the WPA until Monday, Sept. 14th and them were cut off for the simple reason of not taking a job that pay three $3.00 or four $4.00 a week. I have a little granddaughter 8 yrs. old and my father near 90 yrs old to take care of, and how in the world could I support them and myself on such little money, a week? I were working on the sewing project 2189 at the Hartshorn College,[2] in Richmond, Va. and my card had gotten so dilapidated, I stopped by the office where the cards are given and asked for a new card. And the gentleman in there told me that I didnt need a card, what I needed was a place to cook if I knew how. And I told him that I wasnt looking for a job as I had one. Then he said if I couldnt cook, he would give me a job to do something else. I just

11

couldnt tell him a thing. Well, I am a woman of a very few words and I were treated just maybe a little better than some dogs are. He asked about my health and I told him that I couldnt stand very much heat since I have sinus trouble. My teeth are very bad and they have put me in bad health. I have had all taken out except nine, and I were expecting to have the rest or nearly all taken out the next pay day. I couldnt explain any thing at all. He just simply wouldnt listen. And cut me right off saying that I refused to do what he told me. And that I did not want to work. I have been on that ever since last Sept. And only lost a few days.

I guess you can understand why I wouldnt want less than what I were getting. We are getting $35.00 a month and were cut to $31.00 and now am barefooted, I mean my feet is right on the ground. With no help whatever. I know I can do something worth more than 3 or 4 dollars a week. I have never had any of my sewing come back for correction.

I am a seamstress by trade, although I have done housework. But that was 12 years ago since I did any laundering or private work, and only then when my sewing was slow coming in. I have read a good deal about you and I heard the broadcast from Washington on the WPA and that is why I am writing.

Will you or can you please do something for me? I am cut off just in a time of dire need. Will you see that I get something to do? please or see that something is done for me, please.

Most everything I had got burned up including some clothing all the shoes I had worth anything and my bed and bed clothing. I am only asking for what I need, nothing more. If I can get work to do maybe I could get more things from time to time. Work is what I am asking for. I were told if I get a doctor to sign a paper saying that I am disabled to work, I can or might get back on relief tickets. But I dont want that kind of help since I can work at something. I wouldnt dare say that I cant do anything. And I wont swear falsely.

I dont own any property. I have nothing but myself and father and grandchild, to support the best I can.

I have two children of my own, both grown, somewhere in the world. But where I dont know. Please let me hear from you as soon as possible. And I'll be very grateful to you for whatever is done.

Sincerely,
(Mrs.) *Eulalia Foster*
1321 W. Leigh Street
Richmond, Virginia

21 March 1939

President Franklin D. Roosevelt
Washington, D.C.

Dear Sirs,

Please be advised that the unfair supervision of projects by WPA officials of Botetcourt County continues. There is no change, for the better, in their conduct while administering to Negroes. When one is found eligible for, what they call "white collar work," they are refused an opportunity for employment on WPA and should one make a protest and get hold of the work, they do not allow them to work in peace. They take up the task in seizing the work, using every scheme they think should be possible. They do all they are able seemingly, to hinder the worker from making a real success of her undertakings. Their trying to keep the work from Negroes and their fighting those, who have been successful in getting hold of it, keep up a confusion. They soon take the work and have a 403[3] sent to the worker. They give to the Richmond WPA Officials a reason for their cutting off the worker, a statement which is to be concealed, then there is another one, which they have placed upon the 403. . . .

Trusting that I shall hear from you very soon and that conditions shall grow better, I beg to remain,

Very truly yours,
(*Miss*) *Othea E. Randolph*
Glen Wilton, Virginia

11 April 1939

W.P.A. Headquarters
Washington, D.C.

Dear Manager

I am writing you about W.P.A. its so hard for the Negro women to get work yet the paper always say the work is to help the poor people but look to me if I see right they work the ones that have and the poor ones are still left to suffer here in the South. We have tried every way we know to get a project for Negro women in this town and vicinity but it seems impossible. Its (4) four project for white women. Its at least (300) three hundred white women working in this town and vicinity and not one Negro woman. It was (4) four of us Negro women working as maid in the white sewing room and they laid every one of us off and not one of us have any help at all. We knew it would be a lay off but they said in the paper they would cut off the ones that had income enough to live on and not a one out the (4) four have nothing to go upon. We have (30) thirty certified women ready for work but due to the fact that we dont have a project they say they have nothing for the Negro women to do so you see they good as say the Negro women can starve go nacket, her children dont need an education. Oh how I wish you would send out some investigator down here from up there. . . .

I hope I never witness another sumer without food. Oh if you only knew how it felt for a mother to listen to her children cry for bread, and its no bread. Oh I just wish every one of you could just have to feel that way one time, then you have more sympathy for women with children to care for, so please see that we get a project here as we are not allowed to work in the white sewing room. Look into this matter at once, and please help us get work.

Expecting an early reply,

Very truly yours,
Mabel Adams
Elsie Hunter
Charlett Mack
Carrie Turner
Other needy women of
this town and vicinity
915 E. Haines St.
Plant City, Florida

NOTES

1. The Tower Building was erected in downtown Jackson, Mississippi, in 1929 and has served as headquarters for Standard Life Insurance Company for most of its life. That Mary Ramsey was told to write to a life insurance company to ask for relief shows the devious way in which a racist system exploited a poor, defenseless black woman.
2. Hartshorn Memorial College was founded in Richmond, Virginia, in 1833 as a women's Christian school. In 1932 it merged with Virginia Union University, a private black Baptist college.
3. A state form notifying the worker of his or her release from a job based on insufficient job orders.

• • • • •

"The Revenge of Hannah Kemhuff"

Alice Walker

Born in 1944 into a sharecropper family of eight children in Eatonville, Georgia, Alice Walker was the first black woman to receive a Pulitzer Prize for fiction. She was honored in 1986 for her novel *The Color Purple*, published in 1982. Like Walker's other works, *The Color Purple* depicts the pain in black people's lives, especially the pain inflicted on black women by black men. This aspect of the work raised much discord among black males and females, in academic and nonacademic circles alike. One of Walker's statements about intraracial problems sheds some light on her choice of subject matter: "We black women writers know very clearly that our survival depends on trust. We will not have or cannot have anything until we examine what we do to and with each other. There just has not been enough examination or enough application of findings to real problems in our day-to-day living. Black women continue to talk about intimate relationships so that we can recognize what is happening when we see it, then maybe there will be some change in behavior on the part of men *and* women."[1]

Walker's published works include three other novels, *The Third Life of Grange Copeland* (1970), *Meridian* (1976), and *The Temple of My Familiar* (1989); the poetry volumes *Once: Poems* (1968), *Five Poems* (1972), *Revolutionary Petunias and Other Poems* (1973), and *Good Night Willie Lee, I'll See You in the Morning* (1979); two short-story collections, *In Love and Trouble* (1973) and *You Can't Keep a Good Woman Down: Stories* (1981); two collections of essays, *I Love Myself When I Am Laughing . . . and Then Again When I Am Looking Mean and Impressive: A Zora Neale Hurston Reader* (1979) and *In Search of Our Mothers' Gardens and Other Essays* (1983). She has written for such magazines as *Black Collegian, Redbook, Ms.,* and *Mother Jones,* and many of her works have been anthologized. Walker is the recipient of a number of literary awards and the subject of many biographical and critical studies and reviews.

Walker says she based the story "The Revenge of Hannah Kemhuff" (from *In Love and Trouble* [Harcourt Brace Jovanovich]) on "[my] mother's experiences during the Depression, and on Zora Hurston's folklore collection of the 1920s, and on my own response to both out of a contemporary existence." Walker's mother was refused free flour from a distribution center in Georgia because the local white female official was envious of her clothing, which had been sent to her by a relative living in the North. Walker's mother begged for the flour, but the official turned to the next person in line and said, "The *gall* of niggers coming in here dressed better than me!"[2]

In "The Revenge of Hannah Kemhuff" Walker depicts a woman

15

whose children starve to death during the Depression; food is denied them by a white relief worker who believes they do not look hungry or poor enough to qualify for food stamps. Abandoned by her husband, Hannah Kemhuff is unable to save her children. Years later, the broken and lonely Hannah resorts to rootworking to take revenge on the white woman who had denied her family food. Rootworking, is often a substitute for legal assistance, a form of sorcery that has been traditionally used in black culture as an alternative route to power for those unable to find it in the general culture. (Ann Petry in *The Street*, Toni Morrison in *The Bluest Eye*, and Gloria Naylor in *Mama Day* also explore the subject of rootworking.)

Walker's story demonstrates the arbitrariness, the casualness, of racism and its terrible power for destruction, and the pain of being powerless against it. A poor woman alone, Hannah has no one to turn to for help; she is very much trapped by her circumstances. When she finally finds the means to take her revenge, it can bring her little recompense for her many losses.

NOTES

1. Claudia Tate, ed., quoted in *Black Women Writers at Work* (New York: Continuum, 1983), 181.
2. Alice Walker, *In Search of Our Mothers' Gardens and Other Essays* (New York: Harcourt Brace Jovanovich, 1983), 12–13, 16.

In grateful memory
of Zora Neale Hurston

Two weeks after I became Tante Rosie's apprentice we were visited by a very old woman who was wrapped and contained, almost smothered, in a half-dozen skirts and shawls. Tante Rosie (pronounced Ro'*zee*) told the woman she could see her name, Hannah Kemhuff, written in the air. She told the woman further that she belonged to the Order of the Eastern Star.

The woman was amazed. (And I was, too! Though I learned later that Tante Rosie held extensive files on almost everybody in the country, which she kept in long cardboard boxes under her bed.) Mrs. Kemhuff quickly asked what else Tante Rosie could tell her.

Tante Rosie had a huge tank of water on a table in front of her, like an aquarium for fish, except there were no fish in it. There was nothing but water and I never was able to see anything in it. Tante Rosie, of course, could. While the woman waited Tante Rosie peered deep into the tank of water. Soon she said the water spoke to her and told her that although the woman looked old, she was not. Mrs. Kemhuff said that this was true, and wondered if Tante Rosie knew the reason she looked so old. Tante Rosie said she did not and asked if she would mind telling us about it. (At first Mrs. Kemhuff didn't seem to want me there, but Tante Rosie told her I was trying to learn the rootworking trade and she nodded that she understood and didn't mind. I scrooched down as small as I could at the corner of Tante Rosie's table, smiling at her so she wouldn't feel embarrassed or afraid.)

"It was during the Depression," she began, shifting in her seat and adjusting the shawls. She wore so many her back appeared to be humped!

"Of course," said Tante Rosie, "and you were young and pretty."

"How do you know that?" exclaimed Mrs. Kemhuff. "That is true. I had been married already five years and had four small children and a husband with a wandering eye. But since I married young—"

"Why, you were little more than a child," said Tante Rosie.

"Yes," said Mrs. Kemhuff. "I were not quite twenty years old. And it was hard times everywhere, all over the country and, I suspect, all over the world. Of course, no one had television in those days, so we didn't know. I don't even now know if it was invented. We had a radio before the Depression which my husband won in a poker game, but we sold it somewhere along the line to buy a meal. Anyway, we lived for as long as we could on the money I brought in as a cook in a sawmill. I cooked cabbage and cornpone for twenty men for two dollars a week. But then the mill closed down, and my husband had already been out of work for some time. We were on the point of starvation. We was so hungry, and the children were getting so weak, that after I had crapped off the last leaves from the collard stalks I couldn't wait for new leaves to grow back. I dug up the collards, roots and all. After we ate that there was nothing else.

"As I said, there was no way of knowing whether hard times was existing around the world because we did not then have a television set. And we had sold the radio. However, as it happened, hard times hit everybody we knew in Cherokee County. And for that reason the government sent food stamps which you could get if you could prove you were starving. With a few of them stamps you could go into town to a place they had and get so much and so much fat back, so much and so much of corn meal, and so much and so much of (I think it was) red beans. As I say, we was, by then, desperate. And my husband pervailed on me for us to go. I never wanted to do it, on account of I have always been proud. My father, you know, used to be one of the biggest colored peanut growers in Cherokee County and we never had to ask nobody for nothing.

17

"Well, what had happened in the meantime was this: My sister, Carrie Mae—"

"A tough girl, if I remember right," said Tante Rosie.

"Yes," said Mrs. Kemhuff, "bright, full of spunk. Well, she were at that time living in the North. In Chicago. And she were working for some good white people that give her they old clothes to send back down here. And I tell you they were good things. And I was glad to get them. So, as it was gitting to be real cold, I dressed myself and my husband and the children up in them clothes. For see, they was made up North to be worn up there where there's snow at and they were warm as toast."

"Wasn't Carrie Mae later killed by a gangster?" asked Tante Rosie.

"Yes, she were," said the woman, anxious to go on with her story. "He were her husband."

"Oh," said Tante Rosie quietly.

"Now, so I dresses us all up in our new finery and with our stomachs growling all together we goes marching off to ask for what the government said was due us as proud as ever we knew how to be. For even my husband, when he had on the right clothes, could show some pride, and me, whenever I remembered how fine my daddy's peanut crops had provided us, why there was nobody with stiffer backbone."

"I see a pale and evil shadow looming ahead of you in this journey," said Tante Rosie, looking into the water as if she'd lost a penny while we weren't looking.

"That shadow was sure pale and evil all right," said Mrs. Kemhuff. "When we got to the place there was a long line, and we saw all of our friends in this line. On one side of the big pile of food was the white line—and some rich peoples was in that line too—and on the other side there was the black line. I later heard, by the by, that the white folks in the white line got bacon and grits, as well as meal, but that is neither here nor there. What happened was this. As soon as our friends saw us all dressed up in our nice warm clothes, though used and castoff they were, they began saying how crazy we was to have worn them. And that's when I began to notice that all the people in the black line had dressed themselves in tatters. Even people what had good things at home, and I knew some of them did. What does this mean? I asked my husband. But he didn't know. He was too busy strutting about to even pay much attention. But I began to be terribly afraid. The baby had begun to cry and the other little ones, knowing I was nervous, commenced to whine and gag. I had a time with them.

"Now, at this time my husband had been looking around at other women and I was scared to death I was going to lose him. He already made fun of me and said I was arrogant and proud. I said that was the way to be and that he should try to be that way. The last thing I wanted to happen was for him to see me embarrassed and made small in front of a lot of people because I knew if that happened he would quit me.

"So I was standing there hoping that the white folks what give out the food wouldn't notice that I was dressed nice and that if they did they would see how hungry the babies was and how pitiful we all was. I could see my husband over talking to the woman he was going with on the sly. She was dressed like a flysweep! Not only was she raggedy, she was dirty! Filthy dirty, and with her filthy slip showing. She looked so awful she disgusted me. And yet there was my husband hanging over her while I stood in the line holding on to all four of our children. I guess he knew as well as I did what that woman had in the line of clothes at home. She was always much better dressed than me and much better dressed than many of the white peoples. That was because, they say she was a whore and took money. Seems like people want that and will pay for it even in a depression!"

There was a pause while Mrs. Kemhuff drew a deep breath. Then she continued.

"So soon I was next to get something from the young lady at the counter. All around her I could smell them red beans and my mouth was watering for a taste of fresh-water cornpone. I was proud, but I wasn't fancy. I just wanted something for me and the children. Well, there I was, with the children hanging to my dresstails, and I drew my-self up as best I could and made the oldest boy stand up straight, for I had come to ask for what was mine, not to beg. So I wasn't going to be acting like a beggar. Well, I want you to know that that little slip of a woman, all big blue eyes and yellow hair, that little *girl*, took my stamps and then took one long look at me and my children and across at my husband—all of us dressed to kill I guess she thought—and she took my stamps in her hand and looked at them like they was dirty, and then she give them to an old gambler who was next in line behind me! 'You don't need nothing to eat from the way you all dressed up, Hannah Lou,' she said to me. 'But Miss Sadler,' I said, 'my children is hungry.' 'They don't look hungry,' she said to me. 'Move along now, somebody here may really need our help!' The whole line behind me began to laugh and snigger, and that little white moppet sort of grinned behind her hands. She give the old gambler double what he would have got otherwise. And there me and my children about to keel over from want.

"When my husband and his woman saw and heard what happened they commenced to laugh, too, and he reached down and got her stuff, piles and piles of it, it seemed to me then, and helped her put it in somebody's car and they drove off together. And that was about the last I seen of him. Or her."

"Weren't they swept off a bridge together in the flood that wiped out Tunica City?" asked Tante Rosie.

"Yes," said Mrs. Kemhuff. "Somebody like you might have helped me then, too, though looks like I didn't need it."

"So—"

"So after that looks like my spirit just wilted. Me and my children got a ride home with somebody and I tottered around like a drunken woman and put them to bed. They was sweet children and not much trouble, although they was about to go out of their minds with hunger."

Now a deep sadness crept into her face, which until she reached this point had been still and impassive.

"First one then the other of them took sick and died. Though the old gambler came by the house three or four days later and divided what he had left with us. He had been on his way to gambling it all away. The Lord called him to have pity on us and since he knew us and knew my husband had deserted me he said he were right glad to help out. But it was mighty late in the day when he thought about helping out and the children were far gone. Nothing could save them except the Lord and he seemed to have other things on his mind, like the wedding that spring of the mean little moppet."

Mrs. Kemhuff now spoke through clenched teeth.

"My spirit never recovered from that insult, just like my heart never recovered from my husband's desertion, just like my body never recovered from being almost starved to death. I started to wither in that winter and each year found me more hacked and worn down than the year before. Somewhere along them years my pride just up and left altogether and I worked for a time in a whorehouse just to make some money, just like my husband's woman. Then I took to drinking to forget what I was doing, and soon I just broke down and got old all at once, just like you see me now. And I started about five years ago to going to church. I was converted again, 'cause I felt the first time had done got worn off. But I am not restful. I dream and have nightmares still about the little moppet, and always I feel the moment when my spirit was trampled down within me while they all stood and laughed and she stood there grinning behind her hands."

"Well," said Tante Rosie. "There are ways that the spirit can be mended just as there are ways that the spirit can be broken. But one such as I am cannot do both. If I am to take away the burden of shame which is upon you I must in some way inflict it on someone else."

"I do not care to be cured," said Mrs. Kemhuff. "It is enough that I have endured my shame all these years and that my children and my husband were taken from me by one who knew nothing about us. I can survive as long as I need with the bitterness that has laid every day in my soul. But I could die easier if I knew something, after all these years, had been done to the little moppet. God cannot be let to make her happy all these years and me miserable. What kind of justice would that be? It would be monstrous!"

"Don't worry about it, my sister," said Tante Rosie with gentleness. "By the grace of the Man-God I have use of many powers. Powers given me by the Great One Herself. If you can no longer bear the eyes of the enemy that you see in your dreams the Man-God, who speaks to me from the Great Mother of Us All, will see that those eyes are eaten away. If the hands of your enemy have struck you they can be made useless." Tante Rosie held up a small piece of what was once lustrous pewter. Now it was pock-marked and blackened and deteriorating.

"Do you see this metal?" she asked.

"Yes, I see it," said Mrs. Kemhuff with interest. She took it in her hands and rubbed it.

"The part of the moppet you want destroyed will rot away in the same fashion."

Mrs. Kemhuff relinquished the piece of metal to Tante Rosie.

"You are a true sister," she said.

"Is it enough?" Tante Rosie asked.

"I would give anything to stop her grinning behind her hands," said the woman, drawing out a tattered billfold.

"Her hands or the grinning mouth?" asked Tante Rosie.

"The mouth grinned and the hands hid it," said Mrs. Kemhuff.

"Ten dollars for one area, twenty for two," said Tante Rosie.

"Make it the mouth," said Mrs. Kemhuff. "That is what I see most vividly in my dreams." She laid a ten-dollar bill in the lap of Tante Rosie.

"Let me explain what we will do," said Tante Rosie, coming near the woman and speaking softly to her, as a doctor would speak to a patient. "First we will make a potion that has a long history of use in our profession. It is a mixture of hair and nail parings of the person in question, a bit of their water and feces, a piece of their clothing heavy with their own scents, and I think in this case we might as well add a pinch of goober dust; that is, dust from the graveyard. This woman will not outlive you by more than six months."

I had thought the two women had forgotten about me, but now Tante Rosie turned to me and said, "You will have to go out to Mrs. Kemhuff's house. She will have to be instructed in the recitation of the curse-prayer. You will show her how to dress the black candles and how to pay Death for his interception in her behalf."

Then she moved over to the shelf that held her numerous supplies: oils of Bad and Good Luck Essence, dried herbs, creams, powders, and candles. She took two large black candles and placed them in Mrs. Kemhuff's hands. She also gave her a small bag of powder and told her to burn it on her table (as an altar) while she was praying the curse-prayer. I was to show Mrs. Kemhuff how to "dress" the candles in vinegar so they would be purified for her purpose.

She told Mrs. Kemhuff that each morning and evening for nine days she was to light the candles, burn the powder, recite the curse-prayer from her knees and concentrate all her powers on getting her message through to Death and the Man-God. As far as the Supreme Mother of Us All was concerned, She could only be moved by the pleas of the Man-God. Tante Rosie herself would recite the curse-prayer at the same time that Mrs. Kemhuff did, and together she thought the two prayers, prayed with respect, could not help but move the Man-God, who, in turn, would unchain Death who would already be eager to come down on the little moppet. But her death would be slow in coming because first the Man-God had to hear all of the prayers.

"We will take those parts of herself that we collect, the feces, water, nail parings, et cetera, and plant them where they will bring for you the best results. Within a year's time the earth will be rid of the woman herself, even as almost immediately you will be rid of her grin. Do you want something else for only two dollars that will make you feel happy even today?" asked Tante Rosie.

But Mrs. Kemhuff shook her head. "I'm carefree enough already, knowing that her end will be before another year. As for happiness, it is something that deserts you once you know it can be bought and sold. I will not live to see the end result of your work, Tante Rosie, but my grave will fit nicer, having someone proud again who has righted a wrong and by so doing lies straight and proud throughout eternity."

And Mrs. Kemhuff turned and left, bearing herself grandly out of the room. It was as if she had regained her youth; her shawls were like a stately toga, her white hair seemed to sparkle.

2

To The Man God: O great One, I have been sorely tried by my enemies and have been blasphemed and lied against. My good thoughts and my honest actions have been turned to bad actions and dishonest ideas. My home has been disrespected, my children have been cursed and ill-treated. My dear ones have been backbitten and their virtue questioned. O Man God, I beg that this that I ask for my enemies shall come to pass:

That the South wind shall scorch their bodies and make them wither and shall not be tempered to them. That the North wind shall freeze their blood and numb their muscles and that it shall not be tempered to them. That the West wind shall blow away their life's breath and will not leave their hair grow, and that their fingernails shall fall off and their bones shall crumble. That the East wind shall make their minds grow dark, their sight shall fail and their seed dry up so that they shall not multiply.

I ask that their fathers and mothers from their furtherest generation will not intercede for them before the great throne, and the wombs of their women shall not bear fruit except for strangers, and that they shall become extinct. I pray that the children who may come shall be weak of mind and paralyzed of limb and that they themselves shall curse them in their turn for ever turning the breath of life into their bodies. I pray that disease and death shall be forever with them and that their worldly goods shall not prosper, and that their crops shall not multiply and that their cows, their sheep, and their hogs and all their living beasts shall die of starvation and thirst. I pray that their house shall be unroofed and that the rain, the thunder and lighting shall find the innermost recesses of their home and that the foundation shall crumble and the floods tear it asunder. I pray that the sun shall not shed its rays on them in benevolence, but instead it shall beat down on them and burn them and destroy them. I pray that the moon shall not give them peace, but instead shall deride them and decry them and cause their minds to shrivel. I pray that their friends shall betray them and cause them loss of power, of gold and of silver, and that their enemies shall smite them until they beg for mercy which shall not be given them. I pray that their tongues shall forget how to speak in sweet words, and that it shall be paralyzed and that all about them will be desolation, pestilence and death. O Man God, I ask you for all these things because they have dragged me in the dust and destroyed my good name; broken my heart and caused me to curse the day that I was born. So be it.

This curse-prayer was regularly used and taught by rootworkers, but since I did not know it by heart, as Tante Rosie did, I recited it straight from Zora Neale Hurston's book, *Mules and Men,* and Mrs. Kemhuff and I learned it on our knees together. We were soon dressing the candles in vinegar, lighting them, kneeling and praying—intoning the words rhythmically—as if we had been doing it this way for years. I was moved by the fervor with which Mrs. Kemhuff prayed. Often she would clench her fists before her closed eyes and bite the insides of her wrists as the women do in Greece.

3

According to courthouse records Sarah Marie Sadler, "the little moppet," was born in 1910. She was in her early twenties during the

Depression. In 1932 she married Ben Jonathan Holley, who later inherited a small chain of grocery stores and owned a plantation and an impressive stand of timber. In the spring of 1963, Mrs. Holley was fifty-three years old. She was the mother of three children, a boy and two girls; the boy a floundering clothes salesman, the girls married and oblivious, mothers themselves.

The elder Holleys lived six miles out in the country, their house was large, and Mrs. Holley's hobbies were shopping for antiques, gossiping with colored women, discussing her husband's health and her children's babies, and making spoon bread. I was able to glean this much from the drunken ramblings of the Holleys' cook, a malevolent nanny with gout, who had raised, in her prime, at least one tan Holley, a preacher whom the Holleys had sent to Morehouse.

"I bet I could get the nanny to give us all the information and nail parings we could ever use," I said to Tante Rosie. For the grumpy woman drank muscatel like a sow and clearly hated Mrs. Holley. However, it was hard to get her tipsy enough for truly revealing talk and we were quickly running out of funds.

"That's not the way," Tante Rosie said one evening as she sat in her car and watched me lead the nanny out of the dreary but secret-evoking recesses of the Six Forks Bar. We had already spent six dollars on muscatel.

"You can't trust gossips or drunks," said Tante Rosie. "You let the woman we are working on give you everything you need, and from her own lips."

"But that is the craziest thing I have ever heard," I said. "How can I talk to her about putting a fix on her without making her mad, or maybe even scaring her to death?"

Tante Rosie merely grunted.

"Rule number one. OBSERVATION OF SUBJECT. Write that down among your crumpled notes."

"In other words—?"

"Be direct, but not blunt."

On my way to the Holley plantation I came up with the idea of pretending to be searching for a fictitious person. Then I had an even better idea. I parked Tante Rosie's Bonneville at the edge of the spacious yard, which was dotted with mimosas and camellias. Tante Rosie had insisted I wear a brilliant orange robe and as I walked it swished and blew about my legs. Mrs. Holley was on the back patio steps, engaged in conversation with a young and beautiful black girl. They stared in amazement at the length and brilliance of my attire.

"Mrs. Holley, I think it's time for me to go," said the girl.

"Don't be silly," said the matronly Mrs. Holley. "She is probably just a light-skinned African who is on her way somewhere and got lost.'' She nudged the black girl in the ribs and they both broke into giggles.

"How do you do?'' I asked.

"Just fine, how you?'' said Mrs. Holley, while the black girl looked on askance. They had been talking with their heads close together and stood up together when I spoke.

"I am looking for a Josiah Henson''—a runaway slave and the original Uncle Tom in Harriet Beecher Stowe's novel, I might have added. "Could you tell me if he lives on your place?''

"That name sounds awful familiar,'' said the black girl.

"Are you *the* Mrs. Holley?'' I asked gratuitously, while Mrs. Holley was distracted. She was sure she had never heard the name.

"Of course,'' she said, and smiled, pleating the side of her dress. She was a grayish blonde with an ashen untanned face, and her hands were five blunt and pampered fingers each. "And this is my . . . ah . . . my friend, Caroline Williams.''

Caroline nodded curtly.

"Somebody told me ole Josiah might be out this way. . . .''

"Well, we hadn't seen him,'' said Mrs. Holley. "We were just here shelling some peas, enjoying this nice sunshine.''

"Are you a light African?'' asked Caroline.

"No,'' I said. "I work with Tante Rosie, the rootworker. I'm learning the profession.''

"Whatever *for*?'' asked Mrs. Holley. "I would have thought a nice-looking girl like yourself could find a better way to spend her time. I been hearing about Tante Rosie since I was a little bitty child, but everybody always said that rootworking was just a whole lot of n——, I mean colored foolishness. Of course we don't believe in that kind of thing, do we, Caroline?''

"Naw.''

The younger woman put a hand on the older woman's arm, possessively, as if to say "You get away from here, bending my white folks' ear with your crazy mess!'' From the kitchen window a dark remorseful face worked itself into various messages of "Go away!'' It was the drunken nanny.

"I wonder if you would care to prove you do not believe in rootworking?''

"Prove?'' said the white woman indignantly.

"Prove?'' asked the black woman with scorn.

"That is the word,'' I said.

"Why, not that I'm afraid of any of this nigger magic!'' said Mrs. Holley staunchly, placing a reassuring hand on Caroline's shoulder. *I* was the nigger, not she.

"In that case won't you show us how much you don't have fear of it." With the word us I placed Caroline in the same nigger category with me. Let her smolder! Now Mrs. Holley stood alone, the great white innovator and scientific scourge, forced to man the Christian fort against heathen nigger paganism.

"Of course, if you like," she said immediately, drawing herself up in the best English manner. Stiff upper lip, what? and all that. She had been grinning throughout. Now she covered her teeth with her scant two lips and her face became flat and resolute. Like so many white women in sections of the country where the race was still "pure" her mouth could have been formed by the minute slash of a thin sword.

"Do you know a Mrs. Hannah Lou Kemhuff?" I asked.

"No I do not."

"She is not white, Mrs. Holley, she is black."

"Hannah Lou, Hannah Lou . . . do we know a Hannah Lou?" she asked, turning to Caroline.

"No, ma'am, we don't!" said Caroline.

"Well, she knows you. Says she met you on the bread lines during the Depression and that because she was dressed up you wouldn't give her any corn meal. Or red beans. Or something like that."

"Bread lines, Depression, dressed up, corn meal . . . ? I don't know what you're talking about!" No shaft of remembrance probed the depths of what she had done to colored people more than twenty years ago.

"It doesn't really matter, since you don't believe . . . but she says you did her wrong, and being a good Christian, she believes all wrongs are eventually righted in the Lord's good time. She came to us for help only when she began to feel the Lord's good time might be too far away. Because we do not deal in the work of unmerited destruction, Tante Rosie and I did not see how we could take the case." I said this humbly, with as much pious intonation as I could muster.

"Well, I'm glad," said Mrs. Holley, who had been running through the back years on her fingers.

"But," I said, "we told her what she could do to bring about restitution of peaceful spirit, which she claimed you robbed her of in a moment during which, as is now evident, you were not concerned. You were getting married the following spring."

"That was '32," said Mrs. Holley. "Hannah *Lou*?"

"The same."

"How black *was* she? Sometimes I can recall colored faces that way."

"That is not relevant," I said, "since you do not believe. . . ."

"Well, of *course* I don't believe!" said Mrs. Holley.

"I am nothing in this feud between you," I said. "Neither is Tante Rosie. Neither of us had any idea until after Mrs. Kemhuff left that you were the woman she spoke of. We are familiar with the deep and sincere interest you take in the poor colored children at Christmastime each year. We know you have gone out of your way to hire needy people to work on your farm. We know you have been an example of Christian charity and a beacon force of brotherly love. And right before my eyes I can see it is true you have Negro friends.''

''Just what is it you want?'' asked Mrs. Holley.

''What *Mrs. Kemhuff* wants are some nail parings, not many, just a few; some hair (that from a comb will do), some water and some feces—and if you don't feel like doing either number one or number two, I will wait—and a bit of clothing, something that you have worn in the last year. Something with some of your odor on it.''

''What!'' Mrs. Holley screeched.

''They say this combination, with the right prayers, can eat away part of a person just like the disease that ruins so much fine antique pewter.''

Mrs. Holley blanched. With a motherly fluttering of hands Caroline helped her into a patio chair.

''Go get my medicine,'' said Mrs. Holley, and Caroline started from the spot like a gazelle.

''Git away from here! Git away!''

I spun around just in time to save my head from a whack with a gigantic dust mop. It was the drunken nanny, drunk no more, flying to the defense of her mistress.

''She just a tramp and a phony!'' she reassured Mrs. Holley, who was caught up in an authentic faint.

4

Not long after I saw Mrs. Holley, Hannah Kemhuff was buried. Tante Rosie and I followed the casket to the cemetery. Tante Rosie most elegant in black. Then we made our way through briers and grass to the highway. Mrs. Kemhuff rested in a tangly grove, off to herself, though reasonably near her husband and babies. Few people came to the funeral, which made the faces of Mrs. Holley's nanny and husband stand out all the more plainly. They had come to verify the fact that this dead person was indeed *the* Hannah Lou Kemhuff whom Mr. Holley had initiated a search for, having the entire county militia at his disposal.

Several months later we read in the paper that Sarah Marie Sadler Holley had also passed away. The paper spoke of her former beauty and vivacity, as a young woman, and of her concern for those less fortunate than herself as a married woman and pillar of the community and her church. It spoke briefly of her harsh and lengthy illness. It said all who knew her were sure her soul would find peace in heaven, just as her shrunken body had endured so much pain and heartache here on earth.

Caroline had kept us up to date on the decline of Mrs. Holley. After my visit, relations between them became strained and Mrs. Holley eventually became too frightened of Caroline's darkness to allow her close to her. A week after I'd talked to them Mrs. Holley began having her meals in her bedroom upstairs. Then she started doing everything else there as well. She collected stray hairs from her head and comb with the greatest attention and consistency, not to say desperation. She ate her fingernails. But the most bizarre of all was her response to Mrs. Kemhuff's petition for a specimen of feces and water. Not trusting any longer the earthen secrecy of the water mains, she no longer flushed. Together with the nanny Mrs. Holley preferred to store those relics of what she ate (which became almost nothing and then nothing, the nanny had told Caroline) and they kept it all in barrels and plastic bags in the upstairs closets. In a few weeks it became impossible for anyone to endure the smell of the house, even Mrs. Holley's husband, who loved her but during the weeks before her death slept in a spare room of the nanny's house.

The mouth that had grinned behind the hands grinned no more. The constant anxiety lest a stray strand of hair be lost and the foul odor of the house soon brought to the hands a constant seeking motion, to the eyes a glazed and vacant stare, and to the mouth a tightly puckered frown, one which only death might smooth.

• • • • •

"Girl, Colored"

Marian Minus

Mattie Marian Minus was born in 1913 in South Carolina. She dropped her first name after attending Fisk University (1931–35), where she majored in sociology and graduated magna cum laude. In 1935 she received a two-year Julius Rosenwald Scholarship to attend the University of Chicago (1935–37) and study anthropology. She enrolled in a doctoral program, but financial difficulties prevented her from continuing her studies beyond the master's degree. Coeditor with Dorothy West of *New Challenge* magazine in 1937, she began publishing short stories in the 1930s and worked as a clerk for many years at Consumers Union in Mt. Vernon, New York. Minus died in 1973.

The best evidence for Minus's victimization by racism is the public segregation of her own works. To *Woman's Day*, which appealed primarily to a white audience, she contributed stories from 1945 until 1951 about white middle-class America. To African-American magazines such as *Opportunity: A Journal of Negro Life, Black Life*, and *The Crisis: A Record of the Darker Races*, she offered stories and essays about black life.

Opportunity published her stories "The Fine Line" (1939) and "Half Bright" (1940). "Girl, Colored" (*The Crisis* [September 1940]) dramatizes the interplay of racism and capitalism. Carrie, a young black woman, accepts a job as a live-in maid for only $5 a week and one day off a month. Her dismal working conditions reflect the willingness of her new employer, a white woman, to take advantage of Carrie's tenuous position in a competitive work force. Her employer puts before Carrie as a rival for the job a German girl who most likely does not exist. But Carrie's fear that such a girl might exist leads her to take the job and prevents her from pushing for even modest improvements in her working conditions. Minus portrays Carrie as a captive in an economic system that reduces her to the practical equivalent of slave labor.

> Girl, colored, to assist with housework and baby; must be reliable; $20 per month. German girl considered. Clark, 1112 Highdale Rd., Long Island City.   —Advt.

The subway wormed its way through the tunnel that lay below the frenzy and filth of urban streets into the dripping tube that arched its back beneath the river. The air that came in through the half-opened windows was moist and musty, and Carrie's wide brown nostrils flared in sullen offense. She watched the thoughtful contortions of her face reflected in the mirror of the train window, her timid eyes large and staring.

Carrie had come out of the South, the red clay clinging to her misshapen heels, made migrant by the disintegration of a crumbling age. She had been unconscious of the transmission of idea and attitude from age to age until its outworn mechanism and wild momentum had forced her outside the terminals of habit and sour acceptance.

German girl considered. Fear was filling a place which not even thought had filled before.

The train converged on light, and roared upward onto high steel trestles. No longer able to see her face in the window, Carrie gave her attention to the neat brown paper bundle in her lap. Her thin fingers with their big knuckles smoothed out the wrinkles in the package. It held her stiffly starched white work dress, a pair of comfortable shoes, and a thick beef sandwich. Even if she got the job, she might not be provided with lunch. Her memory of fainting from hunger on the first day of her last job, six months before, was bitter-sharp.

As she left the train, Carrie hunched her shoulders in sudden fear that she would soon be retracing her steps. She hugged her parcel close to her breast.

"Number ten's over there," she said softly, gaining the street, "so number two must be down there a way."

She walked with a tread that was firmer than the resolution in her heart in the direction of her reasoning. For six months she had answered advertisements. She had related the necessary details of her life to prospective "madams," and she had returned beaten and cynical to her basement room.

She went through a gate and up a gravel path to a small brick house. Her nervous hands played with a dull knocker until sound was forced from the beat of brass on wood. A pale blond woman opened the door. Wisps of inoffensive hair strayed from the leather thongs of a dozen curlers set at variance on her head.

"Yes?" The woman's voice was spuriously cheerful.

"I come about the job," said Carrie.

The woman opened the door wider. "Come in."

Carrie followed her into an untidy living room.

"We'll go into the kitchen," the woman said, pointing ahead.

Carrie's eyes flickered professionally about the room and her nose lifted on its wide base. They walked through to the kitchen, and she saw the table cluttered with unwashed dishes.

The woman waved her to a seat. "Sit down." she said briefly.

Carrie found a chair and settled on its edge, resting her package on her knees.

"My name is Clark," the woman said. "Mrs. Cado P. Clark."

"I'm Carrie Johnson," Carrie said quickly. She did not have the inclination or energy for a prolonged interview.

"Have you references?" Mrs. Clark asked.

"Yes." A flash of anger that started somewhere deep within her lighted Carrie's eyes. She resented being asked for information before being given any.

"I'll want to see them later," said Mrs. Clark.

Carrie gave her prospective employer an impatient glance. They measured each other in momentary silence. Carrie was the first to speak.

"You want somebody to help with the housework and the baby?" she asked. "At twenty a month?"

"Yes, I do." Mrs. Clark answered. "I want a reliable person. Someone I can put utter trust in."

Carrie did not speak. She smiled wryly and dropped her eyes.

"Have you had much experience?" Mrs. Clark asked. "Have you had to take much responsibility, I mean?"

Carrie shrugged weary shoulders. "I reckon so," she answered shortly. "I been on jobs where I had to do everything under the sun, and I did it. Guess that's being reliable."

Mrs. Clark gave her a sharp look. She murmured unintelligibly.

"Ain't that the right answer to your question?" Carrie parried maliciously.

"Right answer?" Mrs. Clark inquired. "You mean you're trying to give me the answers you think you ought to give, instead of just telling the truth?"

Carrie shrugged again. "I guess I didn't make myself clear," she said in simulated apology.

Mrs. Clark's face brightened. She took a deep breath.

"I want someone to clean, help with the cooking, look after the baby, and do general things about the house," she explained.

"'Bout how long would the hours be?" Carrie asked.

Mrs. Clark calculated quickly. "Well, my husband gets up at seven. He takes breakfast about seven-thirty then he goes to his office. I've been getting his breakfast, but if I get a girl, that'll be changed, of course."

"Oh, certainly," Carrie said with emphasis. "You'll get up 'bout nine then and have your breakfast, won't you, if you get a girl?"

"Yes," Mrs. Clark said eagerly. Then she looked hard at Carrie. She bit her lip and patted the curlers on her head. Carrie snorted audibly.

"Of course, if it'll be too much work for you," Mrs. Clark said waspishly, "I can get a German girl to do it."

The back of Carrie's resentful resistance was broken. She rolled her eyes about the kitchen, seeking some tangible evidence of the competitor whose spirit held nebulous hands at her throat.

"You say you can get a German girl?" she asked uneasily.

"Yes." Mrs. Clark pulled hard at her lip with her even teeth.

Carrie was silent. She did not think for a moment that Mrs. Clark had not already interviewed the omnipresent German girl.

"It's very simple." Mrs. Clark went on. "You see, there are quite a few impoverished refugees in this country now. They can't become public charges so they are very eager to work."

Carrie nodded dumbly. She did not trust herself to speak.

"I think it's wonderful the way they look for work right away after landing in the United States." Mrs. Clark continued, warming to her fantasy. "I've already talked to one of the refugees."

"What'd she say?" Carrie turned miserable eyes on her tormentor.

Mrs. Clark cleared her throat. "She said she'd let me know."

"She didn't think it was too much work for five dollars a week?" Carrie asked in a low voice.

Mrs. Clark looked taken aback. "Why," she stammered, "no."

"I was just wondering."

Carrie looked at the dishes on the table. She saw the smear of childish fingers around the woodwork. She remembered the mussed livingroom.

"I don't see how her decision affects you," Mrs. Clark said slyly.

There was an unexpected hint of hardness in her voice that alarmed Carrie. For the first time she wondered if the German girl were not a bogey set up to frighten her by this wily woman. She shook her head and decided to take no chances.

"What about the baby?" she asked, her voice respectful.

"He's no trouble at all," Mrs. Clark said indulgently. "He's only four."

Carrie nodded wearily. "What would you expect me to do exactly?"

"After breakfast," Mrs. Clark elaborated, "there'd be the cleaning. I would expect you to do the marketing. I have a light lunch. In the afternoons you could rinse out a few pieces and do a bit of ironing. Dinner is usually about six-thirty. So you see you could have some free time between lunch and dinner if you got your other duties finished up. Of course, you'd have to take the baby out in the afternoons. After dinner your evenings would be free. Sometimes there is mending to be done. That would take one or two of your evenings a week."

Her recital finished, she waited for Carrie to speak. Carrie's throat was dry. She did not trust herself to do more than croak if she managed to get her mouth open.

"Would you give a day off a week?" she ventured finally.

"Oh, not a whole day," Mrs. Clark said quickly. "Just one afternoon a week. One day a month would be satisfactory."

"Oh." Carrie lifted her shoulders in a weary hunch. "There ain't much I could do with a day off every week nohow," she said philosophically, "if I ain't gonna be making but twenty a month."

There was a sighing silence into which Carrie's spent breath and Mrs. Clark's anxiety issued like desperate winds.

"Would I have a nice room?" Carrie asked after the pause.

Mrs. Clark rose, victorious, then sat down again. "Before we go that far," she said, "I'd like to see your references."

Carrie pulled a thin packet of letters from her purse. She passed them over silently.

"They're very flattering," Mrs. Clark said when she had finished reading.

"They ain't flattering," Carrie retorted. "They're the gospel truth. I worked hard for every word wrote on that paper."

Mrs. Clark rose hastily. "Your room's this way," she said.

They left the kitchen, and Carrie followed her upstairs to a little, boxlike room. It was bare except for a bed and one chair.

"The last place I worked had a radio," Carrie said unreasonably.

"It did?" Mrs. Clark asked in surprise. She straightened her shoulders. "I don't approve of servants having too many advantages."

"I b'lieves you," Carrie said shortly. She walked around the room. "The floors ain't bad," she volunteered meaninglessly.

"It's a very nice room," Mrs. Clark said defensively. "It could be home."

Carrie looked at her searchingly. "Madam," she said with dignity, "one little room like this couldn't never be home 'less it was in the house of your loved ones."

"There's a table down in the basement," Mrs. Clark said, ignoring Carrie's remark, "that could be brought up here."

"What about a bureau to keep my clothes in?" Carrie asked. She walked to a closet in one corner of the room. "This ain't got no shelf space," she said, looking in, "for me to use."

"You'd have to use your suitcase."

Carrie sighed. The woman knew that she needed the job, and that she would like it. She was too weary to gamble on finding pleasure in upsetting all of Mrs. Clark's calculations by refusing to stay. She could not face the thought of taking the long, fruitless ride back to Harlem.

"You satisfied with my references?" she asked fearfully.

"Your references are satisfactory," Mrs. Clark said, enigmatically stressing the second word.

"You mean you got some doubts about me personally?" Carrie asked meekly.

"Well," Mrs. Clark informed her, "you understand that I must satisfy myself on every score. After all, you'll be coming into constant and close contact with my child."

"Did the German girl satisfy you?" Carrie asked, almost whispering.

Mrs. Clark nodded slowly. "They really work well," she said. "They don't ask for anything but the chance to make an honest living."

"I think I'd like it here," Carrie said quickly, hating her haste. "If it's all right with you, we would call it settled."

"All right," Mrs. Clark said indifferently. Carrie's released breath rushed through her trembling lips. "I think we can call it arranged. Can you begin working immediately?"

Carrie's face broke into a reluctant smile. She was working again.

"Right away," she said. "But I'll have to go up to Harlem tonight after dinner and pick up my belongings."

"You can't go tonight," Mrs. Clark said coldly. "My husband and I are going out after dinner and you'll have to stay with the baby."

"Oh."

Mrs. Clark read the disappointment on Carrie's face. She breathed deeply and smiled inscrutably.

"I know it's difficult for you to make quick adjustments," she said sweetly. "Perhaps I should hire the German girl after all. They don't have any ties in this country. They have fewer arrangements to make than you, for instance."

"That's all right, ma'am," Carrie said quickly. "I can 'tend to it tomorrow night just as easy."

Black Women and Sexism

• • • • •

As with racism, the tradition of sexism toward black women can be traced to its roots in slavery. Slavery legitimized the sexual mistreatment of black women, who were bribed, molested, and raped by slave masters and had no legal recourse, no means to retaliate. Not only were female slaves punished if they resisted the overtures of their masters and other white men, they were also regarded as sinful and held responsible for their victimization. Some were labeled whores as they unwillingly participated in the buying and selling of their bodies for sexual exploitation.

This victimization of black women continued after slavery. In 1874 one black politician boldly proclaimed, ''We want more protection from whites invading our homes and destroying the virtue of our women than they from us.''[1] In 1895 black women formed the National Association of Colored Women (NACW) in formal protest against the slanderous accusation that few black women were virtuous.[2] The perception of black women as whores persisted in the 1930s and 1940s. The economic climate of the Depression perpetuated this assumption, especially when black women found service jobs more often than black men. Saundra Towns explains that black men erroneously equated black women's competitive advantage in the unstable job market with their illicit behavior:

Since [black] men are taught that *things must be earned*, i.e., that one must do something in order to get something, they begin to suspect that what Black women are doing to get jobs . . . is sleeping with white men. It is a logical conclusion, given the fact that in a male-dominated society, all men should be able to work. If Black women were chosen rather than Black men, it was not because of the superior physical strength, or greater intelligence of the former group. From the man's point of view, the woman has only one advantage over him: her sexuality [Towne's italics].[3]

The Department of Commerce census for 1940 indicates that 67.8 percent of employed black women in the South held jobs as service workers (many in private households), compared with 32.8 percent of employed black men. Outside the South 80.3 percent of employed black women held service jobs, compared with 57.1 percent of employed black men.[4] Black women held a greater percentage of service jobs than black men even during the 1930s despite the fact that in 1930, 3,662,893 black males age 10 and older were employed, compared with only 1,840,642 black females age 10 and older.[5] One reason black women were hired in service jobs more often than black men was that lower middle–class white women who previously could not afford the luxury of maid service could now pay as little as 20¢ an hour in wages to a desperate, starving black domestic.[6] Saundra Towns has also suggested that black women held a preponderance of service jobs because whites used black women as foils to avoid giving economic power to black men.[7]

Even intelligent, well-educated black men such as Calvin Hernton have made black women responsible for others' abusive treatment of them. Hernton believes that the black woman took up the role of whore the white South forced on her during slavery because "she had no other morality by which to shape her womanhood."[8] Although trying to exonerate black female slaves, he nevertheless assumes they were immoral.

Just as some white women sought to empower themselves by mistreating their "inferiors," black women, some black men, put upon by white men, vented their anger on and abused black women, who occupied the subordinate position in patriarchal society. After the end of slavery, some black men assumed the position of the old white master, becoming black women's new sexual exploiters, often as pimps who arranged black women's sexual services for white men. "The [black] pimp's dominance over women and his reputation as a lover are especially strong indicators of manhood to Blacks, for they are inextricably associated with a casting off of slave shackles," according to sociologists Richard and Christina Milner. A black pimp may feel that "he can more easily dominate a white woman," and that "a White ho can make more money in prostitution than a black woman"; yet as one black pimp told the Milners, "there are droves of White 'hawks' who will pass up fifty white hos to 'taste the Black fruit.'"[9]

In *The Street,* Ann Petry explores the black-woman-as-whore myth in her portrayal of Lutie Johnson, whose pent-up rage over a lifetime of struggle against exploitation and poverty finally unleashes itself. Marita Bonner's "Patch Quilt" shows us not the woman who is sought for sexual favors but the wife who is betrayed as her husband pursues another woman.

Some of the consequences of childhood rape are depicted in two of the selections in this section. The first, a letter to a relief administrator in Washington, D.C., is a mother's reaction to the rape of her small daughter by her caretaker's husband. Such extreme incidents were not uncommon. Day-care services for working women were nonexistent in the 1930s and 1940s, and children faced innumerable dangers from unscrupulous men. This letter starkly portrays the vulnerability of a poor woman supporting a family alone. The second selection from Maya Angelou's autobiographical *I Know Why the Caged Bird Sings,* vividly describes the experience of rape from the child's point of view, expressing her physical pain, her fear of the rapist, and her guilt and shame for having been raped.

The stereotypical "grand wife" is depicted in an excerpt from Zora Neale Hurston's *Their Eyes Were Watching God.* The marriage of the protagonist, Janie Starks, gives her a secure, respected place in the community and shields her from poverty. But she is confined by her husband's view of her proper role as his wife. In many ways she is the proverbial bird in a gilded cage—well kept and admired but prevented by her keeper, her husband, from fully participating in the life around her. Like all the women presented in this section, Janie suffers from the culture's disregard—embodied largely in her husband—for women.

NOTES

1. Maud White Katz, "The Negro Woman and the Law," *Freedomways* 2 (Summer 1962): 283.
2. John W. Jacks, editor of the *Standard* in Montgomery City, Missouri, assailed the virtue of black women in a letter to Florence Balgarnie, an activist in London, England, who forwarded the letter to Josephine St. Pierre Ruffin, founder of *The Woman's Era,* the first American magazine owned and published by black women. See Wilson Jeremiah Moses, *The Golden Age of Black Nationalism: 1850–1925* (Hamden, Conn.: Archon Books, 1978), 114–16.
3. Saundra Towns, "The Black Woman as Whore: Genesis of the Myth," *Black Position* 3 (1973): 50.
4. John P. Davis, *The American Negro Reference Book,* 2 vols. (Yonkers, N.Y.: Educational Heritage, 1966), I:222.

5. *Abstracts of the Fifteenth Census of the United States* (Washington, D.C.: USGPO, 1933), 330.
6. Baker and Cooke, "Bronx Slave Market," 330.
7. Towns, "Black Woman as Whore," 50.
8. Calvin C. Hernton, *Sex and Racism in America* (New York: Grove Press, 1965), 124.
9. Richard B. Milner and Christina Milner, *Black Players* (Boston: Little, Brown and Co., 1972), 223–24, 210.

● ● ● ● ●

From *The Street*

Ann Petry

Ann Petry currently resides in her native Old Saybrook, Connecticut, where she was born in 1908. She received her Ph.G. degree from the Connecticut College of Pharmacy in 1934 and worked as a pharmacist in her family's drugstore before moving to New York in 1938, where she wrote for the Harlem newspapers *Amsterdam News* and *People's Voice*. Petry is the author of three novels: *The Street* (1946), *Country Place* (1947), and *The Narrows* (1953), the last two being depictions of small-town New England life. She has also published a children's book, *The Drugstore Cat* (1949); two biographies for juvenile readers, *Harriet Tubman, Conductor on the Underground Railroad* (1955) and *Tituba of Salem Village* (1964); and two short-story collections, *Legends of the Saints* (1970) and *Miss Muriel and Other Stories* (1971). Her short stories have appeared in numerous journals and anthologies.

After reading a short story of Petry's, "On Saturday the Siren Sounds at Noon" in *The Crisis*, an editor at Houghton Mifflin Company in Boston suggested that she apply for the Houghton Mifflin Literary Fellowship. Petry submitted the first five chapters and a synopsis of *The Street* and won the $2,400 fellowship for 1945. Houghton Mifflin published the novel in 1946, and it became a best-seller.[1]

The powerful scene at the novel's end that is reprinted here expresses the enormous frustration of the black woman struggling with the multiple stresses of poverty, single motherhood, and sexual exploitation. The protagonist, Lutie Johnson, is an attractive young woman who has left her life as a maid in suburban Connecticut to go to Harlem, where she tries to make a new life for herself and her son Bub. Now in desperate need of money, Lutie is perceived as a whore by Junto, a well-off white man willing to pay Lutie to prostitute herself for him, and by Boots, a black man who has already accepted money for Lutie from Junto but first wants her for himself. "Sure," Boots thinks, "Lutie would sleep with Junto, but he was going to have her first. . . . After all, he's white and this time a white man can have a black man's leavings." Because Junto abused Boots earlier, Boots now feels free to take advantage of Lutie. He sees her not as a fellow victim but as someone— or more accurately, something—for him to use.

The frightful circumstances of Lutie's life in the city have all but overpowered her when she comes to see Boots. The violence of her reaction to his expectation reflects the intensity of the rage that she has contained for a long time, and she is ultimately destroyed by that rage.

NOTE

1. Lorraine Elena Roses and Ruth Elizabeth Randolph, *Harlem Renaissance and Beyond: Literary Biographies of One Hundred Black Women Writers 1900–1945* (Boston: G. K. Hall, 1990), 259.

When she rang the bell of Boots' apartment, he opened the door instantly as though he had been waiting for her.

"Hello, baby," he said, grinning. "Sure glad you got here. I got a friend I want you to meet."

Only two of the lamps in the living room were lit. They were the tall ones on each side of the davenport. They threw a brilliant light on the squat white man sitting there. He got up when he saw Lutie and stood in front of the imitation fireplace, leaning his elbow on the mantel.

Lutie stared at him, not certain whether this was Junto in the flesh or the imaginary one that had been on the studio couch in her apartment. She closed her eyes and then opened them and he was still there, standing by the fireplace. His squat figure partly blocked out the orange-red glow from the electric logs. She turned her head away and then looked toward him. He was still there, standing by the fireplace.

Boots established him as Junto in the flesh. "Mr. Junto, meet Mrs. Johnson. Lutie Johnson."

Lutie nodded her head. A figure in a mirror turned thumbs down and as he gestured the playground for Bub vanished, the nice new furniture disappeared along with the big airy rooms. "A nice white gentleman." "Need any extra money." She looked away from him, not saying anything.

"I want to talk to you, baby," Boots said. "Come on into the bedroom''—he pointed toward a door, started toward it, turned back and said, ''We'll be with you in a minute, Junto.''

Boots closed the bedroom door, sat down on the edge of the bed, leaning his head against the headboard.

''If you'll give me the money now, I'll be able to get it to the lawyer before he closes his office tonight,'' she said abruptly. This room was like the living room, it had too many lamps in it, and in addition there were too many mirrors so that she saw him reflected on each of the walls—his legs stretched out, his expression completely indifferent. There was the same soft, sound-absorbing carpet on the floor.

''Take your coat off and sit down, baby,'' he said lazily.

She shook her head. She didn't move any farther into the room, but stood with her back against the door, aware that there was no sound from the living room where Junto waited. She had brought that awful silence in here with her.

''I can't stay,'' she said sharply. ''I only came to get the money.''

''Oh, yes—the money,'' he said. He sounded as though he had just remembered it. ''You can get the money easy, baby. I figured it out.'' He half-closed his eyes. ''Junto's the answer. He'll give it to you. Just like that''—he snapped his fingers.

He paused for a moment as though he were waiting for her to say something, and when she made no comment he continued: ''All you got to do is be nice to him. Just be nice to him as long as he wants and the two hundred bucks is yours. And bein' nice to Junto pays off better than anything else I know.''

She heard what he said, knew exactly what he meant, and her mind skipped over his words and substituted other words. She was back in the big shabby ballroom at the Casino, straining to hear a thin thread of music that kept getting lost in the babble of voices, in the clink of glasses, in the bursts of laughter, so that she wasn't certain the music was real. Sometimes it was there and then again it was drowned out by the other sounds.

The faint, drifting melody went around and under the sound of Boots' voice and the words that he had spoken then blotted out what he had just said.

''Baby, this is just experience. Be months before you can earn money at it.''

''Nothing happened, baby. What makes you think something happened?''

''I don't have all the say-so. The guy who owns the Casino—guy named Junto—says you ain't ready yet.''

''Christ! he owns the joint.''

The guy named Junto owned the Bar and Grill, too. Evidently his decision that she wasn't to be paid for singing had been based on his desire to sleep with her; and he had concluded that, if she had to continue living in that house where his friend Mrs. Hedges lived or in one just like it, she would be a pushover.

And now the same guy, named Junto, was sitting outside on a sofa, just a few feet away from this door, and she thought, I would like to kill him. Not just because he happens to be named Junto, but because I can't even think straight about him or anybody else any more. It is as though he were a piece of that dirty street itself, tangible, close at hand, within reach.

She could still hear that floating, drifting tune. It was inside her head and she couldn't get it out. Boots was staring at her, waiting for her to say something, waiting for her answer. He and Junto thought they knew what she would say. If she hummed that fragment of melody aloud, she would get rid of it. It was the only way to make it disappear; otherwise it would keep going around and around in her head. And she thought, I must be losing my mind, wanting to hum a tune and at the same time thinking about killing that man who is sitting, waiting, outside.

Boots said, "Junto's a good guy. You'll be surprised how much you'll take to him."

The sound of her own voice startled her. It was hoarse, loud, furious. It contained the accumulated hate and the accumulated anger from all the years of seeing the things she wanted slip past her without her ever having touched them.

She shouted, "Get him out of here! Get him out of here! Get him out of here quick!"

And all the time she was thinking, Junto has a brick in his hand. Just one brick. The final one needed to complete the wall that had been building up around her for years, and when that one last brick was shoved in place, she would be completely walled in.

"All right. All right. Don't get excited." Boots got up from the bed, pushed her away from the door and went out, slamming it behind him.

"Sorry, Junto," Boots said. "She's mad as hell. No use your waiting."

"I heard her," Junto said sourly. "And if this is something you planned, you'd better unplan it."

"You heard her, didnya?"

"Yes. But you still could have planned it," Junto said. He walked toward the foyer. At the door he turned to Boots. "Well?" he said.

"Don't worry, Mack," Boots said coldly. "She'll come around. Come back about ten o'clock."

He closed the door quietly behind Junto. He hadn't intended to in the beginning, but he was going to trick him and Junto would never know the difference. Sure, Lutie would sleep with Junto, but he was going to have her first. He thought of the thin curtains blowing in the wind. Yeah, he can have the leavings. After all, he's white and this time a white man can have a black man's leavings.

Junto had pushed him hard, threatened him, nagged him about Lutie Johnson. This would be his revenge. He locked the door leading to the foyer and put the key in his pocket. Then he headed toward the kitchenette in the back of the apartment. He'd fix a drink for Lutie and one for himself.

The murmur of their voices came to Lutie in the bedroom. She couldn't hear what they said and she waited standing in front of the door, listening for some indication that Junto had gone.

As soon as Junto left, she would go home. But she had to make certain he had gone, because if she walked outside there and saw him she would try to kill him. The thought frightened her. This was no time to get excited or to get angry. She had to be calm and concentrate on how to keep Bub from going to reform school.

She'd been so angry just now she had forgotten that she still had to get two hundred dollars to take to the lawyer. Pop might have some ideas. Yes, he'd have ideas. He always had them. But she was only kidding herself if she thought any of them would yield two hundred dollars.

There was the sound of a door closing, and then silence. She looked out into the living room. It was empty. She could hear the clinking sound of glasses from somewhere in the back of the apartment.

And then Boots entered the room carrying a tray. Ice tinkled in tall glasses. A bottle of soda and a bottle of whiskey teetered precariously on the tray as he walked toward her.

"Here, baby," he said. "Have a drink and get yourself together."

She stood in front of the fireplace, holding the glass in her hand, not drinking it, just holding it. She could feel its coldness through her glove. She would go and talk to Pop. He'd lived three steps in front of the law for so long, he just might have a friend who was a lawyer and if Pop had ever done the friend any favors he might take Bub's case on the promise of weekly payments from her.

And she ought to go now. Why was she standing here holding this glass of liquor that she didn't want and had no intention of drinking? Because you're still angry, she thought, and you haven't anyone to vent your anger on and you're halfway hoping Boots will say something or do something that will give you an excuse to blow up in a thousand pieces.

"Whyn't you sit down?" Boots said.

"I've got to go." And yet she didn't move. She stayed in front of the fireplace watching him as he sat on the sofa, sipping his drink.

Occasionally he glanced up at her and she saw the scar on his cheek as a long thin line that looked darker than she had remembered it. And she thought he's like these streets that trap all of us—vicious, dangerous.

Finally he said, "Listen, you want to get the little bastard out of jail, don't yah? What you being so fussy about?"

She put the glass down on a table. Some of the liquor slopped over, oozing down the sides of the glass, and as she looked at it, it seemed as though something had slopped over inside her head in the same fashion, was oozing through her so that she couldn't think.

"Skip it," she said.

Her voice was loud in the room. That's right, she thought, skip it. Let's all skip together, children. All skip together. Up the golden stairs. Skipping hand in hand up the golden stairs.

"Just skip it," she repeated.

She had to get out of here, now, and quickly. She mustn't stand here any longer looking down at him like this, because she kept thinking that he represented everything she had fought against. Yet she couldn't take her eyes away from the ever-darkening scar that marred the side of his face; and as she stared at him, she felt she was gazing straight at the street with its rows of old houses, its piles of garbage, its swarms of children.

"Junto's rich as hell," Boots said. "What you got to be so particular about? There ain't a dame in town who wouldn't give everything they got for a chance at him." And he thought, Naw, she ain't acting right. And she was all that stood between him and going back to portering or some other lousy, stinking job where he would carry his hat in his hand all day and walk on his head, saying "Yessir, yessir, yessir."

She moved away from the fireplace. There wasn't any point in answering him. Right now she couldn't even think straight, couldn't even see straight. She kept thinking about the street, kept seeing it.

All those years, going to grammar school, going to high school, getting married, having a baby, going to work for the Chandlers, leaving Jim because he got himself another woman—all those years she'd been heading straight as an arrow for that street or some other street just like it. Step by step she'd come, growing up, working, saving, and finally getting an apartment on a street that nobody could have beaten. Even if she hadn't talked to Bub about money all the time, he would have got into trouble sooner or later, because the street looked after him when she wasn't around.

"Aw, what the hell!" Boots muttered. He put his glass down on the table in front of the sofa, got up and by moving swiftly blocked her progress to the door.

"Let's talk it over," he said. "Maybe we can work out something."

43

She hesitated. There wasn't anything to work out or talk over unless he meant he would lend her the money with no strings attached. And if he was willing to do that, she would be a fool not to accept it. Pop was a pretty feeble last resort.

"Come on, baby," he said. "Ten minutes' talk will straighten it out." And she went back to stand in front of the fireplace.

"Ain't no point in your getting mad, baby. We can still be friends," he said softly, and put his arm around her waist.

He was standing close to her. She smelt faintly sweet and he pulled her closer. She tried to back away from him and he forced her still closer, held her hands behind her back, pulling her ever closer and closer.

As he kissed her, he felt a hot excitement well up in him that made him forget all the logical, reasoned things he had meant to say; for her skin was soft under his mouth and warm. He fumbled with the fastenings of her coat, his hand groping toward her breasts.

"Aw, Christ, baby," he whispered. "Junto can get his afterward." And the rhythm of the words sank into him, seemed to correspond with the rhythm of his desire for her so that he had to say them again. "Let him get his afterward. I'll have mine first."

She twisted out of his arms with a sudden, violent motion that nearly sent him off balance. The anger surging through her wasn't directed solely at him. He was there at hand; he had tricked her into staying an extra few minutes in this room with him, because she thought he was going to lend her the money she so urgently needed; and she was angry with him for that and for being a procurer for Junto and for assuming that she would snatch at an opportunity to sleep with either or both of them. This quick surface anger helped to swell and became a part of the deepening stream of rage that had fed on the hate, the frustration, the resentment she had toward the pattern her life had followed.

So she couldn't stop shouting, and shouting wasn't enough. She wanted to hit out at him, to reduce him to a speechless mass of flesh, to destroy him completely, because he was there in front of her and she could get at him and in getting at him she would find violent outlet for the full sweep of her wrath.

Words tumbled from her throat. "You no good bastard!" she shouted. "You can tell Junto I said if he wants a whore to get one from Mrs. Hedges. And the same thing goes for you. Because I'd just as soon get in bed with a rattlesnake—I'd just as soon—"

And he reached out and slapped her across the face. And as she stood there in front of him, trembling with anger, her face smarting, he slapped her again.

"I don't take that kind of talk from dames," he said. "Not even good-looking ones like you. Maybe after I beat the hell out of you a coupla times, you'll begin to like the idea of sleeping with me and with Junto.''

The blood pounding in her head blurred her vision so that she saw not one Boots Smith but three of him; and behind these three figures the room was swaying, shifting, and changing with a wavering motion. She tried to separate the three blurred figures and it was like trying to follow the course of heat waves as they rose from a sidewalk on a hot day in August.

Despite this unstable triple vision of him, she was scarcely aware of him as an individual. His name might have been Brown or Smith or Wilson. She might never have seen him before, might have known nothing about him. He happened to be within easy range at the moment he set off the dangerous accumulation of rage that had been building in her for months.

When she remembered there was a heavy iron candlestick on the mantelpiece just behind her, her vision cleared; the room stopped revolving and Boots Smith became one person, not three. He was the person who had struck her, her face still hurt from the blow; he had threatened her with violence and with a forced relationship with Junto and with himself. These things set off her anger, but as she gripped the iron candlestick and brought it forward in a swift motion aimed at his head, she was striking, not at Boots Smith, but at a handy, anonymous figure—a figure which her angry resentment transformed into everything she had hated, everything she had fought against, everything that had served to frustrate her.

He was so close to her that she struck him on the side of the head before he saw the blow coming. The first blow stunned him. And she struck him again and again, using the candlestick as though it were a club. He tried to back away from her and stumbled over the sofa and sprawled there.

A lifetime of pent-up resentment went into the blows. Even after he lay motionless, she kept striking him, not thinking about him, not even seeing him. First she was venting her rage against the dirty, crowded street. She saw the rows of dilapidated old houses; the small dark rooms; the long steep flights of stairs; the narrow dingy hallways; the little lost girls in Mrs. Hedges' apartment; the smashed homes where the women did drudgery because their men had deserted them. She saw all of these things and struck at them.

Then the limp figure on the sofa became, in turn, Jim and the slender girl she'd found him with; became the insult in the moist-eyed glances of white men on the subway; became the unconcealed hostility in the eyes of white women; became the greasy, lecherous man at the Crosse School for Singers; became the gaunt Super pulling her down, down into the basement.

Finally, and the blows were heavier, faster, now, she was striking at the white world which thrust black people into a walled enclosure from which there was no escape; and at the turn-of-events which had forced her to leave Bub alone while she was working so that he now faced reform school, now had a police record.

She saw the face and head of the man on the sofa through waves of anger in which he represented all these things and she was destroying them.

She grew angrier as she struck him, because he seemed to be eluding her behind a red haze that obscured his face. Then the haze of red blocked his face out completely. She lowered her arm, peering at him, trying to locate his face through the redness that concealed it.

The room was perfectly still. There was no sound in it except her own hoarse breathing. She let the candlestick fall out of her hand. It landed on the thick rug with a soft clump and she started to shiver.

He was dead. There was no question about it. No one could live with a head battered in like that. And it wasn't a red haze that had veiled his face. It was blood.

She backed away from the sight of him, thinking that if she took one slow step at a time, just one slow step at a time, she could get out of here, walking backward, step by step. She was afraid to turn her back on that still figure on the sofa. It had become a thing. It was no longer Boots Smith, but a thing on a sofa.

She stumbled against a chair and sat down in it, shivering. She would never get out of this room. She would never, never get out of here. For the rest of her life she would be here with this awful faceless thing on the sofa. Then she forced herself to get up, to start walking backward again.

The foyer door was closed because she backed right into it. Just a few more steps and she would be out. She fumbled for the knob. The door was locked. She didn't believe it and rattled it. She felt for a key. There was none. It would, she was certain, be in Boots Smith's pocket and she felt a faint stirring of anger against him. He had deliberately locked the door because he hadn't intended to let her out of here.

The anger went as quickly as it came. She had to go back to that motionless, bloody figure on the sofa. The stillness in the room made her feel as though she was wading through water, wading waist-deep toward the couch, and the water swallowed up all sound. It tugged against her, tried to pull her back.

The key was in his pocket. In her haste she pulled all the things out of his pocket—a handkerchief, a wallet, book matches, and the key. She held on to the key, but the other things went out of her hand because as she drew away from him she thought he moved. And all the stories she had ever heard about the dead coming back to life, about the dead talking, about the dead walking, went through her mind; making her hands shake so that she couldn't control them.

As she moved hurriedly away from the couch, she almost stepped on the wallet. She picked it up and looked inside. It bulged with money. He could have given her two hundred dollars and never missed it.

The two hundred dollars she needed was right there in her hand. She could take it to the lawyer tonight. Or could she?

For the first time the full implication of what she had done swept over her. She was a murderer. And the smartest lawyer in the world couldn't do anything for Bub, not now, not when his mother had killed a man. A kid whose mother was a murderer didn't stand any chance at all. Everyone he came in contact with would believe that sooner or later he, too, would turn criminal. The Court wouldn't parole him in her care either, because she was no longer a fit person to bring him up.

She couldn't stop the quivering that started in her stomach, that set up a spasmodic contracting of her throat so that she felt as though her breath had been cut off. The only thing she could do was to go away and never come back, because the best thing that could happen to Bub would be for him never to know that his mother was a murderer. She took half the bills out of the wallet, wadded them into her purse, left the wallet on the sofa.

Getting back to the foyer door was worse this time. The four corners of the room were alive with silence—deepening pools of an ominous silence. She kept turning her head in an effort to see all of the room at once; kept fighting against a desire to scream. Hysteria mounted in her because she began to believe that at any moment the figure on the sofa might disappear into one of these pools of silence and then emerge from almost any part of the room, to bar her exit.

When she finally turned the key in the door, crossed the small foyer, and reached the outside hall, she had to lean against the wall for a long moment before she could control the shaking of her legs, but the contracting of her throat was getting worse.

She saw that the white gloves she was wearing were streaked with dust from the candlestick. There was a smear of blood on one of them. She ripped them off and put them in her coat pocket, and as she did it she thought she was acting as though murder was something with which she was familiar. She walked down the stairs instead of taking the elevator, and the thought recurred.

When she left the building, it was snowing hard. The wind blew the snow against her face, making her walk faster as she approached the entrance to the Eighth Avenue subway.

She thought confusedly of the best place for her to go. It had to be a big city. She decided that Chicago was not too far away and it was big. It would swallow her up. She would go there.

On the subway she started shivering again. Had she killed Boots by accident? The awful part of it was she hadn't even seen him when she was hitting him like that. The first blow was deliberate and provoked, but all those other blows weren't provoked. There wasn't any excuse for her. It hadn't even been self-defense. This impulse to violence had been in her for a long time, growing, feeding, until finally she had blown up in a thousand pieces. Bub must never know what she had done.

In Pennsylvania Station she bought a ticket for Chicago. "One way?" the ticket man asked.

"One way," she echoed. Yes, a one-way ticket, she thought. I've had one since the day I was born.

The train was on the track. People flowed and spilled through the gates like water running over a dam. She walked in the middle of the crowd.

The coaches filled up rapidly. People with bags and hatboxes and bundles and children moved hastily down the aisles, almost falling into the seats in their haste to secure a place to sit.

Lutie found a seat midway in the coach. She sat down near the window. Bub would never understand why she had disappeared. He was expecting to see her tomorrow. She had promised him she would come. He would never know why she had deserted him and he would be bewildered and lost without her.

Would he remember that she loved him? She hoped so, but she knew that for a long time he would have that half-frightened, worried look she had seen on his face the night he was waiting for her at the subway.

He would probably go to reform school. She looked out of the train window, not seeing the last-minute passengers hurrying down the ramp. The constriction of her throat increased. So he will go to reform school, she repeated. He'll be better off there. He'll be better off without you. That way he may have some kind of chance. He didn't have the ghost of a chance on that street. The best you could give him wasn't good enough.

As the train started to move, she began to trace a design on the window. It was a series of circles that flowed into each other. She remembered that when she was in grammar school the children were taught to get the proper slant to their writing, to get the feel of a pen in their hands, by making these same circles.

Once again she could hear the flat, exasperated voice of the teacher as she looked at the circles Lutie had produced. "Really," she said, "I don't know why they have us bother to teach your people to write."

Her finger moved over the glass, around and around. The circles showed up plainly on the dusty surface. The woman's statement was correct, she thought. What possible good has it done to teach people like me to write?

The train crept out of the tunnel, gathered speed as it left the city behind. Snow whispered against the windows. And as the train roared into the darkness, Lutie tried to figure out by what twists and turns of fate she had landed on this train. Her mind balked at the task. All she could think was, It was that street. It was that god-damned street.

The snow fell softly on the street. It muffled sound. It sent people scurrying homeward, so that the street was soon deserted, empty, quiet. And it could have been any street in the city, for the snow laid a delicate film over the sidewalk, over the brick of the tired, old buildings; gently obscuring the grime and the garbage and the ugliness.

* * * * *

"Patch Quilt"

Marita Bonner

Marita Odette Bonner (Occomy) was born in 1898 in Boston, Massachusetts. She attended public schools in Brookline and began her writing career with contributions to her high school student magazine, *Sagamore*. At Radcliffe College she studied writing under the renowned Charles Townsend Copeland, who admired her ability but admonished her as a racial protest writer not to be "bitter." She continued writing while a teacher at Armstrong High School in Washington, D.C., and even after she married William Almy Occomy, moved to Chicago, and had three children. A short-story writer, playwright, and essayist, Bonner published most of her works from 1924 to 1941 in *The Crisis* and *Opportunity*. *Purple Flowers* won the *Crisis* best play award in 1927, the same year that "Drab Rambles" won the *Crisis* best short story prize. Bonner died in 1971.

Lorraine Roses and Ruth Randolph observe that "the writing of Marita Bonner is sensitive to the 'double and triple jeopardies' Afro-American women are exposed to in a society that is race-, sex-, and class-conscious.''[1] Bonner writes about women who are discriminated against as blacks in American society, as women in their black community, and as underpaid workers in a class-conscious economy. Bonner's vision and craft in such short stories as "A Sealed Pod" (1936), "Patch Quilt" (1940), and "One True Love" (1941) link her to contemporary writers like Alice Walker, Gloria Naylor, and Gayle Jones, who also deal with the complex issues of black women's lives.

"Patch Quilt" (*The Crisis* [March 1940]) dramatizes a black woman's victimization by sexism in her own home. It is a simple story of a poor and guileless young woman, Sara, who at the outset is overjoyed because her husband is due home soon with a paycheck for the first time in nearly three years. Her husband betrays her with another woman, however, and Sara reacts violently. As with Lutie Johnson in Ann Petry's *The Street*, Sara's rage gives her no release, no freedom from her trouble. Rather, it entraps her, her husband, and his mistress in a mutual silence of "shame, humiliation, and despair." Sara's eager anticipation of her husband and a brief, joyful reprieve from poverty intensifies the shock of betrayal and the bleakness of her situation once she and her husband resume their life together.

NOTE

1. Roses and Randolph, *Harlem Renaissance and Beyond*, 19.

Sara unrolled a piece of damp clothes from the basket beneath her ironing board and shook it out.

"Another one of them ruffled dresses for Mrs. Brown's Sally. I'clare I can't iron it today." Sara spoke aloud to herself.

She looked at the clock. Twelve o'clock. She should have known that by the sunshine though it was hard to tell time by the sun in March.

Jim ought to be coming any moment now. Jim ought to be coming home from his new job.

"First time in near three years that Jim'll bring home a pay envelope on Saturday. Shore glad the government made them put some of the colored relief men on the new road job along with the white!" Sara had a habit of talking aloud whenever she was alone. She made a half-hearted swoop with her old-fashioned sad-iron over one ruffle before her on the board.

A whistle blew somewhere.

Sara held her iron up from the board and listened. Then walking swiftly to the rusty iron stove that glowed red hot beneath a burden of six irons, she released the one she held in her hand.

"Shame to waste this fire and these clothes all damped just right to iron but I gotta git ready to make market."

She took the board down from its position between two chairs, tossed the dress back into the basket and went into the bedroom.

"I'm going to get me some of the things I been wanting to eat these three years." Sara planned happily as she put on a clean cotton house dress and her only pair of silk stockings.

"Jim's bringing twelve dollars and I got four or five up in the closet. Guess we'll have chicken and yeller yams and greens and ice-cream—if the freezer is still any good—and two kinds of cake for Sunday dinner! Got to celebrate!"

She broke off talking to herself to listen again. Jim ought to be coming into the house right now. Only took fifteen minutes to get home if he took the short cut.

"Guess he gone down town to git his hair cut! Git all prettied up," Sara decided finally.

She went to the cupboard in the kitchen, took down an old tea-pot and drew out four dirty crumpled one dollar bills.

"We can take the ten dollars rent out of Jim's money. I'm going!" she decided recklessly.

She snapped her pocket-book together, unlatched the door and stepped out.

Her house, like all the other houses in the colored district on that hill, stood below the level of the street.

Sara putted a little as she climbed over the ditch where the last night's rain had left a little water.

"Wished they'd let that new road come this side of town," she panted aloud as she came up on the street.

She began to pick the driest spots in the mud to walk through for there were no sidewalks.

"Hi, Sara! Looks like spring's most here!" a voice called.

Sara halted and looked around. A tall, dark colored woman of indeterminate age leaned over the gate of a yard across the road.

"Aw, hi, Miss Susie!" Sara greeted her. She drew nearer to the woman. "I'm 'bout to go to town to make market."

"Jim home yet?"

"Naw, but I can't wait for him to git home! I got right smart buying to do."

"Y'all having company tomorrer?"

Sara drew herself up proudly.

"Naw! Jes' Jim and me but I'clare I feel like eatin' a good dinner like I used to when times was good! I want ice cream and two kinds of cake!"

The other woman did not answer. Instead she looked off toward the top of the hill.

A white cottage stood there.

"Wonder how Miss Drake is?" Miss Susie said after a pause.

Sara looked surprised. "She sick?"

"Naw—! I jes' wondered how she was!"

There was another silence. Sara stirred restlessly and said, "Well—! I'll be gettin' along!"

The other woman did not speak again nor did she look at her.

Sara walked off, down the hill.

Once she looked back. Miss Susie still stood as she had left her, staring down the road after Sara.

"What ails Miss Susie? What she say that 'bout Miss Drake for? She ain't no company of Miss Drake! Jes' said that so's I wouldn't git to tell her what I'se having for dinner! How is Miss Drake!!"

Her mind went back to the house at the crest of the hill, too.

Nobody was Miss Drake's "company." She lived alone with her two children, Sandy and Marie, and earned her living by sewing for white families of the little southern town of Redmond.

"She sews so much for white folks, she thinks she's white too!" was the common belief among the Negroes of the town. "Always stayin' to herself! Keeping that girl and boy cooped up all the time."

"That gal ain't home all the time! She off somewhere passing, workin' in a white store," town gossip proclaimed.

"How anybody going to pass in Redmond where everybody knows everybody else here!" others countered.

Sara thought of all this as she pushed on down the hill toward the shopping district.

She paused once near a clump of bushes to rest.

The shrubbery shook suddenly and a tawny, freckled-face boy in his teens clambered out.

Sara recognized Sandy Drake by the reddish hair.

"Howdy, Miss Sara!" the boy muttered.

"How are you, Sandy! How's your ma and your sister?"

The boy flushed and stuttered something. Sara could not understand him. She tried another tack.

"How they makin' out with the new road? I see you come 'cross the hill from that away? Ain't they knocked off for the day yet?"

Sandy reddened still more. "Yas'm—er—I guess so! I dunno. Ma sent me out to meet sister."

He plunged on up the hill abruptly.

Sara stared after him. "What ails that little fool? Big as any man and can't talk straight so you can get any sense out of it!"

She watched the boy out of sight and quickening her pace set off down the hill until she reached the base where the colored section ended and Market street—the main street—began.

She crossed Market street, lost herself in the midst of the mud and chicken crates, the side-walk vendors and hawkers, the muddy automobiles and crowds of poor whites and Negroes that made Saturday the most exciting day of the week in that town.

With a sort of giddy triumph Sara acquired her chicken and her yellow yams, her fat back and greens, lemons, sugar, flour and vanilla.

At the end of an hour she found herself outside of the Five-and-Ten at the far end of the market, trying to juggle her packages so the oysters would not spill and with but twenty cents in her purse.

"Guess I'll git me an ice-pick! That other thing is enough to try the devil!"

Ten minutes later, with the ice-pick and a pound of pink jaw breakers added to her pack, Sara started back up the hill.

She was heavy with packages—and not one cent was left to her.

She was tired but she was happy. She crunched the candy noisily.

A broad black woman hung across the fence at the first house she reached.

"Hi, Sara!" she called in greeting as Sara came abreast her gate. "Looks like you been doin' right smart buyin'?"

Sara choked hastily over a large piece of candy to make room for a complete answer. "Yas. I been jes' makin' a little market! Spent every bit of fo' dollars for just this one meal, though!" she broke off to giggle and watch the effect of her statement.

The other woman let her eyes sweep up and down Sara's figure.

Then she gazed up the hill toward the top and back down and said, "I hear that one of them travelin' buses done fell over on the new road!"

Startled, Sara forgot to giggle.

"Ain't nobody hurt!" she managed to ask. "You know, Jim's workin' over there."

The other woman shook her head doubtfully. "I ain't heard that. I jes' heard 'bout the bus! Say! Whyn't you cut across the back lots and see?"

Sara shot off without saying goodbye and left the other gazing with veiled eyes after her.

Anxiety and the uneven ground of the fields brought a breathless Sara upon the highway.

A cross-country bus lay on its side in a ditch, a group of people, apparently passengers, and mostly white, stood clumped disconsolately around their bags piled in the road. All the machinery used for excavating the road stood idle. No laborers were in sight.

Uncle Eph, a deaf Negro who claimed to be one hundred and ten, sat on a rock nearby cleaning a red lantern.

Sara approached him.

"Who got hurt!" she screamed, pointing to the bus.

"Ain't nobody hurt!" answered Eph mildly.

Relief loosed Sara's giggles again. "That Annie May Jones had me thinkin' all y'all was kilt out here on the job!" she cried.

Eph rubbed his lamp. "I gotta git these things ready for the night. I keeps the lights on this here job at night."

"So Jim told me. Is Jim gone home?"

Eph scrubbed the lamp in his hand and sat it down on the ground. He did not answer this time.

"I reckon Jim's gone on home!" Sarah screamed again.

Uncle Eph sat back suddenly, shook his rag out and looked Sara directly in the face.

"Go on up to the tool shed!" he said loudly. "Go on up there!"

Sara gaped at him amazed. "Guess the poor soul don' know what I ast him!" She hesitated an instant, thrust her hand in her bag of candy and set two pieces down beside Eph. Then she started off up the hill toward the shed.

The door of the shed was open. Sara peered into the semi-darkness there. She saw nobody and was about to turn back when a sound came from behind the door.

She thrust her head inside, peered around the door.

Something green waved in her face and she heard a low murmuring. "You kin have it all honey. I'm crazy 'bout you!"

It was Jim's voice—Sara's eyes grew accustomed to the gloom. There was Jim's back, and staring with pale stricken fright across Jim's shoulder was Marie Drake. In her hand she clutched a bill.

Sara's bundles hurtled to the ground. Sara's hands snatched up the new ice-pick. Sara lunged and struck and lunged and struck again.

Then she ran screaming and crying aloud back into the sunshine.

Right outside of the door she ran straight into the arms of Uncle Eph.

"I hadn't ought to a tol' you, honey! I hadn't ought to a tol' you, but I couldn't stand no more to see this deceivin' goin' on!"

The bus driver came striding up the hill.

"What's the matter here?" he demanded with that bustling flimsy authority assumed by cheap whites when they want to impress Negroes.

"She busted her eggs and her flour," Uncle Eph replied laconically. "See?"

He pointed to the ground. The driver glanced indifferently, grunted and turning on his heel, strode back to his own troubles.

When he was out of hearing Eph pushed open the door wide. He saw the ice-pick on the ground. He saw the blood on the ice-pick.

"Y'all?" Eph shouted.

There was no reply. Eph drew Sara in, closed the door and struck a match to a candle.

Jim lay across the girl, Marie. Blood was streaming from one of her eyes and she lay staring in terror. In her hands she still held the money.

"You ain't dead! Ain't no use pertendin'." Uncle Eph ordered, "Git up."

"He's bleeding to death on me!" screamed the girl hysterically and began to cry.

"Shet up! Want all them folks from the bus come here and take you to the lock-up?" Eph cried.

Eph knelt beside Jim—rolled him over a little. He beckoned to Sara who leaned, hands clutched at her throat against the door.

"Ain't dead! Neck cut on the side. I'll git some water and we'll lug him cross the fields to Dr. Butler."

Eph stood up, yanked the door open back to its hinges. He pointed to Marie and shouted loudly as if she too were deaf, "Git on out of here! Tell your ma its best to keep young ones like you tied in their own yard!"

And that is how it happened that Marie Drake dropped out of sight. "She gone North to school"—some people said. "Passin'!!"

But Sandy and his mother knew that Marie sat at home with her left eye closed forever and a deep ugly scar marring her left cheek.

Shame made a wall around the house on top of the hill.

And that is how it happened that Jim Brown had to lay off working—"'cause a pick fell on his arm"—a useless arm hanging limp, a tendon cut at the shoulder.

Spring passed, the job on the road ended, but the tendon did not heal. Jim sat listless on the porch and gazed back toward the hills that hid the highway. Sometimes he looked up toward the top of the hill.

He did not say anything. He did not even offer to go fishing any more.

—"And when he did go fishin', that gal was right along with him. He used to come home with scarcely no fish!"

—Like patches in a quilt, Sara could piece the whole story clearly now.

The neighbors had known that day when she went shopping for chicken and oysters, lemonade and a new ice-pick. They had known all this.

That is why they had looked at her so. And she thought it was envy.

And from those fishing trips Jim used to come back absent minded, suddenly irritable, with little red patches—that were made by the im-

print of a mouth coated with lip stick—Sara knew now—on his shirt
. . ."Berries done that!" he had lied.

"You ought to get right smart insurance from Uncle Sam if that pick
fell on him!" the neighborhood declared to Sara.

Sara did not answer. She had to work harder to make ends meet.

Only she and Jim and Marie knew about the ice-pick.

And shame, humiliation, and despair froze them to silence.

Uncle Eph knew, of course, but he never told.

Sometimes he felt sorry because he had been the one who had sent
Sara to the tool shed.

But he always comforted himself with the thought that he had fed
the chicken to his cat.

He could not eat delicacies that had been meant for a feast of rejoicing—and dropped for a maiming—and a slaughter of hopes.

• • • • •

Letter of a Mother in Distress

From the Works Progress Administration Collection, Howard University

The following letter expresses a young mother's unrelenting frustration. Deserted by her husband, left with two small children, and denied
relief, this mother's need to work and her inability to pay for a reliable
babysitter put her children in jeopardy. When her daughter is raped
and contracts a venereal disease, she must cope not only with the existing hardships but with the knowledge that her daughter's future has
been severely damaged.

12 January 1939

Relief Administrator
Washington, D.C.

Dear Administrator—

I'm writing you in regard to a great catastrophe, as you may
read in the article from a local newspaper, which has happened to
me and my little girl.

I am a Mother 25 years old, have two children. I moved to Champaign from Pulaski, Illinois, September, 1935. I was married about two years ago. My husband made a fair stepfather and unfortunately we were separated a few months ago and he has already applied for a divorce, which was published. And I was forced to apply for relief, which has been constantly denied me and my children.

I have lived a respectable life and have connected myself with churches, P.T.A. and representative people although I've little to contribute except my presence.

I even went to State's Attorney Hamill and also to his assistant; I still got no help.

Went back to Mrs. Edna Alexander, to whom we apply for relief, that is she sent for me and when I arrived she told me she could not help me and refused to talk.

I was working that week and had earned $5.00 and I told her I could not pay rent, provide food and clothing and pay someone to look after my children for $5.00 and asked her to please give me groceries and she refused.

I had paid this woman where I was rooming to keep my children. She left them with this man whom she had claimed to be her husband. It was he who *raped* my child and transmitted a venereal disease which your State Health Department shows record for and which may impair my child's health and take from her all social advantages for life.

I feel that the relief authorities in this town are responsible for what happened and if this is proper form of procedure I want to enter it as a complaint against them in this case and ask you to investigate the handling of such in this city for they are rotten.

Very truly,
Dora Hite
1004 N. 6th St
Champaign, Illinois

P.S. I do so much need help with my children. Can you see that I get it?

●　●　●　●　●

From *I Know Why the Caged Bird Sings*

Maya Angelou

An accomplished writer and poet, Maya Angelou has written about
only a small segment of her life in her widely read autobiographies: *I
Know Why the Caged Bird Sings* (1970), *Gather Together in My Name* (1974),
Singing and Swinging and Gettin' Merry Like Christmas (1975), *Heart of a
Woman* (1981), and *All God's Children Need Traveling Shoes* (1986). She
wrote the television screenplays *Georgia, Georgia* (1972), *I Know Why the
Caged Bird Sings* (1978), and *Sister, Sister* (1979) and wrote and produced
for PBS the 10-part series *Blacks, Blues, Blacks* (1979) on the traditions of
African and American life. Her poetry collections are *Just Give Me a Cool
Drink of Water 'fore I Diiie* (1971), *Oh Pray My Wings Are Gonna Fit Me
Well* (1975), *And Still I Rise* (1978), and *Shaker, Why Don't You Sing?*
(1983). Active in the civil rights and feminist movements, Angelou was
appointed northern coordinator of the Southern Christian Leadership
Conference (SCLC) in 1959 and was named woman of the year by *La-
dies' Home Journal* in 1976. She has lectured and taught throughout the
United States and in Africa and has received numerous awards and
honorary doctoral degrees.

Angelou was born in 1928 in St. Louis, Missouri, where she spent
a part of her childhood during the Depression. *I Know Why the Caged
Bird Sings* (Random House) partially focuses on that era as it chronicles
the time of her earliest memories through her teenage years. Reflecting
on her childhood, Angelou remarks that ''the Black female is assaulted
in her tender years by all the common forces of nature at the same time
that she is caught in the tripartite crossfire of masculine prejudice,
white illogical hate and Black lack of power.'' The mission of her autobiography is to show how society violated her as a young black female.

The following excerpt, told from Angelou's point of view at age
eight, centers on her rape by her mother's live-in boyfriend. She clearly
conveys the physical pain of sexual assault and the mental anguish of
not daring to tell. Her timidity and fear of telling magnify the brutality
of the rape. For more than a year after the scene described here took
place she lived in self-imposed silence, speaking only rarely, and then
mostly to her brother.

On a late spring Saturday, after our chores (nothing like those in
Stamps) were done, Bailey and I were going out, he to play baseball and

I to the library. Mr. Freeman said to me, after Bailey had gone downstairs, "Ritie, go get some milk for the house."

Mother usually brought milk when she came in, but that morning
as Bailey and I straightened the living room her bedroom door had been
open, and we knew that she hadn't come home the night before.

He gave me money and I rushed to the store and back to the house.
After putting the milk in the icebox, I turned and had just reached the
front door when I heard, "Ritie." He was sitting in the big chair by the
radio. "Ritie, come here." I didn't think about the holding time until I
got close to him. His pants were open and his "thing" was standing
out of his britches by itself.

"No, sir, Mr. Freeman." I started to back away. I didn't want to
touch that mushy-hard thing again, and I didn't need him to hold me
any more. He grabbed my arm and pulled me between his legs. His face
was still and looked kind, but he didn't smile or blink his eyes. Nothing.
He did nothing, except reach his left hand around to turn on the radio
without even looking at it. Over the noise of music and static, he said,
"Now, this ain't gonna hurt you much. You liked it before, didn't you?"

I didn't want to admit that I had in fact liked his holding me or that
I had liked his smell or the hard heart-beating, so I said nothing. And
his face became like the face of one of those mean natives the Phantom
was always having to beat up.

His legs were squeezing my waist. "Pull down your drawers." I
hesitated for two reasons: he was holding me too tight to move, and I
was sure that any minute my mother or Bailey or the Green Hornet
would bust in the door and save me.

"We was just playing before." He released me enough to snatch
down my bloomers, and then he dragged me closer to him. Turning the
radio up loud, too loud, he said, "If you scream, I'm gonna kill you.
And if you tell, I'm gonna kill Bailey." I could tell he meant what he
said. I couldn't understand why he wanted to kill my brother. Neither
of us had done anything to him. And then.

Then there was the pain. A breaking and entering when even the
senses are torn apart. The act of rape on an eight year-old body is a
matter of the needle giving because the camel can't. The child gives,
because the body can, and the mind of the violator cannot.

I thought I had died—I woke up in a white-walled world, and it had
to be heaven. But Mr. Freeman was there and he was washing me. His
hands shook, but he held me upright in the tub and washed my legs.
"I didn't mean to hurt you, Ritie. I didn't mean it. But don't you tell
. . . Remember, don't you tell a soul."

I felt cool and very clean and just a little tired. "No, sir, Mr. Freeman, I won't tell." I was somewhere above everything. "It's just that
I'm so tired I'll just go and lay down a while, please," I whispered to

him. I thought if I spoke out loud, he might become frightened and hurt me again. He dried me and handed me my bloomers. "Put these on and go to the library. Your momma ought to be coming home soon. You just act natural."

Walking down the street, I felt the wet on my pants, and my hips seemed to be coming out of their sockets. I couldn't sit long on the hard seats in the library (they had been constructed for children), so I walked by the empty lot where Bailey was playing ball, but he wasn't there. I stood for a while and watched the big boys tear around the dusty diamond and then headed home.

After two blocks, I knew I'd never make it. Not unless I counted every step and stepped on every crack. I had started to burn between my legs more than the time I'd wasted Sloan's Liniment on myself. My legs throbbed, or rather the insides of my thighs throbbed, with the same force that Mr. Freeman's heart had beaten. Thrum . . . step . . . thrum . . . step . . . STEP ON THE CRACK . . . thrum . . . step. I went up the stairs one at a, one at a, one at a time. No one was in the living room, so I went straight to bed, after hiding my red-and-yellow-stained drawers under the mattress.

When Mother came in she said, "Well, young lady, I believe this is the first time I've seen you go to bed without being told. You must be sick."

I wasn't sick, but the pit of my stomach was on fire—how could I tell her that? Bailey came in later and asked me what the matter was. There was nothing to tell him. When Mother called us to eat and I said I wasn't hungry, she laid her cool hand on my forehead and cheeks. "Maybe it's the measles. They say they're going around the neighborhood." After she took my temperature she said, "You have a little fever. You've probably just caught them."

Mr. Freeman took up the whole doorway, "Then Bailey ought not to be in there with her. Unless you want a house full of sick children." She answered over her shoulder, "He may as well have them now as later. Get them over with." She brushed by Mr. Freeman as if he were made of cotton. "Come on, Junior. Get some cool towels and wipe your sister's face."

As Bailey left the room, Mr. Freeman advanced to the bed. He leaned over, his whole face a threat that could have smothered me. "If you tell . . ." And again so softly, I almost didn't hear it—"If you tell." I couldn't summon up the energy to answer him. He had to know that I wasn't going to tell anything. Bailey came in with the towels and Mr. Freeman walked out.

Later Mother made a broth and sat on the edge of the bed to feed me. The liquid went down my throat like bones. My belly and behind were as heavy as cold iron, but it seemed my head had gone away and pure air had replaced it on my shoulders. Bailey read to me from *The Rover Boys* until he got sleepy and went to bed.

That night I kept waking to hear Mother and Mr. Freeman arguing. I couldn't hear what they were saying, but I did hope that she wouldn't make him so mad that he'd hurt her too. I knew he could do it, with his cold face and empty eyes. Their voices came in faster and faster, the high sounds on the heels of the lows. I would have liked to have gone in. Just passed through as if I were going to the toilet. Just show my face and they might stop, but my legs refused to move. I could move the toes and ankles, but the knees had turned to wood.

Maybe I slept, but soon morning was there and Mother was pretty over my bed. "How're you feeling, baby?"

"Fine, Mother." An instinctive answer. "Where's Bailey?"

She said he was still asleep but that she hadn't slept all night. She had been in my room off and on to see about me. I asked her where Mr. Freeman was, and her face chilled with remembered anger. "He's gone. Moved this morning. I'm going to take your temperature after I put on your Cream of Wheat."

Could I tell her now? The terrible pain assured me that I couldn't. What he did to me, and what I allowed, must have been very bad if already God let me hurt so much. If Mr. Freeman was gone, did that mean Bailey was out of danger? And if so, if I told him, would he still love me?

After Mother took my temperature, she said she was going to bed for a while but to wake her if I felt sicker. She told Bailey to watch my face and arms for spots and when they came up he could paint them with calamine lotion.

That Sunday goes and comes in my memory like a bad connection on an overseas telephone call. Once, Bailey was reading *The Katzenjammer Kids* to me, and then without a pause for sleeping, Mother was looking closely at my face, and soup trickled down my chin and some got into my mouth and I choked. Then there was a doctor who took my temperature and held my wrist.

"Bailey!" I supposed I had screamed, for he materialized suddenly, and I asked him to help me and we'd run away to California or France or Chicago. I knew that I was dying and, in fact, I longed for death, but I didn't want to die anywhere near Mr. Freeman. I knew that even now he wouldn't have allowed death to have me unless he wished it to.

Mother said I should be bathed and the linens had to be changed since I had sweat so much. But when they tried to move me I fought, and even Bailey couldn't hold me. Then she picked me up in her arms and the terror abated for a while. Bailey began to change the bed. As he pulled off the soiled sheets he dislodged the panties I had put under the mattress. They fell at Mother's feet.

• • • • •

From *Their Eyes Were Watching God*

Zora Neale Hurston

"Zora belongs in the tradition of black women singers, rather than among the 'literati,'" Alice Walker asserts. "Like Billie [Holiday] and Bessie [Smith] she followed her own road, believed in her own gods, pursued her own dreams, and refused to separate herself from 'common' people."[1] Born in Florida in 1891, Hurston began her writing career during the outpouring of creativity among African-American artists in the 1920s known as the Harlem Renaissance. Her work, however, was different; influenced by her anthropological studies at Barnard College and her folklore research, Hurston depicted the folkways of the southern Negro and celebrated the inquisitive and free-thinking black woman. Her early stories, such as "Spunk" (1925), "Sweat" (1926), and "The Gilded Six-Bits" (1933), are set in her all-black hometown, Eatonville, Florida, rather than in the Harlem of the black literati. A prolific and controversial essayist, she often expressed views on race relations that were contrary to the opinions of the general black populace. Her larger works include four novels, *Jonah's Gourd Vine* (1934), *Their Eyes Were Watching God* (1937), *Moses, Man of the Mountain* (1939), and *Seraph on the Suwanee* (1948); an autobiography, *Dust Tracks on a Road* (1943); and two books of folklore, *Mules and Men* (1935) and *Tell My Horse* (1938). Hurston devoted her life to writing, and she depended on grants, white patronage, and odd jobs to hold her from one book to the next. She spent the end of her life as a ward of the state of Florida; living her last days on food vouchers, she died penniless and in obscurity in St. Lucie County in 1960.

Hurston wrote *Their Eyes Were Watching God* (University of Illinois

Press) in seven weeks in Haiti as she was collecting folklore on a Guggenheim fellowship and undergoing the emotional stress of a sagging love affair with a domineering West Indian native much younger than herself. The novel is autobiographical in that it captures the spirit of a love affair between an older woman and a younger man. Lippincott published *Their Eyes Were Watching God* in 1937 with few revisions.

Past and current critics view *Their Eyes Were Watching God* as the best of Hurston's novels. Earlier critics, mostly males, overlooked the gender victimization of the protagonist and instead emphasized the novel's folk elements and social tensions. More recent critics, including Mary Helen Washington and Barbara Christian, have stressed character development—especially that of Janie, the protagonist—her relationship to male characters and her community, and her needs and expectations as a woman. Barbara Christian asserts, "Hurston's Janie not only revised the previously drawn images of the mulatta, the author's rendition of her major characters beautifully revealed the many dimensions of the black woman's soul as well as the restrictions imposed upon her by her own community—that she, like all others, seeks not only security but fulfillment."[2]

The excerpt from Hurston's rich, complex novel reprinted here touches on several aspects of sexism. Janie is well kept by her prosperous husband, the local mayor. He jealously guards her beauty as if it were something he owns but feels free to physically abuse her when supper is badly cooked. He dislikes her speaking up, having opinions, participating in conversation, and taking part in the life outside the store they run together; he prefers her to be set apart from "common" folk and reminds her that she is "Mrs. Mayor Sparks." And he belittles her: "Somebody got to think for women and chillun and chickens and cows," he tells Janie. "I god, they sho don't think none theirselves." After years of struggle, Janie has "pressed her teeth together and learned to hush." She is aware of what is wrong in the way her husband treats her and of the unspoken tensions and desires that make up their relationship, but she keeps much of this knowledge—as she keeps much of her own being, her most genuine thoughts and feelings—to herself.

NOTES

1. Robert Hemenway, noted in *Zora Neale Hurston: A Literary Biography* (Urbana: University of Illinois Press, 1976), *xix*.
2. Barbara Christian, *Black Women, Novelists: The Development of a Tradition, 1892–1976* (Westport, Conn.: Greenwood Press, 1980), 59.

Every morning the world flung itself over and exposed the town to the sun. So Janie had another day. And every day had a store in it, except

Sundays. The store itself was a pleasant place if only she didn't have to sell things. When the people sat around on the porch and passed around the pictures of their thoughts for the others to look at and see, it was nice. The fact that the thought pictures were always crayon enlargements of life made it even nicer to listen to.

Take for instance the case of Matt Bonner's yellow mule. They had him up for conversation every day the Lord sent. Most especial if Matt was there himself to listen. Sam and Lige and Walter were the ringleaders of the mule-talkers. The others threw in whatever they could chance upon, but it seemed as if Sam and Lige and Walter could hear and see more about that mule than the whole county put together. All they needed was to see Matt's long spare shape coming down the street and by the time he got to the porch they were ready for him.

"Hello, Matt."

"Evenin', Sam."

"Mighty glad you come 'long right now, Matt. Me and some others wuz jus' about tuh come hunt yuh."

"Whut for, Sam?"

"Mighty serious matter, man. Serious!!"

"Yeah man," Lige would cut in, dolefully. "It needs yo' strict attention. You ought not tuh lose no time."

"Whut is it then? You oughta hurry up and tell me."

"Reckon we better not tell yuh heah at de store. It's too fur off tuh do any good. We better all walk on down by Lake Sabelia."

"Whut's wrong, man? Ah ain't after none uh y'alls foolishness now."

"Dat mule uh yourn, Matt. You better go see 'bout him. He's bad off."

"Where 'bouts? Did he wade in de lake and uh alligator ketch him?"

"Worser'n dat. De womenfolks got yo' mule. When Ah come round de lake 'bout noontime mah wife and some others had 'im flat on de ground usin' his sides fuh uh wash board."

The great clap of laughter that they have been holding in, bursts out. Sam never cracks a smile. "Yeah, Mat, dat mule so skinny till de women is usin' his rib bones fuh uh rub-board, and hangin' things out on his hock-bones tuh dry."

Matt realizes that they have tricked him again and the laughter makes him mad and when he gets mad he stammers.

"You'se uh stinkin' lie, Sam, and yo' feet ain't mates. Y-y-y-you!"

"Aw, man, 'tain't no use in you gittin' mad. Yuh know yuh don't feed de mule. How he gointuh git fat?"

"Ah-ah-ah- d-d-does feed 'im! Ah g-g-gived 'im uh full cup uh cawn every feedin'."

"Lige knows all about dat cup uh cawn. He hid round yo' barn and watched yuh. 'Tain't no feed cup you measures dat cawn outa. It's uh tea cup."

"Ah does feed 'im. He's jus' too mean tuh git fat. He stay poor and rawbony jus' fuh spite. Skeered he'll hafta work some."

"Yeah, you feeds 'im. Feeds 'im offa 'come up' and seasons it wid raw-hide."

"Does feed de ornery varmint! Don't keer whut Ah do Ah can't git long wid 'im. He fights every inch in front uh de plow, and even lay back his ears tuh kick and bite when Ah go in de stall tuh feed 'im."

"Git reconciled, Matt," Lige soothed. "Us all knows he's mean. Ah seen 'im when he took after one uh dem Roberts chillun in de street and woulda caught 'im and maybe trompled 'im tuh death if de wind hadn't of changed all of a sudden. Yuh see de youngun wuz tryin' tuh make it tuh de fence uh Starks' onion patch and de mule wuz dead in behind 'im and gainin' on 'im every jump, when all of a sudden de wind changed and blowed de mule way off his course, him bein' so poor and everything, and before de ornery varmint could tack, de youngun had done got over de fence." The porch laughed and Matt got mad again.

"Maybe de mule takes out after everybody," Sam said, "'cause he thinks everybody he hear comin' is Matt Bonner comin' tuh work 'im on uh empty stomach."

"Aw, naw, aw, naw. You stop dat right now," Walter objected. "Dat mule don't think Ah look lak no Matt Bonner. He ain't dat dumb. If Ah thought he didn't know no better Ah'd have mah picture took and give it tuh dat mule so's he could learn better. Ah ain't gointuh 'low 'im tuh hold nothin' lak dat against me."

Matt struggled to say something but his tongue failed him so he jumped down off the porch and walked away as mad as he could be. But that never halted the mule talk. There would be more stories about how poor the brute was; his age; his evil disposition and his latest caper. Everybody indulged in mule talk. He was next to the Mayor in prominence, and made better talking.

Janie loved the conversation and sometimes she thought up good stories on the mule, but Joe had forbidden her to indulge. He didn't want her talking after such trashy people. "You'se Mrs. Mayor Starks, Janie. I god, Ah can't see what uh woman uh yo' sability would want tuh be treasurin' all dat gum-grease from folks dat don't even own de house dey sleep in. 'Tain't no earthly use. They's jus' some puny human playin' round de toes uh Time."

Janie noted that while he didn't talk the mule himself, he sat and laughed at it. Laughed his big heh, heh laugh too. But then when Lige or Sam or Walter or some of the other big picture talkers were using a side of the world for a canvas, Joe would hustle her off inside the store to sell something. Look like he took pleasure in doing it. Why couldn't he go himself sometimes? She had come to hate the inside of that store anyway. That Post Office too. People always coming and asking for mail at the wrong time. Just when she was trying to count up something or write in an account book. Get her so hackled she'd make the wrong change for stamps. Then too, she couldn't read everybody's writing. Some folks wrote so funny and spelt things different from what she knew about. As a rule, Joe put up the mail himself, but sometimes when he was off she had to do it herself and it always ended up in a fuss.

The store itself kept her with a sick headache. The labor of getting things down off of a shelf or out of a barrel was nothing. And so long as people wanted only a can of tomatoes or a pound of rice it was all right. But supposing they went on and said a pound and a half of bacon and a half pound of lard? The whole thing changed from a little walking and stretching to a mathematical dilemma. Or maybe cheese was thirty-seven cents a pound and somebody came and asked for a dime's worth. She went through many silent rebellions over things like that. Such a waste of life and time. But Joe kept saying that she could do it if she wanted to and he wanted her to use her privileges. That was the rock she was battered against.

This business of the head-rag irked her endlessly. But Jody was set on it. Her hair was NOT going to show in the store. It didn't seem sensible at all. That was because Joe never told Janie how jealous he was. He never told her how often he had seen the other men figuratively wallowing in it as she went about things in the store. And one night he had caught Walter standing behind Janie and brushing the back of his hand back and forth across the loose end of her braid ever so lightly so as to enjoy the feel of it without Janie knowing what he was doing. Joe was at the back of the store and Walter didn't see him. He felt like rushing forth with the meat knife and chopping off the offending hand. That night he ordered Janie to tie up her hair around the store. That was all. She was there in the store for *him* to look at, not those others. But he never said things like that. It just wasn't in him. Take the matter of the yellow mule, for instance.

Late one afternoon Matt came from the west with a halter in his hand. ''Been huntin' fuh mah mule. Anybody seen 'im?'' he asked.

''Seen 'im soon dis mornin' over behind de schoolhouse,'' Lum said. '' 'Bout ten o'clock or so. He musta been out all night tuh be way over dere dat early.''

''He wuz,'' Matt answered. ''Seen 'im last night but Ah couldn't ketch 'im. Ah'm 'bliged tuh git 'im in tuhnight 'cause Ah got some plowin' fuh tuhmorrow. Done promised tuh plow Thompson's grove.''

"Reckon you'll ever git through de job wid dat mule-frame?" Lige asked.

"Aw dat mule is plenty strong. Jus' evil and don't want tuh be led."

"Dat's right. Dey tell me he brought you heah tuh dis town. Say you started tuh Miccanopy but de mule had better sense and brung yuh on heah."

"It's uh l-l-lie! Ah set out fuh dis town when Ah left West Floridy."

"You mean tuh tell me you rode dat mule all de way from West Floridy down heah?"

"Sho he did, Lige. But he didn't mean tuh. He wuz satisfied up dere, but de mule wuzn't. So one mornin' he got straddle uh de mule and he took and brought 'im on off. Mule had sense. Folks up dat way don't eat biscuit bread but once uh week."

There was always a little seriousness behind the teasing of Matt, so when he got huffed and walked on off nobody minded. He was known to buy side-meat by the slice. Carried home little bags of meal and flour in his hand. He didn't seem to mind too much so long as it didn't cost him anything.

About half an hour after he left they heard the braying of the mule at the edge of the woods. He was coming past the store very soon.

"Less ketch Matt's mule fuh 'im and have some fun."

"Now, Lum, you know dat mule ain't aimin' tuh let hisself be caught. Less watch *you* do it."

When the mule was in front of the store, Lum went out and tackled him. The brute jerked up his head, laid back his ears and rushed to the attack. Lum had to run for safety. Five or six more men left the porch and surrounded the fractious beast, goosing him in the sides and making him show his temper. But he had more spirit left than body. He was soon panting and heaving from the effort of spinning his old carcass about. Everybody was having fun at the mule-baiting. All but Janie.

She snatched her head away from the spectacle and began muttering to herself. "They oughta be shamed uh theyselves! Teasin' dat poor brute beast lak they is! Done been worked tuh death; done had his disposition ruint wid mistreatment, and now they got tuh finish devilin' 'im tuh death. Wisht Ah had mah way wid 'em all."

She walked away from the porch and found something to busy herself with in the back of the store so she did not hear Jody when he stopped laughing. She didn't know that he had heard her, but she did hear him yell out, "Lum, I god, dat's enough! Y'all done had yo' fun now. Stop yo' foolishness and go tell Matt Bonner Ah wants tuh have uh talk wid him right away."

Janie came back out front and sat down. She didn't say anything and neither did Joe. But after a while he looked down at his feet and said, ''Janie, Ah reckon you better go fetch me dem old black gaiters. Dese tan shoes sets mah feet on fire. Plenty room in 'em, but they hurts regardless.''

She got up without a word and went off for the shoes. A little war of defense for helpless things was going on inside her. People ought to have some regard for helpless things. She wanted to fight about it. ''But Ah hates disagreement and confusion, so Ah better not talk. It makes it hard tuh git along.'' She didn't hurry back. She fumbled around long enough to get her face straight. When she got back, Joe was talking with Matt.

''Fifteen dollars? I god you'se as crazy as uh betsy bug! Five dollars.''

''L-l-less we strack uh compermise, Brother Mayor. Les m-make it ten.''

''Five dollars.'' Joe rolled his cigar in his mouth and rolled his eyes away indifferently.

''If dat mule is wuth somethin' tuh *you* Brother Mayor, he's wuth mo' tuh me. More special when Ah got uh job uh work tuhmorrow.''

''Five dollars.''

''All right, Brother Mayor. If you wants tuh rob uh poor man lak me uh everything he got tuh make uh livin' wid, Ah'll take de five dollars. Dat mule been wid me twenty-three years. It's mighty hard.''

Mayor Starks deliberately changed his shoes before he reached into his pocket for the money. By that time Matt was wringing and twisting like a hen on a hot brick. But as soon as his hand closed on the money his face broke into a grin.

''Beatyuh tradin' dat time, Starks! Dat mule is liable tuh be dead befo' de week is out. You won't git no work outa him.''

''Didn't buy 'im fuh no work. I god, Ah bought dat varmint tuh let 'im rest. You didn't have gumption enough tuh do it.''

A respectful silence fell on the place. Sam looked at Joe and said, ''Dat's uh new idea 'bout varmints, Mayor Starks. But Ah laks it mah ownself. It's uh noble thing you done.'' Everybody agreed with that.

Janie stood still while they all made comments. When it was all done she stood in front of Joe and said, ''Jody, dat wuz uh mighty fine thing fuh you tuh do. 'Tain't everybody would have thought of it, 'cause it ain't no everyday thought. Freein' dat mule makes uh mighty big man outa you. Something like George Washington and Lincoln. Abraham Lincoln, he had de whole United States tuh rule so he freed de Negroes. You got uh town so you freed uh mule. You have tuh have power tuh free things and dat makes you lak uh king uh something.''

Hambo said, ''Yo' wife is uh born orator, Starks. Us never knowed dat befo'. She put jus' de right words tuh our thoughts.''

Joe bit down hard on his cigar and beamed all around, but he never said a word. The town talked it for three days and said that's just what they would have done if they had been rich men like Joe Starks. Anyhow a free mule in town was something new to talk about. Starks piled fodder under the big tree near the porch and the mule was usually around the store like the other citizens. Nearly everybody took the habit of fetching along a handful of fodder to throw on the pile. He almost got fat and they took a great pride in him. New lies sprung up about his free-mule doings. How he pushed open Lindsay's kitchen door and slept in the place one night and fought until they made coffee for his breakfast; how he stuck his head in the Pearson's window while the family was at the table and Mrs. Pearson mistook him for Rev. Pearson and handed him a plate; he ran Mrs. Tully off of the croquet ground for having such an ugly shape; he ran and caught up with Becky Anderson on the way to Maitland so as to keep his head out of the sun under her umbrella; he got tired of listening to Redmond's long-winded prayer, and went inside the Baptist church and broke up the meeting. He did everything but let himself be bridled and visit Matt Bonner.

But way after awhile he died. Lum found him under the big tree on his rawbony back with all four feet up in the air. That wasn't natural and it didn't look right, but Sam said it would have been more unnatural for him to have laid down on his side and died like any other beast. He had seen Death coming and had stood his ground and fought it like a natural man. He had fought it to the last breath. Naturally he didn't have time to straighten himself out. Death had to take him like it found him.

When the news got around, it was like the end of a war or something like that. Everybody that could knocked off from work to stand around and talk. But finally there was nothing to do but drag him out like all other dead brutes. Drag him out to the edge of the hammock which was far enough off to satisfy sanitary conditions in the town. The rest was up to the buzzards. Everybody was going to the dragging-out. The news had got Mayor Starks out of bed before time. His pair of gray horses was out under the tree and the men were fooling with the gear when Janie arrived at the store with Joe's breakfast.

"I god, Lum, you fasten up dis store good befo' you leave, you hear me?" He was eating fast and talking with one eye out of the door on the operations.

"Whut you tellin' 'im tuh fasten up for, Jody?" Janie asked surprised.

"'Cause it won't be nobody heah tuh look after de store. Ah'm goin' tuh de draggin'-out mahself."

"'Tain't nothin' so important Ah got tuh do tuhday. Jody. How come Ah can't go long wid you tuh de draggin'-out?"

Joe was struck speechless for a minute. "Why, Janie! You wouldn't be seen at uh draggin'-out, wouldja? Wid any and everybody in uh passle pushin' and shovin' wid they no-manners selves? Naw, naw!''

"You would be dere wid me, wouldn't yuh?"

"Dat's right, but Ah'm uh man even if Ah is de Mayor. But de mayor's wife is something different again. Anyhow they's liable tuh need me tuh say uh few words over de carcass, dis bein' uh special case. But *you* ain't goin' off in all dat mess uh commonness. Ah'm surprised at yuh fuh askin'.''

He wiped his lips of ham gravy and put on his hat. "Shet de door behind yuh, Janie. Lum is too busy wid de hawses.''

After more shouting of advice and orders and useless comments, the town escorted the carcass off. No, the carcass moved off with the town, and left Janie standing in the doorway.

Out in the swamp they made great ceremony over the mule. They mocked everything human in death. Starks led off with a great eulogy on our departed citizen, our most distinguished citizen and the grief he left behind him, and the people loved the speech. It made him more solid than building the schoolhouse had done. He stood on the distended belly of the mule for a platform and made gestures. When he stepped down, they hoisted Sam up and he talked about the mule as a school teacher first. Then he set his hat like John Pearson and imitated his preaching. He spoke of the joys of mule-heaven to which the dear brother had departed this valley of sorrow; the mule-angels flying around; the miles of green corn and cool water, a pasture of pure bran with a river of molasses running through it; and most glorious of all, *No* Matt Bonner with plow lines and halters to come in and corrupt. Up there, mule-angels would have people to ride on and from his place beside the glittering throne, the dear departed brother would look down into hell and see the devil plowing Matt Bonner all day long in a hell-hot sun and laying the raw-hide to his back.

With that the sisters got mock-happy and shouted and had to be held up by the menfolks. Everybody enjoyed themselves to the highest and then finally the mule was left to the already impatient buzzards. They were holding a great flying-meet way up over the heads of the mourners and some of the nearby trees were already peopled with the stoop-shouldered forms.

As soon as the crowd was out of sight they closed in in circles. The near ones got nearer and the far ones got near. A circle, a swoop and a hop with spread-out wings. Close in, close in till some of the more hungry or daring perched on the carcass. They wanted to begin, but the Parson wasn't there, so a messenger was sent to the ruler in a tree where he sat.

The flock had to wait the white-headed leader, but it was hard. They jostled each other and pecked at heads in hungry irritation. Some walked up and down the beast from head to tail, tail to head. The Parson sat motionless in a dead pine tree about two miles off. He had scented the matter as quickly as any of the rest, but decorum demanded that he sit oblivious until he was notified. Then he took off with ponderous flight and circled and lowered, circled and lowered until the others danced in joy and hunger at his approach.

He finally lit on the ground and walked around the body to see if it were really dead. Peered into its nose and mouth. Examined it well from end to end and leaped upon it and bowed, and the others danced a response. That being over, he balanced and asked:

"What killed this man?"

The chorus answered, "Bare, bare fat."

"What killed this man?"

"Bare, bare fat."

"What killed this man?"

"Bare, bare fat."

"Who'll stand his funeral?"

"We!!!!!"

"Well, all right now."

So he picked out the eyes in the ceremonial way and the feast went on. The yaller mule was gone from the town except for the porch talk, and for the children visiting his bleaching bones now and then in the spirit of adventure.

Joe returned to the store full of pleasure and good humor but he didn't want Janie to notice it because he saw that she was sullen and he resented that. She had no right to be, the way he thought things out. She wasn't even appreciative of his efforts and she had plenty cause to be. Here he was just pouring honor all over her; building a high chair for her to sit in and overlook the world and she here pouting over it! Not that he wanted anybody else, but just too many women would be glad to be in her place. He ought to box her jaws! But he didn't feel like fighting today, so he made an attack upon her position backhand.

"Ah had tuh laugh at de people out dere in de woods dis mornin', Janie. You can't help but laugh at de capers they cuts. But all the same, Ah wish mah people would git mo' business in 'em and not spend so much time on foolishness."

"Everybody can't be lak you, Jody. Somebody is bound tuh want tuh laugh and play."

"Who don't love tuh laugh and play?"

"You make out like you don't, anyhow."

"I god, Ah don't make out no such uh lie! But it's uh time fuh all things. But it's awful tuh see so many people don't want nothin' but uh full belly and uh place tuh lay down and sleep afterwards. It makes me sad sometimes and then agin it makes me mad. They say things sometimes that tickles me nearly tuh death, but Ah won't laugh jus' tuh dis-incourage 'em.'' Janie took the easy way away from a fuss. She didn't change her mind but she agreed with her mouth. Her heart said, "Even so, but you don't have to cry about it."

But sometimes Sam Watson and Lige Moss forced a belly laugh out of Joe himself with their eternal arguments. It never ended because there was no end to reach. It was a contest in hyperbole and carried on for no other reason.

Maybe Sam would be sitting on the porch when Lige walked up. If nobody was there to speak of, nothing happened. But if the town was there like on Saturday night, Lige would come up with a very grave air. Couldn't even pass the time of day, for being so busy thinking. Then when he was asked what was the matter in order to start him off, he'd say, "Dis question done 'bout drove me crazy. And Sam, he know so much into things, Ah wants some information on de subject."

Walter Thomas was due to speak up and egg the matter on. "Yeah, Sam always got more information than he know what to do wid. He's bound to tell yuh whatever it is you wants tuh know."

Sam begins an elaborate show of avoiding the struggle. That draws everybody on the porch into it.

"How come you want me *tuh* tell yuh? You always claim God done met you round de cornder and talked His inside business wid yuh. 'Tain't no use in you askin' *me* nothin'. Ah'm questionizin' *you*."

"How you gointuh do dat, Sam, when Ah arrived dis conversation mahself? Ah'm askin' *you*."

"Askin' me what? You ain't told me de subjick yit."

"Don't aim tuh tell yuh! Ah aims tuh keep yuh in de dark all de time. If you'se smart lak you let on you is, you kin find out."

"Yuh skeered to lemme know whut it is, 'cause yuh know Ah'll tear it tuh pieces. You got to have a subjick tuh talk from, do yuh can't talk. If uh man ain't got no bounds, he ain't got no place tuh stop."

By this time, they are the center of the world.

"Well all right then. Since you own up you ain't smart enough tuh find out whut Ah'm talkin' 'bout, Ah'll tell you. Whut is it dat keeps uh man from gettin' burnt on uh red-hot stove—caution or nature?"

"Shucks! Ah thought you had somethin' hard tuh ast me. Walter kin tell yuh dat."

"If de conversation is too deep for yuh, how come yuh don't tell me so, and hush up? Walter can't tell me nothin' uh de kind. Ah'm uh educated man, Ah keeps mah arrangements in mah hands, and if it kept me up all night long studyin' 'bout it, Walter ain't liable tuh be no help to me. Ah needs uh man lak you."

"And then agin, Lige, Ah'm gointuh tell yuh. Ah'm gointuh run dis conversation from uh gnat heel to uh lice. It's nature dat keeps uh man off of uh red-hot stove."

"Uuh huuh! Ah knowed you would going tuh crawl up in dat holler! But Ah aims tuh smoke yuh right out. 'Tain't no nature at all, it's caution, Sam."

"'Tain't no sich uh thing! Nature tells yuh not tuh fool wid no red-hot stove, and you don't do it neither."

"Listen, Sam, if it was nature, nobody wouldn't have tuh look out for babies touchin' stoves, would they? 'Cause dey just naturally wouldn't touch it. But dey sho will. So it's caution."

"Naw it ain't, it's nature, cause nature makes caution. It's de strongest thing dat God ever made, now. Fact is it's de onliest thing God ever made. He made nature and nature made everything else."

"Naw nature didn't neither. A whole healp of things ain't even been made yit."

"Tell me somethin' you know of dat nature ain't made."

"She ain't made it so you kin ride uh butt-headed cow and hold on tuh de horns."

"Yeah, but dat ain't yo' point."

"Yeah it is too."

"Naw it ain't neither."

"Well what *is* mah point?"

"You ain't got none, so far."

"Yeah he is too," Walter cut in, "de red-hot stove is his point.

"He know mighty much, but he ain't proved it yit."

"Sam, Ah say it's caution, not nature dat keeps folks off uh red-hot stove."

"How is de son gointuh be before his paw? Nature is de first of everything. Ever since self was self, nature been keepin' folks off of red-hot stoves. Dat caution you talkin' 'bout ain't nothin' but uh humbug. He's uh inseck dat nothin' he got belongs to him. He got eyes, lak somethin' else; wings lak somethin' else—everything! Even his hum is de sound of somebody else."

"Man, whut you talkin' 'bout? Caution is de greatest thing in de world. If it wasn't for caution—"

"Show me somethin' dat caution ever made! Look whut nature took and done. Nature got so high in uh black hen she got tuh lay uh white egg. Now you tell me, how come, whut got intuh man dat he got tuh have hair round his mouth? Nature!"

"Dat ain't—"

The porch was boiling now. Starks left the store to Hezekiah Potts, the delivery boy, and come took a seat in his high chair.

"Look at dat great big ole scoundrel-beast up dere at Hall's fillin' station—uh great big old scoundrel. He eats up all de folks outa de house and den eat de house."

"Aw 'tain't no sich a varmint nowhere dat kin eat no house! Dat's uh lie. Ah wuz dere yiste'ddy and Ah ain't seen nothin' lak dat. Where is he?''

"Ah didn't see him but Ah reckon he is in de back-yard some place. But dey got his picture out front dere. They was nailin' it up when Ah come pass dere dis evenin'.''

"Well all right now, if he eats up houses how come he don't eat up de fillin' station?''

"Dat's 'cause dey got him tied up so he can't. Dey got uh great big picture tellin' how many gallons of dat Sinclair high-compression gas he drink at one time and how he's more'n uh million years old.''

"'Tain't *nothin'* no million years old!''

"De picture is right up dere where anybody kin see it. Dey can't make de picture till dey see de thing, kin dey?''

"How dey goin' to tell he's uh million years old? Nobody wasn't born dat fur back.''

"By de rings on his tail Ah reckon. Man, dese white folks got ways for tellin' anything dey wants tuh know.''

"Well, where he been at all dis time, then?''

"Dey caught him over dere in Egypt. Seem lak he used tuh hang round dere and eat up dem Pharaohs' tombstones. Dey got de picture of him doin' it. Nature is high in uh varmint lak dat. Nature and salt. Dat's whut makes up strong man lak Big John de Conquer. He was uh man wid salt in him. He could give us flavor to *anything*.''

"Yeah, but he was uh man dat wuz more'n man. 'Tain't no mo' lak him. He wouldn't dig potatoes, and he wouldn't rake hay: He wouldn't take a whipping, and he wouldn't run away.''

"Oh yeah, somebody else could if dey tried hard enough. Me mah-self, Ah got salt in *me*. If Ah like man flesh, Ah could eat some man every day, some of 'em is so trashy they'd let me eat 'em.''

"Lawd, Ah loves to talk about Big John. Less we tell lies on Ole John.''

But here come Bootsie, and Teadi and Big 'oman down the street making out they are pretty by the way they walk. They have got that fresh, new taste about them like young mustard greens in the spring, and the young men on the porch are just bound to tell them about it and buy them some treats.

"Heah come mah order right now,'' Charlie Jones announces and scrambles off the porch to meet them. But he has plenty of competition. A pushing, shoving show of gallantry. They all beg the girls to just buy anything they can think of. Please let them pay for it. Joe is begged to wrap up all the candy in the store and order more. All the peanuts and soda water—everything!

"Gal, Ah'm crazy 'bout you,'' Charlie goes on to the entertainment of everybody. "Ah'll do anything in the world except work for you and give you mah money."

The girls and everybody else help laugh. They know it's not courtship. It's acting-out courtship and everybody is in the play. The three girls hold the center of the stage till Daisy Blunt comes walking down the street in the moonlight.

Daisy is walking a drum tune. You can almost hear it by looking at the way she walks. She is black and she knows that white clothes look good on her, so she wears them for dress up. She's got those big black eyes with plenty shiny white in them that makes them shine like brand new money and she knows what God gave women eyelashes for, too. Her hair is not what you might call straight. It's negro hair, but it's got a kind of white flavor. Like the piece of string out of a ham. It's not ham at all, but it's been around ham and got the flavor. It was spread down thick and heavy over her shoulders and looked just right under a big white hat.

"Lawd, Lawd, Lawd," that same Charlie Jones exclaims rushing over to Daisy. "It must be uh recess in heben if St. Peter is lettin' his angels out lak dis. You got three men already layin' at de point uh death 'bout yuh, and heah's uhnother fool dat's willin' tuh make time on yo' gang."

All the rest of the single men have crowded around Daisy by this time. She is parading and blushing at the same time.

"If you know anybody dat's 'bout tuh die 'bout me, yuh know more'n Ah do," Daisy bridled. "Wisht Ah knowed who it is."

"Now, Daisy, *you* know Jim, and Dave and Lum is 'bout tuh kill one 'nother 'bout you. Don't stand up here and tell dat big ole got-dat-wrong."

"Dey a mighty hush-mouf about it if dey is. Dey ain't never told me nothin'."

"Unhunh, you talked too fast. Heah, Jim and Dave is right upon de porch and Lum is inside de store."

A big burst of laughter at Daisy's discomfiture. The boys had to act out their rivalry too. Only this time, everybody knew they meant some of it. But all the same the porch enjoyed the play and helped out whenever extras were needed.

David said, "Jim don't love Daisy. He don't love yuh lak Ah do."

Jim bellowed indignantly, "Who don't love Daisy? Ah know you ain't talkin' 'bout me."

Dave: "Well all right, less prove dis thing right now. We'll prove right now who love dis gal de best. How much time is you willin' tuh make fuh Daisy?"

Jim: "Twenty yeahs!"

Dave: "See? Ah told yuh dat nigger didn't love yuh. Me, Ah'll beg de Judge tuh hang me, and wouldn't take nothin' less than life."

There was a big long laugh from the porch. Then Jim had to demand a test.

"Dave, how much would you be willin' tuh do for Daisy if she was to turn fool enough tuh marry yuh."

"Me and Daisy done talked dat over, but if you just got tuh know, Ah'd buy Daisy uh passenger train and give it tuh her."

"Humph! Is dat all? Ah'd buy her uh steamship and then Ah'd hire some mens tuh run it fur her."

"Daisy, don't let Jim fool you wid his talk. He don't aim tuh do nothin' fuh yuh. Uh lil ole steamship! Daisy, Ah'll take uh job cleanin' out de Atlantic Ocean fuh you any time you say you so desire." There was a great laugh and then they hushed to listen.

"Daisy," Jim began, "you know mah heart and all de ranges uh mah mind. And you know if Ah wuz ridin' up in uh earoplane way up in de sky and Ah looked down and seen you walkin' and knowed you'd have tuh walk ten miles tuh git home, Ah'd step backward offa dat earoplane just to walk home wid you."

There was one of those big blow-out laughs and Janie was wallowing in it. Then Jody ruined it all for her.

Mrs. Bogle came walking down the street towards the porch. Mrs. Bogle who was many times a grandmother, but had a blushing air of coquetry about her that cloaked her sunken cheeks. You saw a fluttering fan before her face and magnolia blooms and sleepy lakes under the moonlight when she walked. There was no obvious reason for it, it was just so. Her first husband had been a coachman but "studied jury" to win her. He had finally become a preacher to hold her till his death. Her second husband worked in Fohnes orange grove—but tried to preach when he caught her eye. He never got any further than a class leader, but that was something to offer her. It proved his love and pride. She was a wind on the ocean. She moved men, but the helm determined the port. Now, this night she mounted the steps and men noticed her until she passed inside the door.

"I god, Janie," Starks said impatiently, "why don't you go on and see whut Mrs. Bogle want? Whut you waitin' on?"

Janie wanted to hear the rest of the play-acting and how it ended, but she got up sullenly and went inside. She came back to the porch with her bristles sticking out all over her and with dissatisfaction written all over her face. Joe saw it and lifted his own hackles a bit.

Jim Weston had secretly borrowed a dime and soon he was loudly beseeching Daisy to have a treat on him. Finally she consented to take a pickled pig foot on him. Janie was getting up a large order when they came in, so Lum waited on them. That is, he went back to the keg but came back without the pig foot.

"Mist' Starks, de pig feets is all gone!" he called out.

"Aw naw dey ain't, Lum. Ah bought uh whole new kag of 'em wid dat last order from Jacksonville. It come in yistiddy."

Joe came and helped Lum look but he couldn't find the new keg either, so he went to the nail over his desk that he used for a file to search for the order.

"Janie, where's dat last bill uh ladin'?"

"It's right dere on de nail, ain't it?"

"Naw it ain't neither. You ain't put it where Ah told yuh tuh. If you'd git yo' mind out de streets and keep it on yo' business maybe you could git somethin' straight sometimes."

"Aw, look around dere, Jody. Dat bill ain't apt tuh be gone off nowheres. If it ain't hangin' on de nail, it's on yo' desk. You bound tuh find it if you look."

"Wid you heah, Ah oughtn't tuh hafta do all dat lookin' and searchin'. Ah done told you time and time agin tuh stick all dem papers on dat nail! All you got tuh do is mind me. How come you can't do lak Ah tell yuh?"

"You sho loves to tell me whut to do, but Ah can't tell you nothin' Ah see!"

"Dat's 'cause you need tellin'," he rejoined hotly. "It would be ptitiful if Ah didn't. Somebody got to think for women and chillun and chickens and cows. I god, they sho don't think none theirselves."

"Ah knows uh few things, and womenfolks thinks sometimes too!"

"Aw naw they don't. They just think they's thinkin'. When Ah see one thing Ah understands ten. You see ten things and don't understand one."

Times and scenes like that put Janie to thinking about the inside state of her marriage. Time came when she fought back with her tongue as best she could, but it didn't do her any good. It just made Joe do more. He wanted her submission and he'd keep on fighting until he felt he had it.

So gradually, she pressed her teeth together and learned to hush. The spirit of the marriage left the bedroom and took to living in the parlor. It was there to shake hands whenever company came to visit, but it never went back inside the bedroom again. So she put something in there to represent the spirit like a Virgin Mary image in a church. The bed was no longer a daisy-field for her and Joe to play in. It was a place where she went and laid down when she was sleepy and tired.

She wasn't petal-open anymore with him. She was twenty-four and seven years married when she knew. She found that out one day when he slapped her face in the kitchen. It happened over one of those dinners that chasten all women sometimes. They plan and they fix and they do, and then some kitchen-dwelling fiend slips a scrochy, soggy, tasteless mess into their pots and pans. Janie was a good cook, and Joe had looked forward to his dinner as a refuge from other things. So when the bread didn't rise, and the fish wasn't quite done at the bone, and the rice was scorched, he slapped Janie until she had a ringing sound in her ears and told her about her brains before he stalked on back to the store.

Janie stood where he left her for unmeasured time and thought. She stood there until something fell off the shelf inside her. Then she went inside there to see what it was. It was her image of Jody tumbled down and shattered. But looking at it she saw that it never was the flesh and blood figure of her dreams. Just something she had grabbed up to drape her dreams over. In a way she turned her back upon the image where it lay and looked further. She had no more blossomy openings dusting pollen over her man, neither any glistening young fruit where the petals used to be. She found that she had a host of thoughts she had never expressed to him, and numerous emotions she had never let Jody know about. Things packed up and put away in parts of her heart where he could never find them. She was saving up feelings for some man she had never seen. She had an inside and an outside now and suddenly she knew how not to mix them.

She bathed and put on a fresh dress and head kerchief and went on to the store before Jody had time to send for her. That was a bow to the outside of things.

Jody was on the porch and the porch was full of Eatonville as usual at this time of the day. He was baiting Mrs. Tony Robbins as he always did when she came to the store. Janie could see Jody watching her out of the corner of his eye while he joked roughly with Mrs. Robbins. He wanted to be friendly with her again. His big, big laugh was as much for her as for the baiting. He was longing for peace but on his own terms.

"I god, Mrs. Robbins, whut make you come heah and worry me when you see Ah'm readin' mah newspaper?" Mayor Starks lowered the paper in pretended annoyance.

Mrs. Robbins struck her pity-pose and assumed the voice.

"'Cause Ah'm hongry, Mist' Starks. 'Deed Ah is. Me and mah chillun is hongry. Tony don't fee-eed me!"

This was what the porch was waiting for. They burst into a laugh.

"Mrs. Robbins, how can you make out you'se hongry when Tony comes in here every Satitday and buys groceries lak a man? Three weeks' shame on yuh!"

"If he buy all dat you talkin' 'bout, Mist' Starks, God knows whut he do wid it. He sho don't bring it home, and me and mah po' chillun is *so* hongry! Mist' Starks, please gimme uh lil piece uh meat fur me and mah chillun."

"Ah know you don't need it, but come on inside. You ain't goin' tuh lemme read till Ah give it to yuh."

Mrs. Tony's ectasy was divine. "Thank you, Mist' Starks. You'se noble! You'se du most gentlemanfied man Ah ever did see. You'se uh king!"

The salt pork box was in the back of the store and during the walk Mrs. Tony was so eager she sometimes stepped on Joe's heels, sometimes she was a little before him. Something like a hungry cat when somebody approaches her pan with meat. Running a little, caressing a little and all the time making little urging-on cries.

"Yes, indeedy, Mist' Starks, you'se noble. You got sympathy for me and mah po' chillun. Tony don't give us nothin' tuh eat and we'se *so* hongry. Tony don't fee-eed me!"

This brought them to the meat box. Joe took up the big meat knife and selected a piece of side meat to cut. Mrs. Tony was all but dancing around him.

"Dat's right, Mist' Starks! Gimme uh lil piece 'bout dis wide." She indicated as wide as her wrist and hand. "Me and mah chillun is *so* hongry!"

Starks hardly looked at her measurements. He had seen them too often. He marked off a piece much smaller and sunk the blade in. Mrs. Tony all but fell to the floor in her agony.

"Lawd a'mussy! Mist' Starks, you ain't gointuh gimme dat lil teeninchy piece fuh me and all mah chillun, is yuh? Lawd, we'se *so* hongry!"

Starks cut right on and reached for a piece of wrapping paper. Mrs. Tony leaped away from the proffered cut of meat as if it were a rattlesnake.

"Ah wouldn't tetch it! Dat lil eyeful uh bacon for me and all mah chillun! Lawd, some folks is got everything and they's so gripin' and so mean!"

Starks made as if to throw the meat back in the box and close it. Mrs. Tony swooped like lighting and seized it, and started towards the door.

"Some folks ain't got no heart in dey bosom. They's willun' tuh see uh po' woman and her helpless chillun starve tuh death. God's gointuh put 'em under arrest, some uh dese days, wid dey stingy gripin' ways."

She stepped from the store porch and marched off in high dudgeon! Some laughed and some got mad.

"If dat wuz *mah* wife," said Walter Thomas," Ah'd kill her ceme-tery dead."

"More special after Ah done bought her everything mah wages kin stand, lak Tony do," Coker said. "In de fust place Ah never would spend on *no* woman whut Tony spend on *her.*"

Starks came back and took his seat. He had to stop and add the meat to Tony's account.

"Well, Tony tells me tuh humor her along. He moved here from up de State hopin' tuh change her, but it ain't. He say he can't bear tuh leave her and he hate to kill her, so 'tain't nothin' tuh do but put up wid her."

"Dat's 'cause Tony love her too good," said Coker. "Ah could break her if she wuz mine. Ah'd break her or kill her. Makin' uh fool outa me in front of everybody."

"Tony won't never hit her. He says beatin' women is just like step-pin' on baby chickens. He claims 'tain't no place on uh woman tuh hit," Joe Lindsay said with scornful disapproval, "but Ah'd kill uh baby just born dis mawnin' fuh uh thing lak dat. 'Tain't nothin' but low-down spitefulness 'ginst her husband make her do it."

"Dat's de God's truth," Jim Stone agreed. "Dat's de very reason."

Janie did what she had never done before, that is, thrust herself into the conversation.

"Sometimes God gits familiar wid us womenfolks too and talks His inside business. He told me how surprised He was 'bout y'all turning out so smart after Him makin' yuh different; and how surprised y'all is goin' tuh be if you ever find out you don't know half as much 'bout us as you think you do. It's so easy to make yo'self out God Almighty when you ain't got nothin' tuh strain against but women and chickens."

"You gettin' too moufy, Janie," Starks told her. "Go fetch me de checker-board *and* de checkers. Sam Watson, you'se mah fish."

Black Women and Intraracial Prejudice

• • • • •

The stigma associated with a dark complexion in the 1930s and 1940s dates back to colonial times, when the Puritans associated "black" with evil and enslaved blacks as a means of controlling that evil.[1] Whiteness meant intellect, innocence, and piety; blackness connoted ignorance, depravity, and corruption. Writing about color and its impact on slavery in the seventeenth century, John L. Hodge comments that "blackness of color had become an independent reason for enslavement, and a self-fulfilling mark for treating black people as inferior; every slave had black skin and almost every black person was a slave."[2] The practice of miscegenation, usually instigated by white men who forced themselves on black women, led to a lightening of the black race that in turn produced a prejudice against dark skin among African Americans themselves.

Color phobia thoroughly penetrated the psyche of black Americans. Even in the midst of the Depression, and into the 1940s, many adhered to a rigid social structure based on color and economic standing that put darker-skinned women at a decided disadvantage, as Gwendolyn Brooks reveals in her novel *Maud Martha*. The title character knows her husband perceives her as inferior and less attractive because of the darkness of her skin.

William Lloyd Warner identified in the Negro race four categories of color based on social class: dark skin, brown skin, light skin, and passable (for white). According to Warner, dark-skinned and brown-skinned women were usually found in the lower-middle and lower classes because of the social stigma against them. Light-complexioned and "passable" women were usually in the upper or professional class, where "a light complexion is a decided social asset for middle-class women ambitious to improve their status." Although color evaluation in the African-American community was important to a woman's advancement, Warner states that it was "not so crucial in a man's career."[3] A black man's worth was determined by his social behavior and money-making ability; a woman's value was determined by the societally imposed standard of feminine "attractiveness." Thus, dark-skinned women were socially disadvantaged compared not only with light-complexioned women but with equally dark-skinned men. In Dorothy West's "Mammy," a light-complexioned daughter who is ashamed of her mother's dark skin but still wants her near, exploits her mother as a black mammy.

The higher value African Americans placed on Caucasoid features stimulated a profitable cosmetics industry. Understandably, this industry sought the business of all shades of black women who aspired to a lighter hue and a higher social bracket. Newspaper advertisements for products such as Nadinola Bleaching Cream for "white, more charming skin," Fan Tan Skin Whitening Soap for lighter skin—"7 shades in 7 days"—hair straighteners, and skin and hair conditioners were popular in Negro newspapers and magazines of the 1930s and 1940s, even those, like the *Baltimore Afro-American*, that advocated race pride. In Toni Morrison's *The Bluest Eye*, Geraldine teaches her son the difference between colored people and "niggers," carefully lotions his face "to keep the skin from becoming ashen," and cuts his hair "as close to his scalp as possible to avoid any suggestion of wool." Oppressed blacks who attempted to achieve this ideal of whiteness often fell prey to self-hatred and hopelessness when they failed to meet their unrealistic expectations.[4] Morrison's protagonist in *The Bluest Eye*, young Pecola Breedlove, is such a victim.

Color evaluations influenced every aspect of black people's lives, from hiring practices to the choice of friends, dating partners, and spouses. Lip thickness and nostril width were a primary criterion in choosing a mate; the hope was that children would be born with less typically Negroid features. In some families each generation attempted to marry lighter to erase the taint of blackness. The child psychiatrist Margaret Lawrence recalls the subtle influence such thinking had on her when she married in 1938. "I often wonder how it felt for Charles [her husband] to choose a girl darker than his family. . . . These things meant a great deal. . . . I know *I* had some feeling that I had done well to marry lighter."[5]

The hullabaloo over skin color created irreparable animosity within the race and did little to integrate the white and black races. One dark-complexioned female domestic summed up the color mania:

> Our race is so mixed up with the white man we don't know our head from a hole in the ground. The white blood in our race is pulling toward the white and they don't want them, and they think they are better than the Negroes. The brownskin people think they are better than the black people, but that's just the white blood making them think they are so hot. Everything has straight hair; all of the commonest animals. Do you know that the lamb, Jesus Christ, and the Negro are the only ones that have curly, woolly hair? White skin is not healthy and straight hair is common as dirt.[6]

NOTES

1. Winthrop D. Jordan, *White over Black:American Attitudes toward the Negro* (Chapel Hill: University of North Carolina Press, 1968), 91–98.
2. John L. Hodge, et al., *Cultural Bases of Racism and Group Oppression* (Berkeley, Calif.: Two Riders Press, 1975), 62.
3. William Lloyd Warner, et al., *Color and Human Nature. Negro Personality Development in a Northern City* (Washington, D.C.: American Council on Education, 1941), 17–21, 21, 178.
4. Kovel, *White Racism,* 179.
5. Sara Lawrence Lightfoot, *Balm in Gilead: Journey of a Healer,* Radcliffe Biography Series (Reading, Mass.: Addison-Wesley, 1989), 115.
6. Warner, et al., *Color and Human Nature,* 15.

• • • • •

"If You're Light and Have Long Hair" [from *Maud Martha*]

Gwendolyn Brooks

Born in Topeka, Kansas, in 1917 and a resident of Chicago for most of her life, Gwendolyn Brooks is an internationally recognized poet. She submitted poems to the *Chicago Defender* at age 16 and received four poetry awards from the Midwestern Writers Conference prior to the publication of her first volume, *A Street in Bronzeville* (1945). Her second volume of poems, *Annie Allen* (1949), won the Pulitzer Prize in 1950. She was named poet laureate of Illinois in 1968, the same year she published *In the Mecca*. Her other poetry volumes include *The Bean Eaters* (1960), *Riot* (1970), *Aloneness* (1971), *Reckonings* (1975), and *To Disembark* (1981).

Brooks's distinction as a poet lies in her technical dexterity, stark realism, varied content, rich imagery, and wide emotional range. Her poetry gives no small attention to the lives of black women. She reveals the disillusioning realities of married life in "The Anniad" (1945), explores the psychological effects of abortion in "The Mother" (1945), and destroys the myth of the superpowerful black matriarch in "What Shall I Give My Children?" (1945). In addition to her poetry, Brooks has published one novel, *Maud Martha* (1953); an autobiography, *Report from Part One* (1972); and two collections of her works, *The World of Gwendolyn Brooks* (1972) and *Blacks* (1987).

Gwendolyn Brooks's personal experiences with intraracial prejudice as a dark-complexioned young woman no doubt became the impetus for *Maud Martha* (Harper and Row, 1953). Brooks writes in her autobiography:

One of the first "world"-truths revealed to me when I at last became a member of SCHOOL was that, to be socially successful, a little girl must be Bright (of skin). It was better if your hair was curly, too—or at least Good Grade (Good Grade implied, usually, no involvement with the Hot Comb)—but Bright you marvelously *needed* to be. Exceptions? A few. Wealth was an escape passport. If a dusky maiden's father was a doctor, lawyer, City Hall employee, or Post Office man, or if her mother was a School-teacher, there was some hope.

Because Brooks's parents did not fit into these categories (although her mother had been a teacher prior to her marriage), light-complexioned girls rejected her; dark-skinned girls berated her because she dressed

well. "The little Bright ones looked through me if I happened to incon-
venience their vision, and those of my own hue rechristened me Ol'
Black Gal."[1]

The chapter reprinted here articulates the effects of intraracial prejudice on the novel's protagonist, Maud Martha, a dark-complexioned
woman. With her husband, she attends a formal ball at a nightclub
where the candles are white, the rug is white, and her husband leaves
her to dance with a "white as a white" woman. Maud Martha knows
her husband's attraction to this woman is connected to her light skin,
and that her own dark skin alienates him. She describes her color as
"like a wall"; her husband has "to jump over it in order to meet and
touch what I've got for him." Martha is angry at the light-skinned
woman, but she keeps her anger to herself. The problem, she recog-
nizes, is not simply this woman. "If the root was sour," she asks herself, "what business did she have up there hacking at a leaf?"

Like many of the black women of this period, Maud Martha is
affected by an enormous social problem; she is able to articulate the
problem, but she feels there is little she can do about it. She has no one
to even talk to about what she is feeling.

NOTES

1. Gwendolyn Brooks, *Report from Part One* (Detroit: Broadside
   Press, 1972), 37–38, 38.

Came the invitation that Paul recognized as an honor of the first
water, and as sufficient indication that he was, at last, a social somebody. The invitation was from the Foxy Cats Club, the club of clubs. He
was to be present, in formal dress, at the Annual Foxy Cats Dawn Ball.
No chances were taken: "Top hat, white tie and tails" hastily followed
the "Formal dress," and that elucidation was in bold type.

Twenty men were in the Foxy Cats Club. All were good-looking.
All wore clothes that were rich and suave. All "handled money," for
their number consisted of well-located barbers, policemen, "government men" and men with a lucky touch at the tracks. Certainly the Foxy
Cats Club was not a representative of that growing group of South Side
organizations devoted to moral and civic improvements, or to literary
or other cultural pursuits. If that had been so, Paul would have chucked
his bid (which was black and silver, decorated with winking cat faces)
down the toilet with a yawn. "That kind of stuff" was hardly understood by Paul, and was always dismissed with an airy "dicty," "hincty"
or "high-falutin'." But no. The Foxy Cats devoted themselves solely to
the business of being "hep," and each year they spent hundreds of
dollars on their wonderful Dawn Ball, which did not begin at dawn, but

was scheduled to end at dawn. "Ball," they called the frolic, but it served also the purposes of party, feast and fashion show. Maud Martha, watching him study his invitation, watching him lift his chin, could see that he considered himself one of the blessed.

Who—what kind soul had recommended him!

"He'll have to take me," thought Maud Martha. "For the envelope is addressed 'Mr. and Mrs.,' and I opened it. I guess he'd like to leave me home. At the Ball, there will be only beautiful girls, or real stylish ones. There won't be more than a handful like me. My type is not a Foxy Cat favorite. But he can't avoid taking me—since he hasn't yet thought of words or ways strong enough, and at the same time soft enough—for he's kind: he doesn't like to injure—to carry across to me the news that he is not to be held permanently by my type, and that he can go on with this marriage only if I put no ropes or questions around him. Also, he'll want to humor me, now that I'm pregnant."

She would need a good dress. That, she knew, could be a problem, on his grocery clerk's pay. He would have his own expenses. He would have to rent his topper and tails, and he would have to buy a fine tie, and really excellent shoes. She knew he was thinking that on the strength of his appearance and sophisticated behavior at this Ball might depend his future admission (for why not dream?) to *membership*, actually, in the Foxy Cats Club!

"I'll settle," decided Maud Martha, "on a plain white princess-style thing and some blue and black satin ribbon. I'll go to my mother's. I'll work miracles at the sewing machine.

"On that night, I'll wave my hair. I'll smell faintly of lily of the valley."

The main room of the Club 99, where the Ball was held, was hung with green and yellow and red balloons, and the thick pillars, painted to give an effect of marble, and stretching from floor to ceiling, were draped with green and red and yellow crepe paper. Huge ferns, rubber plants and bowls of flowers were at every corner. The floor itself was a decoration, golden, glazed. There was no overhead light; only wall lamps, and the bulbs in these were romantically dim. At the back of the room, standing on a furry white rug, was the long banquet table, dressed in damask, accented by groups of thin silver candlesticks bearing white candles, and laden with lovely food: cold chicken, lobster, candied ham fruit combinations, potato salad in a great gold dish, corn sticks, a cheese fluff in spiked tomato cups, fruit cake, angel cake, sunshine cake. The drinks were at a smaller table nearby, behind which stood a genial mixologist, quick with maraschino cherries, and with lemon, ice and liquor. Wines were there, and whiskey, and rum, and eggnog made with pure cream.

Paul and Maud Martha arrived rather late, on purpose. Rid of their wraps, they approached the glittering floor. Bunny Bates's orchestra was playing Ellington's "Solitude."

Paul, royal in rented finery, was flushed with excitement. Maud Martha looked at him. Not very tall. Not very handsomely made. But there was that extraordinary quality of maleness. Hiding in the body that was not *too* yellow, waiting to spring out at her, surround her (she liked to think)—that maleness. The Ball stirred her. The Beauties, in their gorgeous gowns, bustling, supercilious; the young men, who at other times most unpleasantly blew their noses, and darted surreptitiously into alleys to relieve themselves, and sweated and swore at their jobs, and scratched their more intimate parts, now smiling, smooth, overgallant; the drowsy lights; the smells of food and flowers, the smell of Murray's pomade, the body perfumes, natural and superimposed; the sensuous heaviness of the wine-colored draperies at the many windows; the music, now steamy and slow, now as clear and fragile as glass, now raging, passionate, now moaning and thickly gray. The Ball made toys of her emotions, stirred her variously. But she was anxious to have it end, she was anxious to be at home again, with the door closed behind herself and her husband. Then, he might be warm. There might be more than the absent courtesy he had been giving her of late. Then, he might be the tree she had a great need to lean against, in this "emergency." There was no telling what dear thing he might say to her, what little gem let fall.

But, to tell the truth, his behavior now was not very promising of gems to come. After their second dance he escorted her to a bench by the wall, left her. Trying to look nonchalant, she sat. She sat, trying not to show the inferiority she did not feel. When the music struck up again, he began to dance with someone red-haired and curved, and white as a white. Who was she? He had approached her easily, he had taken her confidently, he held her and conversed with her as though he had known her well for a long, long time. The girl smiled up at him. Her gold-spangled bosom was pressed—was pressed against that maleness—

A man asked Maud Martha to dance. He was dark, too. His mustache was small.

"Is this your first Foxy Cats?" he asked.

"What?" Paul's cheek was on that of Gold-Spangles.

"First Cats?"

"Oh. Yes." Paul and Gold-Spangles were weaving through the noisy twisting couples, were trying, apparently, to get to the reception hall.

"Do you know that girl? What's her name?" Maud Martha asked her partner, pointing to Gold-Spangles. Her partner looked, nodded. He pressed her closer.

"That's Maella. That's Maella."

"Pretty, isn't she?" She wanted him to keep talking about Maella. He nodded again.

"Yep. She has 'em howling along the stroll, all right, all right."

Another man, dancing past with an artificial redhead, threw a whispered word at Maud Martha's partner, who caught it eagerly, winked. "Solid, ol' man," he said. "Solid, Jack." He pressed Maud Martha closer. "You're a babe," he said. "You're a real babe." He reeked excitingly of tobacco, liquor, pinesoap, toilet water, and Sen Sen.

Maud Martha thought of her parents' back yard. Fresh. Clean. Smokeless. In her childhood, a snowball bush had shone there, big above the dandelions. The snowballs had been big, healthy. Once, she and her sister and brother had waited in the back yard for their parents to finish readying themselves for a trip to Milwaukee. The snowballs had been so beautiful, so fat and startlingly white in the sunlight, that she had suddenly loved home a thousand times more than ever before, and had not wanted to go to Milwaukee. But as the children grew, the bush sickened. Each year the snowballs were smaller and more dispirited. Finally a summer came when there were no blossoms at all. Maud Martha wondered what had become of the bush. For it was not there now. Yet she, at least, had never seen it go.

"Not," thought Maud Martha, "that they love each other. It oughta be that simple. Then I could lick it. It oughta be that easy. But it's my color that makes him mad. I try to shut my eyes to that, but it's no good. What I am inside, what is really me, he likes okay. But he keeps looking at my color, which is like a wall. He has to jump over it in order to meet and touch what I've got for him. He has to jump away up high in order to see it. He gets awful tired of all that jumping."

Paul came back from the reception hall. Maella was clinging to his arm. A final cry of the saxophone finished that particular slice of the blues. Maud Martha's partner bowed, escorted her to a chair by a rubber plant, bowed again, left.

"I could," considered Maud Martha, "go over there and scratch her upsweep down. I could spit on her back. I could scream. 'Listen,' I could scream, 'I'm making a baby for this man and I mean to do it in peace.'"

But if the root was sour what business did she have up there hacking at a leaf?

• • • • •

From *The Bluest Eye*

Toni Morrison

Toni Morrison is one of America's outstanding writers of fiction. She is the third black American, and the second black American woman, to receive the Pulitzer Prize for fiction, in 1988 for the best-selling *Beloved* (1987), her fifth novel. *Beloved* and each of her first four novels, *The Bluest Eye* (1970), *Sula* (1973), *Song of Solomon* (1977) (1977 National Book Critics Circle Award), and *Tar Baby* (1981), explore black lives, mostly the lives of women who are in conflict with themselves and others in the community. Among her minor works are such essays as "What the Black Woman Thinks about Women's Lib" (1971) and "Rediscovering Black History" (1974).[1]

Born Chloe Anthony Wofford, Morrison is a native of Lorain, Ohio. She earned her B.A. degree from Howard University and her M.A. degree from Cornell University. Morrison began her writing career in 1957 when she returned to Howard as a lecturer. She has taught at major universities and has held the post of senior editor at Random House.

The Bluest Eye (Henry Holt and Co.) depicts intraracial prejudice in a small Ohio community in the 1940s. Pecola Breedlove, considered an ugly, black child by other members of her race, wants a pair of blue eyes to make herself beautiful. Pecola has internalized the culture's white values and white standards of beauty. Her story is told within a unique structure: the novel's seven sections provide an ironic gloss on various phrases taken from a Dick and Jane reader.

In the following selection, Geraldine, the mother in a "colored" family, explains to her son Junior the difference between being colored and being black, like "niggers": "Colored people were neat and quiet; niggers were dirty and loud." Although Junior is curious about his darker skinned schoolmates and longs to play with them, he soon adopts his mother's superior attitude. He feels free to be extremely cruel and unjust to a lonely, dark-skinned little girl. Pecola is an easy target: she is dark, ugly, poor, friendless, and female. Junior is contemptuous of her weakness, and his mother sees her as the embodiment of everything she hates.

In this excerpt, as in Gwendolyn Brooks's "If You're Light and Have Long Hair," women are both victim and victimizer. Maud Martha's loss is her light-skinned adversary's gain; in *The Bluest Eye* Geraldine feels superior to Pecola and all little girls like her. Accepting either part—the attractive, desirable, and superior, or the undesirable and unworthy—is a kind of self-denial because both roles reflect the white male view of what is attractive and therefore valuable.

NOTE

1. Works by and about Toni Morrison appear in David L. Middleton's *Toni Morrison: An Annotated Bibliography* (*New York: Garland,* 1987).

. . . Geraldine did not allow her baby, Junior, to cry. As long as his needs were physical, she could meet them—comfort and satiety. He was always brushed, bathed, oiled, and shod. Geraldine did not talk to him, coo to him, or indulge him in kissing bouts, but she saw that every other desire was fulfilled. It was not long before the child discovered the difference in his mother's behavior to himself and the cat. As he grew older, he learned how to direct his hatred of his mother to the cat, and spent some happy moments watching it suffer. The cat survived, because Geraldine was seldom away from home, and could effectively soothe the animal when Junior abused him.

Geraldine, Louis, Junior, and the cat lived next to the playground of Washington Irving School. Junior considered the playground his own, and the schoolchildren coveted his freedom to sleep late, go home for lunch, and dominate the playground after school. He hated to see the swings, slides, monkey bars, and seesaws empty and tried to get kids to stick around as long as possible. White kids; his mother did not like him to play with niggers. She had explained to him the difference between colored people and niggers. They were easily identifiable. Colored people were neat and quiet; niggers were dirty and loud. He belonged to the former group: he wore white shirts and blue trousers; his hair was cut as close to his scalp as possible to avoid any suggestion of wool, the part was etched into his hair by the barber. In winter his mother put Jergens Lotion on his face to keep the skin from becoming ashen. Even though he was light-skinned, it was possible to ash. The line between colored and nigger was not always clear; subtle and telltale signs threatened to erode it, and the watch had to be constant.

Junior used to long to play with the black boys. More than anything in the world he wanted to play King of the Mountain and have them push him down the mound of dirt and roll over him. He wanted to feel their hardness pressing on him, smell their wild blackness, and say "Fuck you" with that lovely casualness. He wanted to sit with them on curbstones and compare the sharpness of jackknives, the distance and arcs of spitting. In the toilet he wanted to share with them the laurels of being able to pee far and long. Bay Boy and P. L. had at one time been his idols. Gradually he came to agree with his mother that neither Bay Boy nor P. L. was good enough for him. He played only with Ralph Nisensky, who was two years younger, wore glasses, and didn't want to *do* anything. More and more Junior enjoyed bullying girls. It was easy making them scream and run. How he laughed when they fell down and their bloomers showed. When they got up, their faces red and crinkled, it made him feel good. The nigger girls he did not pick on very much. They usually traveled in packs, and once when he threw a stone at some of them, they chased, caught, and beat him witless. He lied to his mother, saying Bay Boy did it. His mother was very upset. His father just kept on reading the Lorain *Journal*.

When the mood struck him, he would call a child passing by to come play on the swings or the seesaw. If the child wouldn't, or did and left too soon, Junior threw gravel at him. He became a very good shot.

Alternately bored and frightened at home, the playground was his joy. On a day when he had been especially idle, he saw a very black girl taking a shortcut through the playground. She kept her head down as she walked. He had seen her many times before, standing alone, always alone, at recess. Nobody ever played with her. Probably, he thought, because she was ugly.

Now Junior called to her. "Hey! What are you doing walking through my yard?"

The girl stopped.

"Nobody can come through this yard 'less I say so."

"This ain't your yard. It's the school's."

"But I'm in charge of it."

The girl stated to walk away.

"Wait." Junior walked toward her. "You can play in it if you want to. What's your name?"

"Pecola. I don't want to play."

"Come on. I'm not going to bother you."

"I got to go home."

"Say, you want to see something? I got something to show you."

"No. What is it?"

"Come on in my house. See, I live right there. Come on. I'll show you."

"Show me what?"

"Some kittens. We got some kittens. You can have one if you want."

"Real kittens?"

"Yeah. Come on."

He pulled gently at her dress. Pecola began to move toward his house. When he knew she had agreed, Junior ran ahead excitedly, stopping only to yell back at her to come on. He held the door open for her, smiling his encouragement. Pecola climbed the porch stairs and hesitated there, afraid to follow him. The house looked dark, Junior said, "There's nobody here. My ma's gone out, and my father's at work. Don't you want to see the kittens?"

Junior turned on the lights. Pecola stepped inside the door.

How beautiful, she thought. What a beautiful house. There was a big red-and-gold Bible on the dining-room table. Little lace doilies were everywhere—on arms and backs of chairs, in the center of a large dining table, on little tables. Potted plants were on all the windowsills. A color picture of Jesus Christ hung on a wall with the prettiest paper flowers fastened on the frame. She wanted to see everything slowly, slowly. But Junior kept saying, "Hey, you. Come on. Come on." He pulled her into another room, even more beautiful than the first. More doilies, a big lamp with green-and-gold base and white shade. There was even a rug on the floor, with enormous dark-red flowers. She was deep in admiration of the flowers when Junior said, "Here!" Pecola turned. "Here is your kitten!" he screeched. And he threw a big black cat right in her face. She sucked in her breath in fear and surprise and felt fur in her mouth. The cat clawed her face and chest in an effort to right itself, then leaped nimbly to the floor.

Junior was laughing and running around the room clutching his stomach delightedly. Pecola touched the scratched place on her face and felt tears coming. When she started toward the doorway, Junior leaped in front of her.

"You can't get out. You're my prisoner," he said. His eyes were merry but hard.

"You let me go."

"No!" He pushed her down, ran out the door that separated the rooms, and held it shut with his hands. Pecola's banging on the door increased his gasping, high-pitched laughter.

The tears came fast, and she held her face in her hands. When something soft and furry moved around her ankles, she jumped, and saw it was the cat. He wound himself in and about her legs. Momentarily distracted from her fear, she squatted down to touch him, her hands wet from the tears. The cat rubbed up against her knee. He was black all over, deep silky black, and his eyes, pointing down toward his nose, were bluish green. The light made them shine like blue ice. Pecola rubbed the cat's head; he whined, his tongue flicking with pleasure. The blue eyes in the black face held her.

Junior, curious at not hearing her sobs, opened the door, and saw her squatting down rubbing the cat's back. He saw the cat stretching its head and flattening its eyes. He had seen that expression many times as the animal responded to his mother's touch.

92

"Gimme my cat!" His voice broke. With a movement both awkward and sure he snatched the cat by one of its hind legs and began to swing it around his head in a circle.

"Stop that!" Pecola was screaming. The cat's free paws were stiffened, ready to grab anything to restore balance, its mouth wide, its eyes blue streaks of horror.

Still screaming, Pecola reached for Junior's hand. She heard her dress rip under her arm. Junior tried to push her away, but she grabbed the arm which was swinging the cat. They both fell, and in falling, Junior let go the cat, which, having been released in mid-motion, was thrown full force against the window. It slithered down and fell on the radiator behind the sofa. Except for a few shudders, it was still. There was only the slightest smell of singed fur.

Geraldine opened the door.

"What is this?" Her voice was mild, as though asking a perfectly reasonable question. "Who is this girl?"

"She killed our cat," said Junior. "Look." He pointed to the radiator, where the cat lay, its blue eyes closed, leaving only an empty, black, and helpless face.

Geraldine went to the radiator and picked up the cat. He was limp in her arms, but she rubbed her face in his fur. She looked at Pecola. Saw the dirty torn dress, the plaits sticking out on her head, hair matted where the plaits had come undone, the muddy shoes with the wad of gum peeping out from between the cheap soles, the soiled socks, one of which had been walked down into the heel of the shoe. She saw the safety pin holding the hem of the dress up. Up over the hump of the cat's back she looked at her. She had seen this little girl all of her life. Hanging out of windows over saloons in Mobile, crawling over the porches of shotgun houses on the edge of town, sitting in bus stations holding paper bags and crying to mothers who kept saying "Shet up!" Hair uncombed, dresses falling apart, shoes untied and caked with dirt. They had stared at her with great uncomprehending eyes. Eyes that questioned nothing and asked everything. Unblinking and unabashed, they stared up at her. The end of the world lay in their eyes, and the beginning, and all the waste in between.

They were everywhere. They slept six in a bed, all their pee mixing together in the night as they wet their beds each in his own candy-and-potato-chip dream. In the long, hot days, they idled away, picking plaster from the walls and digging into the earth with sticks. They sat in little rows on street curbs, crowded into pews at church, taking space from the nice, neat, colored children; they clowned on the playgrounds, broke things in dime stores, ran in front of you on the street, made ice slides on the sloped sidewalks in winter. The girls grew up knowing nothing of girdles, and the boys announced their manhood by turning the bills of their caps backward. Grass wouldn't grow where they lived. Flowers died. Shades fell down. Tin cans and tires blossomed where they lived. They lived on cold black-eyed peas and orange pop. Like flies they hovered; like flies they settled. And this one had settled in her house. Up over the hump of the cat's back she looked.

"Get out," she said, her voice quiet. "You nasty little black bitch. Get out of my house."

The cat shuddered and flicked his tail.

Pecola backed out of the room, staring at the pretty milk-brown lady in the pretty gold-and-green house who was talking to her through the cat's fur. The pretty lady's words made the cat fur move; the breath of each word parted the fur. Pecola turned to find the front door and saw Jesus looking down at her with sad and unsurprised eyes, his long brown hair parted in the middle, the gay paper flowers twisted around his face.

Outside, the March wind blew into the rip in her dress. She held her head down against the cold. But she could not hold it low enough to avoid seeing the snowflakes falling and dying on the pavement.

●　●　●　●　●

"Mammy"

Dorothy West

A native of Boston, Massachusetts, Dorothy West was born in 1907.[1] She was educated at Boston's Girls' Latin School, Boston University, and the School of Journalism at Columbia University. In 1926 her first short story, "The Typewriter," won one of two second prizes given by *Opportunity*. Other West stories that appeared in *Opportunity* include "The Black Dress" (1934) and "Mammy" (October 1940). She published short fiction in the *Boston Post*, the *Saturday Evening Quill*, and the *New York Daily News* and published one novel, *The Living Is Easy* (1948). From March 1934 until April 1937 West published and edited *Challenge* (later *New Challenge*), a literary journal devoted to the works of young black writers. In addition to her literary accomplishments,

West is known for her association with figures of the Harlem Renaissance and for her photographs of and correspondence with Langston Hughes, Claude McKay, Zora Neale Hurston, and Carl Van Vechten, all of which is housed at Mugar Memorial Library, Boston University (Special Collections).

"Mammy" is based on West's brief experience as a relief investigator in Harlem during the Depression. Three generations of African-American women are painfully estranged, owing to intraracial prejudice. A well-to-do woman who "passes" for white, Mrs. Coleman passes her dark-skinned mother off as a live-in mammy and it seems is responsible for the murder of her grandchild. Mrs. Coleman's daughter is also light enough to pass, but apparently her baby was not.

West's story is extreme, but it does exemplify the pressure to pass for white into a world of greater opportunity, comfort, and financial security. Perhaps more important, it depicts the terrible divisiveness that intraracial prejudice could create even within one family—emblematic of the divisiveness it has created within the larger family of African-Americans.

NOTE

1. According to Roses and Randolph, "West's birth date is often mistakenly given as 1912, but Boston records show she was born in 1907" (*Harlem Renaissance and Beyond*, 343).

The young Negro welfare investigator, carrying her briefcase, entered the ornate foyer of the Central Park West apartment house. She was making a collateral call. Earlier in the day she had visited an aging colored woman in a rented room in Harlem. Investigation had proved that the woman was not quite old enough for Old Age Assistance, and yet no longer young enough to be classified as employable. Nothing, therefore, stood in the way of her eligibility for relief. Here was a clear case of need. This collateral call on her last employer was merely routine.

The investigator walked toward the elevator, close on the heels of a well-dressed woman with a dog. She felt shy. Most of her collaterals were to housewives in the Bronx or supervisors of maintenance workers in office buildings. Such calls were never embarrassing. A moment ago as she neared the doorway, the doorman had regarded her intently. The service entrance was plainly to her left, and she was walking past it. He had been on the point of approaching when a tenant emerged and dispatched him for a taxi. He had stood for a moment torn between his immediate duty and his sense of outrage. Then he had gone away dolefully, blowing his whistle.

The woman with the dog reached the elevator just as the doors slid open. The dog bounded in, and the elevator boy bent and rough-housed with him. The boy's agreeable face was black, and the investigator felt a flood of relief.

The woman entered the elevator and smilingly faced front. Instantly the smile left her face, and her eyes hardened. The boy straightened, faced front, too, and gaped in surprise. Quickly he glanced at the set face of his passenger.

"Service entrance's outside," he said sullenly.

The investigator said steadily, "I am not employed here. I am here to see Mrs. Coleman on business."

"If you're here on an errand or somethin' like that," he argued doggedly, "you still got to use the service entrance."

She stared at him with open hate, despising him for humiliating her before and because of a woman of an alien race.

"I am here as a representative of the Department of Welfare. If you refuse me the use of this elevator, my office will take it up with the management."

She did not know if this was true, but the elevator boy would not know either.

"Get in then," he said rudely, and rolled his eyes at his white passenger as if to convey his regret at the discomfort he was causing her.

The doors shut and the three shot upward, without speaking to or looking at each other. The woman with the dog, in a far corner, very pointedly held the small harmless animal on a tight leash.

The car stopped at the fourth floor, and the doors slid open. No one moved. There was a ten-second wait.

"You getting out or not?" the boy asked savagely.

There was no need to ask who he was addressing.

"Is this my floor?" asked the investigator.

His sarcasm rippled. "You want Mrs. Coleman, don't you?"

"Which is her apartment?" she asked thickly.

"Ten-A. You're holding up my passenger."

When the door closed, she leaned against it, feeling sick, and trying to control her trembling. She was young and vulnerable. Her contact with Negroes was confined to frightened relief folks who did everything possible to stay in her good graces, and the members of her own set, among whom she was a favorite because of her two degrees and her civil service appointment. She had almost never run into Negroes who did not treat her with respect.

In a moment or two she walked down the hall to Ten-A. She rang, and after a little wait a handsome middle-aged woman opened the door.

"How do you do?" the woman said in a soft drawl. She smiled. "You're from the relief office, aren't you? Do come in."

"Thank you," said the investigator, smiling, too, relievedly.

"Right this way," said Mrs. Coleman, leading the way into a charming living-room. She indicated an upholstered chair. "Please sit down."

The investigator, who never sat in overstuffed chairs in the homes of her relief clients, plumped down and smiled again at Mrs. Coleman. Such a pleasant woman, such a pleasant room. It was going to be a quick and easy interview. She let her briefcase slide to the floor beside her.

Mrs. Coleman sat down in a straight chair and looked searchingly at the investigator. Then she said somewhat breathlessly, "You gave me to understand that Mammy has applied for relief."

The odious title sent a little flicker of dislike across the investigator's face. She answered stiffly, "I had just left Mrs. Mason when I telephoned you for this appointment."

Mrs. Coleman smiled disarmingly, though she colored a little.

"She has been with us ever since I can remember. I call her Mammy, and so does my daughter."

"That's a sort of nurse, isn't it?" the investigator asked coldly. "I had thought Mrs. Mason was a general maid."

"Is that what she said?"

"Why, I understood she was discharged because she was no longer physically able to perform her duties."

"She wasn't discharged."

The investigator looked dismayed. She had not anticipated complications. She felt for her briefcase.

"I'm very confused, Mrs. Coleman. Will you tell me just exactly what happened then? I had no idea Mrs. Mason was—was misstating the situation." She opened her briefcase.

Mrs. Coleman eyed her severely. "There's nothing to write down. Do you have to write down things? It makes me feel as if I were being investigated."

"I'm sorry," the investigator said quickly, snapping shut her briefcase. "If it would be distasteful—. I apologize again. Please go on."

"Well, there's little to tell. It all happened so quickly. My daughter was ill. My nerves were on edge. I may have said something that upset Mammy. One night she was here. The next morning she wasn't. I've been worried sick about her."

"Did you report her disappearance?"

"Her clothes were gone, too. It didn't seem a matter for the police. It was obvious that she had left of her own accord. Believe me, young woman, I was relieved when you telephoned me." Her voice shook a little.

"I'm glad I can assure you that Mrs. Mason appears quite well. She only said she worked for you. She didn't mention your daughter. I hope she has recovered.''

''My daughter is married,'' Mrs. Coleman said slowly. ''She had a child. It was stillborn. We have not seen Mammy since. For months she had looked forward to nursing it.''

''I'm sure it was a sad loss to all of you,'' the investigator said gently. ''And old Mrs. Mason, perhaps she felt you had no further use for her. It may have unsettled her mind. Temporarily,'' she added hastily. ''She seems quite sane.''

''Of course, she is,'' said Mrs. Coleman with a touch of bitterness. ''She's old and contrary. She knew we would worry about her. She did it deliberately.''

This was not in the investigator's province. She cleared her throat delicately.

''Would you take her back, Mrs. Coleman?''

''I want her back,'' cried Mrs. Coleman. ''She has no one but us. She is just like one of the family.''

''You're very kind,'' the investigator murmured. ''Most people feel no responsibility for their aging servants.''

''You do not know how dear a mammy is to a southerner. I nursed at Mammy's breast. I cannot remember a day in my life without her.''

The investigator reached for her briefcase and rose.

''Then it is settled that she may return?''

A few hours ago there had been no doubt in her mind of old Mrs. Mason's eligibility for relief. With this surprising turn there was nothing to do but reject the case for inadequate proof of need. It was always a feather in a field worker's cap to reject a case that had been accepted for home investigation by a higher paid intake worker.

Mrs. Coleman looked at the investigator almost beseechingly.

''My child, I cannot tell you how much I will be in your debt if you can persuade Mammy to return. Can't you refuse to give her relief? She really is in need of nothing as long as I am living. Poor thing, what has she been doing for money? How has she been eating? In what sort of place is she staying?''

''She's very comfortable, really. She had three dollars when she came uptown to Harlem. She rented a room, explained her circumstances to her landlady, and is getting her meals there. I know that landlady. She has other roomers who are on relief. She trusts them until they get their relief checks. They never cheat her.''

''Oh, thank God! I must give you something to give to that woman. How good Negroes are. I am so glad it was you who came. You are so sympathetic. I could not have talked so freely to a white investigator. She would not have understood.''

The investigator's smile was wintry. She resented this well-meant restatement of the trusted position of the good Negro.

She said civilly, however, "I'm going back to Mrs. Mason's as soon as I leave here. I hope I can persuade her to return to you tonight."

"Thank you! Mammy was happy here, believe me. She had nothing to do but a little dusting. We are a small family, myself, my daughter, and her husband. I have a girl who comes every day to do the hard work. She preferred to sleep in, but I wanted Mammy to have the maid's room. It's a lovely room with a private bath. It's next to the kitchen, which is nice for Mammy. Old people potter about so. I've lost girl after girl who felt she was meddlesome. But I've always thought of Mammy's comfort first."

"I'm sure you have," said the investigator politely, wanting to end the interview. She made a move toward departure. "Thank you again for being so cooperative."

Mrs. Coleman rose and crossed to the doorway.

"I must get my purse. Will you wait a moment?"

Shortly she reappeared. She opened her purse.

"It's been ten days. Please give that landlady this twenty dollars. No, it isn't too much. And here is a dollar for Mammy's cab fare. Please put her in the cab yourself."

"I'll do what I can." The investigator smiled candidly. "It must be nearly four, and my working day ends at five."

"Yes, of course," Mrs. Coleman said distractedly. "And now I just want you to peep in at my daughter. Mammy will want to know how she is. She's far from well, poor lambie."

The investigator followed Mrs. Coleman down the hall. At an open door they paused. A pale young girl lay on the edge of a big tossed bed. One hand was in her tangled hair, the other clutched an empty bassinet. The wheels rolled down and back, down and back. The girl glanced briefly and without interest at her mother and the investigator, then turned her face away.

"It tears my heart," Mrs. Coleman whispered in a choked voice. "Her baby, and then Mammy. She has lost all desire to live. But she is young and she will have other children. If she would only let me take away that bassinet! I am not the nurse that Mammy is. You can see how much Mammy is needed here."

They turned away and walked in silence to the outer door. The investigator was genuinely touched, and eager to be off on her errand of mercy.

Mrs. Coleman opened the door, and for a moment seemed at a loss as to how to say good-bye. Then she said quickly, "Thank you for coming," and shut the door.

The investigator stood in indecision at the elevator, half persuaded to walk down three flights of stairs. But this, she felt, was turning tail, and pressed the elevator button.

The door opened. The boy looked at her sheepishly. He swallowed and said ingratiatingly, "Step in, miss. Find your party all right?"

She faced front, staring stonily ahead of her, and felt herself trembling with indignation at this new insolence.

He went on whiningly, "That woman was in my car is mean as hell. I was just puttin' on to please her. She hates niggers 'cept when they're bowin' and scraping'. She was the one had the old doorman fired. You see for yourself they got a white one now. With white folks needin' jobs, us niggers got to eat dirt to hang on."

The investigator's face was expressionless except for a barely perceptible wincing at his careless use of a hated word.

He pleaded, "You're colored like me. You ought to understand. I was only doing my job. I got to eat same as white folks, same as you."

They rode the rest of the way in a silence interrupted only by his heavy sighs. When they reached the ground floor, and the door slid open, he said sorrowfully, "Good-bye, miss."

She walked down the hall and out into the street, past the glowering doorman, with her face stern and her stomach slightly sick.

The investigator rode uptown on a northbound bus. At One Hundred and Eighteenth Street she alighted and walked east. Presently she entered a well-kept apartment house. The elevator operator deferentially greeted her and whisked her upwards.

She rang the bell of number fifty-four, and visited briefly with the landlady, who was quite overcome by the unexpected payment of twenty dollars. When she could escape her profuse thanks, the investigator went to knock at Mrs. Mason's door.

"Come in," called Mrs. Mason. The investigator entered the small, square room. "Oh, it's you, dear," said Mrs. Mason, her lined brown face lighting up.

She was sitting by the window in a wide rocker. In her black, with a clean white apron tied about her waist, and a white bandanna bound around her head, she looked ageless and full of remembering.

Mrs. Mason grasped her rocker by the arms and twisted around until she faced the investigator.

She explained shyly, "I just sit here for hours lookin' out at the people. I ain' seen so many colored folks at one time since I left down home. Sit down, child, on the side of the bed. Hit's softer than that straight chair yonder."

The investigator sat down on the straight chair, not because the bedspread was not scrupulously clean, but because what she had come to say needed stiff decorum.

"I'm all right here, Mrs. Mason. I won't be long."

"I was hopin' you could set awhile. My landlady's good, but she's got this big flat. Don't give her time for much settin'."

The investigator, seeing an opening, nodded understandingly.

"Yes, it must be pretty lonely for you here after being so long an intimate part of the Coleman family."

The old woman's face darkened. "Shut back in that bedroom behin' the kitchen? This here's what I like. My own kind and color. I'm too old a dog to be learnin' new tricks."

"Your duties with Mrs. Coleman were very slight. I know you are getting on in years, but you are not too feeble for light employment. You were not entirely truthful with me. I was led to believe you did all the housework."

The old woman looked furtively at the investigator. "How come you know diff'rent now?"

"I've just left Mrs. Coleman."

Bafflement veiled the old woman's eyes. "You didn' believe what all I tol' you?"

"We always visit former employers. It's part of our job, Mrs. Mason. Sometimes an employer will re-hire our applicants. Mrs. Coleman is good enough to want you back. Isn't that preferable to being a public charge?"

"I ain't a-goin' back," said the old woman vehemently.

The investigator was very exasperated. "Why, Mrs. Mason?" she asked gently.

"That's an ungodly woman," the old lady snapped. "And I'm God-fearin'. 'Tain't no room in one house for God and the devil. I'm too near the grave to be servin' two masters."

To the young investigator this was evasion by superstitious mutterings.

"You don't make yourself very clear, Mrs. Mason. Surely Mrs. Coleman didn't interfere with your religious convictions. You left her home the night after her daughter's child was born dead. Until then, apparently, you had no religious scruples."

The old woman looked at the investigator wearily. Then her head sank forward on her breast.

"That child warn't born dead."

The investigator said impatiently, "But surely the hospital—?"

"'T'warnt born in no hospital."

"But the doctor—?"

"Little sly man. Looked like he'd cut his own throat for a dollar."

"Was the child deformed?" the investigator asked helplessly.

"Hit was a beautiful baby," said the old woman bitterly.

"Why, no one would destroy a healthy child," the investigator cried indignantly. "Mrs. Coleman hopes her daughter will have more children." She paused, then asked anxiously, "Her daughter is really married, isn't she? I mean, the baby wasn't—illegitimate?"

"It's ma and pa were married down home. A church weddin'. They went to school together. They was all right till they come up N'th. Then *she* started workin' on 'em. Old ways wasn't good enough for her."

The investigator looked at her watch. It was nearly five. This last speech had been rambling gossip. Here was an old woman clearly unoriented in her northern transplanting. Her position as mammy made her part of the family. Evidently she felt that gave her a matriarchal right to arbitrate its destinies. Her small grievances against Mrs. Coleman had magnified themselves in her mind until she could make this illogical accusation of infanticide as compensation for her homesickness for the folkways of the South. Her move to Harlem bore this out. To explain her reason for establishing a separate residence, she had told a fantastic story that could not be checked, and would not be recorded, unless the welfare office was prepared to face a libel suit.

"Mrs. Mason," said the investigator, "please listen carefully. Mrs. Coleman has told me that you are not only wanted but very much needed in her home. There you will be given food and shelter in return for small services. Please understand that I sympathize with your— imaginings, but you cannot remain here without public assistance, and I cannot recommend to my superiors that public assistance be given you."

The old woman, who had listened worriedly, now said blankly, "You mean I ain't a-gonna get it?"

"No, Mrs. Mason, I'm sorry. And now it's ten to five. I'll be glad to help you pack your things, and put you in a taxi."

The old woman looked helplessly around the room as if seeking a hiding place. Then she looked back at the investigator, her mouth trembling.

"You're my own people, child. Can' you fix up a story for them white folks at the relief, so's I could get to stay here where it's nice?"

"That would be collusion, Mrs. Mason. And that would cost me my job."

The investigator rose. She was going to pack the old woman's things herself. She was heartily sick of her contrariness, and determined to see her settled once and for all.

"Now where is your bag?" she asked with forced cheeriness. "First I'll empty these bureau drawers." She began to do so, laying things neatly on the bed. ''Mrs. Coleman's daughter will be so glad to see you. She's very ill, and needs your nursing.''

The old woman showed no interest. Her head had sunk forward on her breast again. She said listlessly, ''Let her ma finish what she started. I won't have no time for nursin'. I'll be down on my knees rasslin' with the devil. I done tol' you the devil's done eased out God in that house.''

The investigator nodded indulgently, and picked up a framed photograph that was lying face down in the drawer. She turned it over and involuntarily smiled at the smiling child in old-fashioned dress.

''This little girl,'' she said, ''it's Mrs. Coleman, isn't it?''

The old woman did not look up. Her voice was still listless.

''That *was* my daughter.''

The investigator dropped the photograph on the bed as if it were a hot coal. Blindly she went back to the bureau, gathered up the rest of the things, and dumped them over the photograph.

She was a young investigator, and it was two minutes to five. Her job was to give or withhold relief. That was all.

''Mrs. Mason,'' she said, ''please, please understand. This is my job.''

The old woman gave no sign of having heard.

103

PART 2

Black Women and the Civil Rights and Black Power Movements

Oh, the blues has got me on the go.
They've got me on the go.
They roll around my house, in and out
of my front door.

—Bessie Smith
In the House Blues

Black Women Against Racism

• • • • •

After we found out that Christian love
wouldn't cure the [racial] sickness in
Mississippi, then we knew we had other
things to do.
—Fannie Lou Hamer, civil rights advocate

A decade before the civil rights movement got under way, the U.S. Supreme Court handed down several important legal decisions against racial discrimination related to voting (*Smith v. Allwright*, 1944), interstate
travel (*Morgan v. Virginia*, 1946), housing (*Shelley v. Kraemer*, 1948), and
education (*Sipuel v. Board of Regents of the University of Oklahoma*, 1948).[1]
These positive rulings had little bearing, however, on the masses of
black women in the 1950s who rode segregated buses to and from work,
sent their children to segregated schools, and stayed away from the voting polls for fear of reprisals from white southern racists.

Rosa Parks, quiet-spoken seamstress, created the spark that ignited
the civil rights movement when she refused to give up her bus seat
to a white man as she rode home from work on 1 December 1955 in
Montgomery, Alabama. Parks was not the first black woman that year
to challenge segregated seating on Montgomery's buses; Claudette Col-
vin, Mary Louise Smith, and Aurelia Browder had earlier refused to
relinquish their seats to whites.[2] The Women's Political Council (WPC),

under the presidency of JoAnn Robinson, an Alabama State College professor, decided that Rosa Parks was the ideal woman to rally around. Parks was a churchgoer, a respected citizen, and a former secretary for the local NAACP chapter. After she was arrested, the WPC initiated plans for a boycott of Montgomery's city buses. The Montgomery Improvement Association (MIA) took up the WPC's plans and organized the boycott. The MIA advised black boycotters, "If cursed, do not curse back. If struck, do not strike back, but evidence love and goodwill at all times."[3]

Parks's explanation for her refusal to vacate her seat was simply that she was "tired," but Martin Luther King, Jr., later said that her refusal to move arose from her dissatisfaction with "the accumulated indignities of days gone by and the boundless aspirations of generations yet unborn."[4] Nevertheless, Parks's nonviolent protest caused her much distress. She lost her job as a seamstress in a local department store and endured bomb threats to her person and property; she finally moved to Detroit. She was among the first in a long line of black women to influence every front of the civil rights movement. Southern black women played a particularly strong role in the struggle for equal education, having inherited from slavery a legacy of educational deprivation that they were trying to overcome. As slaves, black women and men were forbidden to read and write because whites feared that, if educated, their slaves might rise up against them. The Freedmen's Bureau, a government agency established after the Civil War to aid the newly emancipated slaves, erected schools for blacks, many of which remained segregated until (and in some instances, after) the 1954 Supreme Court decision on *Brown v. Board of Education of Topeka, Kansas* prohibited separate schools for the races. Most of the black schools were vocational; white southerners believed that vocational training would prepare blacks for their "place," with black women concentrating on cooking, sewing, and other service-related tasks. Not only did this belief provide the white South with "an excuse to neglect expensive Negro high school construction altogether," but it severely limited the education of black women in a society that already devalued all women because of their gender.[5]

Black women during the civil rights movement followed the tradition of their African-American foremothers who, both before and after slavery, had attempted to eradicate the race's illiteracy by founding schools, establishing literary societies, and devoting their lives to teaching. These foremothers included Mary S. Peake, who secretly taught school in her home in Hampton, Virginia, in the 1850s; Susie King Taylor, an ex-slave who opened a night school in Liberty County, Georgia, in the 1860s; Lucy Lany, who founded Haines Normal Institute in Augusta, Georgia, in 1886; Charlotte Hawkins, who opened Palmer Memorial Institute, a finishing school for girls in Sedalia, North Carolina, in 1902; and Mary McLeod Bethune, who founded the Daytona Educational and Industrial School for Negro Girls in Daytona, Florida, in 1904. Teaching was the primary profession in which black women were accepted by a race- and sex-conscious society. But unlike most white women who improved their status by becoming teachers, black women had the added burden of teaching in poorly funded, segregated schools.

In poorer black communities, a greater value was generally placed on women, not men, getting an education. According to Bob Smith, ''It was the old Southern Negro story of the women's getting the education that would help them stay South and teach or go north and get jobs as secretaries. . . . What point was there in educating Negro boys for nonexistent jobs?''[6] More black women than black men have received a grade school education because society has offered them, rather than black men, greater economic opportunities. In 1960, 14.3 percent of black females age 25 and older completed 4 years of high school, compared with 11.3 percent of black males in the same age group.[7] Consequently, black women were more likely to know what unequal education meant—outdated textbooks, leaky old buildings, underpaid teachers. The deprivations they suffered themselves fomented southern black women's discontent and precipitated their desire for educational changes. Septima Poinsette Clark, Autherine Lucy, Barbara Rose, and Daisy Bates are among the many women who fought for equal education for black Americans.

In her autobiography, *The Long Shadow of Little Rock*, Daisy Bates recalls the agonizing confrontations with die-hard segregationists to attain equal education for black children in Little Rock, Arkansas, in 1957. She confronted local officials when they refused to desegregate Little Rock public schools according to the 1954 Supreme Court decision. Gov. Orval Faubus called out the National Guard to prevent the schools from being integrated, but Bates countered by securing the aid of President Eisenhower, who appropriated the Arkansas National Guard and ordered more troops to the city to enforce federal law.

In the 1960s black women from high schools and colleges joined the ranks of various civil rights organizations to fight racism in all segments of American life. They affiliated with CORE (Congress of Racial Equality), NAACP (National Association for the Advancement of Colored People), SCLC (Southern Christian Leadership Conference), SNCC (Student Nonviolent Coordinating Committee), and the Urban League. They desegregated lunch counters and churches, marched for equal wages, and rode ''freedom trains.'' Many were publicly humiliated by white racists, as Anne Moody recounts in her autobiography, *Coming of Age in Mississippi*. Others were physically wounded while protesting.

Black women made up a large segment of the contingency that traveled by mule carts from the South to pitch tents in foot-deep mud on the grounds of the Washington Monument to protest discrimination in the famous 1963 march on Washington, D.C. supported by Martin Luther King, Jr. The government's response was encouraging. After John F. Kennedy's assassination in November 1963, Lyndon B. Johnson secured the passage of the Civil Rights Act of 1964, which, among other provisions, authorized federal action against discrimination and segregation in public facilities and in the workplace. It was the most far-reaching civil rights legislation ever approved by Congress.

Although there were growing grass-roots movements outside the South—such as the one focusing on poor economic conditions for blacks in Cambridge, Maryland, led by Gloria Richardson in 1962—[8]the civil rights movement turned its attention in the early 1960s to voter registration in the Deep South. Southern blacks had been consistently disenfranchised since Reconstruction, and the one-party (Democrat) South ensured their disenfranchisement through the white primary, which prevented blacks from registering and voting. CORE and SNCC organized intensive voting rights activity in Mississippi, the most challenging of the southern states; because of the fear of white intimidation and extralegal procedures, only 5 percent of Mississippi blacks had registered to vote.[9] When SNCC volunteers and field secretaries spread into Ku Klux Klan–infested backwoods to organize local blacks, many courageous older black women, such as Fannie Lou Hamer of Sunflower County, Mississippi, welcomed the activists into their homes. Thousands of the northern white college students who came to Mississippi during Freedom Summer 1964 to assist with registration efforts met "some of the 'mamas' in the community" and believed they were "in touch with the core of the local civil rights insurgency."[10] The voter registration drive led to the passage on 6 August 1965 of the Voting Rights Act, which abolished discriminatory practices and literacy examinations at the polls and installed federal registers in all states where blacks had been prohibited from voting.

At the same time that the civil rights movement was reaching its peak in the mid-1960s, another movement in the black community's struggle for freedom was stirring. The black power or black liberation movement was at once a call to militant action and a call for unity and pride in being black. Unlike the civil rights movement, it was more popular in the urban North than in the rural South, was inspired more by African culture than by the church, and espoused Malcolm X's philosophy of separatism and black nationalism more than Martin Luther King, Jr.'s philosophy of integration.[11] Angry riots by black urban youth and the rise of black militant groups—Revolutionary Action Movement (RAM),[12] Republic of New Africa (RNA),[13] and the Black Panther Party

110

for Self Defense[14]—ended the reign of nonviolent protest that Martin Luther King, Jr., had initiated.

Some black women joined these militant groups organized to fight racism, and a few, including Assata Shakur and Angela Davis, gained national attention because of their affiliation with the Black Panther party.[15] They functioned mainly as clerical auxiliaries to the male Panthers, but when the party was placed in the FBI's counterintelligence program (COINTELPRO) as a black nationalist hate group, both male and female members were regarded as dangerous. Even city police departments expanded their counterinsurgency forces to annihilate the Panthers. In her autobiography, Davis describes the police brutality of Los Angeles police officers who physically attacked a black crowd at a peace rally and, after identifying her, came after her with drawn billy clubs. Sympathizing with the defenseless, scattered protesters, some local black women, much like the women in the earlier voter registration drives in the South, gave these young activists shelter in their homes.

Many other black women were absorbed with the concept of black nationalism. Like their black male counterparts, they embraced Africa as their motherland and idealized all aspects of that continent. Their new image manifested pride in their African heritage and a greater sense of self-worth as black women. They wore African hairstyles, jewelry, tribal dress, and bright colors. They embraced "black" instead of "Negro" or "colored" as a race designation, and some even took on African names and gave their children African names. Their new cultural image was a direct strike against the culture of Western white racist imperialists.[16]

Mary Helen Washington relays Alice Walker's comment that, before the Civil Rights Movement," she walked in the white world 'less real to them than a shadow,' that the Civil Rights Movement gave her history, heroes, and hope, that it *literally* called her to life [italics mine].[17] From the 1950s to the early 1970s, the civil rights and black power movements brought considerable psychological liberation to African-Americans. This period's spirit of confrontation, black solidarity, race pride, and cultural self-esteem are manifested in the selections in this part of the book.

NOTES

1. In *Smith v. Allwright*, the Supreme Court ruled that the exclusion of Negroes from voting in state primaries is unconstitutional (*United States Reports: Cases Adjudged in the Supreme Court*, vol. 321 [Washington, D.C.: Government Printing Office, 1944], 649–70). In 1946 Irene Morgan, a black

woman, refused to surrender her seat to a white man while traveling by bus from Gloucester, Virginia, to Baltimore, Maryland. In *Morgan v. Virginia,* the Supreme Court ruled that the state legislation regarding race "unduly burdens interstate commerce," and that passengers have a right to travel without abiding by the segregation laws of the states through which public conveyances pass (*United States Supreme Court Reports.* Lawyers' ed., 2d series, vol. 90 (Rochester, N.Y.: Lawyer's Cooperatives, 1946), 1317). In *Shelley v. Kraemer,* the Supreme Court ruled that restrictive covenants designed to exclude a race from home ownership or occupation of real estate are unconstitutional (*Supreme Court Reports.* 92:1161–62). In *Sipuel v. Board of Regents of the University of Oklahoma,* Ada Louise Sipuel, a black woman, sued for her right to attend the University of Oklahoma Law School. The Supreme Court ruled that "a Negro, concededly qualified to receive professional legal education offered by a state, cannot be denied such education because of her color." The court ordered the University of Oklahoma to provide an education for Sipuel "as soon as it does for applicants of any other group" (*U.S. Reports* (1948), 332:631–33).

2. JoAnn Gibson Robinson, *The Montgomery Bus Boycott and the Women Who Started It,* ed. David Garrow (Knoxville: University of Tennessee Press, 1987), 37–39, 43, 136.

3. David Levering Lewis, *King: A Critical Biography* (New York: Praeger, 1970), 50, 81.

4. Ibid., 50.

5. Bob Smith, *They Closed Their Schools: Prince Edward County, Virginia, 1951–1964* (Chapel Hill: University of North Carolina Press, 1965), 14.

6. Ibid., 77.

7. *Statistical Abstract of the United States 1977* (Washington, D.C.: Bureau of the Census, 1977), 136.

8. Gloria Richardson was born in 1922 in Baltimore and reared in Cambridge, Maryland. As cochair of the Cambridge Nonviolent Action Committee (CNAC) she rallied the second ward of Cambridge in 1962 to challenge black poverty and unemployment and segregated housing and schools. With the assistance of freedom riders from New York City, the CNAC was the first major civil rights organization in the 1960s to be led by a woman. See Annette K. Brock, "Gloria Richardson and the Cambridge Movement," *Black Women in United States History,* 16 vols., ed. Darlene Clark Hine (Brooklyn: Carlson, 1990), 16:122–25.

9. Rhoda Lois Blumberg, *Civil Rights: The 1960s Freedom Struggle* (Boston: Twayne, 1984), 85.

10. Sara Evans, *Personal Politics: The Roots of Women's Liberation in the Civil Rights Movement and the New Left* (New York: Vintage, 1980), 51.

11. Stewart Burns, *Social Movements of the 1960s: Searching for Democracy* (Boston: Twayne, 1990), 50.

12. RAM, founded in 1963 by Robert Williams (who subsequently fled to Tanzania after he was charged with kidnapping a white couple), was a Marxist-Leninist group whose members instigated various guerrilla warfare campaigns in large cities. See Robert H. Brisbane, *Black Activism: Racial Revolution in the United States 1954–1970* (Valley Forge, N.Y.: Judson Press, 1974), 180–81.

13. RNA was organized by former RAM members in 1968 in Detroit after the demise of RAM. With exiled Robert Williams as its president, the group first demanded that the U.S. government cede to it five southern states (South Carolina, Georgia, Alabama, Mississippi, and Louisiana) for the creation of an independent black nation. The strategy was for blacks to take control of these states via the ballot and then wage guerrilla warfare if the federal government objected. The group disbanded in 1971 when its members were charged with murder and treason by the state of Mississippi, which had become its headquarters in 1970. See Brisbane, *Black Activism*, 183–85.

14. The Black Panther Party for Self Defense was founded in Oakland, California, in 1966 by Huey P. Newton and Bobby Seale. Made up of political nationalists whose militaristic ideology paralleled the Marxist-Leninist creed of Mao Tse-tung, the Panthers fought against class oppression, enforced civil rights laws, and demanded constitutional guarantees.

15. Assata Shakur, also known as Joanne Chesimard, was born Joanne Deborah Byron on 16 July 1947 in Jamaica, New York. An avowed revolutionary and a member of the New York Black Panther party, she was considered armed and dangerous and was placed on the FBI's most-wanted list for bank robbery, kidnapping, murder, and attempting to overthrow the U.S. government. She was shot and captured on the New Jersey Turnpike on 2 May 1973 and became a pretrial detainee for several years in the basement of the men's jail in Middlesex, New Jersey, where she was given inadequate medical attention and was kept under 24-hour surveillance. During this time the prosecutions of many previous charges against her in New York were either dropped for insufficient evidence or resulted in her being acquitted. She was eventually convicted in New Jersey for killing a policeman because, even though she did not pull the trigger, she was present at the time of the shooting. See Assata Shakur, *Assata: An Autobiography* (Westport, Conn.: Lawrence Hill, 1987), vi–18.

16. Brisbane, *Black Activism* 179.

17. Washington, *Black-Eyed Susans, Midnight Birds*, 14.

• • • • •

"The Volcano of Hate Erupts" [from *The Long Shadow of Little Rock*]

Daisy Bates

Born in Huttig, Arkansas, in 1922, Daisy Bates was familiar with southern prejudice long before her dramatic entry into the civil rights movement. She became orphaned after three white men raped and killed her mother. Bates and her husband began in 1941 to publish a newspaper, the *State Press*, and in 1942 lost their advertising from local white businessmen when she protested the killing of a black soldier by a white policeman. By 1957 white segregationists had successfully conspired to shut the paper down.

Daisy Bates gained international attention in September 1957 when, as head of the Arkansas branch of the NAACP, she defied Gov. Orval Faubus's attempts to prevent the integration of all-white Central High School in Little Rock. For her desegregation efforts she endured bomb threats to her home and was hanged in effigy by white segregationists. The NAACP awarded Bates the Spingarn medal in 1958 for her pioneering role in the Little Rock incident. She recounts her painful, frightening ordeal in her moving autobiography, *The Long Shadow of Little Rock* (David McKay, 1962), coauthored with her husband, L. Christopher Bates.

The following excerpt from Bates's autobiography tells the story of the day and night of 23 September 1957, when she helped to escort nine black children to their classes at Central High. Although her efforts would eventually be supported by Pres. Dwight D. Eisenhower, who used the National Guard to enforce the integration of Central High, Bates, her coworkers, and the schoolchildren had only each other to turn to at the outset. Bates's simply told narrative powerfully conveys the close, ever-present threat of violence from white racists and the remarkable courage required to persist in spite of them.

On Monday morning, September 23, all nine children, accompanied by their parents, arrived at my home before eight o'clock. All but two parents had to leave for work immediately. The two who remained were Oscar Eckford, a night worker, and Mrs. Imogene Brown, an unemployed practical nurse.

Reporters came and went. They wanted to know whether the children were going to school. A few of the newspapermen called me aside, lowered their voices, and asked, "Mrs. Bates, are you really sending the children to Central? The mob there is really vicious now."

There were several radio outlets in our home and the children stationed themselves all over the house to listen. Radio commentators were broadcasting sidewalk interviews with men and women in the mob gathered in front of Central. A man was saying, "Just let those niggers show up! Just let 'em try!" Someone else said, "We won't stand for our schools being integrated. If we let 'em in, next thing they'll be marrying our daughters."

None of us said anything, but all of us were watching the hands of the clock move closer to eight thirty. The radios blared, but the children were strangely silent. Elizabeth sat alone, almost motionless. Carlotta and Ernest walked restlessly from room to room. The faces of all were solemn but determined.

Once when I entered the living-room I saw Mrs. Brown seated on the sofa, her hands clasped tightly in her lap, her eyes closed, her lips moving in prayer. Across the room Mr. Eckford sat with bowed head. For the first time I found that I was praying, too.

At last the call came from the police. They told us it would be safer to take a roundabout route to the school. They would meet us near Central and escort the children through a side entrance.

The white newsmen left my home for Central High. The Negro reporters remained, seating themselves around the kitchen table drinking coffee. They were: L. Alex Wilson, general manager and editor of the *Tri-State Defender,* of Memphis, Tennessee; James Hicks, managing editor of the *New York Amsterdam News;* Moses J. Newsome of the *Afro-American,* of Baltimore, Maryland; and Earl Davy, *State Press* photographer.

I told them they must take a different route from the one the children would take, but that if they were at the Sixteenth Street and Park Avenue entrance to Central, they would be able to see the nine enter the school.

We had two cars. I went in the first car with some of the children and C. C. Mercer. Frank Smith, field secretary of the NAACP, followed with the rest of the nine. To this day I cannot remember which of the nine were in our car. Nor can they.

As we approached the side entrance to the school, the main body of the mob was moving away from us. I got out of the car and told the children to go quickly. From the sidewalk I watched the police escort them through the door of the school. Someone in the mob saw them enter and yelled, "They're in! The niggers are in!"

The people on the fringes of the mob started moving toward us. A policeman rushed up to me. "Get back in the car, Mrs. Bates. Drive back the way you came, and fast!"

115

I tumbled into the car. Mr. Mercer was waiting at the wheel. The car radio was on and a hoarse-voiced announcer was saying: "The Negro children are being mobbed in front of the school." I knew the children were in the school and, for the moment, at least, safe. But who was being mobbed?

We sped back to the house to reassure Mrs. Brown and Mr. Eckford. Then I called the other parents at work to quiet their fears.

A series of false radio reports followed. Newscasters, broadcasting from the school grounds, reported that the children were being beaten and were running down the halls of the school, bloodstained; that the police were trying to get them out, but the nine children, hysterical with fright, had locked themselves in an empty classroom.

A young white lawyer, who was very close to Assistant Chief of Police Gene Smith, devised a plan by which he would keep me informed of the goings on inside the school. When I called him, he assured me that the reports were false. After each report I would check with him, then call the parents. Once Mr. Eckford screamed at me in exasperation, "Well, if it's not true why would they say such things on the air?"

"The children have barricaded themselves inside the school, the mob is breaking through the barricades, and the police are powerless to rescue the children," we heard one breathless newscaster announce. Again I called and demanded to know what was going on. I was told that the children were safe, but the police didn't know how much longer their forces could control the mob, which had now grown to over a thousand.

Later that day we learned that a white teen-age girl had been slipping in and out of the school, issuing false reports to the radio broadcasters. They had put her statements on the air without checking them. Gene Smith, Assistant Chief of Police, had finally caught up with her and ordered her arrested.

One could say it was the answer to Mrs. Brown's prayer that the Negro reporters arrived at Central about five minutes ahead of us. Jimmy Hicks of the *Amsterdam News* later told me just what did happen that morning.

"We parked our car near the school and made a dash for the Sixteenth Street entrance. When the mob saw us, they yelled, 'Here they come!' and came rushing at us. The women screamed, 'Get the niggers! Get 'em!' About a thousand folk blocked the streets. One big burly guy swung at my head. I ducked. The blow landed on my shoulder, spinning me around. I ran between two parked cars which concealed me from the mob. Two men jumped on top of Earl Davy, dragging him into a bank of high grass. Others were kicking and beating him while the two held him. They took his press camera and threw it to the sidewalk and smashed it flat with their feet. Several men jumped on Alex Wilson,

116

knocking him to the ground and kicking him in the stomach. As he was getting up, one of the mobsters hollered, 'Run, nigger!' Alex wouldn't run. The brute, with a brick in his hand, jumped on Alex's back, and raised the brick to crush Alex's skull.

"'The niggers are in the school! The niggers are in the school!'

"The man jumped off Alex's back, calling to the others, 'Come on! The niggers are in!' The mobsters beating Davy, Newsome, and Wilson all charged toward the school like a pack of wild animals.

"We probably saved you and the children, but I know you saved us. Some of the mob had spotted me between the cars and were advancing on me with sticks and clubs. And when they charged toward the school, we got the hell out of there. But you know, during all that beating, Alex never let go of his hat."

The frenzied mob rushed the police barricades. One man was heard to say, "So they sneaked them in behind our back. That's all we need. Let's go get our shotguns!" Hysterical women helped to break the barricades and then urged the men to go in and "get the niggers out!" Some of the women screamed for their children to "Come out! Don't stay in there with those niggers!" About fifty students rushed out, crying, "They're in! They're in!"

Around eleven thirty, Gene Smith realized his police force was inadequate to hold the mob. He ordered the nine removed from the school. They were taken out through a delivery entrance in the rear of the school, placed in police cars and driven to their homes. When it was announced that the children had been removed, the reporters rushed to my home and asked me what was our next step. Would the nine return to Horace Mann, the all-Negro school? I said No, they were going to remain out of the school until the President of the United States guaranteed them protection within Central High School. This was interpreted by the reporters as my having requested troops.

The mob, thwarted in its attempt to put its hands on the Negro children, switched momentarily to another field of battle. They went after the "Yankee" reporters.

The entire *Life* magazine staff on the scene was beaten. Photographers Francis Miller and Gray Villet were slugged in the mouth. Writer Paul Welch was beaten in the face and cut on the neck. All three men were arrested for inciting a riot. After their release Mr. Miller said, in bitter sarcasm, that he was evidently arrested for striking a man's fist with his face.

Most of the citizens of Little Rock were stunned as they witnessed a savage rebirth of passion and racial hatred that had lain dormant since Reconstruction days. As dusk was falling, tension and fear grew. The mob spread throughout the city, venting its fury on any Negro in sight.

Two Negro women driving through the city were pulled from their car and beaten. Two Negro men in a truck were surrounded by the mob near the school and beaten, and their truck windows smashed with rocks. Mayor Woodrow Mann wired President Eisenhower for protection. The Justice Department called Harry Ashmore, editor of the *Arkansas Gazette*, and asked him to describe the situation. He said, "I'll give it to you in one sentence. The police have been routed, the mob is in the streets and we're close to a reign of terror."

That evening I sat in the semidarkened living-room with L. C. and reporters, watching the empty quiet street through our broken living-room window. The police car that had been assigned to guard our house was barely visible across the street. A cab stopped in front of the house. All of us stood up. I heard a soft click. L. C. had released the safety on his .45 automatic. Dr. G. P. Freeman, our next-door neighbor and dentist, was aimlessly running his hand along the barrel of a shotgun he held in his left hand. When Alex Wilson of the Memphis *Tri-State Defender* stepped from the cab, I breathed a sigh of relief. As he entered the house Alex said, "I had planned to return earlier, but the story of the mob was a little difficult to write." He took L. C.'s gun, saying, "I'll watch for a while." He took a seat in front of the window. I watched him place his light gray hat on the table near him. I thought, "What a guy! He took the brunt of the mob today, yet here he is, holding a gun to help protect *us*."

The radio commentator reported that teen-age mobs had taken to cars and were driving wildly through the streets throwing bottles and bricks into Negroes' homes and places of business. One of the white reporters jumped out of his seat. "Ye gods!" he demanded. "Aren't they *ever* going to stop? Such hate! I heard a woman say today, 'I hope they drag out nine dead niggers from that school.'"

I left the room to call the parents of the pupils to see whether they had adequate protection. They reported that the city police were on the job. About 10:30 P.M., I returned to the living-room. Brice Miller, reporter for the United Press International, was talking to L. C. I saw his photographer in the shadows across the street.

"What's up, Brice?" I asked.

"Oh, nothing. Just checking."

"Oh, come now," I said. "We've all heard the rumor that the mob would ride tonight, and this will probably be their first stop. Isn't that the reason your photographer is across the street?"

"Well, yes," he admitted.

"Where did you hear the rumor?"

"One of the segregationist students told me. She was so pleased to have a reporter hanging on her words. I, of course, notified the police and the FBI."

L. C. broke into the conversation. "Something's up—things are too quiet." He asked Brice Miller about the radio reports.

"Oh, they're just a bunch of wild kids getting in on the act. They're not the real dangerous ones," he guessed.

"Say, Freeman," said L. C., "maybe we should stand guard outside for a while."

L. C. got a shotgun from the closet and, with Dr. Freeman, went outside. I went into the kitchen to make coffee. Brice Miller followed. "Since I'm here," he said, "maybe you can give me the reaction of the parents to today's mob."

Just then L. C. rushed back into the house. "Something's up! A car just passed driving slow with its lights off and a bunch of tough-looking characters in it. And the police car outside is following it."

Miller plunged past L. C., calling his photographer. "Come on! This might be it." Not only his photographer but all the reporters except Alex Wilson followed him.

"Do you have plenty of ammunition for these guns?" Alex asked.

"Yes," L. C. said.

"Well, we'll be ready for them if they show up."

Dr. Freeman stood guard at the bedroom window, Alex Wilson at the living-room, and L. C. at the kitchen window. L. C. told me to turn out the lights and go downstairs. I turned out the lights and sat on the top step of the stairway. We heard the wail of sirens approaching us. The minutes seemed like hours as I sat in the darkened stairway waiting for something to happen.

"The police are back," said L. C. He opened the door and turned on the lights.

"Turn that light off!" commanded the policeman as he entered. "And stay away from the window." The policeman, a big, red-haired man, was tense with excitement. "We just stopped a motorcade of about one hundred cars, two blocks from here. When we followed that car that passed, we ran into the mob head on. We radioed for help and a whole group of city and Federal agents showed up. We found dynamite, guns, pistols, clubs, everything, in the cars. Some of the mob got away on foot, leaving their cars. We don't know what will happen tonight, so no one is to leave the house."

No one slept that night.

At about 2:30 A.M. the phone rang. I answered. A man's voice said, "We didn't get you last night, but we will. And you better not try to put those coons in our school!"

Just before dawn I went to the kitchen to make a fresh pot of coffee. L. C. was sitting by the window, his shotgun cradled in his arm. Dawn was breaking. I watched the sky turn from dull gray to pale pink as the sun's rays flashed across the horizon. The aroma of the coffee aroused

Wilson and Freeman from their cramped sitting positions. They entered the kitchen looking tired and worn.

"And I thought I had it tough as a correspondent during the Second World War," said Alex.

"I'm going to stick to pulling teeth, myself," said Freeman.

• • • • •

From *Coming of Age in Mississippi*

Anne Moody

Anne Moody gained prominence as a writer with the publication of her award-winning autobiography, *Coming of Age in Mississippi* (1969). Winner of the Brotherhood Award from the National Council of Christians and Jews and of the best book of the year award from the National Library Association in 1969, Moody's autobiography vividly chronicles her participation in the civil rights struggles in her native Mississippi while she was a student at Tougaloo College. In addition to organizing and fund-raising for CORE, she worked as a civil rights project coordinator at Cornell University. Before her graduation in 1964, however, she left the movement disillusioned, concluding that "no matter how hard we in the Movement worked, nothing seemed to change; . . . we made a few visible little gains, yet at the root, things always remained the same." Divorced with one daughter, Moody has published a short-story collection, *Mr. Death: Four Stories* (1975), and has contributed articles to *Ms.* and *Mademoiselle*.

The excerpt reprinted here focuses on Moody's experiences in the days surrounding the assassination of NAACP leader Medgar Evers in the summer of 1963. Moody participated in a sit-in at the Woolworth's lunch counter, where local whites tore her off a stool, dragged her by her hair, and smeared her with mustard and ketchup; she joined a march and was hauled off by police with hundreds of other protesters to be held in the oppressively hot buildings used to house cattle during the auctions at the annual state fair. Her straightforward, detailed account leaves an indelible impression of the remarkable, persistent courage displayed by those who joined the cause for civil rights.

120

In mid-September I was back on campus. But didn't very much happen until February when the NAACP held its annual convention in Jackson. They were having a whole lot of interesting speakers: Jackie Robinson, Floyd Patterson, Curt Flood, Margaretta Belafonte, and many others. I wouldn't have missed it for anything. I was so excited that I sent one of the leaflets home to Mama and asked her to come.

Three days later I got a letter from Mama with dried-up tears on it, forbidding me to go to the convention. It went on for more than six pages. She said if I didn't stop that shit she would come to Tougaloo and kill me herself. She told me about the time I last visited her, on Thanksgiving, and she had picked me up at the bus station. She said she picked me up because she was scared some white in my hometown would try to do something to me. She said the sheriff had been by, telling her I was messing around with that NAACP group. She said he told her if I didn't stop it, I could not come back there any more. He said that they didn't need any of those NAACP people messing around in Centreville. She ended the letter by saying that she had burned the leaflet I sent her. "Please don't send any more of that stuff here. I don't want nothing to happen to us here," she said. "If you keep that up, you will never be able to come home again."

I was so damn mad after her letter, I felt like taking the NAACP convention to Centreville. I think I would have, if it had been in my power to do so. The remainder of the week I thought of nothing except going to the convention. I didn't know exactly what to do about it. I didn't want Mama or anyone at home to get hurt because of me.

I had felt something was wrong when I was home. During the four days I was there, Mama had tried to do everything she could to keep me in the house. When I said I was going to see some of my old class-mates, she pretended she was sick and said I would have to cook. I knew she was acting strangely, but I hadn't known why. I thought Mama just wanted me to spend most of my time with her, since this was only the second time I had been home since I entered college as a freshman.

Things kept running through my mind after that letter from Mama. My mind was so active, I couldn't sleep at night. I remembered the one time I did leave the house to go to the post office. I had walked past a bunch of white men on the street on my way through town and one said, "Is that the gal goin' to Tougaloo?" He acted kind of mad or something, and I didn't know what was going on. I got a creepy feeling, so I hurried home. When I told Mama about it, she just said, "A lotta people don't like that school." I knew what she meant. Just before I went to Tougaloo, they had housed the Freedom Riders there. The school was being criticized by whites throughout the state.

The night before the convention started, I made up my mind to go, no matter what Mama said. I just wouldn't tell Mama or anyone from home. Then it occurred to me—how did the sheriff or anyone at home know I was working with the NAACP chapter on campus? Somehow they had found out. Now I knew I could never go to Centreville safely again. I kept telling myself that I didn't really care too much about going home, that it was more important to me to go to the convention.

I was there from the very beginning. Jackie Robinson was asked to serve as moderator. This was the first time I had seen him in person. I remembered how when Jackie became the first Negro to play Major League baseball, my uncles and most of the Negro boys in my home-town started organizing baseball leagues. It did something for them to see a Negro out there playing with all those white players. Jackie was a good moderator, I thought. He kept smiling and joking. People felt re-laxed and proud. They appreciated knowing and meeting people of their own race who had done something worth talking about.

When Jackie introduced Floyd Patterson, heavyweight champion of the world, the people applauded for a long, long time. Floyd was kind of shy. He didn't say very much. He didn't have to, just his being there was enough to satisfy most of the Negroes who had only seen him on TV. Archie Moore was there too. He wasn't as smooth as Jackie, but he had his way with a crowd. He started telling how he was run out of Mississippi, and the people just cracked up.

I was enjoying the convention so much that I went back for the night session. Before the night was over, I had gotten autographs from every one of the Negro celebrities.

I had counted on graduating in the spring of 1963, but as it turned out, I couldn't because some of my credits still had to be cleared with Natchez College. A year before, this would have seemed like a terrible disaster, but now I hardly even felt disappointed. I had a good excuse to stay on campus for the summer and work with the Movement, and this was what I really wanted to do. I couldn't go home again anyway, and I couldn't go to New Orleans—I didn't have money enough for bus fare.

During my senior year at Tougaloo, my family hadn't sent me one penny. I had only the small amount of money I had earned at Maple Hill. I couldn't afford to eat at school or live in the dorms, so I had gotten permission to move off campus. I had to prove that I could finish school, even if I had to go hungry every day. I knew Raymond and Miss Pearl were just waiting to see me drop out. But something happened to me as I got more and more involved in the Movement. It no longer seemed important to prove anything. I had found something outside myself that gave meaning to my life.

I had become very friendly with my social science professor, John

Salter, who was in charge of NAACP activities on campus. All during the year, while the NAACP conducted a boycott of the downtown stores in Jackson, I had been one of Salter's most faithful canvassers and church speakers. During the last week of school, he told me that sit-in demonstrations were about to start in Jackson and that he wanted me to be the spokesman for a team that would sit-in at Woolworth's lunch counter. The two other demonstrators would be classmates of mine, Memphis and Pearlena. Pearlena was a dedicated NAACP worker, but Memphis had not been very involved in the Movement on campus. It seemed that the organization had had a rough time finding students who were in a position to go to jail. I had nothing to lose one way or the other. Around ten o'clock the morning of the demonstrations, NAACP headquarters alerted the news services. As a result, the police department was also informed, but neither the policemen nor the newsmen knew exactly where or when the demonstrations would start. They stationed themselves along Capitol Street and waited.

To divert attention from the sit-in at Woolworth's, the picketing started at J. C. Penney's a good fifteen minutes before. The pickets were allowed to walk up and down in front of the store three or four times before they were arrested. At exactly 11 A.M., Pearlena, Memphis, and I entered Woolworth's from the rear entrance. We separated as soon as we stepped into the store, and made small purchases from various counters. Pearlena had given Memphis her watch. He was to let us know when it was 11:14. At 11:14 we were to join him near the lunch counter and at exactly 11:15 we were to take seats at it.

Seconds before 11:15 we were occupying three seats at the previously segregated Woolworth's lunch counter. In the beginning the waitresses seemed to ignore us, as if they really didn't know what was going on. Our waitress walked past us a couple of times before she noticed we had started to write our own orders down and realized we wanted service. She asked us what we wanted. We began to read to her from our order slips. She told us that we would be served at the back counter, which was for Negroes.

"We would like to be served here," I said.

The waitress started to repeat what she had said, then stopped in the middle of the sentence. She turned the lights out behind the counter, and she and the other waitresses almost ran to the back of the store, deserting all their white customers. I guess they thought that violence would start immediately after the whites at the counter realized what was going on. There were five or six other people at the counter. A couple of them just got up and walked away. A girl sitting next to me finished her banana split before leaving. A middle-aged white woman who had not yet been served rose from her seat and came over to us. "I'd like to stay here with you," she said, "but my husband is waiting."

The newsmen came in just as she was leaving. They must have discovered what was going on shortly after some of the people began to leave the store. One of the newsmen ran behind the woman who spoke to us and asked her to identify herself. She refused to give her name, but said she was a native of Vicksburg and a former resident of California. When asked why she had said what she had said to us, she replied, "I am in sympathy with the Negro movement." By this time a crowd of cameramen and reporters had gathered around us taking pictures and asking questions, such as Where were we from? Why did we sit-in? What organization sponsored it? Were we students? From what school? How were we classified?

I told them that we were all students at Tougaloo College, that we were represented by no particular organization, and that we planned to stay there even after the store closed. "All we want is service," was my reply to one of them. After they had finished probing for about twenty minutes, they were almost ready to leave.

At noon, students from a nearby white high school started pouring in to Woolworth's. When they first saw us they were sort of surprised. They didn't know how to react. A few started to heckle and the newsmen became interested again. Then the white students started chanting all kinds of anti-Negro slogans. We were called a little bit of everything. The rest of the seats except the three we were occupying had been roped off to prevent others from sitting down. A couple of the boys took one end of the rope and made it into a hangman's noose. Several attempts were made to put it around our necks. The crowds grew as more students and adults came in for lunch.

We kept our eyes straight forward and did not look at the crowd except for occasional glances to see what was going on. All of a sudden I saw a face I remembered—the drunkard from the bus station sit-in. My eyes lingered on him just long enough for us to recognize each other. Today he was drunk too, so I don't think he remembered where he had seen me before. He took out a knife, opened it, put it in his pocket, and then began to pace the floor. At this point, I told Memphis and Pearlena what was going on. Memphis suggested that we pray. We bowed our heads, and all hell broke loose. A man rushed forward, threw Memphis from his seat, and slapped my face. Then another man who worked in the store threw me against an adjoining counter.

Down on my knees on the floor, I saw Memphis lying near the lunch counter with blood running out of the corners of his mouth. As he tried to protect his face, the man who'd thrown him down kept kicking him against the head. If he had worn hard-soled shoes instead of sneakers, the first kick probably would have killed Memphis. Finally a man dressed in plain clothes identified himself as a police officer and arrested Memphis and his attacker.

124

Pearlena had been thrown to the floor. She and I got back on our stools after Memphis was arrested. There were some white Tougaloo teachers in the crowd. They asked Pearlena and me if we wanted to leave. They said that things were getting too rough. We didn't know what to do. While we were trying to make up our minds, we were joined by Joan Trumpauer. Now there were three of us and we were integrated. The crowd began to chant, "Communists, Communists, Communists." Some old man in the crowd ordered the students to take us off the stools.

"Which one should I get first?" a big husky boy said.

"That white nigger," the old man said.

The boy lifted Joan from the counter by her waist and carried her out of the store. Simultaneously, I was snatched from my stool by two high school students. I was dragged about thirty feet toward the door by my hair when someone made them turn me loose. As I was getting up off the floor, I saw Joan coming back inside. We started back to the center of the counter to join Pearlena. Lois Chaffee, a white Tougaloo faculty member, was now sitting next to her. So Joan and I just climbed across the rope at the front end of the counter and sat down. There were now four of us, two whites and two Negroes, all women. The mob started smearing us with ketchup, mustard, sugar, pies, and everything on the counter. Soon Joan and I were joined by John Salter, but the moment he sat down he was hit on the jaw with what appeared to be brass knuckles. Blood gushed from his face and someone threw salt into the open wound. Ed King, Tougaloo's chaplain, rushed to him.

At the other end of the counter, Lois and Pearlena were joined by George Raymond, a CORE field worker and a student from Jackson State College. Then a Negro high school boy sat down next to me. The mob took spray paint from the counter and sprayed it on the new demonstrators. The high school student had on a white shirt; the word "nigger" was written on his back with red spray paint.

We sat there for three hours taking a beating when the manager decided to close the store because the mob had begun to go wild with stuff from other counters. He begged and begged everyone to leave. But even after fifteen minutes of begging, no one budged. They would not leave until we did. Then Dr. Beittel, the president of Tougaloo College, came running in. He said he had just heard what was happening.

About ninety policemen were standing outside the store; they had been watching the whole thing through the windows, but had not come in to stop the mob or do anything. President Beittel went outside and asked Captain Ray to come and escort us out. The captain refused, stating the manager had to invite him in before he could enter the premises, so Dr. Beittel himself brought us out. He had told the police that they had better protect us after we were outside the store. When we got outside, the policemen formed a single line that blocked the mob from us. However, they were allowed to throw at us everything they had collected. Within ten minutes, we were picked up by Reverend King in his station wagon and taken to the NAACP headquarters on Lynch Street.

After the sit-in, all I could think of was how sick Mississippi whites were. They believed so much in the segregated Southern way of life, they would kill to preserve it. I sat there in the NAACP office and thought of how many times they had killed when this way of life was threatened. I knew that the killing had just begun. "Many more will die before it is over with," I thought. Before the sit-in, I had always hated the whites in Mississippi. Now I knew it was impossible for me to hate sickness. The whites had a disease, an incurable disease in its final stage. What were our chances against such a disease? I thought of the students, the young Negroes who had just begun to protest, as young interns. When these young interns got older, I thought, they would be the best doctors in the world for social problems.

Before we were taken back to campus, I wanted to get my hair washed. It was stiff with dried mustard, ketchup and sugar. I stopped in at a beauty shop across the street from the NAACP office. I didn't have on any shoes because I had lost them when I was dragged across the floor at Woolworth's. My stockings were sticking to my legs from the mustard that had dried on them. The hairdresser took one look at me and said, "My land, you were in the sit-in, huh?"

"Yes," I answered, "Do you have time to wash my hair and style it?"

"Right away," she said, and she meant right away. There were three other ladies already waiting, but they seemed glad to let me go ahead of them. The hairdresser was real nice. She even took my stockings off and washed my legs while my hair was drying.

There was a mass rally that night at the Pearl Street Church in Jackson, and the place was packed. People were standing two abreast in the aisles. Before the speakers began, all the sit-inners walked out on the stage and were introduced by Medgar Evers. People stood and applauded for what seemed like thirty minutes or more. Medgar told the audience that this was just the beginning of such demonstrations. He asked them to pledge themselves to unite in a massive offensive against segregation in Jackson, and throughout the state. The rally ended with "We Shall Overcome" and sent home hundreds of determined people. It seemed as though Mississippi Negroes were about to get together at last.

Before I demonstrated, I had written Mama. She wrote me back a letter, begging me not to take part in the sit-in. She even sent ten dollars for bus fare to New Orleans. I didn't have one penny, so I kept the money. Mama's letter made me mad. I had to live my life as I saw fit. I had made that decision when I left home. But it hurt to have my family prove to me how scared they were. It hurt me more than anything else—I knew the whites had already started the threats and intimidations. I was the first Negro from my hometown who had openly demonstrated, worked with the NAACP, or anything. When Negroes threatened to do anything in Centreville, they were either shot like Samuel O'Quinn or run out of town, like Reverend Dupree.

I didn't answer Mama's letter. Even if I had written one, she wouldn't have received it before she saw the news on TV or heard it on the radio. I waited to hear from her again. And I waited to hear in the news that someone in Centreville had been murdered. If so, I knew it would be a member of my family.

On Wednesday, the day after the sit-in, demonstrations got off to a good start. Ten people picketed shortly after noon on Capitol Street, and were arrested. Another mass rally followed the demonstrations that night, where a six-man delegation of Negro ministers was chosen to meet Mayor Thompson the following Tuesday. They were to present to him a number of demands on behalf of Jackson Negroes. They were as follows:

1. Hiring of Negro policemen and school crossing guards
2. Removal of segregation signs from public facilities
3. Improvement of job opportunities for Negroes on city payrolls—Negro drivers of city garbage trucks, etc.
4. Encouraging public eating establishments to serve both whites and Negroes
5. Integration of public parks and libraries
6. The naming of a Negro to the City Parks and Recreation Committee
7. Integration of public schools
8. Forcing service stations to integrate rest rooms

After this meeting, Reverend Haughton, the minister of Pearl Street Church, said that the Mayor was going to act on all the suggestions. But the following day, Thompson denied that he had made any promises. He said the Negro delegation "got carried away" following their discussion with him.

"It seems as though Mayor Thompson wants to play games with us," Reverend Haughton said at the next rally. "He is calling us liars and trying to make us sound like fools. I guess we have to show him that we mean business."

When Reverend Charles A. Jones, dean and chaplain at Campbell College, asked at the close of the meeting, "Where do we go from here?" the audience shouted, "To the streets." They were going to prove to Mayor Thompson and the white people of Jackson that they meant business.

Around ten the next morning, an entire day of demonstrations started. A little bit of everything was tried. Some Negroes sat-in, some picketed, and some squatted in the streets and refused to move.

All of the five-and-ten stores (H. L. Green, Kress, and Woolworth) had closed their lunch counters as a result of the Woolworth sit-in. However, this did not stop the new sit-ins. Chain restaurants such as Primos Restaurant in downtown Jackson were now targets. Since police brutality was the last thing wanted in good, respectable Jackson, Mississippi, whenever arrested demonstrators refused to walk to a paddy wagon, garbage truck, or whatever was being used to take people to jail, Negro trusties from Jackson's city jail carted them away. Captain Ray and his men would just stand back with their hands folded, looking innocent as lambs for the benefit of the Northern reporters and photographers.

The Mayor still didn't seem to be impressed with the continuous small demonstrations and kept the streets hot. After eighty-eight demonstrators had been arrested, the Mayor held a news conference where he told a group of reporters, "We can handle 100,000 agitators." He also stated that the "good colored citizens are not rallying to the support of the outside agitators" (although there were only a few out-of-state people involved in the movement at the time) and offered to give Northern newsmen anything they wanted, including transportation, if they would "adequately" report the facts.

During the demonstrations, I helped conduct several workshops, where potential demonstrators, high school and college students mostly, were taught to protect themselves. If, for instance, you wanted to protect the neck to offset a karate blow, you clasped your hands behind the neck. To protect the genital organs you doubled up in a knot, drawing the knees up to the chest to protect your breasts if you were a girl.

The workshops were handled mostly by SNCC and CORE field secretaries and workers, almost all of whom were very young. The NAACP handled all the bail and legal services and public relations, but SNCC and CORE could draw teen-agers into the Movement as no other organization could. Whether they received credit for it or not, they helped make Jackson the center of attention throughout the nation.

During this period, civil rights workers who had become known to the Jackson police were often used to divert the cops' attention just before a demonstration. A few cops were always placed across the street from NAACP headquarters, since most of the demonstrations were organized there and would leave from that building. The "diverters" would get into cars and lead the cops off on a wild-goose chase. This would allow the real demonstrators to get downtown before they were noticed. One evening, a group of us took the cops for a tour of the park. After giving the demonstrators time enough to get to Capitol Street, we decided to go and watch the action. When we arrived there ourselves, we met Reverend King and a group of ministers. They told us they were going to stage a pray-in on the post office steps. "Come on, join us," Reverend King said. "I don't think we'll be arrested, because it's federal property."

By the time we got to the post office, the newsmen had already been informed, and a group of them were standing in front of the building blocking the front entrance. By now the group of whites that usually constituted the mob had gotten smart. They no longer looked for us, or for the demonstration. They just followed the newsmen and photographers. They were much smarter than the cops, who hadn't caught on yet.

We entered the post office through the side entrance and found that part of the mob was waiting inside the building. We didn't let this bother us. As soon as a few more ministers joined us, we were ready to go outside. There were fourteen of us, seven whites and seven Negroes. We walked out front and stood and bowed our heads as the ministers began to pray. We were immediately interrupted by the appearance of Captain Ray. "We are asking you people to disperse. If you don't, you are under arrest," he said.

Most of us were not prepared to go to jail. Doris Erskine, a student from Jackson State, and I had to take over a workshop the following day. Some of the ministers were in charge of the mass rally that night. But if we had dispersed, we would have been torn to bits by the mob. The whites standing out there had murder in their eyes. They were ready to do us in and all fourteen of us knew that. We had no other choice but to be arrested.

We had no plan of action. Reverend King and some of the ministers who were kneeling refused to move; they just kept on praying. Some of the others also attempted to kneel. The rest of us just walked to the paddy wagon. Captain Ray was using the Negro trusties. I felt so sorry for them. They were too small to be carrying all these heavy-ass demonstrators. I could tell just by looking at them that they didn't want to, either. I knew they were forced to do this.

After we got to jail we were mugged and fingerprinted, then taken to a cell. Most of the ministers were scared stiff. This was the first time some of them had seen the inside of a jail. Before we were mugged, we were all placed in a room together and allowed to make one call. Reverend King made the call to the NAACP headquarters to see if some of the ministers could be bailed out right away. I was so glad when they told him they didn't have money available at the moment. I just got my kicks out of sitting there looking at the ministers. Some of them looked so pitiful, I thought they would cry any minute, and here they were, supposed to be our leaders.

When Doris and I got to the cell where we would spend the next four days, we found a lot of our friends there. There were twelve girls altogether. The jail was segregated. I felt sorry for Jeanette King, Lois Chaffee, and Joan Trumpauer. Just because they were white they were missing out on all the fun we planned to have. Here we were going to school together, sleeping in the same dorm, worshipping together, playing together, even demonstrating together. It all ended in jail. They were rushed off by themselves to some cell designated for whites.

Our cell didn't even have a curtain over the shower. Every time the cops heard the water running, they came running to peep. After the first time, we fixed them. We took chewing gum and toilet tissue and covered the opening in the door. They were afraid to take it down. I guess they thought it might have come out in the newspaper. Their wives wouldn't have liked that at all. Peep through a hole to see a bunch of nigger girls naked? No! No! They certainly wouldn't have liked that. All of the girls in my cell were college students. We had a lot to talk about, so we didn't get too bored. We made cards out of toilet tissue and played Gin Rummy almost all day. Some of us even learned new dance steps from each other.

There were a couple of girls in with us from Jackson State College. They were scared they would be expelled from school. Jackson State, like most of the state-supported Negro schools, was an Uncle Tom school. The students could be expelled for almost anything. When I found this out, I really appreciated Tougaloo.

The day we were arrested one of the Negro trusties sneaked us a newspaper. We discovered that over four hundred high school students had also been arrested. We were so glad we sang freedom songs for an hour or so. The jailer threatened to put us in solitary if we didn't stop. At first we didn't think he meant it, so we kept singing. He came back with two other cops and asked us to follow them. They marched us down the hall and showed us one of the solitary chambers. ''If you don't stop that damn singing, I'm gonna throw all of you in here together,'' said the jailer. After that we didn't sing any more. We went back and finished reading the paper.

We got out of jail on Sunday to discover that everyone was talking about the high school students. All four hundred who were arrested had been taken to the fairgrounds and placed in a large open compound without beds or anything. It was said that they were getting sick like flies. Mothers were begging to have their children released, but the NAACP didn't have enough money to bail them all out.

The same day we went to jail for the pray-in, the students at Lanier High School had started singing freedom songs on their lunch hour. They got so carried away they ignored the bell when the break was over and just kept on singing. The principal of the high school did not know what to do, so he called the police and told them that the students were about to start a riot.

When the cops came, they brought the dogs. The students refused to go back to their classrooms when asked, so the cops turned the dogs loose on them. The students fought them off for a while. In fact, I was told that mothers who lived near the school had joined the students in fighting off the dogs. They had begun to throw bricks, rocks, and bottles. The next day the papers stated that ten or more cops suffered cuts or minor wounds. The papers didn't say it, but a lot of students were hurt, too, from dog bites and lumps on the head from billy clubs. Finally, one hundred and fifty cops were rushed to the scene and several students and adults were arrested.

The next day four hundred of the high school students from Lanier, Jim Hill, and Brinkley High schools gathered in a church on Farish Street, ready to go to jail. Willie Ludden, the NAACP youth leader, and some of the SNCC and CORE workers met with them, gave a brief workshop on nonviolent protective measures and led them into the streets. After marching about two blocks they were met by helmeted police officers and ordered to disperse. When they refused, they were arrested, herded into paddy wagons, canvas-covered trucks, and garbage trucks. Those moving too slowly were jabbed with rifle butts. Police dogs were there, but were not used. From the way everyone was describing the scene it sounded like Nazi Germany instead of Jackson, USA.

On Monday, I joined a group of high school students and several other college students who were trying to get arrested. Our intention was to be put in the fairgrounds with the high school students already there. The cops picked us up, but they didn't want to put us so-called professional agitators in with the high school students. We were weeded out, and taken back to the city jail.

I got out of jail two days later and found I had gotten another letter from Mama. She had written it Wednesday the twenty-ninth, after the Woolworth sit-in. The reason it had taken so long for me to get it was that it came by way of New Orleans. Mama sent it to Adline and had Adline mail it to me. In the letter she told me that the sheriff had stopped by and asked all kinds of questions about me the morning after the sit-in. She said she and Raymond told them that I had only been home once since I was in college, that I had practically cut off all my family connections when I ran away from home as a senior in high school. She said he said that that he knew I had left home. "He should know," I thought, "because I had to get him to move my clothes for me when I left." She went on and on. She told me he said I must never come back there. If so he would not be responsible for what happened to me. "The whites are pretty upset about her doing these things," he told her. Mama told me not to write her again until she sent me word that it was O.K. She said that I would hear from her through Adline.

I also got a letter from Adline in the same envelope. She told me what Mama hadn't mentioned—that Junior had been cornered by a group of white boys and was about to be lynched, when one of his friends came along in a car and rescued him. Besides that, a group of white men had gone out and beaten up my old Uncle Buck. Adline said Mama told her they couldn't sleep, for fear of night riders. They were all scared to death. My sister ended the letter by cursing me out. She said I was trying to get every Negro in Centreville murdered.

I guess Mama didn't tell me these things because she was scared to. She probably thought I would have tried to do something crazy. Something like trying to get the organizations to move into Wilkinson County, or maybe coming home myself to see if they would kill me. She never did give me credit for having the least bit of sense. I knew there was nothing I could do. No organization was about to go to Wilkinson County. It was a little too tough for any of them. And I wasn't about to go there either. If they said they would kill me, I figured I'd better take their word for it.

Meantime, within four or five days Jackson became the hotbed of racial demonstrations in the South. It seemed as though most of the Negro college and high school students there were making preparations to participate. Those who did not go to jail were considered cowards by those who did. At this point, Mayor Allen Thompson finally made a decisive move. He announced that Jackson had made plans to house over 12,500 demonstrators at the local jails and at the state fairgrounds. And if this was not enough, he said, Parchman, the state penitentiary, 160 miles away, would be used. Governor Ross Barnett had held a news conference offering Parchman facilities to Jackson.

An injunction prohibiting demonstrations was issued by a local judge, naming NAACP, CORE, Tougaloo College, and various leaders. According to this injunction, the intent of the named organizations and individuals was to paralyze the economic nerve center of the city of Jackson. It used as proof the leaflets that had been distributed by the NAACP urging Negroes not to shop on Capitol Street. The next day the injunction was answered with another mass march.

The cops started arresting every Negro on the scene of a demonstration, whether or not he was participating. People were being carted off to jail every day of the week. On Saturday, Roy Wilkins, the National Director of NAACP, and Medgar Evers were arrested as they picketed in front of Woolworth's. Theldon Henderson, a Negro lawyer who worked for the Justice Department, and had been sent down from Washington to investigate a complaint by the NAACP about the fairgrounds facilities, was also arrested. It was said that when he showed his Justice Department credentials, the arresting officer started trembling. They let him go immediately.

Mass rallies had come to be an every night event, and at each one the NAACP had begun to build up Medgar Evers. Somehow I had the feeling that they wanted him to become for Mississippi what Martin Luther King had been in Alabama. They were well on the way to achieving that, too.

After the rally on Tuesday, June 11, I had to stay in Jackson. I had missed the ride back to campus. Dave Dennis, the CORE field secretary for Mississippi, and his wife put me up for the night. We were watching TV around twelve-thirty, when a special news bulletin interrupted the program. It said, "Jackson NAACP leader Medgar Evers has just been shot."

We didn't believe what we were hearing. We just sat there staring at the TV screen. It was unbelievable. Just an hour or so earlier we were all with him. The next bulletin announced that he had died in the hospital soon after the shooting. We didn't know what to say or do. All night we tried to figure out what had happened, who did it, who was next, and it still didn't seem real.

First thing the next morning we turned on the TV. It showed films taken shortly after Medgar was shot in his driveway. We saw the pool of blood where he had fallen. We saw his wife sobbing almost hysterically as she tried to tell what had happened. Without even having breakfast, we headed for the NAACP headquarters. When we got there, they were trying to organize a march to protest Medgar's death. Newsmen, investigators, and reporters flooded the office. College and high school students and a few adults sat in the auditorium waiting to march.

Dorie Ladner, a SNCC worker, and I decided to run up to Jackson State College and get some of the students there to participate in the march. I was sure we could convince some of them to protest Medgar's death. Since the march was to start shortly after lunch, we had a couple of hours to do some recruiting. When we got to Jackson State, class was in session. "That's a damn shame," I thought. "They should have dismissed school today, in honor of Medgar."

Dorie and I started going down each hall, taking opposite classrooms. We begged students to participate. They didn't respond in any way.

"It's a shame, it really is a shame. This morning Medgar Evers was murdered and here you sit in a damn classroom with books in front of your faces, pretending you don't even know he's been killed. Every

Negro in Jackson should be in the streets raising hell and protesting his death," I said in one class. I felt sick, I got so mad with them. How could Negroes be so pitiful? How could they just sit by and take all this shit without any emotions at all? I just didn't understand.

"It's hopeless, Moody, let's go," Dorie said.

As we were leaving the building, we began soliciting aloud in the hall. We walked right past the president's office, shouting even louder. President Reddix came rushing out, "You girls leave this campus immediately," he said, "You can't come on this campus and announce anything without my consent."

Dorie had been a student at Jackson State. Mr. Reddix looked at her. "You know better than this, Dorie," he said.

"But President Reddix, Medgar was just murdered. Don't you have any feelings about his death at all?" Dorie said.

"I am doing a job. I can't do this job and have feelings about everything happening in Jackson," he said. He was waving his arms and pointing his finger in our faces. "Now you two get off this campus before I have you arrested."

By this time a group of students had gathered in the hall. Dorie had fallen to her knees in disgust as Reddix was pointing at her, and some of the students thought he had hit her. I didn't say anything to him. If I had I would have been calling him every kind of fucking Tom I could think of. I helped Dorie off the floor. I told her we'd better hurry, or we would miss the demonstration.

On our way back to the auditorium we picked up the Jackson *Daily News*. Headlines read JACKSON INTEGRATION LEADER EVERS SLAIN.

> Negro NAACP leader Medgar Evers was shot to death when he stepped from his automobile here early today as he returned home from an integration strategy meeting.
>
> Police said Evers, 37, was cut down by a high-powered bullet in the back of the driveway of his home.

I stopped reading. Medgar was usually followed home every night by two or three cops. Why didn't they follow him last night? Something was wrong. "They must have known," I thought. "Why didn't they follow him last night?" I kept asking myself. I had to get out of all this confusion. The only way I could do it was to go to jail. Jail was the only place I could think in.

When we got back to the auditorium, we were told that those who would take part in the first march had met at Pearl Street Church. Dorie and I walked over there. We noticed a couple of girls from Jackson State. They asked Dorie if President Reddix had hit her, and said it had gotten out on campus that he had. They told us a lot of students had planned to demonstrate because of what Reddix had done. "Good enough," Dorie said, "Reddix better watch himself, or we'll turn that school out."

I was called to the front of the church to help lead the marchers in a few freedom songs. We sang "Woke Up This Morning With My Mind on Freedom" and "Ain't Gonna Let Nobody Turn Me 'Round." After singing the last song we headed for the streets in a double line, carrying small American flags in our hands. The cops had heard that there were going to be Negroes in the streets all day protesting Medgar's death. They were ready for us.

On Rose Street we ran into a blockade of about two hundred policemen. We were called to a halt by Captain Ray, and asked to disperse. "Everybody ain't got a permit get out of this here parade," Captain Ray said into his bull horn. No one moved. He beckoned to the cops to advance on us.

The cops had rifles and wore steel helmets. They walked right up to us very fast and then sort of engulfed us. They started snatching the small American flags, throwing them to the ground, stepping on them, or stamping them. Students who refused to let go of the flags were jabbed with rifle butts. There was only one paddy wagon on the scene. The first twenty of us were thrown into it, although a paddy wagon is only large enough to seat about ten people. We were sitting and lying all over each other inside the wagon when garbage trucks arrived. We saw the cops stuff about fifty demonstrators in one truck as we looked out through the back glass. Then the driver of the paddy wagon sped away as fast as he could, often making sudden stops in the middle of the street so we would be thrown around.

We thought that they were going to take us to the city jail again because we were college students. We discovered we were headed for the fairgrounds. When we got there, the driver rolled up the windows, turned the heater on, got out, closed the door and left us. It was over a hundred degrees outside that day. There was no air coming in. Sweat began dripping off us. An hour went by. Our clothes were now soaked and sticking to us. Some of the girls looked as though they were about to faint. A policeman looked in to see how we were taking it. Some of the boys begged him to let us out. He only smiled and walked away.

Looking out of the back window again, we noticed they were now booking all the other demonstrators. We realized they had planned to do this to our group. A number of us in the paddy wagon were known to the cops. After the Woolworth sit-in, I had been known to every white in Jackson. I can remember walking down the street and being pointed out by whites as they drove or walked past me.

Suddenly one of the girls screamed. Scrambling to the window, we saw John Salter with blood gushing out of a large hole in the back of his head. He was just standing there dazed and no one was helping him. And we were in no position to help either.

After they left everyone else out of the garbage trucks, they decided to let us out of the paddy wagon. We had now been in there well over two hours. As we were getting out, one of the girls almost fell. A guy started to help her.

"Get ya hands off that gal. Whatta ya think, ya goin' to a prom or somethin'?" one of the cops said.

Water was running down my legs. My skin was soft and spongy. I had hidden a small transistor radio in my bra and some of the other girls had cards and other things in theirs. We had learned to sneak them in after we discovered they didn't search the women but now everything was showing through our wet clothes.

When we got into the compound, there were still some high school students there, since the NAACP bail money had been exhausted. There were altogether well over a hundred and fifty in the girls' section. The boys had been put into a compound directly opposite and parallel to us. Some of the girls who has been arrested after us shared their clothes with us until ours dried. They told us what had happened after we were taken off in the paddy wagon. They said the cops had stuffed so many into the garbage trucks that some were just hanging on. As one of the trucks pulled off, thirteen-year-old John Young fell out. When the driver stopped, the truck rolled back over the boy. He was rushed off to a hospital and they didn't know how badly he had been hurt. They said the cops had gone wild with their billy sticks. They had even arrested Negroes looking on from their porches. John Salter had been forced off some Negro's porch and hit on the head.

The fairgrounds were everything I had heard they were. The compounds they put us in were two large buildings used to auction off cattle during the annual state fair. They were about a block long, with large openings about twenty feet wide on both ends where the cattle were driven in. The openings had been closed up with wire. It reminded me of a concentration camp. It was hot and sticky and girls were walking around half dressed all the time. We were guarded by four policemen. They had rifles and kept an eye on us through the wired sides of the building. As I looked through the wire at them, I imagined myself in Nazi Germany, the policemen Nazi soldiers. They couldn't have been any rougher than these cops. Yet this was America, "the land of the free and the home of the brave."

About five-thirty we were told that dinner was ready. We were lined up single file and marched out of the compound. They had the cook from the city jail there. He was standing over a large garbage can stirring something in it with a stick. The sight of it nauseated me. No one was eating, girls or boys. In the next few days, many were taken from the fairgrounds sick from hunger.

When I got out of jail on Saturday, the day before Medgar's funeral, I had lost about fifteen pounds. They had prepared a special meal on campus for the Tougaloo students, but attempts to eat made me sicker. The food kept coming up. The next morning I pulled myself together enough to make the funeral services at the Masonic Temple. I was glad I had gone in spite of my illness. This was the first time I had ever seen so many Negroes together. There were thousands and thousands of them there. Maybe Medgar's death had really brought them to the Movement, I thought. Maybe his death would strengthen the ties between Negroes and Negro organizations. If this resulted, then truly his death was not in vain.

Just before the funeral services were over, I went outside. There was a hill opposite the Masonic Temple. I went up there to watch the procession. I wanted to see every moment of it.

As the pallbearers brought the body out and placed it in a hearse, the tension in the city was as tight as a violin string. There were two or three thousand outside that could not get inside the temple, and as they watched, their expression was that of anger, bitterness, and dismay. They looked as though any moment they were going to start rioting. When Mrs. Evers and her two older children got into their black limousine, Negro women in the crowd began to cry and say things like "That's a shame,". . . "That's a young woman,". . . "Such well-looking children,". . . "It's a shame, it really is a shame."

Negroes formed a seemingly endless line as they began the march to the funeral home. They got angrier and angrier; however, they went on quietly until they reached the downtown section where the boycott was. They tried to break through the barricades on Capitol Street, but the cops forced them back into line. When they reached the funeral home, the body was taken inside, and most of the procession dispersed. But one hard core of angry Negroes decided they didn't want to go home. With some encouragement from SNCC workers who were singing freedom songs outside the funeral home, these people began walking back toward Capitol Street.

Policemen had been placed along the route of the march, and they were still there. They allowed the crowd of Negroes to march seven blocks, but they formed a solid blockade just short of Capitol Street. This was where they made everyone stop. They had everything—shotguns, fire trucks, gas masks, dogs, fire hoses, and billy clubs. Along the sidewalks and on the fringes of the crowd, the cops knocked heads, set dogs on some marchers, and made about thirty arrests, but the main body of people in the middle of the street was just stopped.

They sang and shouted things like "Shoot, shoot" to the police, and then the police started to push them back slowly. After being pushed back about a block, they stopped. They wouldn't go any farther. So the cops brought the fire trucks up closer and got ready to use the fire hoses on the crowd. That really broke up the demonstration. People moved back faster and started to go home. But it also made them angrier. Bystanders began throwing stones and bottles at the cops and then the crowd started too; other Negroes were pitching stuff from second- and third-story windows. The crowd drew back another block, leaving the space between them and the fire trucks littered with rocks and broken glass. John Doar came out from behind the police barricade and walked toward the crowd of Negroes, with bottles flying all around him. He talked to some of the people at the front, telling them he was from the Justice Department and that this wasn't "the way." After he talked for a few minutes, things calmed down considerably, and Dave Dennis and a few others began taking bottles away from people and telling them they should go home. After that it was just a clean-up operation. One of the ministers borrowed Captain Ray's bull horn and ran up and down the street telling people to disperse, but by that time there were just a few stragglers.

After Medgar's death there was a period of confusion. Each Negro leader and organization in Jackson received threats. They were all told they were "next on the list." Things began to fall apart. The ministers, in particular, didn't want to be "next"; a number of them took that long-promised vacation to Africa or elsewhere. Meanwhile SNCC and CORE became more militant and began to press for more demonstrations. A lot of the young Negroes wanted to let the whites of Jackson know that even by killing off Medgar they hadn't touched the real core of the Movement. For the NAACP and the older, more conservative groups, however, voter registration had now become number one on the agenda. After the NAACP exerted its influence at a number of strategy meetings, the militants lost.

The Jackson *Daily News* seized the opportunity to cause more fragmentation. One day they ran a headline THERE IS A SPLIT IN THE ORGANIZATIONS, and sure enough, shortly afterward, certain organizations had completely severed their relations with each other. The whites had succeeded again. They had reached us through the papers by letting us know we were not together. "Too bad," I thought. "One day we'll learn. It's pretty tough, though, when you have everything against you, including the money, the newspapers, and the cops."

Within a week everything had changed. Even the rallies were not the same. The few ministers and leaders who did come were so scared— they thought assassins were going to follow them home. Soon there were rallies only twice a week instead of every night.

The Sunday following Medgar's funeral, Reverend Ed King organized an integrated church-visiting team of six of us from the college. Another team was organized by a group in Jackson. Five or six churches were hit that day, including Governor Ross Barnett's. At each one they had prepared for our visit with armed policemen, paddy wagons, and dogs—which would be used in case we refused to leave after "ushers" had read us the prepared resolutions. There were about eight of these ushers at each church, and they were never exactly the usherly type. They were more on the order of Al Capone. I think this must have been the first time any of these men had worn a flower in his lapel. When we were asked to leave, we did. We were never even allowed to get past the first step.

A group of us decided that we would go to church again the next Sunday. This time we were quite successful. These visits had not been publicized as the first ones were, and they were not really expecting us. We went first to a Church of Christ, where we were greeted by the regular ushers. After reading us the same resolution we had heard last week, they offered to give us cab fare to the Negro extension of the church. Just as we had refused and were walking away, an old lady stopped us. "We'll sit with you," she said.

We walked back to the ushers with her and her family. "Please let them in, Mr. Calloway. We'll sit with them," the old lady said.

"Mrs. Dixon, the church has decided what is to be done. A resolution has been passed, and we are to abide by it."

"Who are we to decide such a thing? This is a house of God, and God is to make all of the decisions. He is the judge of us all," the lady said.

The ushers got angrier then and threatened to call the police if we didn't leave. We decided to go.

"We appreciate very much what you've done," I said to the old lady.

As we walked away from the church, we noticed the family leaving by a side entrance. The old lady was waving to us.

Two blocks from the church, we were picked up by Ed King's wife, Jeanette. She drove us to an Episcopal church. She had previously left the other two girls from our team there. She circled the block a couple of times, but we didn't see them anywhere. I suggested that we try the church. "Maybe they got in," I said. Mrs. King waited in the car for us. We walked up to the front of the church. There were no ushers to be seen. Apparently, services had already started. When we walked inside, we were greeted by two ushers who stood at the rear.

"May we help you?" one said.

"Yes," I said. "We would like to worship with you today."

"Will you sign the guest list, please, and we will show you to your seats," said the other.

I stood there for a good five minutes before I was able to compose myself. I had never prayed with white people in a white church before. We signed the guest list and were then escorted to two seats behind the

139

other two girls in our team. We had all gotten in. The church service was completed without one incident. It was as normal as any church service. However, it was by no means normal to me. I was sitting there thinking any moment God would strike the life out of me. I recognized some of the whites, sitting around me in that church. If they were praying to the same God I was, then even God, I thought, was against me.

When the services were over the minister invited us to visit again. He said it as if he meant it, and I began to have a little hope.

• • • • •

From *Angela Davis: An Autobiography*

Angela Davis

Angela Yvonne Davis was born in 1944 in Birmingham, Alabama, to schoolteachers, B. Frank and Sally E. Davis. She attended the Sorbonne in Paris, graduated magna cum laude from Brandeis University in 1965, received her master's degree from the University of California at San Diego in 1968, and was awarded an honorary doctorate from Lenin University in Germany. In 1968 she became an acting assistant professor of philosophy at the University of California at Los Angeles but was dismissed when the Board of Regents discovered that she was a member of the Communist party. When the university did not renew Davis's contract in 1970, it was censured by the American Association of University Professors. In 1970 Angela Davis was placed on the FBI's most-wanted list for murder, kidnapping, and interstate flight. She was accused of planning the alleged kidnapping of three black San Quentin prisoners from the Marin County Hall of Justice in San Rafael, California, and of supplying the gun that killed four people, including a judge. After her capture in New York City, Davis spent 16 months in jail; in 1972 she was tried and acquitted of all charges. Well known on the lecture circuit, Davis also has written several books in addition to her autobiography—*If They Come in the Morning: Voices of Resistance* (1971), edited with Ruchell Magee, and others, *Women, Race, and Class* (1983), and *Women, Culture, and Politics* (1989).

Racism was very much a part of Angela Davis's background, even though she was born into a middle-class family. As a child she lived on "Dynamite Hill," where white night riders bombed the homes of black civil rights advocates, and she knew the four black girls killed in Sunday school when the Ku Klux Klan bombed a black Birmingham church in September 1963. "My political involvement," Davis said, "stems from my existence in the South."[1] Politically involved with the Communist party and various black grass-roots organizations, such as the Black Panther party, Davis was genuinely concerned about the oppression of the poor. She worked with various groups to raise their consciousness about their oppression and to indicate how they could rise above it.

In the following excerpt from *Angela Davis: An Autobiography* (Random House, 1974), Davis focuses on her experiences in Los Angeles in 1969 working with grass-roots black activist organizations to rid the black community of white racism. With the Black Student Alliance,[2] the Che-Lumumba Club,[3] and the Black Panther party (BPP), she planned a massive peace rally to protest an unwarranted police raid on the Los Angeles headquarters of the Black Panthers. As a champion of the Black Panthers, she distributed leaflets and recorded radio announcements about the rally. Two days before the rally, while keeping watch outside the Panther headquarters, she and others were dispersed and attacked at random by police officers. Davis's account of her involvement in the black liberation struggle vividly reflects the dangers she faced as a black woman committed to overcoming the oppression of black people.

NOTES

1. "The Angela Davis Case," *Newsweek*, 26 October 1970, 20.
2. The Black Student Alliance was a leftist student group established in 1967 at San Diego State College.
3. The Che-Lumumba Club was formed in 1967 in Los Angeles as the black cell of the Communist party; its primary responsibility was to convey Marxist-Leninist ideas to the black liberation struggle.

. . . In order to organize the resistance, a coalition was established between the Black Panther Party, the Black Student Alliance and our Che-Lumumba Club. On the basis of this coalition of the Black Left, we felt we could call for a broad united resistance emanating from all sectors of the Black community.

That night we sponsored a meeting, attended by delegates from

Black organizations throughout the city. This body approved a call for a general strike two days later in the Black community. On that day, we would hold a massive protest rally on the steps of City Hall. We had about thirty-six hours to put the rally together. It was no time at all, but the quicker the community reacted in an organized way, the more effective our protest would be.

That very night, thousands of leaflets were printed. The next morning, teams saturated the community with literature about the attack and the need to resist. The local Black radio station and an underground FM station gave us free time to issue the strike call and to publicize the rally. Others announced the rally as a part of the news.

I personally recorded spot announcements and held press conferences, since my name was known in the community. Yet I also felt the need to involve myself on a grass-roots level. I needed to acquire a sense of the mood of the community—and that could not be done from behind a microphone.

A team was on its way to Jordon Down Projects in Watts to distribute leaflets. I decided to go along. In all my experience of door-to-door community work, never had I seen such unanimous acceptance of our appeal. Literally no one was abrupt, no one tried to shut us out, and all agreed that we had to resist the attack on the Panthers. Many of the people recognized me, and I was surprised that they also volunteered their support for me in the fight for my job. Virtually every person with whom I spoke made a firm promise to observe the general strike and to attend the rally the next morning.

There were problems back at the Panther office. The woman who lived in the house behind the office had reported that early in the morning the police had returned and shot tear-gas cartridges into the office. The fumes were stronger now than shortly after the attack had halted. It was impossible to remain inside for any length of time without becoming sick.

It was decided, as a result, to hold a vigil in front of the office at all times. Participants in the vigil would form themselves into shifts in order to clean out all the debris. When the sun went down, there were still more than a hundred people taking part in the vigil. The tear-gas fumes had not abated and most of the group was clustered at the end of the block so no one would be overcome by the gas. The plans were to keep the vigil going throughout the night. Franklin led the group in freedom songs.

While the singers were warming up, I noticed some strange movements in the area: police cars creeping by—unmarked, but unmistakably police cars with agents peering out at us. I assumed that this was the normal surveillance. It seemed unlikely that they would try anything on a group which included not only the usual young movement people, but ministers, professors, politicians as well.

The singing broke into full blast. Perhaps the police felt affronted by the words of "Freedom Is a Constant Struggle" and "I Woke up This Morning with My Mind Staid on Freedom" because they abruptly interrupted with a voice projected through a loudspeaker. "The Los Angeles Police Department [LAPD] has declared this an illegal assembly. If you do not move out, you will be subject to arrest. You have exactly three minutes to disperse."

Even if we had tried, we could not have dispersed in three minutes. We decided immediately not to disperse, but rather to form ourselves into a moving picket line. As long as we kept moving, we would not be an "assembly" and would theoretically have the right to remain. Senator Mervyn Dymally, a Black state senator, decided that he was going to speak to the policeman in charge, thinking he could calm them down.

The line stretched from the corner where the group had been singing, well past the office, which was near the next corner.

I moved toward the end nearest the Panther office. It was dark and difficult to determine exactly what was happening at the other corner. Suddenly there was a dash of the crowd. Thinking that this had been precipitated by nothing more serious than a show of force at the other end, I turned to calm everybody and tell them not to run. But at that moment, I saw a swarm of the black-suited cops who had executed the attack on the office the day before. They were already beating people further down, and some of them were about to converge on us.

I had been facing the crowd. I turned quickly, but before I could break into a run, I was knocked to the ground. I hit my head on the pavement and was momentarily stunned. During those seconds of semiconsciousness, I felt feet trampling on my head and body and it flashed through my mind that this was a terrible way to die.

A brother screamed, "Hey, that's Angela down there." Immediately, hands were pulling me up. I could see the billy clubs smashing into these brothers' heads. Someone told me later that as soon as the police realized who I was, they had come after me with their sticks.

Once on my feet, I ran as fast as I could.

This was insane. Clearly, the police had no intention of arresting us. They only wanted to beat us. Even Senator Dymally hadn't been immune. After his futile conversation with the chief of police, I learned later, he had been the first to be hit.

We raced through the neighborhood, across lawns, through alleys, wherever it seemed we could find temporary refuge. As I ran across a front yard with some sisters and brothers I didn't even know, I heard a voice coming from the dark porch, telling us to come in. We ran into

143

the house, lay down on the floor and tried to catch our breath. It was a middle-aged Black woman who had opened her doors to us. When I tried to thank her, she said that after what had happened the day before, this was the very least she could do.

We were on a side street, off Central Avenue. I looked through the draperies in the front room and could see nothing except a police car cruising by. Then I noticed some of our people on a porch across the street and decided I would try to get over to that house.

In all the excitement, I hadn't noticed how badly I had been bruised by the fall. Blood was streaming down my leg and my knee was throbbing with pain. But there was no time to think about that now. I thanked the woman, said good-bye and ran toward the house across the street as fast as I could.

The family who lived there had allowed a comrade from our Party to organize a first-aid station in the house. People with blood all over their faces were already waiting to be tended, and a squad had gone out searching for others who were wounded. Apparently, people throughout the neighborhood had opened their doors. Their spontaneous show of solidarity had saved us from a real massacre.

I was worried about Kendra, Franklin, Tamu, Taboo and the rest of my Che-Lumumba comrades whom I had not yet seen. The Panther leaders not under arrest as a result of the original assault were also missing, as were key members of the Black Student Alliance. A brother from the BSA said he would accompany me around the neighborhood in order to determine what had happened to our friends. People were crowded in the storefronts along Central Avenue. By hiding in the shadows along the way, we were able to reach one of the storefronts without incident. The people we were worried about were among the crowds in the storefronts. One person had been arrested.

On Central Avenue, a squadron of cops in black jumpsuits was marching in formation. When they saw one of our people in the street, several of them would jump out of line, swing at the person with their billy clubs and then calmly fall back into the march. It appeared they were determined to hold us prisoner indefinitely in these houses and storefronts.

Later, we learned that the police in the black jumpsuits were members of the Los Angeles Police Department's counterinsurgency force— the Special Weapons and Tactical Squad. Subsequent research determined that the SWAT Squad was composed primarily of Vietnam veterans. For over a year, they had been in training, learning how to wage counterurban guerrilla warfare, learning how to "quell" riots, and obviously also how to provoke them. They had made their public debut with the attack on the Panther office. Their offensive against our vigil was their second official appearance.

The attack on us had begun around six o'clock in the evening. It wasn't until ten-thirty or eleven that it appeared we might be able to leave the houses and storefronts. Around that time, one of Senator Dymally's aides got word to us that the police were prepared to retreat if we all left the area immediately. Whether or not his guarantee was good was a matter for speculation.

Even in this moment of crisis, our most important concern was making the rally a success. Most of the organizers and speakers for the meeting were down on Central Avenue. There was only one logical explanation for this ruthless siege: the police were trying to sabotage our rally. We had to take the chance of trying to get people out of the area so that we could go on with preparations for the mass meeting.

The exit took place without incident. After almost everyone had left, Kendra and I, together with other comrades, headed for a house to hold an emergency Che-Lumumba meeting. Everyone was cautioned to shake off all police tails before arriving.

There we discussed a proposal we were going to present to other members of the coalition the next morning: a march, at the conclusion of the rally, to the county jail where the Panthers were being held. The march would culminate in a demonstration raising the demand for their immediate freedom.

In the middle of our discussions, the brother on security out front rushed into the room to tell us that the police were cruising by in unusual numbers. They had discovered our meeting place, and we had no idea what they would try to do. Our uncertainty, our firm belief based on previous experience that the Los Angeles police would stop at nothing to crush their adversaries meant that we would have to prepare for the worst.

Weapons were checked out, loaded and distributed. In the formidable silence, in the tension-laden room, we waited in readiness. Fortunately, the attack did not materialize. Despite the excitement and the threat of an assault looming over us, we managed to get through our meeting early enough to catch a few hours' sleep before the rally. Everyone else was going home. But it was too dangerous to go to my house on Raymond Street. I had to resign myself to sleeping on Kendra and Franklin's floor.

I woke up the next morning with a terrible feeling of apprehension that only a few hundred people might show up. If the rally were poorly attended, then L.A. ruling circles, particularly the LAPD, might take it as a sign that the Black community was accepting the repression without resisting it. The police could therefore claim a mandate to escalate their aggression. They would attempt to totally obliterate the Black Panther Party and would move on to other militant Black organizations. The arbitrary police violence in the ghetto would mount.

145

With these fears digging at my stomach, I drove down to City Hall with Kendra, Franklin and other members of the club. It was about an hour and a half before the meeting was scheduled to begin. We arrived early to see that equipment was set up and raise the question of the march with the others.

What we saw when we arrived made us all feel euphoric. At least a thousand people were already on the steps—and four-fifths of them were Black. People were still steadily streaming into the area.

By the time the first speaker took the microphone, the crowd had swelled to eight or ten thousand strong. It was a magnificent multitude, studded with signs and banners demanding an end to police repression, demanding a halt to the offensive against the Panthers, demanding immediate release of the captured Panthers.

The speeches were powerful. As we had previously agreed, the theme of the rally—the theme of all the speeches—was genocide. The aggression against the Panthers embodied the racist policy of the U.S. government toward Black People. Carried to its logical conclusion, this policy was a policy of genocide.

The Panthers had been charged with conspiracy to assault police officers. In my speech, I turned the idea of conspiracy around and charged Ed Davis, the Chief of Police, and Sam Yorty, the mayor of L.A., with conspiring with U.S. Attorney General John Mitchell and J. Edgar Hoover to decimate and destroy the Black Panther Party.

Months later, the existence of just such a plan was revealed to the public. The government had decided to wipe out the BPP throughout the entire country. J. Edgar Hoover had called the Panthers "the greatest threat to the internal security of the country," and police forces in most of the major cities had moved on local Panther chapters.

As I emphasized in my speech, our defense of the Panthers had to be a defense of ourselves as well. If the government could carry out its racist aggression against them without fearing resistance, then it would soon be directed against other organizations and would finally engulf the entire community.

We needed more than a one-day stand. Papers circulated in the crowd to be signed by those who wanted to play an active role in organizing the mass movement we needed. By the time the speeches were over, the people were in a fighting mood. Franklin took the microphone and called for the march and demonstration. It was instantly approved with unanimous and roaring applause. We set out for the jail.

When we reached the County Courthouse where the jail was located, the collective anger was so great that the people could not be contained. Defiant throngs pressed forward through the doors of the building. So great was their rage that they began to destroy everything in sight. As they attacked the coin machines in the lobby, they were probably fantasizing about ripping down the iron bars of the jail upstairs.

There were only two ways out of the lobby—one exit on each side. If the police decided to attack, if would be a blood-bath, without a doubt. They only had to lock off the exits and we would be bottled in the building, with no place to run, no room for maneuvering.

But the crowd was ungovernable. I tried to get their attention. But my voice does not carry well without the aid of a microphone and it was drowned out in the clamor. It was Franklin who eventually assumed the role he always seems to excel in: he stood at the top of the lobby steps and with his voice blasting forth like a trumpet, he elicited complete silence from the raging demonstrators. He explained our immediate tactical disadvantages. The police had already sealed off one of the entrances. They were stationed throughout the area and could fall upon us in just a matter of minutes.

It was not enough to explain the dangers of the moment. What had to be emphasized was that the Panther prisoners would be freed by the actions of a *mass movement*. The militant protests of a movement of masses, the determined thrust of thousands of people, could force our enemy to release the sisters and brothers upstairs. Rather than waste our energies giving vent to our frustrations, we should be trying to organize ourselves into a permanent movement to defend our fighters and to defend ourselves.

The people left the courthouse and the demonstration continued outside in full force and with unabated enthusiasm. Thousands marched around the jailhouse chanting slogans of resistance.

Later, the street in front of the Panther office was overflowing with people who came down to assist in the ongoing work of this movement. In all respects, this had been an extraordinarily triumphant day. The rally had more than served its purpose. But in order to realize the potential of what we had just witnessed, much day-to-day organizing was needed. Sisters and brothers would have to commit themselves to work that might not be as visible or dramatic as what we had just done, but which, in the final analysis, would be infinitely more effective.

In the aftermath of the rally, its immediate effects could already be seen. For a while, at least, there was a noticeable let-up of police violence in the community. If you were stopped, you could see that the L.A. police were not as self-confident and certainly not as arrogant as they had been before. By the same token, the collective confidence, pride and courage of the community was definitely on the rise. I felt deeply gratified each time someone in the community expressed his satisfaction to me that something was finally being done about the brutality and insanity of the police.

Black Women Against Sexism

• • • • •

The notable absence of black women in decision-making roles during the civil rights movement is aptly described by Michele Wallace: "Although usually grudgingly respected by men for the contribution they made to the movement's work, black women were never allowed to rise to the lofty heights of a Martin Luther King or a Roy Wilkins, or even a John Lewis. Not a single black woman was allowed to make one of the major speeches or to be part of the delegation of leaders that went to the White House during the March on Washington."[1] Many of the men devoted to the movement were also devotees of the Christian church, and a fair number of the movement's leaders were ministers. These men brought to the movement the patriarchal values sanctioned by the black church and as a rule were unconcerned about equal treatment on the basis of sex. In 1964 Ruby Doris Smith Robinson confronted the male leadership of SNCC with a position paper on the lowly roles of women in the organization, and Stokely Carmichael responded with what became perhaps the most notorious sexist remark of the time: "The only position of women in SNCC is prone—with the exception of women who either dress or look like men."[2]

The attitude of black men toward black women during the civil rights movement was not unlike that of nineteenth-century black activists. Historically, black male political activists did not even acknowledge the sex and class oppression of black women in their fight against racism. Manning Marable states that, even before 1865, ''the problem stemmed from the evolution of patriarchal institutions within Black civil society.'' Through such institutions as the church, mutual benefit societies, newspapers, and the Negro Convention Movement, the black male activist responded to white patriarchy by ''identif[ying] the cause of Black liberation with the ultimate attainment of 'black manhood.'''[3] In 1843, when Henry Highland Garnet delivered before the Negro Convention his ''Address to the Slaves of the United States,'' he urged black *men* to oppose white aggression and eulogized those who had: ''Noble men! Those who have fallen in freedom's conflict, their memories will be cherished by the true-hearted and the God-fearing in all future generations; those who are living, their names are surrounded by a halo of glory.''[4] Garnet's glorification of the black man is echoed in Martin Luther King, Jr.'s appraisal of the Negro in the civil rights struggle: ''Once plagued with a tragic sense of inferiority resulting from the crippling effects of slavery and segregation, the Negro has now been driven to reevaluate *himself. He* has come to feel that *he* is somebody. *His* religion reveals to *him* that God loves all His children and that the important thing about a man is not *his* specificity but *his* fundamentum [italics added].''[5]

Black women also encountered intense discrimination in the black power movement as they worked alongside black men. Black Muslims (Malcolm X), the Black Panther party (Eldridge Cleaver), and Spirit House (Imamu Amiri Baraka) specifically recognized the black woman's role in building a black nation as invaluable but nevertheless secondary. Leaders viewed the assertion of manhood as the primary goal in the liberation struggle and publicly reminded black women of their responsibilities to black men, as Stokely Carmichael did in a speech he made at Morgan State College in January 1967: ''Girls . . . What is your responsibility to your fellow black brothers? So that you can become a social worker or so that you can kick down a door in the middle of the night to look for a pair of shoes?''[6] William A. Blakey, the black director of congressional liaison for the U.S. Commission on Civil Rights, admits that ''the attitude of many black men toward black women is one of disrespect and a desire to dominate'' and suggests that men believe they must persecute black women to repudiate the myth of the ''castrating black matriarch.''[7]

One form of persecution during the black power movement was flaunting the white woman in the black woman's face. Some black male revolutionaries, as the saying goes, ''talked black and slept white.'' When black women questioned them about the obvious contradiction between an espousal of black power and cohabitation with white women, many black men either saw no contradiction or chose to deny it, like the black male revolutionary in Ann Allen Shockley's ''Is She

Relevant?'' Some males apparently agreed with the playwright and prominent black power activist Imamu Amiri Baraka: "The fact that she happens to be black or white is no longer impressive to anybody, but a man who gets himself a woman is what's impressive."[8] This attitude is offensive not only for its sexism but for its dismissal of the abuse black women have suffered from white women.

Joseph L. White lays some of the blame for the sexism in the black power movement on "self-inflated brothers," members of the Me Generation afflicted with the "I am the great god-damn syndrome."[9] Extremely narcissistic and fixated on sexual gratification, they entered relationships with women for what they could get out of them, as Sonia Sanchez portrays them in her play *Uh, Uh; But How Do It Free Us?* Sanchez focuses on single black women dealing with black male revolutionaries who pit them against white women, use them as whores, and goad them to make babies for the revolution. The desire of some black male revolutionaries to increase the black population led them to value women only for their capacity to breed, a disturbing throwback to the attitude held by slave owners more than 100 years earlier.

Black male activists were also all too likely to displace their anger and humiliation in defeat onto women. Ann Allen Shockley's "To Be a Man" depicts a somewhat broken revolutionary whose beating in a bar by a white policeman leaves him feeling powerless, stripped of his manhood. His attempt to regain it by raping his wife is met by her response, "It takes more than that to be a man."

Black women suffered considerably from the sexism of black men during the civil rights and black liberation struggles. While a few confronted and demanded respect from black men, the majority subordinated their feelings as women while forging ahead to fight the battle against racism. Both movements had conflicting consequences for black women. As blacks they contributed to the struggle for freedom and reaped some of the benefits; as women they had to deal with the tendency of black men to control or diminish their contribution and to withhold those benefits.

NOTES

1. Michele Wallace, *Black Macho and the Myth of the Super-Woman* (New York: Warner, 1979), 223–24.
2. Quoted in Evans, *Personal Politics*, 239.
3. Manning Marable, "Groundings with My Sisters: Patriarchy and the Exploitation of Black Women," in Hine, *Black Women in U.S. History*, 10:412, 412–13.
4. Henry Highland Garnet, "An Address to the Slaves of the United States

of America," reprinted in *Black Nationalism in America,* ed. John H. Bracey, Jr., et al., (New York: Bobbs-Merrill, 1970), 75.

5. Martin Luther King, Jr., *Stride toward Freedom: The Montgomery Story* (New York: Harper & Row, 1958), 190.

6. Quoted in Marable, "Groundings with My Sisters," 432.

7. William A. Blakey, "Everybody Makes the Revolution: Some Thoughts on Racism and Sexism," *Civil Rights Digest* 6 (Spring 1974): 19.

8. Quoted in Bell Hooks, *Ain't I a Woman: Black Women and Feminism* (Boston: South End Press, 1981), 97.

9. Joseph L. White, *The Psychology of Blacks: An Afro-American Perspective* (Englewood Cliffs, N.J.: Prentice-Hall, 1984), 77.

● ● ● ● ●

"Is She Relevant"

Ann Allen Shockley

An essayist, short-story writer, novelist, and newspaper columnist, Ann Allen Shockley, who was born in 1927 in Louisville, Kentucky, has been a writer for five decades. She is also the librarian of special collections at Fisk University in Nashville, Tennessee. While a student at Fisk from 1944 to 1948, she wrote short stories and essays for the *Fisk Herald* and feature articles, a column for teenagers, news articles, short stories, and a social column for the *Louisville Defender.* In 1949 she was a columnist for the *Federalsburg Times* in Maryland, and from 1950 to 1954 she wrote a column, "Ebony Topics," for the *Bridgeville News* in Delaware. She has published two reference guides, *Living Black American Authors: A Biographical Directory* (1973) and *Handbook of Black Librarianship* (1977); two novels, *Loving Her* (1978) and *Say Jesus and Come to Me* (1982); a short-story collection, *The Black and White of It* (1980); and a critical anthology, *Afro-American Women Writers: 1746–1933* (1988). Shockley's writings have an ethnocentric focus, and her fiction often addresses issues seldom broached, such as the tranquilizing effects of the black church, homophobia in the black community, and the black lesbian minister.

The theme of sexism permeates several of Shockley's earlier short stories, which depict intraracial and interracial relationships. In "Ain't

151

No Use in Crying" (1967), "End of an Affair" (1969), and "To Be a Man" (1969), Shockley writes eloquently of the systematic victimization of black women by black and white men. "Is She Relevant" (*Black World* [January 1971]) reflects Shockley's continuing concern, even during the black liberation movement, for the black woman's oppression in the black-white racial war.

"Is She Relevant," in its unblinking look at some of the dynamics of attraction between white women and black men, is a good example of Shockley's willingness to enter controversial territory. The main character, Eli, is a leading force in the black power movement. He is alternately attracted and repelled by aspects of his girlfriend's whiteness. He has a personal need for her, yet as an advocate of black power he is embarrassed by his involvement with her. She is "relevant"— important—to him, but not to the movement. When an old friend and an attractive young black woman, both activists, pay Eli and his girlfriend a surprise visit, Eli is confronted with the hypocrisy of "talking black" while "sleeping white." Like Eli, the young black woman, Flo, is a powerful, gifted speaker for the movement. Her anger at finding him living with a white woman is explosive. Unlike Gwendolyn Brooks's Maud Martha, a woman of an earlier era who resented her husband's pursuit of a light-skinned woman but felt that expressing her anger would be futile, Flo does not hesitate to confront Eli. Both are women of their time: the unpoliticized Maud Martha is repressed, and the politicized Flo is completely liberated.

"Power is what we need—" he shouted, voice sonorously ascending to the beamed rafters of the old Elk's Hall, "*Black Power!*" He stepped back from the lectern, a smile of triumph glowing from the sharply molded dark handsome face. The sleeves of his dashiki fell back as he gave the clenched fist gesture of strength and togetherness. He basked and gloried in the cheers and applause emanating from the beautiful sea of Black brothers and sisters.

"Right on!"

"Tell it like it is!"

The flashes of lightning coming from cameras licked quick tongues of white heatless flames across his face. He felt good. He always felt good after his speeches. Perspiration glistened on his forehead like sharp fragments of slivery glass.

Deliberately he took the wooden forked comb from his back pocket and ran it through the mountain-high pyramid Afro hairdo. This was a favorite gimmick with him—especially devised to impress the sisters.

"Great, Eli, just *great!*" Jackson hopped on the platform to put his thick arms about Eli's shoulders, hugging him ecstatically.

Hell, he *knew* that was great. Wasn't that why they called upon him to travel around and spread the Black gospel? That was his job. His *thing*. He had a natural knack for it.

"Got to split now, Jackson," he said, carefully moving down

from the rickety rostrum weakened by the weight of other ghostly Black speakers before him in ages past. "Speeches are *work*, man. Getting old, I guess—" He winked to show he really didn't feel that way. But he *was* getting older. A veteran now who only made speeches—not war.

"Yeah, I know you tired," Jackson agreed sympathetically, taking his arm to help maneuver him through the throngs of handshaking, backslapping well-wishers. "But it's all for the cause. 'Member all them freedom rides and voting drives we done been on? Well, this is the work we got to do now. *Organize* for power. Let the man know where it's at. And *you*, Eli, are one of the top brothers who's doing this. You helping to set the pace. Just *look* at all the faces filled with what you done told them," he whispered.

Sure, sure, he thought tiredly, look at all them brothers and sisters still sweating it out. What is meaningful about beating a stalwart rock. If the rock refuses to move, the best thing to do is blast it away.

Jackson's short chunky figure in tight faded blue jeans followed him to the side door. Another figure had taken his place now on the platform, a young woman with soft curly *au naturel* hair dressed in a colorful buba. Wide-hooped gold earrings made great round double o's against her rich black velvety skin. She was a beautiful sister. Her voice was loud and clear as a bell, ringing out like Gloria Lynne's. The audience was already captured. He was impressed. It was hard to grab them after he finished.

Jackson's eyes followed his gaze. "That's Flo. She's real great. Why'n you stay and hear her?"

"Sorry—" he said, shaking his head, "I'm tired." After all, he had driven over 300 miles today to make the speech. Besides, he was beginning to feel irritable, wanting to get away from the oppressive southern heat and the decaying smell of the sagging building.

"I understand," Jackson said, squeezing his arm. "See you later, maybe—hun?"

"Right." Again he clenched his fist as he slipped out the door into the cool night air. He walked hurriedly down the broken sidewalk, going by the brown anonymous figures sitting on steps and on the ledges of window sills of old forsaken houses. Children played away the night while the adults rapped and talked-the-talk above soul music blasting from radios to beat the asphalt with black rhythmic sounds.

His car was parked two blocks down the street. He did that when he drove away to make speeches so they couldn't see his pride and joy, a sleek new red Jaguar. After all, well, who would understand? But life was to live. Wasn't he, a Black man, entitled to those things, too?

He unlocked the door and slid into the car's luxurious elegance. The smell of newness was still fresh in its womb. Lord, if only his momma could see him now. Little snot-nosed Eli Thomas, Junior, all grown-up. He never knew why she named him after a mythical father—a senior whom he never knew existed.

Starting the motor with loving care, he pulled out into the heavy magic traffic of Friday night. He drove skillfully, weaving in and out of the stream of cars with ease. His thoughts returned to Jackson. Good old Larry Jackson whom everybody called by his last name. How many Friday nights had he and Jackson spent in stinking white southern jails with cracked heads, closed eyes, and split lips while lying in their own vomit. Younger, tougher, taking it and giving a lot too. Following Martin, Stokely . . . her.

Her. His thoughts shifted to her. She wanted to come with him on this trip. To get away, she said. She *did* stay cooped up in the apartment all the time, hidden away. New York was a good place to hide.

He saw the hotel looming in front of him, a huge monstrosity of gilded modern architectural living with hundreds of lights gleaming from square shaped windows. The building beckoned to him like a fat lazy whore.

The white doorman, elaborately adorned in a pompous red suit with gold braid, tipped his cap and greeted him by name. He got out, leaving the motor running. The car would be parked for a Black man who had just cussed out all their white asses.

He rode the tomblike elevator to the sixteenth floor where he had a suite. He unlocked the door and walked into the living room, sinking his feet into the thick carpet. She was still awake, sitting on the couch watching television, waiting patiently as she always waited for him. Why couldn't she for once—

Upon seeing him, she got up quickly, smiling, her blue eyes large with the image of him. Her long sun-colored hair sprayed in cords of straw down and over her pale white face. She was thin, and seemed to be getting thinner. Her tiny shoulders were beginning to droop now, like bearing an extra weight of pain. She wore a white negligee that made her seem bleached. He wished for an unknown reason that she had put on a black one.

"Darling—" she kissed him lightly. "You look tired."

Christ! Always you look tired. It wasn't that. He was just keyed up from the speech, the Black faces worshipping him. *Him!* Eli Thomas, Junior, who five years ago was just a young Black nigger attending a small Black Georgia state college because it was cheap and he lived there. Now he was *made.* His picture stared out at him from newspapers and magazines and over television. Eli Thomas, Junior—maker of the Black revolution—made by the Black revolution.

"Fix me a drink, Stell." He snapped off the black and white TV set, cutting off the movements, sounds, and faces framed in the square box. Wearily, he flopped down on the couch, leaning his head back.

He listened to the sounds of her dropping ice cubes in the glasses from the small wall refrigerator in the bathroom. God, the great white fathers thought of all conveniences to make money. Money. The word invaded his mind. He was living high. Money, fame, and his own white broad. White pussy was a give-away now. For the cause. Made them think they were atoning for all the Black wrongs by giving what had so long been forbidden—the fruit of themselves.

He'd had *his* share and *more*. Only Stell had lingered and hung around longer than the others. An innocent from Oberlin who had gone South one summer like all the other pale young white warriors armed with righteousness. At nights, under brilliant star-crossed skies, hidden in the soft damp earth where slave masters had once raped slave women, the pious do-goodness became human frailty spun in a cocoon of summer lightning sex.

"Here—"

She startled him with the glass. He tasted the drink. Just as he liked it. The scotch eased slothfully down his throat, zigzagging a path of warmth to his nervous system. He closed his eyes, wishing now he had his records of Aretha, Coltrane, and Miles to weave black satiny tones of shaded beauty to bounce him off a soft wall.

"Well, what did you accomplish?" she asked brightly, nestling beside him on the couch.

Accomplish? Something always had to be accomplished with her. Like settling a business deal. Erecting a building. Something to be seen. Concrete. In the Movement, just a good old soul inspiring white cuss-out was an accomplishment. The fact that it even could be *had*. Wasn't that what he got paid for?

"We got a lot done," he said, filling his mouth and body with more of the liquor. Good expensive Ambassador.

Reflectively, she sucked on her glass before saying quietly: "Eli when are we going to get married?"

Damn! As always out of the clear blue sky. She had been alone thinking too much again—too long and too hard. Her middle-class mind was rearing its ugly moralistic head. Wanting to live by the rules. White rules of the do's and don't's of her conformist daddy, who owned a string of hardware stores, and Congregationalist mother, whose tight cunt hadn't had anything slipped in or out except Stell.

"Baby," he made his voice smoothly wheedling, "that don't count no more. What can a few words make us do or *be* what we ain't already been to each other?" Hell, his daddy—nor all the other phantomlike daddies who followed and slept in the bed in checkerboard fashion where daddies are supposed to sleep—married his mother.

He felt her move away. He had hurt her. A perverted sense of glee swept over him like a fun-town orgasm in the house of mirrors.

"Eli, you don't ever intend to marry me," she said quietly, the words cat's paws on the brim of night.

"Baby, sure, sure I do," he protested quickly, soothingly, bringing her head down on his shoulder. Maybe someday he would. If not *her*, someone like her.

Lightly he kissed her eyes, the tip of her nose, and then her thin lips, probing his tongue between her tiny sharp teeth. He felt her tremble and knew that the power was still there despite the now frequent outbursts of dissatisfaction. She was after all *his*. What whitey had baited the Black brothers with for timeless ages, and what so many had needlessly died about. The white goddess was now off her pedestal, toppled off upon Black pricks to kick, beat, curse—love?

His hand slipped beneath her robe to her breasts—they felt too small—and on to the flat stomach which needed more fullness to cushion him, and down to the pubic hair which he wished was a little more brittle. What did he want? A big, Black woman to engulf and smother him with the bed of Africa?

A knock sounded on the door. An unexpected intrusion dividing the moment in time.

"Damn, who's that?" He straightened up quickly.

She primly pulled the robe down over her knees. "I'll see."

"No," he said curtly, getting up. "I'll answer it."

Jackson's squat form stood in the doorway with the speaker Flo beside him. Their warm smiles broke off when they saw Stell in the background.

"Hi, man," Jackson said finally, a little too loudly, "thought I'd stop by for old time's sake and have a goodbye drink before you cooled town. Brought Flo along. She wanted to meet you."

"Yeah, groovy, brother. Com'on in." He broadened his face into what he hoped was a welcoming smile.

"This is *the* man, Flo," Jackson said, "old brother Eli."

Flo looked at Stell and frowned. "We didn't know you had company."

"That's all right. Stell's with me." He reached for her, putting his arm around her waist to show them how it was with them. "Stell, this is Jackson, a longtime friend, and Flo," he introduced offhandedly. "We got some scotch—" The *we* was emphasized too, and Jackson's facial expression of knowingness showed he had caught the message.

"Nice hotel," Flo commented, settling down in one of the overflowing chairs. Her short dress swept above her knees, exposing silken raven bare thighs. She saw Eli gazing at them and languidly wound one leg slowly around the other—curled snakes at rest. "*Real* nice. Right in the heart of town, too." She stared meaningfully back at him.

"It's close to the stores. Stell wanted to shop," he added lamely. What business was it of hers? He had the money. If his woman wanted to pick up a few things, that was his business. "Stell, get some glasses and stuff."

Jackson sat down opposite Flo in the chair surrounding the coffee table. "Your speech was great, Eli."

"Sure, just *great*. Down with the establishment and home to the *established* hearth," Flo croned, lips spread in a vinegary smile.

"No digs, please, Stell's all right," Eli heard himself saying defensively, answering the dark girl with the accusing eyes.

"Humph! *I'm* beginning to think *all* white women are fine with the Black brothers but not the white *men*. I guess the revolution ends at night. After all, you can't screw a revolution."

Stell returned with the bottle of scotch and glasses. "I'll be right back with the ice and soda." Her mouth formed an outline of a smile at Eli. An air of innocence surrounded her. This was what had attracted him in the beginning.

Flo poured a heavy-handed glass of scotch. "I'll take mine without anything."

When Stell left the room again, Jackson asked: "How long's this been going on, Eli?"

"Two years," he said quietly, focusing on his drink.

"Whe-e-e," Jackson whistled between his teeth. "Hope it ain't too *pub-lic*."

Suddenly Eli felt anger spread hot tentacles through him. "Shit, Jackson!" he snapped fiercely. "What the hell you putting on about? Remember back there on that march in Alabama? You took all the white pussy thrown at you and then some!"

"Ain't seen a nigger man that won't yet!" Flo snorted over the rim of her glass.

"Shut the fuck up!" Jackson shouted back.

Suddenly Flo leaned forward, shaking with rage, her earrings dangling furiously against her cheeks. "Now *you* listen here, Jackson, you talking to a big, brassy Black revolutionary woman who's been through shit, too! And ain't no white *or* Black sonofabitching man telling *me* to shut up! It's all the Flo's who's been holding up your Black male asses for centuries. Working for you, having your babies, taking your goddam awful crap, and being your wailing wall against whitey.

"Now you gotten up, you got short memories and missing with thanks. You think you're *men* now. Sure, you might be men, but damn if you all ain't thinking you're *supermen* just because you can get all the white women without getting lynched for wanting it, looking at it, breathing it, smelling it, and balling it!"

Stell came back into the room. He knew she had heard. Her cheeks seemed flushed, and she didn't look at them but concentrated on the glass coffee table where she set the ice and soda. Eli saw Jackson watching her speculatively. Jealousy flared up in him. He thought of the night the two of them had shared one together under a blanket beside the mules. The girl had thought she was purging the world of racism.

The room held a chilled quiet until Stell began haltingly: "I—I wanted so much to go and hear Eli's speech." She was seated beside him now, holding the same warm neglected drink she had prepared before they came.

Flo and Jackson glanced quickly at each other. Jackson twisted his glass as Flo's bell voice rang out too shrilly: "No white folks allowed at that one, honey. Not even the press."

Stell reddened and looked down at her glass which she mechanically lifted to her mouth. Jackson's eyes appeared trapped at the milky whiteness of her throat. Suddenly she set her glass down as if a decision had been made.

"Excuse me. I feel tired. I think I'll go to bed. It was nice meeting both of you."

They said nothing. What was there to say? The room was then a blade of silent steel. They waited for her to close the bedroom door. Eli was certain he had seen tears in her eyes.

"Well, well. How interesting," Flo commented sarcastically. "The great Black honky-hater has a white bitch. Talk Black—sleep white. Slogan of the Black man's revolution. Which makes me wonder, do you really mean what you're saying?"

"You jealous?" Eli shot back, incensed by her taunts.

Her eyes widened. "Me? Jealous of *her* having something like *you?* You who haven't yet learned how to treat your own Black women right? Baby, don't make me laugh!"

"I ought to knock your goddam teeth down your throat!" he snarled hotly, standing menacingly.

She stood up too, facing him, head bobbing in tune with her anger. "You just *try* it. And see if all the Black sisters will be peeing in your pot after I tell them how it is with you!"

"Look, you two," Jackson intervened quickly, stepping between them. "Let's all cool it. We can't fight among ourselves." He put his arms around both their shoulders. "We've had a busy night. I think we all need to get some rest."

Jackson held Flo's arm, guiding her to the door. "Thanks for coming to speak for us, Eli."

Flo's dark eyes spat jungles of primitive fire at him. Jackson paused by the door, still holding tightly to Flo. "Eli," he began reflectively, "I felt like that about an ofay chick once. Real hungup—uptight. Then I got deeper in the Movement, and I asked myself, man, is she relevant? To me. To what I'm doing."

Flo, breathing hard, shrugged off Jackson's restraining grip. "Long's pussy's involved, I ain't seen that make no difference with *no* man. Whether somebody's *relevant* or not!" she mocked.

"So long, brother," Jackson smiled thinly. "Keep in touch."

They were gone. He went into the bedroom. She was lying in bed waiting patiently for him. He wondered how she felt, after hearing. She must have heard. Why couldn't she explode at him like Black women who can burst into a demon of rage. He remembered his mother's curses at the parade of faceless men whom she spat and breathed fire at over the boiling smell of cabbage.

If only she weren't so damn *nice*. Didn't she ever want to swear at him? If only for a moment? The only time he had seen her angry was down South where he first met her on the march. She was angry then—about race. But after she met him, the anger left. As if meeting him had solved everything. Hell, she wasn't all that exciting to screw—even placid sometimes. But the color—the color always made him come.

He fell wearily on top of the covers beside her with his clothes and shoes still on.

"Aren't you getting in?" she asked, the words coming through a veil.

"After a while." He stayed there quietly. The room was empty of sound and movement.

Finally, her hand crept timidly above the covers to grasp his. "I love you, Eli," she said softly.

"Do you?" he asked. Did she love him or was it what he stood for and what this made him seem in her eyes? A new black tower? A Black superman, as Flo had called him. Would she have loved him 10 or 15 years ago in another period of time?

His fingers suddenly tightened around hers. He looked at her, the paleness against the pillow, and smelled the funny white female smell that always was strangely exciting to his senses. His free hand combed through the silky hair and touched her face. He marvelled at the darkness of him touching her.

Was she relevant? This whiteness belonging to him. He bent over her, nestling his face against her breasts. She was his calm after the storm. A place where his Black soul could rest. She was relevant to *him*. His needs. His ego. His lifestyle. He had to live *his* life too, didn't he? Didn't he?

● ● ● ● ●

Uh, Uh; But How Do It Free Us?

Sonia Sanchez

Born in Birmingham, Alabama, in 1934, Sonia Sanchez is a writer of considerable talent. She has a perceptive eye and a keen ear for the nuances and rhythms of black folk speech and music, and she explores issues pertinent to the black community, some controversial, nationalistic, and topical. Whether the topic is black liberation, black love, sexism, drugs, or interracial affairs, she writes to educate and to correct misconceptions. Her published poetry includes *Homecoming* (1969), *We a BaddDDD People* (1970), *A Blues Book for Magical Women* (1974), *I've Been a Woman: New and Selected Poems* (1978), and *homegirls & handgrenades* (1984). She has also published the plays *The Bronx Is Next* (1970), *Sister Son/ji* (1972), *Malcolm Man Don't Live Here No More* (1972), *Uh, Uh; But How Do It Free Us?* (1974), and *I'm Black When I'm Singing, I'm Blue When I Ain't* (1982); and two books for children, *The Adventures of Fat Head, Small Head, and Square Head* (1974) and *A Sound Investment and Other Stories* (1979). Her plays and poems have been reprinted in numerous anthologies and magazines, and she has been the recipient of the PEN Writing Award (1967), an honorary doctorate from Wilberforce University (1972), the National Endowment for the Arts Award (1978–79), the Tributes to Black Women Award (1984), and the American Book Award (1985) for *homegirls & handgrenades*. The mother of three daughters, Sanchez is a professor at Temple University.

In a sense, the question Sanchez asks in the title of her three-part play *Uh, Uh; But How Do It Free Us?* (published in Ed Bullins, ed., *The New Lafayette Theater Presents* [Anchor]) is the question each of her black women characters asks of the black power movement: how does a movement dominated by black men and their interests free *us*? The female characters appear in three "groups," which are presented successively. In the first group, two black women, one traditional, one more contemporary, live with one black man. The sexually liberated times make such a living arrangement acceptable, but who benefits? Essentially, a man is now being taken care of by two women instead of one. The women play certain roles largely for his satisfaction, not their own. Even the more contemporary woman seems to value her own education only as it benefits the man—"I saved him from the boredom that is you," she tells her rival. How has the movement freed these women?

In the second group, a black prostitute being harshly mistreated by several drug dealers, most of them black, tells them that black people have in them more power than they know, that black women are queens. "Yeah," she says. "Some of the younger dudes talk to me sometimes. Say I should stop this stuff. They say I'm a queen, the mother of the universe." But in a farcical response to this modern notion, the drug dealers make the only white man among them "queen." This act is emblematic of a culture that places black women at the bottom of the power structure and white men at the top: the black woman, a prostitute, is devalued, and the white male, a drug dealer, is enthroned. How has the black power movement—as represented by the words of "the younger dudes"—freed this black woman?

In the final group, a young black woman is betrayed by her lover, an up-and-coming leader in the black power movement who has had a long-standing affair with a white woman. He wants the black woman in his life largely for show, not for herself. As his white mistress tells him, "Since you're moving up in the movement out here, you do need a Blk/woman image." The black power movement has not freed this black woman; instead, through one of its young leaders, it has entrapped her.

As the play progresses the black female characters increasingly question their treatment and confront their abusers. The two women in the first group seem to accept their position and argue only with each other. The black prostitute in the second group voices objections about her place in the world, but the words she speaks are not her own; she repeats the ideas she has heard others talk about, without believing them. The black woman in the third group directly confronts her lover with his betrayal, and her instinct is to escape from him. Once she thinks things through, however, she decides to stay; she feels too humiliated to go back home in defeat.

Sanchez's play explores the enormous hole in the black power movement that women fell through.

CHARACTERS

GROUP I: *(Brother is stretched out across the bed and sisters are seated on outer side of bed. One sister is reading)*
MALIK: *twenty years old, dressed in traditional clothes*
WALEESHA: *twenty-one years old, pregnant, sitting on the left side of the bed*
NEFERTIA: *eighteen years old, in traditional dress, sitting on the right side of the bed, reading a book*

GROUP II: *(Four brothers, one devil, sitting on five/white/rocking/horses. A sister/whore and white whore stand on either side with whips)*
SISTER WHORE: *about twenty-five years old in tight/mini/dress/long/knee/boots, black stockings and an expensive red/colored wig on her head*
WHITE WHORE: *about twenty-four years old in purple/see/-through/shirt and bell-bottom pants. Has on boots and blond hair*

THREE BROTHERS AND ONE WHITE MAN: *ranging in ages twenty-six to thirty-four, dressed in bell bottoms, cowboy hats, big ties and jewelry*

BROTHER: *about thirty-eight years old, dressed in dashiki with tiki and African hat*

GROUP III: *(A screen separates a sister and a devil/woman [white woman]. On the sister's side of the screen are African masks and she sits on an African stool; there are suitcases on the floor. A table with phone. On the devil/woman's side is pop art, a table with phone and phonograph, and a butterfly chair, where she lounges. The brother sits on pillows in the middle of the floor. In front of the pillows is a table with liquor)*

BROTHER: *about thirty-four years old, has on two/toned suit, one side is brown suede with a big yellow flower in the center. One side is an orange dashiki with a brown/embroidered map of Africa, wears a talisman, tight/ brown/suede/pants and sandals, shades and a floppy/suede hat*

SISTER: *about thirty-two years old, big natural, dresses in long dress*

DEVIL/WOMAN: *about thirty-three years old, plain-looking, light brown hair, dressed simply but richly*

DANCERS: *(Two brothers and two sisters, stretched out on the floor observing the three groups)*

SETTING

The lights are low at the beginning, just light enough to see the arrangement of the ACTORS *in the three groups. The* DANCERS *are stretched out in front of the group as if waiting. . . . As each group speaks the light is directed on them and the* DANCERS *move conspicuously/inconspicuously in front of them and watch and listen. When the talking ceases, the* DANCERS *begin their talking.*

TIME

Now

(*The light moves to* GROUP 1)

WALEESHA: Are you goin' out again tonight, Malik?

MALIK: Yea. Got a lot a people to see tonight 'bout the play we doing; then we have a rehearsal. Why, what's the matter? (*Raises up from the bed and looks in her direction*)

WALEESHA: Oh. I just wondered if you were gonna be home or not. (*Stands up, stretches; we see* SHE'S *about seven or eight months pregnant*) I just thought you might want to go to a show or something. Felt like doin' something this evening. I guess I'll knit. (*Picks up her knitting*

162

and for a few minutes the quiet sound of needles pierces the ears) Are you
going also, Nefertia?

NEFERTIA: *(Looks up from her book)* Uh, huh. We're rehearsing again tonight. But the play is real baddddd. And Malik is the best. He's beautiful, Waleesha. You should see how the others just stop when he's
onstage and just listen to him. It's like the brother who wrote the play
was writing it just for Malik.

MALIK: *(Turns toward NEFERTIA)* Do you really think so? I mean, I don't
really feel that I have the necessary fire or depth for the second act. I
mean, I say the words, but they don't feel true inside. You know what
I mean? It . . . sometimes I think an older dude should play the part.

NEFERTIA: It sounds fine to me. You are just a perfectionist, Malik. Always pushing yourself. You are a brilliant man. The part is you.

MALIK: *(Gets up and walks around the room and stops in front of a long/
mirror, turns and swaggers slightly)* Do you really think so?

NEFERTIA: Man. You simply too much in it. Don't you remember when
they were giving out parts they kept looking at you. I knew then that
it was going to be yours. Remember how you thought at first that
they hadn't cast you for anything. I saw you get uptight when some
of the better roles were given. I knew then. Mannnnnn, I knew then
that the part was yours. That my Malik had gotten the best, the main
part of the play and was gon' to tear it up, he mean. The meanest. *(Is
laughing at the end)*

WALEESHA: Are you in the play also, Nefertia? I mean, now that you
are three months pregnant it might be too much for you. Goin' to
school and all.

NEFERTIA: Girl, no. I ain't tired at all. *(Stands up and walks across the
room slowly)* And, no one knows I'm pregnant yet. I haven't told them
a word. As long as I'm small they won't know and have to be concerned.

WALEESHA: But, sister, you should tell everyone, after all, it is an occasion for rejoicing. Is it not so, my husband? (MALIK *is looking at himself
in the mirror)* Malik, I said is it not so that Nefertia's pregnancy should
be a time of rejoicing?

MALIK: *(Turns around)* Yeah, and she don't even look pregnant, does
she? I remember when you were three months pregnant, Waleesha,
you were bigggggg. The doctor had to put you on a diet at three
months. *(Laughs)* Do you remember?

WALEESHA: *(Stops knitting)* Yes. I ate a lot during those early months. It
was around that time that Nefertia first moved in with us. Remember?
(Begins knitting again, and the sound of the needles clicking is heavy)

MALIK: Yeah. I remember. Well, I'm gonna split now. *(Goes to closet and
gets his jacket)*

NEFERTIA: Wait a minute. I'll get my coat, too.

MALIK: No. I have a couple of stops to make. I'll be moving too fast for you. You come on later to the theatre. I'll meet you there.

WALEESHA: Do you want somethin' to eat before you go?

MALIK: Naw, I'll be eating where I'm goin'. Hey, I need a couple of dollars. Nefertia, did your school check come?

NEFERTIA: Yes. But I didn't git a chance to cash it. And I have only two dollars.

MALIK: That'll do. (*Walks over and takes two dollars*) See y'all later. (*Exists*)

WALEESHA: Yes. I was huge, wasn't I, when I wuz three months. No, it was really four months. Don't youuuu remember, Nefertia?

NEFERTIA: Uh huh. (*Reading again*)

WALEESHA: Yes, he is right. I was really big. Don't you think so, Nefertia?

NEFERTIA: (*Without looking up*) Uh huh.

WALEESHA: (*Raises her voice slightly*) Say something besides uh huh. I'm just trying to have some kind of conversation.

NEFERTIA: (*Without looking up*) No, you ain't. You just trying to start an argument. You know it. I know it. We both know it. That's why I don't answer ya.

WALEESHA: An argument? An argument 'bout what, Nefertia? What do we have to argue about?

NEFERTIA: (*Finally looks up*) 'Bout me. That's what. ''Bout Malik and me. That's what. You mad cuz I'm the second wife. You still mad at me, sister, and you know it.

WALEESHA: Why should I be mad at you? Just tell me why, Nefertia. Malik brought you here—you were his choice. His decision. And since I love him I have to abide by his choice, no matter how unwise it may be. (*Stands up*) I guess I'll fix something to eat now. (*Stretches*) Ah. This warrior is kicking me hard. He's gon' be bad cuz he's bad already. Ah. He's moving again. (*Puts hands on stomach*) You want to feel little Maliki, Nefertia? You want to hear him running around this house of mine, playing his warrior games?

NEFERTIA: What I want to feel yo/stomach for? No. I got to finish this reading for tomorrow's class.

WALEESHA: (*Gets a can of beans and begins to open it. Begins to speak softly*) One thing's for sure, though. When I have my warrior the burden will be on you. Oh, yes. When I have my sweet Maliki, you'll be big and fat like me and you (*Great laughs*) will have a longgggggg nine months. Just you wait, just you wait . . .

NEFERTIA: You a bitch, you know, Waleesha. You and yo quiet/sneaky ways. How you know fo sure you gon' have a male/child? And what if it's a girl? Huh? What if it's a girl/child? And so what if you do have a male/child? I can have one too. Or even if I have a girl, Malik will love her just like he loves me now. Just like he loved me befo I came here to this house. He used to tell me about you. You and yo/knitting and going to the movies. And hardly ever interested in him, he said. He said you never saw him, never. He said you never read anything, not even a newspaper. We love each other becuz we have everything in common. Theatre, school, poetry. Ours is not just physical love, he says. It's mental, too. So it's you who don't really stand a chance here. I might have been chosen second, but he told me I saved him from you and yo/non/interest in anything. (*During the above,* WA-LEESHA *has warmed the beans and is making a salad.* NEFERTIA *moves over to her, still talking*) Yes, Waleesha, I saved him from the boredom that is you. You dig? I am the second choice, but first in his heart. You dig it, sistuh?

WALEESHA: (*Sits down and begins to eat, and just before eating, looks up and slowly smiles*) Just you wait and see, sister. Just you wait and see. . .

(*Light fades and moves to* DANCERS. *One* MALE DANCER *stays stretched out watching. Moving to see better.* DANCERS: MALE DANCER *walks across stage. Two* SISTER DANCERS *sitting down on imaginary chairs,* ONE *knitting, the* OTHER *reading. When* HE *passes the* KNITTING SISTER, HE *beckons to her and* SHE *gets up and follows him, knitting. Then, looking at him, knitting.* MALE DANCER *passes the* SECOND SISTER *reading. Stops. Turns around, escorts the* FIRST KNITTING SISTER *back to other side of stage, constantly straining his neck to see* OTHER SISTER, HE *turns the* KNITTING SISTER *around, back to him and audience.* SHE *stands mutely, knitting.* MALE DANCER *turns, jumps up and down joyously, walks, stops. Look in make-believe mirror. Flexes left leg, then the right leg. Combs his natural. Turns quickly around to look at the* KNITTING SISTER. HE *sits down next to* READING SISTER. *Begins to read with her. Starts to rap.* SHE *looks up. Listens. He raps more. And still rapping,* HE *removes her book. Touches her body, still rapping. Holds her as they dance a love dance. When* SHE *becomes mesmerized,* HE *takes her and puts her next to the* KNITTING SISTER. HE *lines them up behind him and begins to walk around the stage, stopping at a mirror to preen.* HE *returns to get the other two* SISTERS, *the* KNITTING SISTER *behind him and the* READING SISTER *behind the* KNITTING SISTER. *The* READING SISTER *keeps trying to move in front of the* KNITTING SISTER *but* SHE *is blocked each time. And the* MALE DANCER *never looks around. As the* MALE DANCER *walks,* HE *keeps turning his head as* HE *sees some other sisters, beckons, like as to ''I'll see you later'' look, spruces up. Stops at mirror again and does a preening dance. The* SECOND MALE DANCER *on the floor laughs, rolls over the floor and laughs. Laughs. Laughs.*

Light moves to GROUP II. ALL MEN *riding their horses*)

FIRST BROTHER: This horse is good.

SECOND BROTHER: The best ever.

THIRD BROTHER: Yeah. Giddap, you goddamn horse. Faster. You too slow today. Gots to ride my horse a little higher today. Gots to go to the moooonnn. Soooonnnn. Boommmm. Boommmm. (*Laughs*)

WHITE DUDE: It's good being out that joint. It's gooood being free again. After two years. It's good being out. Ain't it, men?

BROTHER MAN: Yeah, mannnn. That place was a M.F. Eight years there. Amid everything. But I'm out now. And the first thing I said I wuz gon' do wuz to get the biggest fix in the world. It wuz gon' be so big that I would be the world. You diggit. I would be the world. Cuz, man, I got the biggest hustle in the whole wide world today. I found Blackness in the joint, you dig, and I wrote a book and everything I write is licked up by everyone. The Blk/prison/writer is a hero. All thanks is due to Malcolm/man, Eldridge/man for making this all so simple. Man, I got it made after all these thirty-eight years of little hustles, little busts. I got it made. All praises is due to Blackness.

FIRST BROTHER: Hey, you Black/bitch. Git over here and do yo/job. What you gittin' paid for? You broken down whore. Git over here and pree-form. Right now. You ain't gittin' paid to stand around.

SECOND BROTHER: Yeah, make it over here, tootie suitie or we'll re-move y'all. Cuz we some bad ones right here. We the new breed, ain't we, man. (*This section is spoken fast. A climax of sorts. At the conclusion* THEY *return to their pleasant light/high*)

THIRD BROTHER: The new Black man raging in the land. We the orga-nized/gangster/Blk/man. We mean. We do what's to be done. We dealing. We the new Blk/mafia. We dealing.

FIRST BROTHER: Dealing? Man, do we deal. Look around ya and you see us. Dealing from city to city. Making money, bread. Controlling an entire Blk/community.

SECOND BROTHER: Yeah. We keep coming up four aces and the only thing beat four aces is a flush.

THIRD BROTHER: And if that shows, y'all knows toilets is for flushes! (*Laughs*)

FIRST BROTHER: We badddddd.

SECOND BROTHER: Baddddddder than bad.

THIRD BROTHER: Baddddddder than a dude's bad breath.

FIRST BROTHER: We meannnnn.

SECOND BROTHER: Meaner then MEANNN.

THIRD BROTHER: Meaner than a dude whose corn you done stepped on.

FIRST BROTHER: We Blk/mafia/men.

SECOND BROTHER: Blk/on/Blk/mafia men.

THIRD BROTHER: Blacker than Blk/mafia/men. Bother us and you'll see!

WHITE MAN: Come here, you. (*Beckons to* WHITE WHORE) Come here now. I want you to beat me again while I'm riding.

WHITE WHORE: No. I ain't coming this time. The last time you hurt me.

You paying me to beat you. O.K. That's it. Nothing else. I won't do anything else. (*Turns to* BROTHER MAN) You said only the beating, nothing more, since y'all already had your lady. (*Points to the horse*) You promised. The last time he was awful. What's wrong with him? Do he hate women or something?

WHITE MAN: What you calling me, whore? You trying to call me something, you think something wrong with me? I got my stable together already. Out one week and I got three bitches breathing their desire over me already. They humpin' for me. Bring me all their money. They can do more than you can anyday, you anemic-looking witch.

BROTHER MAN: (*Laughs softly*) Take it slow, man. She just a little scared of you. You did take her through some deep changes. We had to pull you off her. Now, didn't we?

WHITE MAN: She weak. She weak like all women. Don't need them, though. Got my girl. Cumon, girl. Let's go. Let's you and me git a thing going. I want to feel you in my guts. Warming my insides. Making me feel good. Warm. Secure. Manly. Gots to git that again. C'mon over here, you purple bitch. Help me to come. Hit me, hurt me. Turn me inside out with pain. C'mon you dead-lookin' whore. (WHITE WHORE *moves over slowly. Begins to beat him softly.* HE *screams. Harder. Beats him harder. And on the last hit,* HE *grabs the whip and pulls her toward him.* SHE *screams.*

WHITE MAN *gets off the horse. His movement is like a slow memory of death*) What you doin' beating me, Momma? I didn't do anything. Really, I didn't say no dirty/bad/words, Momma. Please don't beat me. Please pull up my pants, Momma. You get so carried away you hit me all over.

WHITE WHORE: There he goes again. Git him away from me. He's crazy.

BLACK WHORE: Help her, you dudes. He crazier than you think. He gon' kill her. (*Moves to help and is blocked by* BROTHER MAN)

WHITE WHORE: Help me. Don't let him hit me again. (*Tries to run away but is caught in the* WHITE DUDE'S *massive arms*) I didn't mean to hit you. Please excuse me. Let me go now. I really have to go. Don't hit me again.

WHITE MAN: (*Oblivious to all that has happened*) Momma. Why you always hitting me. I am good. I ain't gon' turn out bad. There ain't no evil spirits inside me. Momma, don't hit me. I'm just seven years old. I wasn't doing nothing. Dottie and I were just playing house. OWWWW. Momma, I'm bleeding. Don't hit me so hard. I'll never play house again. Help me. Somebody help me. Daddy, come back and help me. Help me. (*Sobs*)

WHITE WHORE: (*Is on her knees now and her cries mingle with the* WHITE MAN'S *cries*) Help me. (*Sobs*) Help me, somebody, help me, help me.

BROTHER MAN: (*Still on horse*) They a sorry sight, you know.

FIRST BROTHER: Why you always letting him hang around here, man?

SECOND BROTHER: Yeah. It's one thing to do the biz—another to social- ize with the dude. I mean, brother/man, he be weird.

THIRD BROTHER: You know when we wuz in the joint they caught him being somebody's ''kid''—so what good is he anyway?

BROTHER MAN: I don't know. Perhaps you right. He's always hanging around. I guess I feel sorry for him in a way. I owe him something. When I first got out the joint, he saw me through till I could move around—got my thing straight. Look at the po/sorry/bastard. With a mama complex or something. Guess I should stop this madness. (*Turns and looks at* BLACK WHORE) What you think over there, Blk/ whore? Should I stop it now? (*Moves over and puts* WHITE DUDE *back on horse. Talking softly to* WHITE DUDE. *Hands whip to* WHITE WHORE. WHITE WHORE *slides on away to the* THIRD BLACK DUDE *who helps her*)

BLACK WHORE: Y'all some crazy dudes, but ya paying me so that's all I'm gon' say.

BROTHER MAN: (*Moving toward* BLACK WHORE) What's yo name, girl?

BLACK WHORE: Ain't got no name. Lost my name when I was eleven years old. I became just a body then so I forgot my name. Don't no- body want to know a Black woman's name anyway. You gon' take me home with ya to keep? Put me in your pocket to hold/touch when you need some warmth? No? Well, since you ain't, then there ain't no reason to tell ya my name. All ya need to know is on my face and body. If you can read a map you can read me.

BROTHER MAN: Yeah. Well, it's well traveled. But don't get smart with us. You are what you are cuz you wants to be. Don't go telling us nothing 'bout some dude turning you on when you was young. Every whore in the world says the same thing. Can't no dude in the world make you want to turn a trick less you inclined to do so. But y'all always blaming us. Blk/men for your whoring whore. You a whore cuz you wants to be, now ain't that so?

BLACK WHORE: Uh huh.

FIRST BROTHER: Is that all you gots to say is uh huh?

BLACK WHORE: Uh huh. Amen. And yassuh, boss.

SECOND BROTHER: You a smart whore, ain't ya?

THIRD BROTHER: (*Still helping the* WHITE WHORE) Too smart, if you ask me. Never could stand no smart Black women anyhow. Always open- ing they mouths.

BROTHER MAN: Come over here, Black Whore.

BLACK WHORE: Yeah. I'm coming. I'm coming to receive my payment as usual on time, on schedule. For showing you just a little of your- selves whenever you see me.

BROTHER MAN: Get down on all fours.

BLACK WHORE: Yassuh, boss.

FIRST BROTHER: Man. Let me get down from my horse and git her.

BROTHER MAN: No, she's mine. (*Puts a collar on her neck and climbs on her back and begins to ride her as* HE *was riding the wooden horses*) What kind of a day is it today, Black Whore?

BLACK WHORE: How in the hell I'm spoze to know, man, since I've been in here with ya crazy dudes all day.

BROTHER MAN: (*Pulls collar hard till* BLACK WHORE *cries out*) Would you say the sun is shining?

BLACK WHORE: (*Quickly, sensing danger*) Yes, it is. The sun is shining.

BROTHER MAN: How is that so when I wore my raincoat in here today? Are you suggesting I'm crazy or something for wearing my raincoat, Black Whore? You think you know better than me, Black/woman/whore?

BLACK WHORE: I mean the sun was shining for a while but it started to rain. Now it's raining. It's steady raining outside.

BROTHER MAN: (*Smiles*) Is it still raining, Black Whore?

BLACK WHORE: Yessir. Mr. Brother man. It's raining.

BROTHER MAN: Still raining? I can't believe that for this time of year. Take me over to the window so I can see if it's raining or not. Giddap now, blk/horse. Giddap. I know you ain't gon' take me higher cuz only the white horse can do that. Hey, stop here for a minute. Them dudes got some coke that look goooood. Gots to git some of that now. (BLACK WHORE *takes him slowly over to the three* BLACK DUDES *and the* WHITE DUDE) Is it any good?

FIRST BROTHER: I'm ten feet tall and gittin' taller.

SECOND BROTHER: I am god. I am god. I am god.

THIRD BROTHER: Get me a woman. No, get me five women. I need five women to satisfy what I see in my mind. Send out for some more women. Ya hear me?

WHITE DUDE: I rule the universe. I am the universe. The universe revolves around me. I am the universe. I am a man. A man. A man. Can't no one surpass me. I am a man. The man. A man. The man.

BROTHER MAN: This stuff must be good. Give me some. Now (*Smiles a long smile*) here's some for you, Black Whore. I know you just itching for some. Here, have some of mine.

BLACK WHORE: (*Reaches for it hesitantly, then takes it greedily. Becomes more relaxed*) Thank you, Brother Man.

BROTHER MAN: Think nothing of it, Black Whore. Now, let us continue our trip toward weatherland. (*Laughs*) Whew. That stuff is baddddd. Whoa. Blk/whore. (*Turns*) Man, is that any of our stuff? It is. That too good for the niggers outside. They don't need that stuff at all. Whew! That's goooood, lady. Awright. Giddap, Black Whore. We got a destiny with the weather.

BLACK WHORE: (*Softly, mumblingly*) Our destiny is over, my man. We're yesterday.

BROTHER MAN: (*Stops the* BLACK WHORE) Whoa! What you say, whore? What you mumbling, ain't you satisfied? Didn't I just give ya some coke? Now, didn't I? I mean, ain't ya satisfied? Are you just the typical Black/woman? Always complaining, never satisfied. Always bitching about something. What's wrong, you want some more coke, don't ya? Yeah, that's it. C'mon. Ima gonna see to it that you personally get more coke. (*Turns*) Hey, you dudes, c'mon off and get some more coke for the lady here. I mean, let's share it with this no-name whore here. Why she could be your sister. Maybe somebody's momma? Hey, whore, is you somebody's momma? Huh? You somebody's momma? You got a kid? (*Pulls collar tightly*) Answer me, bitch. I'm talking to you. The new Blk/man in America. The successful Blk/man in America. Answer me now.

BLACK WHORE: Yes. I have a kid.

BROTHER MAN: You a mother. It figures, though. You all have one kid or something living with some old woman or something and you visit there on holidays and bring presents and hugs and kisses and promises of an earlier visit, right?

BLACK WHORE: That's right.

FIRST BROTHER: Hey, how you know that, man? That sounds like my ole lady. I didn't know what she was 'til someone told me 'bout her. I always thought she was a teacher or something.

SECOND BROTHER: She was a teacher all right, man. She was steady teaching dudes all they needed to know to git by. She still humping, man?

FIRST BROTHER: Man, she died last year. O.D. When I got in the bizness, I had one of my boys run her some good stuff. Guess it was too much for her. They found her in her room, sleeping like a baby. In fact, when I saw her laid out she looked like I remembered her to be when I was little and thought she was a queen. A beautiful queen.

BROTHER MAN: They saying today that Blk/women are queens. Did y'all know that? Have you heard any of that stuff, Blk/whore?

BLACK WHORE: Yeah. Some of the younger dudes talk to me sometimes. Say I should stop this stuff. They say I'm a queen, the mother of the universe. A beautiful Blk/woman/queen.

BROTHER MAN: Do you believe it?

BLACK WHORE: No. I know I ain't no queen. Look at me. I'm a whore. I know it. It just that they young. They see Blk/women differently. They say I'm not responsible for what I am. They say . . . (*Stops*)

BROTHER MAN: Don't stop. Continue on.

BLACK WHORE: Aww, it ain't nothing but a lot of talk.

BROTHER MAN: Some call it rhetoric. Go on, finish it. I want to hear who is responsible.

BLACK WHORE: They say—it ain't me saying it, now, they say that we're the way we are because the men, the dudes, the brothers our age couldn't see us as anything else except whores, suz they couldn't see theyselves as anything else except pimps or numbers runners or junkies or pushers, or even . . . (*Stops*)

BROTHER MAN: Don't stop now. Hey, y'all. C'mon over here, y'all are missing a education. Git your behinds over here and listen to our Blk/whore. She gon' rap on what's wrong with us all. Continue now. Or even—

BLACK WHORE: Awwww, man. It ain't me. I'm just repeating what they done told me. It ain't my words.

BROTHER MAN: Continue, I said.

BLACK WHORE: Or even the Blk/gangsters who go round thinking they baddddd. All they doing is repeating themselves out loud. Cuz they still hurting, killing, selling dope to our people, and they don't know that instead of having a little bit of the planet, that the planet earth is ours. All ours just waiting to be taken over.

BROTHER MAN: You believe that, girl?

BLACK WHORE: No. Course not. Just some young punks rapping hard.

BROTHER MAN: Would you like to believe it, girl? I mean, would you like to be a queen of the universe, c'mon on. Get up off ya knees. Ya, a queen. Hey, White Whore, bring the fur coat out the closet and some makeup. Hurry up. We got a queen here, waiting to be fixed up. (EVERYONE *moves around the* BLACK WHORE, *fixing her up till* THEY *step back and see her dressed up*) Everyone bow. No. Altogether. On the count of three. Everyone bow and say yo/majesty, one, two, three, yo/majesty. C'mon. Louder than that. One. Two. Three, yo/majesty. Yeah. That's better now, yo/majesty. Walk around and view your subjects. Walk around and see what's your kingdom's about. Go ahead, now, we ain't gon' hurt you any, go on now.

(*The* BLACK WHORE *begins to walk shakily.* SHE'S *obviously scared. But as* SHE *walks,* SHE *relaxes, and as* SHE *passes by the second time, her face changes and her body seems taller.* SHE *looks queenly, like a latter day Lady Day looked on TV, nervous and unsure but queenly*)

WHITE DUDE: Stop it. What is this sheeeeet. Who she think she is anyway? If anyone's gon' be queen of the universe around here, it's gon' be me. (*Goes to closet, puts on coat, high-heel shoes, wig, earrings. Turns around slowly and walks sensuously toward the* GROUP) Here now. Look at me. I'm your queen of the universe. (*Begins to switch all around the room. The* DUDES *begin to laugh. Loudly clap*) See, I'm the real queen. I am the universe. And I'm a queen, too. I'm the queen of the universe.

Look at me, everybody. Don't look at her. She's Black. I'm white. The rightful queen. Look at me, everybody. Your queen for today, for tomorrow, forever. The only queen for America. You get your queen some coke right now. (WHITE WHORE *brings some coke from one of the* DUDES) And don't you forget that I'm the queen, you hear? Get back over there, you purple witch you. (*Takes his coke*)

BROTHER MAN: All right, we have two contestants for the prize of "queen of the universe." Here they are, America. Look at them. Hear ye, hear ye. All you dudes, c'mon over here. You, too, White Whore. We're having a contest to find out which one is the true queen of the universe. The decision of us the judges will be final. All right, the contest begins. Begin your walk, all you would-be queens.

(*The* TWO QUEENS *walk around the room. As* THEY *move, the* BLACK WHORE *becomes more regal and silent and the switching sounds and sighs of the* WHITE DUDE *become shrill. As* THEY *make a final turn, the* WHITE DUDE *moves in front of the* BLACK WHORE *and blocks her path.* SHE *moves aside and* HE *moves in front of her.* SHE *moves aside and* HE *moves in front of her again.* SHE *moves aside and* HE *moves in front of her and as* SHE *moves* HE *punches her in the stomach and face.* SHE *falls to the floor. And the* WHITE/ DUDE/QUEEN *continues his walk and each time* HE *passes the* BLK/WHORE HE *kicks her*)

WHITE DUDE: It is obvious that I'm the queen. Is that right?

BROTHER MAN: Without a doubt. You've proved the point, man. The only queens in the world are white. And probably men. It's a good lesson for sorry whores who listen to young dudes rapping 'bout nothing, cuz me and my men are the time. It's the 1970s, and don't ya forget it. The decade of the hustles. The hustlers. The decade of easy/good/long/bread if you willing to take chances. We know who we are. We take off banks now. Run the whole dope operation in the Black communities. We run it and we run it well. (*Turns to the* THREE BROTHERS) Where y'all going to tomorrow?

FIRST BROTHER: Detroit, man. A big shipment tomorrow.

SECOND BROTHER: Chicago. Got a meeting going with some Black cops who'll make sure things stay cool.

THIRD BROTHER: Louisville. Having a little trouble with one of the lieutenants there. Nothing too serious. If need be, he goes.

BROTHER MAN: C'mon. Let's take off one more time before we split. Queens. Not in my time. Get off the floor, Blk/whore. C'mon, do yo/ preordained/work.

(MEN *get on their horses and wait. The* WHORES *come over and begin to beat/hit them with a rhythm and* THEY *ride their horses. Quietly staring out at the audience,* EACH ONE *involved with his own orgiastic dreams.*

Light moves to the DANCERS. DANCERS: MALE DANCER *is obviously a* LITTLE BOY. *Looks lost. Alone. Moving around stage. Looks up and sees a*

"MAMMA" FEMALE DANCER. *Runs toward her but* SHE *knocks him down.* HE *runs toward her again, but* SHE *knocks him down.* HE *runs toward her again, but* SHE *knocks him down. Keeps going, begins to play with other* FEMALE DANCER. SHE'S *a* LITTLE GIRL. *Playing house—mama and daddy.* SHE *hugs him.* HE *hugs her. The* MAMMA FEMALE *walks past. Pulls them apart. Begins a thrashing, killing dance, and leaves the* YOUNG BOY *sitting alone. Within himself. And as* HE *sits,* HE *grows older. Becomes a* MAN. *And a* "LITTLE GIRL" *female dancer, about eleven years old, passes by him, and* HE *watches her. Sees* SHE *is being stalked by an* OLDER MALE DANCER. HE *watches, fascinated by it all. The two* DANCERS [LITTLE GIRL/OLDER MAN] *return now together.* SHE *is following. The* OLDER MALE DANCER *comes over to* MALE DANCER [*sitting down*] *and offers him the* YOUNG GIRL. *The three* DANCERS *dance a new/orgiastic/blue-bird-blue-bird through my window dance and the* LITTLE GIRL DANCER *goes mad and becomes a* WOMAN *and we'll never know the exact moment her childhood ends. The three* DANCERS *move down the street and the two* MALE DANCERS *turn the* YOUNG CHILD WOMAN DANCER *over to another* FEMALE DANCER *who begins to console her caressingly. The two* MALE DANCERS *move off together and shyly begin to touch each other. Discordant music is heard!*

Light fades and moves to GROUP III.

GROUP III: *The* BROTHER *slowly moves from the pillows.* HE *has a disturbed look on his face.* HE *mixes himself a long drink, turns around and looks at the two* WOMEN *in each separate room.* THEY *are both reading.* HE *shakes his head, turns, and finishes his drink.* HE *picks up a red/blk/green pillow and goes to the* SISTER *side first, and* HE *must stand or sit always with the dashiki side showing and never show the other side while visiting the* SISTER)

SISTER: (*Walks to the* BROTHER) Well, I'm here. I finally made it. Three thousand miles from cold NYC to you and San Francisco.

BROTHER: Uh huh. I thought once that you wouldn't but you did. You a strong sister.

SISTER: I have to be, man. You a strong brother and you ain't got no time for nobody who's weak.

BROTHER: Uh huh.

SISTER: What's wrong, honey? You seem distant. Is something wrong?

BROTHER: No. Well, not wrong, but I have to go out tonight. To see this dude about something. Ain't sure I'm gon' git back tonight. And this yo/second night in town. Just wanted to be with you every night since you've finally come to me.

SISTER: Business is business, my man. I still have a lot of unpacking to do. The movement comes before you and, me, love/making all. When you have to TCB you have to. (SHE *moves away from him and begins to busy herself*) Now you git stepping and if you git a chance, call me. I'll be okay. Man, don't look so sad. We've got a whole lifetime of touching, loving, ahead of us.

BROTHER: I just want you to know, lady. You'll never regret coming out here to me. I'll take good care of you. Your family still mad about your coming?

SISTER: And how. They said you just can't pick up and go three thousand miles to a man you've only known six months. My father said, he needs to shave off that big beard of his. He looks like Castro. And what does he do? When I told them, you were in school getting your master's, they wanted to know then how would you support me. I told them that the new/Blk/woman didn't worry about a man taking care of her. She and her man work together. If he had no job she worked and let him do the work of organizing the people. Since the money came from the oppressor, it didn't matter who made it. My mother stared at me in disbelief. Well, girl, she said, the new/Blk/woman, as you call her, is a first-class fool and had better git that part 'bout support straight right away cuz any Blk/man who don't think he has to support you will eventually begin to think you a fool, too, for letting him get away with it. You gon' end up in a heap of trouble. And it went on and on like that every day till I left. My mother finally told me that it would have been better if I hadn't read all those books. She finally hugged me and said if I got into trouble to call her right away cuz wuzn't no—what's that he calls himself?—I said, revolutionary Black man—well, wasn't no revolutionary Black man gon' hurt her one and only daughter with no foreign talk. She said we Blk/women been fighting a long time just to get Blk/men to take care of us now you and yo/kind gon' to take us back. Girl, I think we older women needs to talk to y'all 'bout something called common sense. Then we hugged again and that's all. (*Goes to* BROTHER *and hugs him and becomes playful*) Then I jumped on a plane, no wagon train for this sister, and California here I wuz. And you were at the airport with a rose, one lone red rose. And I thought, man, that's beautiful. I'm going to press that rose in the first book you sent me. Do you remember?

BROTHER: Yeah. It was Fanon's *Studies in a Dying Colonialism*, wasn't it?

SISTER: Uh huh.

BROTHER: Well, baby. I gots to split, but bizness is calling me tonight. I'll try to call you. If I don't, I'll send some sisters over to bring you out to the school tomorrow. All right? (*Kisses her and picks up the red/ blk/green pillow and leaves. For a moment* SHE *stands as if waiting, then begins quick movements. Goes over to one of the suitcases and begins to unpack.* BROTHER *returns to the middle of stage and puts the red/blk/green pillow down. Crosses to table, pours himself another drink, turns, peers to the right, picks up a red velvet pillow and enters the* WHITE WOMAN'S *apartment*)

BROTHER: Grettings from afar. Your boy/wonder has returned.

WHITE WOMAN: How was your trip down the peninsula?

BROTHER: Not bad. We'll talk about that later, but now some food and drink for one who has traveled so far to partake of your charms. (*Slightly drunk*)

WHITE WOMAN: (*Smiling but serious*) Ah, my man, you are most definitely mad. And didn't you promise me that you would cut down on your drinking? You got blotto, no. Now what is it you say . . . ?

BROTHER: Wasted, my love.

WHITE WOMAN: Yes. You got wasted night before last. I had to put you to bed. That's no good. How are we going to change this diseased world if you're drunk?

BROTHER: I know. You know it's just these recent happenings. Like you know, it's hard to leave you sometimes, and you know I'll have my new family starting next week. It's just so hard. You see, she doesn't know anything about you. She could never understand you and me and her and me at the same time, you being white and all.

WHITE WOMAN: Now, my man, it's your decision to make. (*Gets up and fixes two drinks*) If it's too much we can stop seeing each other. I'm not here to destroy you or make you feel guilty. I love you, my man, and whatever decision you make I'll abide by. (*Hands drink to* BROTHER) But since you're moving up in the movement out here, you do need a Blk/woman image. She's cute looking. Small. Compact, with a good/ growing/awareness of what's to be done. You made a good choice and she obviously adores you. I say how she was watching you in New York. You are her life. So she'll be dedicated to you and you need a Blk/woman who will dedicate her life to you, for you are becoming a very important man out here. But people are noticing that you don't have a Blk/woman.

BROTHER: You're a rare woman, you know. Not many women would share their man the way you do. You know, I wuz coming here tonight to say that we had to stop seeing each other. That since she's coming next week it wouldn't be fair to both of you, that you both would be cheated in some way. But you've made it so simple. Since we understand, we can keep this just between us. And she'll never know. (*Hands empty glass to* WHITE WOMAN) How's about another one of those goodie good drinks you fix for your VIP's, huh? Then some good dinner for a hard-working revolutionary. (BROTHER *sits on pillow*)

WHITE WOMAN: (*Moves over to* BROTHER *and sits down next to him*) After we eat, could we go to the club and see John Handy? I haven't seen him since your birthday. Let's go out tonight. Make it a grand celebration since my wandering warrior has returned from the peninsulan wars.

BROTHER: Girl, I'm tired. Just wants to sleep for a coupla days. (*Turns and sees her face)* But . . . all right. I tell ya not for long. Just for one set. Now go fix my food. RAT NOW! Y'all hear? This nigger is ready to grease out loud.

(WHITE WOMAN *gets up and moves behind the screen. The* BROTHER *goes over to phone and dials a number. We see the* SISTER *stretched out on the floor and* SHE *picks up the phone on the first ring)*

BROTHER: How you doing, baby? Were you sleeping?

SISTER: No. Just dreaming, 'bout you and me, and us, 'bout our yet unborn children waiting for us. To be born. Just thinking good things 'bout us, man. 'Bout what will be cuz we, this new Blk/man Blk/woman will finally put to rest the thoughts that we can't/don't git along. It wuz good news, man, just like you good news for me.

BROTHER: Yeah. I feel the same way 'bout you. You beautiful people and I'm happy you here. We got a whole lot of work to do and to do it with someone like you should be a gasssss. Look, baby, this meeting is taking longer than I thought. I won't be able to get back over to ya. I gots a lot of talking to do this night so you close yo/eyes and continue to dream 'bout me. Us. Our future, just continue to dream 'bout us. Don't let nothing interfere with that. Yo/dreams of us. Me and you. As long as we're together in yo/dreams we will BE. Remember that, baby. Just remember that. Don't you ever forget that you my woman. My Black woman. The woman I'ma gonna show to the world. My choice for the world to see.

SISTER: I love you, man. I love only you. Been waiting for you for a long time and now that we together time had better git stepping cuz it's you and me now and nothing's gon' git in our way.

BROTHER: Git some sleep now, baby. I'll see you tomorrow. Later on.
(BROTHER *hangs up and moves behind the screen.*

SISTER *hangs up, gets up and happiness is on her face.* SHE *does a quick spin and lets out a loud laugh. Stretches out on floor and goes to sleep. At the same time, you see the* BROTHER *and* WHITE WOMAN *dancing past. Talking. Laughing)*

WHITE WOMAN: And I thought you had forgotten my birthday.

BROTHER: *(Smiles)* I thought you thought that. I just didn't mention it to you because I wasn't sure if I would be able to buy you what I wanted to. I solved it all, however. I wrote a bad check that's so full of rubber it'll bounce from here to the Golden Gate Bridge.

WHITE WOMAN: *(Laughs)* You're incorrigible. *(Moves away from him and hands him a letter)* Here you are. On time as usual, my man. Now, don't you do that again.

BROTHER: *(Doesn't raise his hand to accept the letter. Turns away and flops down in the chair)* I ain't gon' take no more of yo/money, girl. I'll/we'll, she and I will have to make it on her check and the school check. It was all right befo but no mo. Not now. It wouldn't seem right.

WHITE WOMAN: Ahhhhh, my man. That's what I love about you. Your values. You know you two can't get along on the money you're both making, that part-time teaching job she has can't/won't really help. I mean the money is rightfully yours. I told you that a long time ago, it's the money that my father got by underpaying Black people for years. It's rightfully yours. It should go to a Black man twisting and turning to be someone. Twisting and turning to survive it all. (*Moves to table and puts the check down. Pours two drinks*) It's really amusing. The estate sends me all this money and I give it to you and you travel around. Talk. Organize. Get people to change the world so no more men like my father will exist. If my mother only knew she would have one very real attack instead of one of her many fake ones. (*Hands* BROTHER *a drink*)

BROTHER: Yeah. It just seems weird taking care of her with your checks.

WHITE WOMAN: But, baby, she deserves it, too. After all, she's Black and she works hard, too. She's a sort of inspiration to Black women.

BROTHER: (*Taking a sip*) Don't you . . . well, don't you envy her or hate her at all? She comes down hard on white women, you know.

WHITE WOMAN: Yes, she does. But I understand her bitterness, loneliness. She's had a very hard life. Not many people would have survived it. No. I don't hate her. After all, she says a lot of truth. (*Crosses over and sits down in front of* BROTHER) A lot of white women do love Blk/men. She feels threatened by this. (*Kisses him, then takes down her hair. Lets it flow on him, his face, as* HE *stretches out and pulls her on top of him*)

BROTHER: I don't know what I'd do without you, baby. You good to me.

WHITE WOMAN: Don't try to. Everything is as it should be. I can share you any time as long as you always turn up here. Drunk or sober. You hear? (*Holds his head as* SHE *talks*) You are mine, my man. I found life, a reason for living, when I found you. I live from the light you bring me. When you stand up to talk and I hear you telling your brothers and sisters what we've discussed, I feel all warm inside. I see me up there on stage and it's so goood.

BROTHER: Come here, you, and say it's so goooood again.

WHITE WOMAN: (*Moves on him and covers his face with her hair*) It's so goooooooood, my man.

(*Light moves to the* BLACK WOMAN'S *side,* SHE'S *on the floor, exercising. Her rhythm on the floor corresponds to the sounds coming from the* WHITE WOMAN'S *side. When* SHE'S *finished,* SHE *relaxes at the same time the* WHITE WOMAN *and* BLACK MAN *separate and rest alongside each other.* BLACK WOMAN *stands up and you see* SHE'S *pregnant. Early stages of pregnancy. Holds up a beautiful long dress and puts it on a hanger. Turns when* SHE *hears the door open*)

SISTER: Hey. What's happening? Look at this dress. I made it this morning. (*Holds it up to her body*) How do you like it?

BROTHER: You'll be tough, baby. Are you speaking tonight?

SISTER: Yes, at the cultural center. It should be a good crowd. Imagine having five crazy poets onstage together. The Black Experience indeed! It's gon' be smoking tonight. I just did a new poem tonight for the sisters at San Francisco State. It's called "To All Sisters." Listen to it. (*As the* SISTER *reads the poem, the* BROTHER'S *face and body tense. When* SHE *finishes,* HE *sits down*)

BROTHER: You coming down kinda hard, ain't you, baby?

SISTER: Hard. Can't nobody be too hard on a devil/woman. She's the same as the devil/man, ain't she? One of the sisters came into my office today saying her old man has won. He said that it was a political move. So she asked him what's political about a devil/woman since she thought we were talking about all white people, not just white men. She said he looked at her and said you don't know what's happening. That the only way he as a Black man could maneuver would be to have a well/to/do/white chick in his corner. Man, she's all torn up so when I come home I wrote this poem. That's why it's got to be baddddddd—baddddddder than bad so we can put that white woman in her proper perspective, you dig? Tell me, man, what's happening with Greg, huh? Frances is a beautiful sister. Loyal, hardworking. What is on his mind, man?

BROTHER: (*Looks up. Worried*) How in the hell should I know? I don't know what's on that nigger's mind. It's his business, not ours. (*Stands up*) Look, baby. I got a whole lot on my mind. Johnny and I are leaving tomorrow night for Mexico to hook up with some revolutionaries down there so I ain't got no time to figure out the workings of some dude's mind.

SISTER: Oh, I'm sorry, man, but you know what's happening here. It was just on my mind and I had to spit it out. Had to. Sometimes this is just so unreal. I mean, sisters really working hard at being true Black women. Really hard. And then some dude takes them out, so far out to lunch that they might never come back. Couldn't you speak to him, mannn?

BROTHER: (*Impatient*) Yeah. When I come back I'll talk to him, O.K.? Now miss do-good lady, would you please pack me a bag before you go out?

SISTER: (*A worried look*) You not coming with me tonight? Oh no. But you promised, mannnnnnnnn. Our last night together, you promised it would be our night. You'll be gone a whole week.

BROTHER: Too tired, baby. Had meetings all day with the people here who are to hook us up in Mexico.

SISTER: (*Sulking*) I know, but you promised.

BROTHER: So what? What you sulking 'bout? So I promised. I'm here, ain't I? I ain't goin' no place tonight. When you come back I'll be here waiting for you. I just don't feel like hearing no poets up on a stage talking bad. (*Smiles*) It's just hard for me, you know, to see you up there on stage gittin' all that applause. Makes me begin to wonder why you chose me. After all, I'm not really famous yet. I'm working on it. But you, everybody knows you so . . .

SISTER: Ah, man. I understand now. It's alright. Look, I'll leave as soon as I read. So I can come home to you, man, to one who has chosen me from afar. (*The bell rings*) There they are. I'll run on downstairs. They'll bring me home. You get some rest, mannn, cuz when I come back . . . (*Smiles*)

BROTHER: Do it to them, baby. See you soon.

(BROTHER *fixes drink and picks up the phone,* HE *hesitates. A worried look on his face. Dials the phone. Phone rings. On the* WHITE WOMAN'S *side the phone rings and rings and rings and* SHE *looks up and continues to read.* BROTHER *puts down the receiver and dials again. The phone rings and rings and the* WHITE WOMAN *gets up and fixes herself a drink. Puts some music on and picks up the phone and dials.* BROTHER *jumps for the phone*)

WHITE WOMAN: Greetings, my man. How are you? Thought I'd take a chance and call you there.

BROTHER: Uh huh. Where are you? I've been trying to get you all night.

WHITE WOMAN: Why, I'm home. I've been here all night. Thinking about you.

BROTHER: I've been calling you all night. And the phone just rang and rang. Where you been?

WHITE WOMAN: I told you. No place, just here. You must have dialed a wrong number.

BROTHER: Bitch. What you take me for, a fool?

WHITE WOMAN: (*Coldly*) Impregnating women is a criteria for revolution?

BROTHER: You think Black babies ain't part of the change?

WHITE WOMAN: How are we going to have time for a baby? There's no place for children now. I thought you had better sense than that. There's too much work to be done to stop and have a baby. Too much hard work to be done. That baby will tie you down, my mannn. You been together six months and she's pregnant already.

BROTHER: Just leave her out of this. She's happy about the baby. Just leave her out of this. (*Coldly*) If you worried about supporting us all, just stop worrying. When I return from Mexico, I'm gon' git a part/time/job to tide us over. Don't you worry about us at all. Look. I better hang up. Got some packing to do tonight. I'll call you from Mexico. (*There's no answer*) Are you there? Hey. What's wrong?

WHITE WOMAN: I'm crying.

179

BROTHER: Why? I've been away before.

WHITE WOMAN: I'm crying because for the first time I was being a bitch. I was jealous of her. She's carrying your child inside her. She's tied to you forever. You can leave anytime you want to. You just need . . . want . . . me for my money. That's all you want me for is my money. (*Begins to scream. Cry*)

BROTHER: Stop that now. Get yourself together and stop! Hear me? Do you hear me? Answer me. Do you hear me? (WHITE WOMAN *sits crying by the phone. Listens to him calling her. Lights a cigarette and listens.* SHE *stops crying and sits silently*) Answer me. Do you hear me? Are you all right? Speak to me. Answer me. Are you all right? Don't do anything silly now, you still got those sleeping tablets in your house? Answer me. Do you hear me? Do you still have those sleeping tablets in your house? Hey, answer me! (BROTHER *hangs up phone, takes a drink, walks back and forth. Drinking. Thinking.* WHITE WOMAN *takes a drink. Walks back and forth. Finally stretches out on the floor and waits.* BROTHER *leaves the* SISTER'S *house and enters the* WHITE WOMAN'S *house, sees her on the floor and tries to wake her up.* SHE'S *motionless*) Hey, lady. Wake up. Are you all right? Hey, lady. C'mon now. I'm sorry for making you cry. Did you take anything, huh? I'm sorry it took me so long to get here. Couldn't get a cab. I finally had to walk/run here. Are you all right, baby? My baby. (*Puts her hand in his lap and kinda croons the words ''my baby'' over and over again like a chant*) My baby. You gon' be all right. You not gon' leave me. Your mannn. We're together forever. I am committed to you, lady. Don't nobody mean to me what you mean to me. C'mon, baby, you gonna be all right. I'm yo/mannnn. Nothing can change that, you know. So what if she's having a baby. It's something she wanted. I guess it fulfills her as a Black woman, but it didn't bother you and me, baby. Not us. We were together before she came and we'll stay together. Why, lady, you've made me all that I am. I'm almost finished with school because of you. I can travel whenever I want to because of you. I dress well because of you. I never want for money because of you. I'm a man because you've allowed me to be a man. Say you all right, baby. (*Moves her head back and forth*) C'mon, baby, speak to me.

WHITE WOMAN: (*Speaks dully*) Where am I?

BROTHER: Ah. Thank God, here with me. What did you take, lady?

WHITE WOMAN: (*Slowly*) I took some sleeping tablets with a glass of scotch.

BROTHER: Lady. What you do that for? You had no reason to do that. What would I do if something happened to you? How would I make it without you? I neeed you, lady. Don't scare me like that.

WHITE WOMAN: (*Slowly*) I just felt so lonely. So all alone. And I thought, he'll leave me one day. (*Tries to sit up and* BROTHER *helps her*)

He'll leave me one day just with the memory of three years together. Just with the sound of my door opening and shutting. He'll leave me and I'll dry up without his light. Without his sun. And I didn't want to see that day, my mannn. Do you understand? Don't be mad at me. You called me a bitch and I knew you were mad at me and I am a bitch . . .

BROTHER: No, not you. You're my life. I was just mad at you because you weren't home on my last night.

WHITE WOMAN: I was home, my love. I was just trying to make you jealous. Forgive me, my mannn. Forgive this foolish honky/woman. Devil/woman as yo/Black/woman calls me.

BROTHER: Hush now. And don't call yo/self those names.

WHITE WOMAN: But I am a honky. A devil. Am I not? Isn't she talking about me, mannn?

BROTHER: No, she ain't. Not about you. You exceptional, lady. There ain't nobody like you. You no honky, or devil or none of those names. You're my woman. You understand that? If she has to call names and identify whites by certain names that's her business. But you and I know it's not you she's talking about. You're the most humane person in the world.

WHITE WOMAN: Ah, man. Say you love me.

BROTHER: I love you.

WHITE WOMAN: Say you're all mine.

BROTHER: I'm all yours, all yours.

WHITE WOMAN: And you'll need me always.

BROTHER: I'll need you always.

WHITE WOMAN: (*Stretches back out and puts her head in his lap*) Stay the night with me, man.

BROTHER: I can't. I promised . . .

WHITE WOMAN: Say you'll stay the night with me until I go to sleep. Please. It's your last night. If you stay I'll be able to get myself straight. Please.

BROTHER: All right, baby. Let me call home. O.K.? (WHITE WOMAN *gets up. Slowly. And moves behind the screen.* BROTHER *goes to the phone and dials and the phone rings at the same time the* BLACK WOMAN *enters her apartment.* SHE *picks up the phone*) Hey. You just get in? How was the reading?

SISTER: Oh, fine. Mannn. Where are you?

BROTHER: I got a call from one of the organizers of the trip. Something came up, I can't talk about it on the phone. Look. I should be home soon. Would you start packing my clothes for me? I'll be there soon.

SISTER: But—but—but—why?

BROTHER: Now, no questions. Just do as you're told. And we'll talk when I get there. Later. (*Hangs up the phone*)

(SISTER *stands with the phone in her hand. Finally hangs it up. Moves and takes three suitcases out and opens them and methodically begins to pack each one of them. Slowly. Crooning a low mournful song. Maybe "Sometimes I Feel Like a Motherless Child."* BROTHER *is fixing himself a drink when* WHITE WOMAN *comes from behind the screen.* SHE *has on a natural wig and a long dress*)

WHITE WOMAN: Well, how do I look?

BROTHER: Fine. Just fine, lady. You lookin' good.

WHITE WOMAN: I wanted to surprise you. Do I have that natural look she's always talking about?

BROTHER: Yes, you do.

WHITE WOMAN: Come here, my man. (BROTHER *moves to her and kisses her*) Who do you love?

BROTHER: You, lady.

WHITE WOMAN: And who am I?

BROTHER: My woman.

WHITE WOMAN: And thou should have no other woman besides me. For I am all that you need. I can be all that you want. (*Spins away from him*) I can be natural when you need naturalness. (*Takes off wig*) Or I can be me when you want me. I am all things for you. (*Moves back to him excitedly*) I know, let's get married. Right here, tonight. Let us marry one another to each other.

BROTHER: Aw, lady, I don't know, that sounds, well, I don't know.

WHITE WOMAN: What's wrong with vowing to each other to love eternally? You didn't mean what you said, evidently.

BROTHER: No. It just seems unnecessary. But if you want to, why not?

WHITE WOMAN: Good. You go over to that side and I'll walk from this side. We'll kneel together and say our vows.

BROTHER: What should I say?

WHITE WOMAN: Just say what I say. All right? (BOTH *move to a separate part of the room and walk toward each other. Meet. And kneel, facing the audience*) We have come to declare our love. This white woman and Black man. We have come to speak out loud our love so that the night will hear us and know. (*Turns to* BROTHER) I love you, Black man.

BROTHER: (*Turns to* WHITE WOMAN) I love you, White woman.

WHITE WOMAN: And the words are spoken. And what can take back the words which represent the feelings, time and place and the words will travel throughout the land and make this universe stop and listen because I have said I love you Black man and his reply was love. The words have been spoken. And we are. Now. We have spoken in the night but the morning light will know. For the night and the morning are one. As we are one and our love shall be eternal.

BROTHER: And our love shall be eternal.

WHITE WOMAN: For you are the light. The energy. The sun. And I re-

182

ceive your light and live. And grow stronger each day. For you are my light, otherwise I shall dwell in darkness. And together we are the universe. Light and darkness, strength and weakness. One and two. (*Turns to* BROTHER) Say we are one.

BROTHER: We are one.

WHITE WOMAN: You are the light and I am your darkness.

BROTHER: I am yo/light and you are my darkness.

WHITE WOMAN: We need each other to be.

BROTHER: We would be lost without each other.

WHITE WOMAN: And the universe has joined us together, and the universe will curse those who try to deny us, the universe will pour out her anger on those who would separate the darkness from the sun for naturalness is the order of the day. (*Takes from her pocket two onyxes. Hands one to* BROTHER, *puts one around his neck*) I bring you eternal darkness.

BROTHER: I bring you eternal light.

BROTHER/WHITE WOMAN: We are one. As the morning and night are one. As life and death are one. We are one. (THEY *stand as* THEY *say the above*)

WHITE WOMAN: (*Almost hysterically*) All those who move to destroy this will be damned. Shall be damned. You are warned. My focus will destroy you. (*Laughs a rasping laugh*) Now, my husband of one minute. Let us rest for a while. We need to rest. It's been a long night, hasn't it, my man.

BROTHER: Yes, My wife of one and a half minutes. Let us rest for I gots to split and pack for the trip today. C'mon, lady, let's rest for a while. (BROTHER *and* WHITE WOMAN *stretch out,* SHE *on top of him, and light fades.*

The SISTER *is sitting on the stool. Three bags are packed.* SHE *waits. The* BROTHER *enters the room hurriedly.* HE *looks somewhat tired. Disheveled. Obviously worried*)

SISTER: Who is she? I just want to know who she is.

BROTHER: What are you talkin' 'bout?

SISTER: (*Rises*) Who is she, mannn? Just tell me who she is. What she is. What she is that she can get you to stay out till 6 A.M. in the morning. Who is she, mannnnn?

BROTHER: I don't know what you're talking about.

SISTER: I'ma talking about you, mannn. I'ma talking about you leaving me here alone on our last night together. I'ma talking about you not coming to the poetry reading, I'ma talking about me anxious to get home rushing up the stairs to you. To the silence of a room, to a telephone call that told me nothing, I'ma talking about lies and more lies, I'ma talking about us, mannn. (*Moves up to his face*) Who is she, man? Is she prettier than me? Is she blacker than me? Is the taller than me?

Does she make love better to you than me? I just want to know who she is.

BROTHER: (*Coolly*) You're hysterical. Why don't you calm down. Just shut up and calm down. I told you where I was. I was taking care of some business.

SISTER: (*Moving away with back to audience*) With whom?

BROTHER: With someone who is organizing the trip.

SISTER: What's her name?

BROTHER: It's a he.

SISTER: What's his name?

BROTHER: What his name? Girl, what's yo/problem. I told you from the git go that when I'm on business it's private. When I'm on business in the movement it's very private. And don't be asking me. I'll tell you what I want you to know. No mo, now stop this nonsense and help me pack. I'm gon' be late for my plane. (SISTER *turns and runs over to him and hits him—the slap is loud and there is a momentary silence.* [BROTHER] *backs away*) Don't do that again, you hear me? What you tryin' to start. You want me to beat you up so you can show everybody what a no/good/nigger I am? Is that what you want? Lookie here, baby. (*Moves to her*) Lookie here, girl, I had to leave. It was urgent business. I don't like telling you everything cuz it could be dangerous for you and . . .

SISTER: You're lying. I know it. I feel it inside that you're lying. You got another woman. I know it. Tell me who she is, man? Is she younger than me? Is her stomach flatter than mine? (*Turning around*) What's wrong with me now? You don't like my getting big with the baby? Is that it? Why mannnnn, why another woman, when you told me I was all that you needed. That yo/life was complete now that you had a Black woman. Were they all lies too? Just a six-month year-old lie. Not even a year-old lie. Just a six/month/year-old lie. Well. That's it. I'm leaving. My bags are packed. I'm going back home.

BROTHER: Just like that. (*Has moved over and poured himself a drink*) You just gonna pack up and leave. Go back to mommy and daddy so they can say/remind you every day with I told you so, I told you he was a no/good/nigger. I told you he meant you no good, him with that Big Castro beard. I told you so. I told you so. And I thought you were a mature Black woman. Ready for the unknown. Ready for the fight, ready to run at the first sign of trouble. You gon' go home cuz you can't figure it all out. You don't have all the right answers.

SISTER: (*Hesitates slightly*) But this isn't the first time you've done this. This is just the first time it's been so blatant. I've gotten so many phone calls from you explaining why you couldn't come this way that I began to think you and that telephone were one. I am a Black woman, but that don't mean I should be a fool. To you being a Black woman means I should take all the crap you can think of and any extra crap just hanging loose. That ain't right, man, and you know it too.

BROTHER: Well. Let's stop this now. You unpack yo/clothes. I need one of the suitcases for my trip.

SISTER: I'm going, I'm leaving you.

BROTHER: You ain't going no place.

SISTER: I'm going back to New York.

BROTHER: *(Moves to suitcases and opens them, begins to throw her clothes out of cases)* You ain't going nowhere now. You are officially unpacked. So just sit down and keep quiet since you acting like such a fool. (SHE *stands up and* HE *pushes her back down on the stool)* Stay seated and keep quiet. I got too much on my mind to listen to this foolishness.

SISTER: That's the way my life is now. Scattered just like those clothes on the floor. And I'm pregnant too. What a trick bag I'm in. It's funny, you know. Don't you think it's funny, mannnn? And we ain't even legally married.

BROTHER: You sound like one of those TV/soap operas. *(Sings a Hearts and Flowers song)* "Tune in tomorrow and see how our dear sister turns out. When last we left her her life was scattered out on the floor like leftover stale potato chips, pregnant, alone, unmarried, standing with her face to the sun. What more could happen to our courageous hero-ine? Tune in tomorrow and find out." SHEEEEET. Everytime one of you bourgie bloods decide to become Black you act like people owe you something. Well, I've been Black ALL my life. Done struggled all my life in Louisville. My mother and all her different men. All my brothers and sisters with different daddies. Girl, you don't know what hard times is all about. Just because you decided to wade into Blackness and you found the water steaming not from the sweat of yo/brothers and sisters, you gon' turn around and go back to N.Y.C. you bourgie/Black/bitch. Who do you think you are? Just because you're well known you think you an exception. You get what all the other Black/women of yo/time gon' git. Stand up. (SISTER *doesn't move*, SHE'S *thinking quietly.* HE *moves over and pulls her up)* I said stand up. Who do you think you are? Just because they applaud you for some words, some poems, you say, you still gon' git what every Blk/wom-an's getting, you ain't no different from them at all. This is 1967. Don't you forget that. Let me help you remember who you are. *(Slaps the right side of her face)* You a Black woman bitch. *(Slaps the left side of her face)* You the same as every Black woman. *(Slaps the right side of her face)* You were born to cry in the night. *(Slaps the left side of her face)* You ain't no different from any Black woman. *(Slaps the right side of her face)* You're my mother, and my mother's mother every Blk/man's mother I've ever seen. *(Slaps the left side of her face)* You like all Blk/

women, ain't no difference. (*Then he kisses her. Long and hard*) Now. Pack my bag like I told you to. I got just a few minutes to make the plane. (SISTER *picks up one bag and begins to pack the bag in silence*) Anything special you want from Mexico.

SISTER: Nothing.

BROTHER: Well. I'll choose you something nice. Hey. Maybe if Johnny and I save on some of our expenses, maybe by Friday we could send for you. How about a weekend in Mexico with yo/old/man? How would you like that?

SISTER: Yes. I'd like to be someplace with MY old man.

BROTHER: I'll see if I can work it out. Maybe with a few calls here and there I can work it out. (*Fingers the onyx as* HE *talks*) Yes. Maybe it can be done.

SISTER: You know, I didn't think too much about it night before last. But I had this dream. It seems that we went to the hospital together. It was time for the baby and I had two babies, one white and one Black. I kept saying the white one wasn't mine. The hospital nurses and doctors kept smiling. No, it's yours. They said in fact we almost missed it. Thought it was the after/birth until we looked and saw this baby. It's yours. I screamed, but it's deformed. It's deformed. It's ugly. I don't want it. And their grinning faces grew bigger and bigger as they said two for one. We've got two babies for you. You can't have one without the other. That's the way it goes in this hospital. Take the two babies or none at all. I remember they were laughing as they left my room. (*Hands suitcase to the* BROTHER *and stands up*)

BROTHER: It's just a dream. Nothing to it. Some dreams are just weird. That's all. But sometimes, baby, you try to live too Blackly. Like giving up yo/wine and not smoking and no more pork. Girl, it don't matter what we eat as long as we do it to this man. As long as we upset his system it don't matter what we eat.

SISTER: But we are what we eat, mannnnn. And drinking is slow death. And smoking. No mo cigarettes. No mo weed for me. It's all wrong. How can we change things doing it the same way he's doing it. How can we be different being like him. Look. When some of us in New York first got our naturals people said they weren't important—that they didn't make no difference. But they have made a difference, you know. We've made people change their minds about the beauty of their hair.

BROTHER: Aw right. I know. I know. Another time we'll argue this out. It's time for this ole dude to make it on outa here. I'll call you tonight from the hotel. Okay? And stop looking so lost. So sad. I still love you in spite of your foolishness. I forgive you. C'mon and give me a kiss.

SISTER: (*Moves toward the* BROTHER *and kisses him*) Goodbye, mannnnnnnn.

BROTHER: Maybe I'll see you on Friday night. (*Exits*)

SISTER: (*Stands for a while and stares. Then turns around and begins to pick up her clothes. She puts them in the two bags. Then she moves/walks around the room, stopping first one place then another*) There must be a place for me somewhere. Let me continue walking. Ah. Here's a corner for me. (*Gets on her knees, begins to pray hesitantly*) Oh Lord, Help me, this poor Blk/woman/sinner sitting here. Help me out of this misery. I know I have done wrong and all, but help me, dear Lord, help me, yo/poor servant here in the wilderness of California, help me . . . (*Begins to laugh*) Help me to . . . (*Bursts out laughing*) Girl, ain't no Lord gon' help you, at least not one that we've been taught to pray to, git off your knees. You look like some fool asking for help from one who ain't never helped Black people do anything 'cept stay on their knees. But you do need some kind of help. You made a mistake and you don't know what to do about it. What about yo/child? What about yo/child rushing out of the darkness of yo/womb into light. You've got to give him light. No madness. But light. What you gon' do, Black girl? (SISTER *goes over and picks up the two bags and starts out. Sits down and begins to unpack. Slowly*) How can I go home with this big stomach? How can I? I'll forget it, that's what I'll do. I'll forget it happened and wait for him to change. He'll get over whatever she is. He'll change. He'll stop drinking. And smoking. He'll understand why a Black man must be faithful to his woman, so she'll stop the madness of our mothers repeating itself out loud. He just needs time. I just got to rock myself in Blackness, insulate my soul with righteousness and that will sustain us both. Gots to. Yeah. (*Begins to rock bath and forth*) Gots to rock myself in Blackness. In sweet, sweet Blackness, cuz I am the new Black woman. I will help the change to come. Just gots to rock myself in Blackness in the knowledge of womanly Blackness and I shall be. (*Begins to sing a tune as* SHE *continues to rock*)

I'm a Black woman,
gon' get Blacker than the nite
become one with my man
I'm a Black woman
mother of the sun,
Gon' become one with my man
and get Blacker.

Yeah. Yeah. (*Continues to rock*)

Gots to rock myself in Blackness
Gots to rock myself in Blackness
Gots to rock myself in Blackness

(*Lights fades to* DANCERS. MALE DANCER *turns and faces the audience. The two* FEMALE DANCERS, *one with black mask on, the other with white mask, sit in back—one to the right and one to the left.* MALE DANCER *stands. Walks around and drinks a drink. Turns and looks at* BOTH *of them, tosses a coin to see which one* HE'LL *visit.* HE *walks a hip/walk to the* FEMALE DANCER *wearing the black mask, holds out his hand. Kisses her and leaves hiply. Goes to* FEMALE DANCER *with the white mask on and* THEY *circle each other.* THEY'RE *apparently equals.* THEY *dance.* HE *leads. Then* SHE *leads.* HE *leads then* SHE *leads.* HE *leads then* SHE *leads.* HE *finally gives up and* SHE *heads the dance. The* MALE DANCER *returns to the* FEMALE DANCER *with black mask and her stomach is now big, and as* THEY *dance* THEY *can't touch till finally* THEY'RE *dancing without touching each other.* HE *returns to the* FEMALE DANCER *with the white mask.* HE *finds her stretched out lifeless on the floor.* HE *tries to wake her up—*HE *drags her back and forth trying to wake her up. When* HE *fails* HE *sits and waits, and waits.* SHE *turns.* SHE *twists her body snakelike and slides up to him and curls herself round him.* HE *is hypnotized and* HE *begins to follow her snakelike on the floor, moving in and out finally touching.* THEY *stick out their tongues and kiss and the* FEMALE DANCER *with white mask becomes lifeless again. The* MALE DANCER'S *body becomes like the sun warming her till* SHE *begins to stir again and* THEY *dance a sensuous dance. When the* MALE DANCER *returns to the* FEMALE DANCER *with black mask on* HE *is shaking. Chilled, tired to the bone.* SHE *greets him discordantly. Moving around, dissatisfied. And* HE *is so tired that* HE *begins to shake. The slow movement from the feet to his shoulders and* HE *knocks her down as* HE *spins with each quiver of his body.* HE *picks up his bag and moves slowly out, body twitching from the cold that* HE *feels. The* FEMALE DANCER *with black mask on rolls across the floor, trying to find a comforting place. Gets on her knees and prays. First one place then another until* SHE *can clasp her hands not longer. And* SHE *laughs. Her body laughs and* SHE *becomes still. Finally* SHE *rises and straightens out her black mask. Her long dress, her natural. And* SHE *begins to march at first in a tired manner, but as* SHE *passes,* SHE *becomes upright in her Blackness and* SHE *smiles, slightly. Stage darkens. There is no beginning or end*)

• • • • •

"To Be a Man"

Ann Allen Shockley

"To Be a Man" (*Negro Digest* [July 1969]) is another strong articulation by Ann Allen Shockley of the black woman's role as a sexual scapegoat in the racial war between black and white men. When I asked Shockley why she wrote this story, she said simply, "there is more to being a man than being a stud," and, " 'To Be a Man' still stands the test of time."[1]

Claude, a black male activist, is harassed and beaten in a bar by a racist white policeman who is looking for a mugger. Claude goes home bloodied and defeated. Later, when his wife gets home and asks him what has happened, he does not tell her; they had fought earlier, and he defensively steels himself against her. Feeling stripped of his manhood by the white policeman and desperately wanting it back, wanting revenge, Claude tries to accomplish both by "being a man" to his wife. "He could make babies like the white man," he thinks. "He could and *should* make hundreds of babies to create an army to fight the white man. . . . He *could*. He was a man. *Wasn't he?*" Claude cannot regain his manhood by raping his wife, as she tells him. But his act fits a pattern of abuse that has a long history: men taking out the abuses and failures they have suffered on women.

NOTE

1. Ann Allen Shockley, letter to the author, 13 January 1991.

Anita followed her movements in the bureau mirror as she deftly applied pink lipstick to the full Cupid's bow of her mouth. Then pausing, she gazed critically back at her reflection. The off-shoulder black cocktail dress fitted snugly over her round curved hips, while the white pearl necklace and earrings set off the creamy tan of her skin. She decided that she looked very chic and smart.

"I'm sorry you won't go with me, Claude," she said, turning now to the man seated at a make-shift card table desk in the corner of the bedroom.

"I got more important things to do," he grumbled sullenly, bent over the mound of papers.

A frown wrinkled tiny delicate lines between her wide-spaced eyes as she stared long at him. Sometimes—like now—he looked so forbidding to her with all that fierce black hair worn stiff and high and long. Bushy hair growing down his dark brown face into sideburns which ended in an entangled brush of beard. With all that hair covering his face and arching above the thick full lips, he looked like a Black Samson. A Black Samson who needed hair to give him his man-strength.

She sighed, reaching to struggle her fingers one by one into the white linen gloves. "You never go anyplace with me anymore." Not since he had gotten so wrapped up in the Movement. The Movement—almost an obsession with him now.

He lit a cigarette from the crumpled pack of Larks on the table, flicking the match into the already overflowing ash tray. "I got better things to do. Right now, the Movement—"

"The *Movement!*" she almost shouted at him. "That's all you *think* about. Hell! I believe in the Movement too, but Christ, I can't *live* the Movement. I'm also an *individualist*. A *person*. Not just a *Negro* person. I can't eat, sleep, and go to the toilet with Civil Rights and hating the white man with each breath I take. I can't *submerge* the fact that I *also* like to have *fun* once in a while. I like to enjoy a good book not soused with racism, listen to pretty music, walk in the park and admire the natural green of the grass and blue of the sky. I like to look up at the strength of the trees growing high, and I like to look down and gaze into the coolness of a spring brook. I like to *see* and *do* those things as a *person* without their being marred all the time by hating and thinking about the white man!"

She stopped, feeling out of breath like the words had drained her. Slowly she went over to him, caressing his hard broad back outlined in the colorful summer African shirt with geometric patterns of spears and masks surrounding a lion. "Can't you relax—sometimes?" It was a plea.

He tensed beneath her touch, not turning to her, not looking. "Hell no! That's the trouble now—we been relaxing too long. Your daddy and my daddy—relax—ing. Uncle Toming all those years. Letting things get tougher and tougher."

"Claude, that's not true. You know how our parents—"

"Yeah, I *know*. By buying lifetime memberships in the NAACP! *You* go on to that cocktail party with all those mealy-mouth white liberals who're going to do this-and-that for the brother until they get out in the air and back to the suburbs!"

"I *work* with those people. I can't refuse their invitations *all* the time. Besides, in my line of work, it gives me an opportunity to meet others and make significant contacts."

"Significant contacts," he sneered. "Excuses—excuses—excuses. *You* just want to be *with* them, and *act* like them, and wish you were *like* them. You can't forget your little black *bourgeois* upbringing about how great it is being *in* with white people. Like a status symbol—''

She stepped back as if struck. ''You had the same so-called black *bourgeois* background as I.''

''Yeah, baby, but I got *out*. That second year in that middle-class snooty college, I got out and joined the Movement. I left my doctor daddy and my social sprinting mother be-e-e-hind!''

''There *are* times when I think you're jealous because at least I *did* finish—''

His hands tightened on the chair, the knuckles showing like taut knobs through his skin. She knew the lance had pierced. Always between them now were angry, hate-filled words making them no longer one, but two, divided into sharp, brittle separate pieces blown by different winds and guided by different stars.

''Go on where you going,'' he muttered thickly. ''I got work to do.''

''Work—'' she repeated bitterly, watching him shut himself away from her over the desk. Her eyes swept the papers before him, the array of pencils, and the old-fashioned battered typewriter. ''What *kind* of work? *I* work. *I* keep us going. And I work because my black skin *still* doesn't deter me from liking good scotch, good steaks, living in a decent neighborhood, and seeing a good play. And it's *my* work that's doing it.'' She watched him puff heavily on the cigarette, knowing she had wounded this time—struck where the sore was like a cancer eating him.

Finally he laughed shortly. ''*Some* work! The only nigger in a Government Job Placement Center. A showpiece to prove nobody's prejudice. A nigger behind a desk who's pretty and looks white with a forever Florida suntan. Big deal! *Me*—I'm out in the street working *with* the brothers. Out there where the nitty gritty is fighting Mister Charlie. *I'm* going to make whitey realize I'm a *man*. I want to be treated as a man. And baby, I *am* going to be treated like a man!''

''Takes a lot to make a man,'' she scoffed, slamming the door hard behind her.

The door's slam was like a slap. A burning sting pierced the tips of his forefinger and thumb. The cigarette had burned down to a pinpoint heat. He dropped it in the burial ground of others. A sharp recurring pain streaked across his forehead, blurring his vision and the words on the paper. She had caused him to lose his thought. Just when his pencil had moved and written a wonderful spring of free flowing words. He was certain this one was *the* one—the essay that the Atlantic Monthly or New Yorker would publish. He was sure because he *knew* it was good. It was just as good as any of Baldwin's or Jones' or Cleaver's. Wasn't he socking it to whitey? Spilling out his seething hatred and venom and

frustrations? Making whitey feel guilt. Making whitey want to feel punished by the hot word lava flung at him by a black writer. Now was the
time for the black writer to emerge because whitey was a masochist who
wanted to be verbally whipped by the black man for his guilt. Whitey
wanted the Negro to tell him like it is. Tell him that he wasn't shit, never
was shit, and never would *be* shit! But the black man *was* some shit!
And even if blood had to flow, the black man would *prove* he was some
good shit!

He stared down at the papers and rejection slip that had come in
the morning's mail—the telltale slip he had tried to hide from her. The
stock words swam before him: "Thank you for your submittal which
we are returning to you. Please don't consider this a reflection on the
quality of your work . . ."

He crumpled up the letter. Damn them! Whitey wouldn't even *give*
him a chance to tell it like it is. He got up stiffly, noticing the soft summer evening rapidly fading into night. A mauve twilight streaked pink
and lilac ridges across the blue sky.

What he needed was a drink. He went to the kitchen where a bottle
of Cutty Sark was on the sink. He got a glass from the cabinet and half
filled it with the clear brown liquid. Raising the glass to his lips, he
savored the rich expensive odor of the scotch. Then suddenly, in revenge, he flung the glass across the room. It made a dull thud against
the wall before crashing into pieces on the floor. The ache in his head
flared anew. He closed his eyes, thinking he had to get out—away from
here—if only for a while.

He had to walk a block down the neat well-kept residential street
with rows of modern one-story box houses and green carpets of mani-
cured lawns before he could board the bus. He felt the eyes upon him
as he took a seat midway by the window. The people on the bus stared
furtively at him because they were used to seeing clean-shaven Negro
men in well-pressed suits, dress shirts, and carefully matching ties in
this neighborhood. This amused him, so he always played a game with
the passengers.

First he would glare at the white women: gazing boldly to frighten
them through his boring eyes with all those stories about the black
man's sex powers. Some of the women would look away nervously,
averting the black-eyed spotlight beaming upon them, while others
would squirm uneasily on their seats, as if what his gaze was divulging
made them want to masturbate.

Then tiring of this, he would turn his fierce threatening look to the
pale-faced, washed-out, cleanly scrubbed dickless white men, and
watch them wither as they wondered if he were there to start a riot or

rob them or rape their women. It was a tough, hard, funny, well-played game that he enjoyed very much.

But tonight, he didn't feel like playing. Instead of staring at them, he simply ignored them by looking out the window and down at the cars appearing like miniature bugs darting in and out of the traffic. Soon the white people began to empty the bus, and after a while, he was left alone to travel into the belly of the ghetto where the seats would then be taken by others like himself.

He felt a surge of exhilaration when the first sister got on: a large, black perspiring woman grunting up the steps, flopping down tiredly on the seat in front of him. Her hair was short and shot straight up as beads of sweat sprinkled the bare crinkled kitchen of her neck. He smelled her sweat, felt her tiredness, wallowed in her big, black brassiness, and felt suddenly hilariously drunk.

"You won't be tired long. We black men are going to take up for you," he thought he had said to himself. But when the woman turned, stared at him, and back, he wondered if he had said it aloud.

The ghetto noises began to drift in and rock with the rhythm of the bus. Flashing neon signs shattered kaleidoscopic shock waves of pawn shops, bars, furniture outlets, and all-night grocery stores. Soul music spilled from the sleazy bars and shabby, mountainous hollow-eyed-tenements into the streets, bouncing off the hot pavements with its loud soaring beat. Home. He wished Anita would move here where his work was, his heart lay, and where his pain could be borne with a little more ease. But no, *she* wanted to stay where they were because it was closer to her work and she liked it there.

The streets were taking on the evening's life. Men lounged on the corners cracking jokes and making passes at the pliant flashing swell of brown, yellow, black feminine pulchritude floating by in gales of teasing laughter. He breathed deeply, soaking in the fetid air and the sounds and sights. He liked it *here*.

He got off the bus and walked back to the Movement's office. A few people who knew him waved. He waved back, bracing his shoulders in a swagger, making the lion on his shirt stretch as he smiled broadly at them. The office was locked. He stood at the door for a moment, then decided to go to Tubby's Black Bar across the street.

The place was deserted except for two men in dingy T-shirts and faded pants at the bar drinking beer. An old man half-slept in a corner by the juke-box blaring James Brown's wailing blues shout. The man's muddy face sank heavily in deep valley folds. He was dressed in overalls that fell over and hid his shoes. From time to time, he would awaken, sip from a glass of beer gone flat, and nod again.

"Hi, Claude—" the shiny, dark, bald-headed man behind the bar greeted him.

"Hey, Tubby. Whiskey." He perched on the bar stool, glancing around at the shabby booths and worn wooden floor which had held and showed the weight and scuffle of many souls long gone. Friday and Saturday, there was hardly room to get in. The whiskey was set before him. It was cheap and raw and burned like a blaze going down his throat. But it warmed him and he began to feel mellow inside. He reached in his pocket and pulled out a crumpled $10 bill, the week's pay from the Movement. "Slow night," he commented, picking up the change.

"Yeah. Too hot to stir. Anyway, I got no air conditioner." Tubby's head jerked back to a lone fan in the window whirling a bee sound to make a faint breeze.

Suddenly a police siren screamed outside, reaching high above the wailing of James Brown. The two men further down the bar turned quickly, trying to peer out the dirt-streaked plate glass window. A quick visible chill of fear iced their eyes. The loud whine ceased, but from the proximity of it's subsidence, they could tell it had stopped somewhere near.

Claude kept his eyes on the glass. He had to drink slowly to make the liquor and the money and companionship last. James Brown's bellow ended in a crying moan, leaving the room silent and each man's thoughts naked to the other.

"Trouble—" Tubby said, frowning. "Too hot a night for trouble."

The police car's siren squealed again and faded away. The old man's eyes opened as if on signal, and he reached for the beer glass that was encircled with skimmed foam.

"Well!" Tubby smiled, relief flooding his face. "Gone. Pro'bly nothing much. Next round on the house, brothers."

Then the police's warning song shrilled again, coming closer and louder like a screaming angry hyena. The scream stopped in front of the bar. The door swung back and two uniform policemen entered.

"Everybody up and over against the wall," the big, stout one ordered, standing spraddle-legged with gun drawn in the middle of the room. "Search 'em, Ed," he said to the tall, thin young one who looked and acted like a rookie.

The two men at the bar, resembling well-trained robots, moved simultaneously to stand against the pock-marked wall scribbled with countless names and addresses and epithets. The old man half stood obediently in his corner, then through no volition of his own, swayed back down in his chair, too drunk to stand.

"You too, Pops," the big officer snapped, pushing the bill of his cap back to unmask small narrow eyes. Then, moving uncannily fast across the room, he jerked the old man to his feet and shoved his dead weight against the wall. The man bent his will to blend into the scars of the wall's legacy of past histories.

"What's wrong, officer?" Tubby asked quickly. "I ain't had no trouble in here—"

"But *we've* had trouble. White man was mugged down the street. We're looking for the nigger who done it." It was then his eyes discovered Claude still sitting firmly on the bar stool. Their eyes met: the white man's cold grey steel of a winter's sky, and the angry, black man's storm of inbred hate. "Goddamnit! You get over there to that wall like the rest."

Claude steeled himself against the bar, planting his feet solidly on the rungs of the stool. Who the hell did they think they were bursting in here like this. They had no right. That white man who got mugged had no right—being here in *their* world. Words came out, revealing his thoughts.

"What was that white man doing down here anyway? Looking for black pussy?"

The policeman's mouth opened in surprise, his thin lips folding like a tent against the flabbiness of his face. For a stilled deathlike moment, he was too shocked to say anything. Then giving an angry bellow, his meaty hands seized Claude by his shirt, ripping the African symbols and tearing the lion into shreds. Furiously he slammed him against the wall.

The hardness struck his head, stunning him for a moment. He knew he had fallen because he felt the floor and grit under the palms of his hands. Dazed, he saw the big black shoes of the policeman shift, and before he could roll out of the way, felt the hard weight of the lawman's foot plunging into his side. Pain gripped him as his body was left as breathless as a deflated balloon.

"Black bastard! I believe *you* the one done it. Get the Goddam hell up. *Get up!*"

He got up slowly, the hurt bursting through him. The room swirled in a circular motion, reminding him of the ferris wheel he rode on when he was a boy that went around and around, and when he closed his eyes, he could yet feel the revolving sensation in the blackness. He felt numbed and on another planet where there was nothing and even the nothing would not keep still. The cheap rotgut whiskey rose to his throat. He wanted to vomit. But he swallowed and swallowed the bile to keep it down. He couldn't do *that*. Not before *him*.

"Don't this one look like the one he described, Ed?"

"Naw, Bull," the young cop replied, shaking his head, eyes nervously skirting Claude. "He said the guy was little and yellow with—"

"*He* looks like him to *me*," Bull growled, spittle making bubbles at the corners of his mouth. His tone became wheedling. "Now don't he to *you?*"

The young one looked down and away as if studying the thought, but said nothing. The men against the wall stood motionless like a shadow of silent ghosts.

Claude guardedly watched the cop called Bull, thinking if that white son-of-a-bitch hit him again, he'd kill him. So help him, he'd kill that white motherfucker!

"I'm goin' to take *this* nigger in—" Bull said, pointing to Claude. "Com'on. Let's go—"

Claude worked his lips. They felt cracked and he could taste the salt of blood around them. The movement of his mouth to speak hurt, but the words came out strong, not betraying the inward pain. "How you going to take *me* in? He just said I didn't fit—"

"Shut up, nigger! I can take you in for anything I Goddam got a mind to. We ought to take all you black coons in and kill ever' last one of you. Pow! Pow! Like *that!*" He waved his pistol menacingly, shoving it into Claude's face.

Suddenly, upon seeing the beefy face and the wild grey eyes so near, the old familiar ache crossed his forehead as a rushing tide of black ancient fires of loathing seared through him. His black fist clenched, doubled hard and drew back. The white target wavered like a leering pendulum before him. It seemed like a time without beginning or end, but it was only a second before his right fist raised, ladened with the weight of his rage. Suddenly there was a weakness in his arm like a pressure was holding it back, subconsciously restraining it, making his arm not a part of him but a separate entity. The fist shot out, lightly grazing the fleshy white chin.

"Goddam black bastard!" the policeman roared.

He saw the cop's gun handle raise in the air and pause for a blinding moment before he closed his eyes and waited to go down in darkness.

He awakened in the back room of Tubby's on a hard dirty cot. A cold towel was over his forehead, and he felt the bandage behind his ear. The pallid yellow naked bulb shone above him, making him aware that he had entered the now.

"You goin' to be all right, man," Tubby said soothingly, standing above him, face anxious. "That other cop grabbed his arm just in time to keep him from *really* knockin' your brains out."

"They didn't take me in—"

"Naw. They too scared, I guess. The skinny one said sumpin' 'bout the chief wanting 'em to lay off crackin' niggers' heads for a while. Guess they scared we might start a riot—" He laughed a dim sound.

"Can you make it home by yourself? I'll call a cab—" Gently he removed the towel.

"I can make it." He shifted his legs over the side of the bed, and with effort, stood up groggily. "I'm O.K.—" Aside from a pain in his head and the blood caking his lips, making them heavy and swollen. "Only thing—only thing, I sure wished I had knocked the Goddam pure white shit out of that motherfucker—" But he hadn't. He hadn't, or was it that he *couldn't* . . .

A chilling helplessness invaded him, blown by the winds of past ancient black futility. He suddenly wanted to go home.

At home he didn't bother to wash. He simply stepped out of his tattered clothes and got between the clean white sheets in his shorts.

It was early but seemed late to him. It was early when she came home, yet seemed late to him. He closed his eyes when he heard her key, pretending to be asleep. His ears followed her movements from the living room to the bathroom where he heard the running water, the flushing of the toilet, then her foot sounds in the soft mules coming into the room. The bed dipped slightly as she slid in beside him. He could smell the peppermint toothpaste and the Avon cream she applied to her face at night, as well as the faint odor of her perfume still clinging to her. He wondered why it hadn't taken her as long as usual to go through her nightly rituals. Without opening his eyes, he knew it was because she hadn't put her curlers on—she hadn't planted the garden rows of wires to make her hair bloom round soft ringlets in the morning.

He heard her turn over on her side and sigh. Soon she would be asleep. Listening to her steady breathing, he thought: she hadn't spoken to him or even tried to awaken him and talk with him. She hadn't noticed the bloody bandage behind his ear or the cakey brown crust on his mouth. It was as though he wasn't there—wasn't there like the white policeman had acted—like he was nothing, a nameless phantom to be pushed and cursed and ignored. He was nothing at all. Absolutely *nothing.*

Suddenly he opened his eyes to shout at her as the white policeman had at him. *Make* her notice him—see him—realize he was *there.*

The darkness met his eyes first. Upon seeing it, he felt inept, frustrated in the mire of his thoughts. Somehow he knew she hadn't even bothered to turn *on* the light in the room at all. Simply undressed in the bathroom and followed her instinct around the darkened bedroom to the bed. She hadn't *wanted* to see him.

"Anita!" he shouted, sitting up angrily. "*Anita!*"

She stirred, moving a little. "What is it, Claude?" The words were even estranged from him, coming sleepy and muffled in her pillow.

197

He swallowed hard. What *was* it? What *did* he want? To tell her about the evening—his failure. A failure because of a yet alive age-old fear of the white man still ghosting his black mind and making him ineffectual. Was that what had caused his abortive effort to strike back the way he really wanted to? Hard, strong, like a man—not a feeble man.

"How were the nice white people?" he finally asked, the question meaningless to him, but it was an attempt, a start. For wasn't *she* there eating and drinking and laughing with *them*, while others of *them* were beating *him* up?

"Oh, God, Claude. Not tonight—again. I'm sleepy."

He moved closer to where she was lying with her back to him. A perverse anger made him want to continue: "Did you sneak out in the car with any of those faggot blonde boys who're always trying to get you in bed behind my back?"

She did not answer, her back and her silence a barrier to him.

"They almost killed a white son-of-a-bitch downtown tonight for that thing—after black women."

"Is that so—?"

"And the police thought *I* was the one who did it!" Now! Hear that? He thought gleefully. The police thought someone like *him* could do that—was capable of defending his black women.

"Well—did you?"

Had he detected a note of sarcasm in her words? The derision dripped over him like smoldering hot honey. Was it her cool contempt that made him feel she knew him too well?

"I *could* have—"

"Hum-m-m. With your black power, I suppose."

"Damnit, Anita. LOOK AT ME!" The words spewed out a belch of fire before he realized she couldn't look at him because of the darkness. Even if she did look, there would only be the dark outline of him that was a man.

"All right, Claude," she murmured in exasperation, turning towards him. "So a white man was half killed—"

"And I was involved. The police beat me up in a bar—" The words were hesitant—the story not coherent. Puzzle pieces which he couldn't put together for her. Snatches of thoughts and actions left hanging in the air.

"So? What's so new about that? The white man's been beating nigger heads since slave time and will *still* do it whenever they can get a chance. It just happened that you were there at that time in that particular situation." Suddenly her voice softened: "Claude, I'm sorry. Are you hurt bad?"

She reached for the light on the bedstand, but he stopped her. He didn't want the light. The light and its harshness would destroy the mood and the moment and turn his feelings inside out. The sudden concern of her began to anger him. But wasn't that what he had wanted? Her sympathy, kindness—the protective shelter of his black woman, as all black men had wanted and gotten at some time?

"What's there to be sorry about?" he snapped defensively. "We're all going to get bloody fighting the system. In the Movement, we *expect* those things—*welcome* them. Roll with the punches and give out some too. You dig me, baby?"

"Un-huh," she yawned, shifting back to her side of the bed.

To him, the disdain was there in the mocking aloofness. The ache in his head began again, slowly, intensifying the pain from the cut on his head. He had been a buffoon all night—a black travesty beaten by what he was trying to beat, destroyed by what he was trying to destroy. And now, he was being 'buked and scorned by what he imagined her to be all in one: a black tribe of Amazons towering in statuesque dominance over the black male pygmies stunted by the white man's nurturing.

The ache increased as pain and heated resentment flowed hotly through his loins. The boiling blood caused his manhood to rise stiff and long. The throbbing elongated maleness of him made him passionately aware again of what he was and of what he could do. He could make babies like the white man. He could and *should* make hundreds of babies to create an army to fight the white man. Hundreds of black babies to make the white man's milk black. He *could*. He was a man. *Wasn't he?*

Uttering a harsh desperate cry, his arms reached out to grab her, to pull her savagely against him. He wanted *her* to feel and know the strength of him, the depth, the height, the power and the glory. His bruised sore lips smashed against hers.

Then tearing the flimsy material of her gown, he covered her with his stink and beard, anger and wretchedness. He entered her before she was ready and was hardly conscious of what he was doing. He heard and didn't hear her cries to cease, for him to stop, get up, get off. He had caught her by surprise.

She stiffened beneath him, trying to close the entrance to her against him. But he swelled and gloried in the battle that he fought now without gun or fist—only with the spear of him stabbing again and again into her until finally he felt her weaken and grow pliant under his warriorlike strokes to make her submissive to his will and strength and manhood. He fought and fought, marvelling at his staying power, pridefully thinking he could go on and on like this all night.

But when he felt the moistness of her beginning to receive him, bringing him into the hot deep well of her that claimed him now and made him feel caught and obliviously lost, he realized the battle was over. And in the end, he cried out in triumph—in defeat.

After a quivering moment that froze him, he rolled off her, breathing heavily, expelling the last of his strength.

Before he closed his eyes to give up to the tiredness, he heard her say in a voice that made him know she knew: "It takes more than that to be a man—"

Then he thought he never wanted to awaken again.

Black Mothers and Daughters in Conflict

• • • • •

The conflicts between black mothers and daughters manifested during the civil rights and black power movements can be explained to some extent by a pattern of mothering that began during slavery becoming outdated as black young people fought for racial equality and individual identity and as America became more liberalized in the 1950s, 1960s, and early 1970s. A major socializing agent for their children in a racist environment, black mothers often concentrated on the protection and survival of their children rather than encourage their self-fulfillment. Because the white power structure regarded black males as a threat, many black mothers nurtured their daughters by training them to be strong, "take-charge" black women within the home but gave their sons little or no responsibilities to check their aggression against whites. Janice S. Laws and Joyce Strickland conclude:

> This mothering process, born out of a slave mentality resulted in the training of Black children for sociological survival or adjustment at the expense of a positive psychological self-concept. [It] created a fear syndrome which paralyzes us and perpetuates the condition of external as opposed to internal self-control. Our psycho-social-historical perspective has been grounded to a greater extent in racial absorption and

201

assimilation rather than self-determination, self-realization, self-love, and self-empowerment.[1]

Laws and Strickland imply that the nurturing method of black mothers needs to change if young black men and women are to be able to work together for the improvement of the family and the race. Black sons and daughters need to be taught a new concept of manhood and womanhood, one that erases the fear of blacks' alleged "racial inferiority" and the stigma of "black powerlessness."

Not all black mothers, of course, perverted the roles of their children and denied their children freedom of expression by encouraging them to take a defensive approach to racism rather than mount political or psychological attacks on it. Many mothers marched and protested alongside their black daughters and sons. Nevertheless, the mother-daughter conflict is a problem in the black community that has often been ignored and that inhibited some black women from taking full control of their lives during the 1950s and 1960s, a time when the race was emphasizing self-determination. It is no less important than the conflict between black women and black men. The mother-daughter conflict, most often brought on by the daughter's rebellion not only against racism but against her traditional upbringing, gives us a more comprehensive view of the struggle in the black community, which has worked to resolve generational hostilities as well as racial and sexual ones. Although it is natural for each generation to rebel against the previous one, the climate of the 1950s, 1960s, and early 1970s was particularly rebellious, fueling the natural tendency of the young to seek something beyond the scope of their parents' world.

When four black male college students first sat-in at a segregated lunch counter in Greensboro, North Carolina, on 31 January 1960, an older black woman cook scolded them: "You're acting stupid, ignorant! That's why we can't get anywhere today. You know you're supposed to eat at the other end."[2] Like the prototypical black mother, this woman was surprised at the male students' boldness in defying the white system and was trying to reinforce the traditional expectation that they would remain subservient.

Similarly, the mother-daughter conflict often stemmed from the mother's simple fear for her daughter's life. Participants in the protest marches and demonstrations for civil rights in the South were often physically harmed, and mothers wanted to protect their daughters. In the selection from *Coming of Age in Mississippi*, her mother was anxious about Anne Moody's activism. Fearful not only for Anne's safety but for that of her entire family, she worried that word of her daughter's role in the civil rights movement would spark reprisals from local white racists. Before attending a rally led by NAACP leader Medgar Evers,

Moody recalls, "I had written Mama. She wrote me back a letter, begging me not to take part in the sit-in. . . . Mama's letter made me mad. I had to live my life as I saw fit. I had made that decision when I left home. But it hurt to have my family prove to me how scared they were. It hurt me more than anything else—I knew the whites had already started the threats and intimidations."[3]

The mother-daughter conflict was also precipitated when the assimilationist mother opposed her nationalist daughter's espousal of an African role as a carrier of black culture and as what Laws and Strickland call an "impetus for black power." Such a mother was simply out of touch with the emotional value of the black liberation movement, which boosted black egos, altered black roles and images, and celebrated an African heritage. The outlook that young women assumed during the black liberation movement was crucial because, as Laws and Strickland remind us, the daughters, as future mothers, would become through their own children "the catalyst to change the course of our history. . . . This generational cycle holds the key to the psychological liberation of black people and our ultimate sociological power as a people."[4]

"Women who write fiction write stories about mothers and daughters," comments Susan Koppelman in the introduction to her anthology *Between Mothers and Daughters*, ". . . women of every race, ethnicity, religion, region, and historical period."[5] Women writing from and about the experience of the civil rights and black power movements of the 1960s and 1970s are no different. The tumultuous public events often gave rise to private struggles among family members whose views on how to respond, or even whether to respond, differed. The selections that follow look at the struggles between mothers and daughters, or mother and daughter figures, wrought by the public struggles of their time. They are stories of daughters' rebellions and their search for their own identity and of their mothers' resistance to these rebellions, their desires to have their daughters see things their way. Black women writers tend to write from a daughter's perspective while acknowledging their need, as Mary Helen Washington asserts, "to piece together the story of a viable female culture, one in which there is generational continuity."[6]

For many young women of this period, joining the civil rights or black power movement represented a decision to lead their lives differently from the way their mothers had led theirs. It was a decision to confront and protest the denial of opportunity not only to their race but to themselves as individual women. In Alice Walker's *Meridian*, the title character pursues the betterment of the lives of black people by joining the civil rights movement and seeks self-betterment by attending college. Her mother, Mrs. Hill, criticizes her for both pursuits: "You've wasted a year of your life, fooling around with those people. . . . It never bothered *me* to sit in the back of the bus, you get just as good a view and you don't have all those nasty white asses passing you." Later, when Meridian insists on going to college even though she has had a baby and will have to give it up for adoption to get her education, her mother says, "Everybody else that slips up like you did *bears* it. You're the only one that thinks you can just outright refuse." Mrs. Hill is tied to the old, segregated, private existence most women of her time and circumstances knew; she cannot imagine the value of the progressive, integrated, public life her daughter imagines for herself.

The mother of Kiswana Browne in Gloria Naylor's *The Women of Brewster Place* also resists the change in her daughter's values. She appreciates the middle-class comforts and security she and her husband have attained, their ability to afford good college educations for their children and to make contributions to the NAACP. She cannot understand why her daughter has changed her name to an African one, wears her hair in an Afro, and is determined to live in a black ghetto. In a heated argument with her mother, Kiswana explains, "[I'm] trying to be proud of my heritage and the fact that I was of African descent. . . . I'd rather be dead than be like you—a white man's nigger who's ashamed of being black!"

There is the same kind of misunderstanding between the old woman, Mother McCullum, and the young woman, Tisha Dees, in Arthenia Bates Millican's *The Deity Nodded*. Here the difference arises over choice of religion, Mother McCullum being a devoted follower of the Baptist church and Tisha a convert to the Black Muslim faith. Tisha rejects Christianity as a religion "the slave masters gave us" and embraces the Muslim faith for being authentically derived from the African heritage of black people.

The rise in interest in the Muslim faith attended the rise of the black power movement. The Black Muslims, a religious sect that began in the early 1930s in Detroit, Michigan, opposed white racist imperialism and advocated racial separation and black unity. The message of race pride and a united black front in the late 1950s and early 1960s was especially appealing to young, idealistic inner-city militants who had tired of racial discrimination and the ambivalence of black leaders about racial issues. In addition, the Muslims' anti-Christian tone appealed to "increasing numbers of Negroes [who were] . . . disillusioned by the continuation of racial segregation in the church" and who identified "the church with social apathy and racial subordination."[7] There was no mass exodus from Christian churches, but in 1959 membership in the Nation of Islam grew from 30,000 to more than 100,000, accompanied by the growing popularity of Malcolm X, the chief spokesman for Black Muslims.[8] Often young converts who had not regularly attended church came from Christian homes. Young blacks regarded their defection from their parents' faith as an opportunity to defy pressures toward religious, racial, and gender conformity, but to some older blacks their children's decision was devastating.

The young women in these stories share a willingness to confront the values imposed on them by the white patriarchal world and the assumptions of their mothers about how to live in that world. Opportunities to make choices open up to them not only because of the inroads of the civil rights and black power movements but because of their own courage in participating in these events. Conflict arises when the daughters reject what their mothers consider important elements of a black woman's identity.

In the selections by Naylor and Walker, the daughters are uneasy about their decisions; it is difficult for them to tolerate their mothers' distress over their choices, and they are unable to integrate into their new lives the essential, life-giving elements from their past. "The romantic illusion that a woman can 'find herself' in isolation from her community has been dangerous for women. It tricks a young woman into abandoning the world that has nurtured her," writes Koppelman.[9] In the excerpt from *Meridian* and in "Kiswana Browne," the author seems to side with the daughter, to make the story hers, not the mother's. Yet both stories give the mother her due; each mother is a strong character who has lived her life in accordance with traditional principles of child rearing, responsibility, and self-pride. Consequently, both Naylor and Walker manage to convey that the daughter is giving up something of value to attain her new identity and place in the world.

Arthenia Bates Millican has also created a strong, principled mother figure for whom the daughter figure, Tisha, has a genuine affection. But Tisha is more at peace with her new way of life than Meridian and Kiswana are, largely because the Christian life she has rejected, as embodied in mother McCullum, seems to her so bleak and unappealing. Unlike Meridian and Kiswana, however, Tisha is able to acknowledge what she believes to be good in Mother McCullum and takes comfort in that knowledge.

NOTES

1. Janice S. Laws and Joyce Strickland, "Black Mothers and Daughters: A Clarification of the Relationship as an Impetus for Black Power," *Black Books Bulletin* 6 (1980): 29, 33.

2. Brisbane, *Black Activism*, 45.

3. Anne Moody, *Coming of Age in Mississippi* (New York: Doubleday, 1969), 240.

4. Laws and Strickland, "Black Mothers and Daughters," 28.

5. Susan Koppelman, ed., *Between Mothers and Daughters: Stories across a Generation* (New York: Feminist Press, 1985), xv.

6. Mary Helen Washington, "I Sign My Mother's Name: Alice Walker, Dorothy West, Paule Marshall," in *Mothering the Mind*, ed. Ruth Perry and Martine Watson Brownly, (New York: Holmes and Meier, 1984), 147.

7. C. Eric Lincoln, *The Black Muslims in America* (Boston: Beacon Press, 1961), 28.

8. Brisbane, *Black Activism,* 112.

9. Koppelman, *Between Mothers and Daughters,* xx.

• • • • •

"Battle Fatigue" [from *Meridian*]

Alice Walker

Alice Walker took five years to complete *Meridian* (Harcourt Brace Jovanovich, 1976); from 1965 to 1970 she was also quilting, writing a history book for preschool children in Jackson, Mississippi, and trying to become pregnant. Her daughter Rebecca was born three days after she completed *Meridian*. In the 1960s Walker actively participated in civil rights marches. One week after she walked four miles across Atlanta in Martin Luther King, Jr.'s funeral procession, she miscarried; she recalls, "I did not even care. It seemed to me, at the time, that if 'he' (it was weeks before I could form his name) must die no one deserved to live, not even my own child."[1] Walker's commitment to the civil rights struggle, to what Martin Luther King, Jr., stood for, and later to her own career as a writer, links her to Meridian, the revolutionary protagonist in her novel *Meridian*.

In both Walker's life and Meridian's there is a relationship between personal development and social conditions. Each daughter departed from her mother's expectation of her to pursue her own personal development. Walker's mother offered her "uncharacteristically bad advice" about having children, even when Walker wanted to pursue a writing career; her mother told her, "You married a man who's a wonderful fatherly type. He has so much love in him he should have fifty children running around his feet." In response, Walker thought, "If they're running around his feet for the two hours between the time

206

he comes home from the office and the time we put them to bed . . . they'd be underneath my desk all day. Sweep. Sweep."[2]

"Battle Fatigue" tells of the high price young women have sometimes paid in breaking from the past and their mothers' way of life. In deciding to give up her child so she can go away to college, Meridian must bear a sense of alienation not only from her mother, who bitterly opposes her choice, but from the generations of black mothers before her who in slavery thought "their greatest blessing from 'Freedom' was that it meant they could keep their own children."

NOTES

1. Walker, *In Search of Our Mothers' Gardens,* 148.
2. Ibid., 364.

Truman Held was the first of the Civil Rights workers—for that's what they were called—who began to mean something to her, though it was months after their initial meeting that she knew. It was not until one night when first he, then she, was arrested for demonstrating outside the local jail, and then beaten.

There had been a Freedom march to the church, a prayer by the Reverend in charge, Freedom songs, several old women testifying (mainly about conditions inside the black section of the jail, which caused Meridian's body to twitch with dread) and finally, a plan of what their strategy was to be, and the singing of "Ain't Gonna Let Nobody Turn Me Round."

The strategy was for a midnight march, with candles, across the street from the jail by the people who had not been arrested earlier, of whom Truman was one. The strategy was, in fact, for everyone not formerly arrested to be so. This was in protest against the town's segregated hospital facilities. It was also an attempt to have the earlier demonstrators released from jail. But even as she marched, singing, to the courthouse square, which was across from the jail, Meridian could not figure out how it was supposed to work. The earlier demonstrators, she felt sure, would not be set free because a few singing people stood peacefully across from the jail. And the jail was too small to accommodate any more bodies. It must already be jammed.

They had been singing for only a few minutes when the town became alive with flashing lights. Police cars came from everywhere. Dozens of state troopers surrounded them, forming a wall between them and the jail. She noticed they really *did* have crew cuts, they really *did* chew gum. Next, the jailhouse door was opened and the earlier demonstrators came wearily out, their faces misshapen from swellings and discolored from bruises. Truman limped along with the rest, moving in great pain and steadily muttering curses as the line of troopers hurried them relentlessly out of the square. It was a few seconds before Meridian understood that it was now their turn.

As soon as this line was out of sight, the troopers turned on them, beating and swinging with their bludgeons. One blow knocked Meridian to the ground, where she was trampled by people running back and forth over her. But there was nowhere to run. Only the jail door was open and unobstructed. Within minutes they had been beaten inside, where the sheriff and his deputies waited to finish them. And she realized why Truman was limping. When the sheriff grabbed her by the hair and someone else began punching her and kicking her in the back, she did not even scream, except very intensely in her own mind, and the scream was Truman's name. And what she meant by it was not even that she was in love with him: What she meant by it was that they were at a time and a place in History that forced the trivial to fall away— and they were absolutely together.

Later that summer, after another demonstration, she saw him going down a street that did not lead back to the black part of town. His eyes were swollen and red, his body trembling, and he did not recognize her or even see her. She knew his blankness was battle fatigue. They all had it. She was as weary as anyone, so that she spent a good part of her time in tears. At first she had burst into tears whenever something went wrong or someone spoke unkindly or even sometimes if they spoke, period. But now she was always in a state of constant tears, so that she could do whatever she was doing—canvassing, talking at rallies, tying her sneakers, laughing—while tears rolled slowly and ceaselessly down her cheeks. This might go on for days, or even weeks. Then, suddenly, it would stop, and some other symptom would appear. The shaking of her hands, or the twitch in her left eye. Or the way she would sometimes be sure she'd heard a shot and feel the impact of the bullet against her back; then she stood absolutely still, waiting to feel herself fall.

She went up to a yard with an outdoor spigot and soaked the bottom of her blouse in water. When she came back down to the street to wipe the tear gas from Truman's eyes, he was gone. A police car was careening down the street. She stood in the street feeling the cool wet spot on her side, wondering what to do.

The majority of black townspeople were sympathetic to the Movement from the first, and told Meridian she was doing a good thing: typing, teaching illiterates to read and write, demonstrating against segregated facilities and keeping the Movement house open when the other workers returned to school. Her mother, however, was not sympathetic.

"As far as I'm concerned," said Mrs. Hill, "you've wasted a year of your life, fooling around with those people. The papers say they're crazy. God separated the sheeps from the goats and the black folks from the white. And me from anybody that acts as foolish as they do. It never bothered *me* to sit in the back of the bus, you get just as good a view and you don't have all those nasty white asses passing you.''

Meridian attempted to ignore her, but her mother would continue. ''If somebody thinks he'll have to pee when he gets to town, let him use his own toilet before he leaves home! That's what we did when I was coming up!'' Eventually Mrs. Hill would talk herself out.

It had taken Meridian a long time to tell her mother she *was* in the Movement, and by the time she did, her mother already knew. Now she had news that was even more likely to infuriate her. To deliver it, she brought Delores Jones (another Movement worker) and Nelda Henderson, an old playmate, with her. It was cowardly of her, but Meridian could not face her mother alone.

While Meridian was still a student in high school she was tested and informed that, for her area and background, her IQ of 140 was unusually high. She was pregnant at the time, sick as a dog and about to be expelled from school; she had shrugged her shoulders at the news. But now, though she had not completed high school, she was to have— if she wanted it—a chance to go to college. Mr. Yateson told her this, explaining that a unique honor was being bestowed upon her—who might or might not be worthy; after all, nice girls did not become pregnant in high school—and that he expected her to set a high moral standard because she would be representing the kind of bright ''product'' his ''plant'' could produce.

He spoke so proprietarily she thought at first he intended to send her to college with his own money. But no. He explained that a generous (and wealthy) white family in Connecticut—who wished to help some of the poor, courageous blacks they saw marching and getting their heads whipped nightly on TV—had decided, as a gesture of their liberality and concern, to send a smart black girl to Saxon College in Atlanta, a school this family had endowed for three generations.

''You don't mean I'm the smartest one you've got!'' said Meridian, humbly. But then the thought that this might be true simply because Mr. Yateson's ''plant'' generally produced nothing among its ''products'' but boredom tickled her and she smiled.

Mr. Yateson was annoyed. ''In my day,'' he said, ''we didn't reward bad behavior—nor did we think it was funny!''

So then Meridian felt she had to apologize for her smile, even though it had been such a pathetic one, and some of the joy of the experience went out of it for her.

It was Truman who put it back by telling her Saxon College was only two hours away, and just across the street from his own school, R. Baron College, which he attended when he was not working in the

Movement out of town. Because of course there was an Atlanta Movement, in which he had already been involved. He and Meridian would see each other every day.

"*Mais oui,*" Truman kept saying, as she looked shyly but happily up at him, "you will be just the Saxon type!"

But then, she had never told him she had a child.

"You have a right to go to college," said Delores. "You're lucky to have the chance." She was slender and brown, with a strong, big nose and eyebrows like black wings. She wore jeans and flowered shirts and was unafraid of everything. "Listen," she said, "it's not every day that somebody's going to care about your high IQ and offer you a scholarship. You ain't no dummy, girl, and don't you even consider acting like one now." They walked up to the front door, Nelda Henderson reaching out to squeeze Meridian's hand.

"No matter what your mother says," Delores continued, "just remember she spends all her time making prayer pillows."

Nelda said nothing about Meridian going to college because she wanted to save her words for Meridian's mother. Nelda cried easily and looked at Delores and Meridian with sad envy. She was pregnant again and it was just beginning to show. When Mrs. Hill came to the door there was a coolness in her response to Nelda's greeting, which brought the always close tears to the surface.

The Hills' house was white on the outside with turquoise shutters. It was cluttered with heavy brown furniture, white porcelain dolls, and churns filled with paper flowers. Dozens of snapshots of other people's children grinned down at them from the walls.

"Well, it can't be moral, that I know. It can't be right to give away your own child." They say around the dining room table drinking tea. "If the good Lord gives you a child he means for *you* to take care of it."

"The good Lord didn't give it to her," muttered Delores. Delores was intrepid. Meridian loved her.

"But this is the only chance I have, Mama," she said.

"You should have thought about that before."

"I didn't *know* before," she said, looking into her glass. "How can I take care of Eddie Jr. anyway?" she asked. "I can't even take care of myself."

Mrs. Hill frowned. "Do you know how many women have thought that and had to have God make a way? You surprised me," she continued, sighing, "I always thought you were a *good* girl. And all the time, you were fast."

"I was something," said Meridian. "But I didn't even know what fast was. You always talked in riddles. 'Be sweet.' 'Don't be fast.' You never made a bit of sense."

"That's right," said Mrs. Hill. "Blame me for trusting you. But I know one thing: Everybody else that slips up like you did *bears* it. You're the only one that thinks you can just outright refuse . . ." Mrs. Hill stopped and wiped her eyes.

"Look at Nelda," she began, " I know *she'd* never . . ."

But Nelda interrupted. "Don't say that, Mrs. Hill," she said, her eyes tearing. "I'd do anything to have a chance to go to college like Meridian. I wish to God I could have made it to junior high."

For a moment, as she looked at Meridian's mother, there was hatred in her sad eyes. Hatred and comprehension of betrayal. She had lived across the street from the Hills all her life. She and Meridian played together in the Hills' back yard, they went to school together. Nelda knew that the information she had needed to get through her adolescence was information Mrs. Hill could have given her.

There had been about Nelda in those days a naïve and admirable sweetness, but there was also apparent, if one knew how to recognize such things (and Mrs. Hill might certainly have done so), a premonition of her fall, which grew out of her meek acceptance of her family's burdens. She had been left in charge of her five younger brothers and sisters every day while her mother worked. On Saturdays she struggled to town to do the shopping, the twins racing ahead of her down the street, the two toddlers holding to her arms and the baby strapped to her back. This was Nelda—as pretty, the boys used to say, as an Indian— at fourteen, just before she became pregnant herself.

On Sundays Nelda was free to do as she liked. Her mother did not work then, but spent most of the day—with all her other children neatly dressed and combed—in church. (She was a large, "bald-headed" woman, with massive breasts and a fine contralto singing voice. Her husband had been lost in France during the Second World War, and though only two of her children were his—Nelda and the next oldest child, a boy—they all carried his name. She had lost her hair, bit by bit, during each pregnancy.) Nelda was allowed to spend the day at home washing her hair, making dinner and doing her homework (she made it to school perhaps six times a month, and no truant officer ever knocked on her door), and in the late afternoons she went, with Meridian and Delores, to a movie in town, where the three of them sat in the gallery above the heads of the white movie goers and necked with their boyfriends of the moment.

Meridian knew the father of Nelda's first baby. He was an older boy, in high school, a gentle boy who treated Nelda as if he loved her more than life, which he might have. He bought her combs and blouses and Bermuda shorts, and her first pair of stockings—all from the three-dollar allowance his mother gave him each week plus his earnings from cutting lawns during the summer. While her mother was at work he

211

often came by to cut their grass and stayed to help Nelda give the children supper, baths and put them to bed. Nelda was well into her third month before she realized something was wrong. It started, she confided to Meridian, by her noticing her pee smelled different.

"What do you mean, your *pee* smells different?" Meridian laughed.

"I don't know," Nelda giggled, "but this ain't its usual smell." They sat on the toilets at school and laughed and laughed.

"You should *want* Eddie Jr.," said Mrs. Hill, "Unless you're some kind of monster. And no daughter of mine is a monster, surely."

Meridian closed her eyes as tight as she could.

Delores cleared her throat. "The only way Meridian can take care of Eddie Jr. is if she moves in here with you and gets a job in somebody's kitchen while you take care of the kid."

"Of course I'll help out," said Mrs. Hill. "I wouldn't let either one of 'em starve, but—" she continued, speaking to Delores as if Meridian were not present, "this is a clean, upright, *Christian* home. We believe in God in this house."

"What's that got to do with anything?" asked Delores, whose face expressed belligerence and confusion. "The last time God had a baby he skipped, too."

Mrs. Hill pretended she wasn't angry and insulted. She smiled at this girl she wanted to hit. "You're not from around here," she said, "everybody knows people from up Atlanta have strange ideas. A lot of you young people have lost your respect for the church. Do you even believe in God?"

"I give it some thought," said Delores.

Mrs. Hill drew in her stomach and crossed her plump arms over it. "I just don't see how you could let another woman raise your child," she said. "It's just selfishness. You ought to hang your head in shame. I have six children," she continued self-righteously, "though I never wanted to have any, and I have raised every one myself."

"You probably could have done the same thing in slavery," said Delores.

"Let's all be monsters!" Delores joked as she and her friends left Mrs. Hill's house, but Meridian and Nelda did not laugh.

She might not have given him away to the people who wanted him. She might have murdered him instead. Then killed herself. They would all have understood this in time. She might have done it that way except for one thing: One day she really looked at her child and loved him with as much love as she loved the moon or a tree, which was a considerable amount of impersonal love. She wanted to know more about his perfect, if unplanned-for, existence.

"Who are you?" she asked him.

"Where were you when I was twelve?"

"Who *are* you?" she persisted, studying his face for signs of fire, watermarks, some scar that would intimate a previous life.

"Were there other people where you were? Did you come from a planet of babies?" She thought she could just imagine him there, on such a planet, pulling the blue grass up by the handfuls.

Now that she looked at him, the child was beautiful. She had thought him ugly, like a hump she must carry on her back.

"You will no longer be called Eddie Jr." she said. "I'll ask them to call you Rundi, after no person, I hope, who has ever lived."

When she gave him away she did so with a light heart. She did not look back, believing she had saved a small person's life.

But she had not anticipated the nightmares that began to trouble her sleep. Nightmares of the child, Rundi, calling to her, crying, suffering unbearable deprivations because she was not there, yet she knew it was just the opposite: Because she was not there he needn't worry, ever, about being deprived. Of his life, for instance. She felt deeply that what she'd done was the only thing, and was right, but that did not seem to matter. On some deeper level than she had anticipated or had even been aware of, she felt condemned, consigned to penitence, for life. The past pulled the present out of shape as she realized that what Delores Jones had said was *not*, in fact, true. If her mother had had children in slavery she would not, automatically, have been allowed to keep them, because they would not have belonged to her but to the white person who "owned" them all. Meridian knew that enslaved women had been made miserable by the sale of their children, that they had laid down their lives, gladly, for their children, that the daughters of these enslaved women had thought their greatest blessing from "Freedom" was that it meant they could keep their own children. And what had Meridian Hill done with *her* precious child? She had given him away. She thought of her mother as being worthy of this maternal history, and of herself as belonging to an unworthy minority, for which there was no precedent and of which she was, as far as she knew, the only member.

After she had figuratively kissed the ground of the campus and walked about its lawns intent on bettering herself, she knew for certain she had broken something, for she began hearing a voice when she studied for exams, and when she walked about the academic halls, and when she looked from her third-floor dormitory window. A voice that cursed her existence—an existence that could not live up to the standard of motherhood that had gone before. It said, over and over, until she would literally reel in the streets, her head between her hands: Why don't you die? Why not kill yourself? Jump into the traffic! Lie down under the wheels of that big truck! Jump off the roof, as long as you're up there! Always, the voice. Mocking, making fun. It frightened her because the voice urging her on—the voice that said terrible things about her lack of value—was her own voice. It was talking to her, and it was full of hate.

Her teachers worked her hard, her first year at Saxon. She read night and day, making up for lost time. But no matter how hard she labored she was always willing to tackle more, because she knew almost no one there, and because Saxon was a peaceful but strange, still, place to her, and because she was grateful to be distracted. She was not to pause long enough to respond to this spiritual degeneration in herself until she was in her second year.

● ● ● ● ●

"Kiswana Browne" [from *The Women of Brewster Place*]

Gloria Naylor

Born in New York City in 1950 to Roosevelt and Alberta Naylor, Gloria Naylor received her B.A. degree in 1981 from Brooklyn College and her M.A. degree in 1983 from Yale University. Her debut as a novelist came with the publication of *The Women of Brewster Place* (Viking Penguin, 1983), which received the American Book Award for best first novel. It depicts the struggles of seven black women who differ in age, political consciousness, and sexual preference but who share the common oppressions of poverty, sexism, and racism. Her two subsequent novels, *Linden Hills* (1985) and *Mama Day* (1988), are also concerned with black women's struggles. Naylor has written essays and articles for the *New York Times, Essence, Ms., People,* and *Southern Review.* She is the recipient of the Distinguished Writer Award (1983) from the Mid-Atlantic Writers Association, the Candace Award (1986) from the National Coalition of 100 Black Women, and a Guggenheim Fellowship (1988).

Gloria Naylor is quick to say, "I had a marvelous mother at home who would have done anything for us," yet she just as quickly says sections of *The Women of Brewster Place* "were written as a catharis for the various types of pain I may have been going through at the moment." She grew up as a very shy child unable to talk to her parents about her problems, which she daily conveyed to her diary. Conflict, for Naylor, is necessary for personal growth, and she believes that whether or not ties with family, community, and religious or spiritual values are weakened, a woman often relinquishes something to expand her horizons.[1]

In *The Women of Brewster Place*, Kiswana, a separatist, works with an unstable grass-roots coalition; her mother leads a secure, middle-class life. In their words and lifestyles, the two women reveal fundamental differences in outlook that are largely generational; they have different value systems and favor different solutions to the race problem. Kiswana, as she attempts to genuinely live out the principle of integrating her African heritage into her own life and promoting it to others, is more vulnerable. She is faced with the problem of supporting herself while not compromising her ideals, and she ends up depending on unemployment checks. "Kiswana Browne" conveys the difficulty black daughters encountered when they repudiated conventional solutions to race problems.

NOTES

1. Gloria Naylor, address at the Black Cultural Center, Atlanta, Georgia, 1 April 1988.

From the window of her sixth-floor studio apartment, Kiswana could see over the wall at the end of the street to the busy avenue that lay just north of Brewster Place. The late-afternoon shoppers looked like brightly clad marionettes as they moved between the congested traffic, clutching their packages against their bodies to guard them from sudden bursts of the cold autumn wind. A portly mailman had abandoned cart and was bumping into indignant window-shoppers as he puffed behind the cap that the wind had snatched from his head. Kiswana leaned over to see if he was going to be successful, but the edge of the building cut him off from her view.

A pigeon swept across her window, and she marveled at its liquid movements in the air waves. She placed her dreams on the back of the bird and fantasized that it would glide forever in transparent silver circles until it ascended to the center of the universe and was swallowed up. But the wind died down, and she watched with a sigh as the bird beat its wings in awkward, frantic movements to land on the corroded top of a fire escape on the opposite building. This brought her back to earth.

Humph, it's probably sitting over there crapping on those folks' fire escape, she thought. Now, that's a safety hazard. . . . And her mind was busy again, creating flames and smoke and frustrated tenants whose escape was being hindered because they were slipping and sliding in pigeon shit. She watched their cussing, haphazard descent on the fire escapes until they had all reached the bottom. They were milling around, oblivious to their burning apartments, angrily planning to march on the mayor's office about the pigeons. She materialized placards and banners for them, and they had just reached the corner, boldly sidestepping fire hoses and broken glass, when they all vanished.

A tall copper-skinned woman had met this phantom parade at the corner, and they had dissolved in front of her long, confident strides. She plowed through the remains of their faded mists, unconscious of the lingering wisps of their presence on her leather bag and black fur-trimmed coat. It took a few seconds for this transfer from one realm to another to reach Kiswana, but then suddenly she recognized the woman.

"Oh, God, it's Mama!" She looked down guiltily at the forgotten newspaper in her lap and hurriedly circled random job advertisements.

By this time Mrs. Browne had reached the front of Kiswana's building and was checking the house number against a piece of paper in her hand. Before she went into the building she stood at the bottom of the stoop and carefully inspected the condition of the street and the adjoining property. Kiswana watched this meticulous inventory with growing annoyance but she involuntarily followed her mother's slowly rotating head, forcing herself to see her new neighborhood through the older woman's eyes. The brightness of the unclouded sky seemed to join forces with her mother as it highlighted every broken stoop railing and missing brick. The afternoon sun glittered and cascaded across even the tiniest fragments of broken bottle, and at that very moment the wind chose to rise up again, sending unswept grime flying into the air, as a stray tin can left by careless garbage collectors went rolling noisily down the center of the street.

Kiswana noticed with relief that at least Ben wasn't sitting in his usual place on the old garbage can pushed against the far wall. He was just a harmless old wino, but Kiswana knew her mother only needed one wino or one teenager with a reefer within a twenty-block radius to decide that her daughter was living in a building seething with dope factories and hang-outs for derelicts. If she had seen Ben, nothing would have made her believe that practically every apartment contained a family, a Bible, and a dream that one day enough could be scraped from those meager Friday night paychecks to make Brewster Place a distant memory.

216

As she watched her mother's head disappear into the building, Kiswana gave silent thanks that the elevator was broken. That would give her at least five minutes' grace to straighten up the apartment. She rushed to the sofa bed and hastily closed it without smoothing the rumpled sheets and blanket or removing her nightgown. She felt that somehow the tangled bedcovers would give away the fact that she had not slept alone last night. She silently apologized to Abshu's memory as she heartlessly crushed his spirit between the steel springs of the couch. Lord, that man was sweet. Her toes curled involuntarily at the passing thought of his full lips moving slowly over her instep. Abshu was a foot man, and he always started his lovemaking from the bottom up. For that reason Kiswana changed the color of the polish on her toenails every week. During the course of their relationship she had gone from shades of red to brown and was now into the purples. I'm gonna have to start mixing them soon, she thought aloud as she turned from the couch and raced into the bathroom to remove any traces of Abshu from there. She took up his shaving cream and razor and threw them into the bottom drawer of her dresser beside her diaphragm. Mama wouldn't dare pry into my drawers right in front of me, she thought as she slammed the drawer shut. Well, at least not the *bottom* drawer. She may come up with some sham excuse for opening the top drawer, but never the bottom one.

When she heard the first two short raps on the door, her eyes took a final flight over the small apartment, desperately seeking out any slight misdemeanor that might have to be defended. Well, there was nothing she could do about the crack in the wall over that table. She had been after the landlord to fix it for two months now. And there had been no time to sweep the rug, and everyone knew that off-gray always looked dirtier than it really was. And it was just too damn bad about the kitchen. How was she expected to be out job-hunting every day and still have time to keep a kitchen that looked like her mother's, who didn't even work and still had someone come in twice a month for general cleaning. And besides . . .

Her imaginary argument was abruptly interrupted by a second series of knocks, accompanied by a penetrating, "Melanie, Melanie, are you there?"

Kiswana strode toward the door. She's starting before she even gets in here. She knows that's not my name anymore.

She swung the door open to face her slightly flushed mother. "Oh, hi, Mama. You know, I thought I heard a knock, but I figured it was for the people next door, since no one hardly ever calls me Melanie." Score one for me, she thought.

"Well, it's awfully strange you can forget a name you answered to for twenty-three years," Mrs. Browne said, as she moved past Kiswana into the apartment. "My, that was a long climb. How long has your elevator been out? Honey, how do you manage with your laundry and groceries up all those steps? But I guess you're young, and it wouldn't bother you as much as it does me." This long string of questions told Kiswana that her mother had no intentions of beginning her visit with another argument about her new African name.

"You know I would have called before I came, but you don't have a phone yet. I didn't want you to feel that I was snooping. As a matter of fact, I didn't expect to find you home at all. I thought you'd be out looking for a job." Mrs. Browne had mentally covered the entire apartment while she was talking and taking off her coat.

"Well, I got up late this morning. I thought I'd buy the afternoon paper and start early tomorrow."

"That sounds like a good idea." Her mother moved toward the window and picked up the discarded paper and glanced over the hurriedly circled ads. "Since when do you have experience as a fork-lift operator?"

Kiswana caught her breath and silently cursed herself for her stupidity. "Oh, my hand slipped—I meant to circle file clerk." She quickly took the paper before her mother could see that she had also marked cutlery salesman and chauffeur.

"You're sure you weren't sitting here moping and daydreaming again?" Amber specks of laughter flashed in the corner of Mrs. Browne's eyes.

Kiswana threw her shoulders back and unsuccessfully tried to disguise her embarrassment with indignation.

"Oh, God, Mama! I haven't done that in years—it's for kids. When are you going to realize that I'm a woman now?" She sought desperately for some womanly thing to do and settled for throwing herself on the couch and crossing her legs in what she hoped looked like a nonchalant arc.

"Please, have a seat," she said, attempting the same tones and gestures she'd seen Bette Davis use on the late movies.

Mrs. Browne, lowering her eyes to hide her amusement, accepted the invitation and sat at the window, also crossing her legs. Kiswana saw immediately how it should have been done. Her celluloid poise clashed loudly against her mother's quiet dignity, and she quickly uncrossed her legs. Mrs. Browne turned her head toward the window and pretended not to notice.

"At least you have a halfway decent view from here. I was wondering what lay beyond that dreadful wall—it's the boulevard. Honey, did you know that you can see the trees in Linden Hills from here?"

Kiswana knew that very well, because there were many lonely days that she would sit in her gray apartment and stare at those trees and think of home, but she would rather have choked than admit that to her mother.

"Oh, really, I never noticed. So how is Daddy and things at home?"

"Just fine. We're thinking of redoing one of the extra bedrooms since you children have moved out, but Wilson insists that he can manage all that work alone. I told him that he doesn't really have the proper time or energy for all that. As it is, when he gets home from the office, he's so tired he can hardly move. But you know you can't tell your father anything. Whenever he starts complaining about how stubborn you are, I tell him the child came by it honestly. Oh, and your brother was by yesterday," she added, as if it had just occurred to her.

So that's it, thought Kiswana. That's why she's here.

Kiswana's brother, Wilson, had been to visit her two days ago, and she had borrowed twenty dollars from him to get her winter coat out of layaway. That son-of-a-bitch probably ran straight to Mama—and after he swore he wouldn't say anything. I should have known, he was always a snotty-nosed sneak, she thought.

"Was he?" she said aloud. "He came by to see me, too, earlier this week. And I borrowed some money from him because my unemployment checks hadn't cleared in the bank, but now they have and everything's just fine." There, I'll beat you to that one.

"Oh, I didn't know that," Mrs. Browne lied. "He never mentioned you. He had just heard that Beverly was expecting again, and he rushed over to tell us."

Damn. Kiswana could have strangled herself.

"So she's knocked up again, huh?" she said irritably.

Her mother started. "Why do you always have to be so crude?"

"Personally, I don't see how she can sleep with Willie. He's such a dishrag."

Kiswana still resented the stance her brother had taken in college. When everyone at school was discovering their blackness and protesting on campus, Wilson never took part; he had even refused to wear an Afro. This had outraged Kiswana because, unlike her, he was dark-skinned and had the type of hair that was thick and kinky enough for a good "Fro." Kiswana had still insisted on cutting her own hair, but it was so thin and fine-textured, it refused to thicken even after she washed it. So she had to brush it up and spray it with lacquer to keep it from lying flat. She never forgave Wilson for telling her that she didn't look African, she looked like an electrocuted chicken.

"Now that's some way to talk. I don't know why you have an attitude against your brother. He never gave me a restless night's sleep, and now he's settled with a family and a good job."

"He's an assistant to an assistant junior partner in a law firm. What's the big deal about that?"

"The job has a future, Melanie. And at least he finished school and went on for his law degree."

"In other words, not like me, huh?"

"Don't put words into my mouth, young lady. I'm perfectly capable of saying what I mean."

Amen, thought Kiswana.

"And I don't know why you've been trying to start up with me from the moment I walked in. I didn't come here to fight with you. This is your first place away from home, and I just wanted to see how you were living and if you're doing all right. And I must say, you've fixed this apartment up very nicely."

"Really, Mama?" She found herself softening in the light of her mother's approval.

"Well, considering what you had to work with." This time she scanned the apartment openly.

"Look, I know it's not Linden Hills, but a lot can be done with it. As soon as they come and paint, I'm going to hang my Ashanti print over the couch. And I thought a big Boston Fern would go well in that corner, what do you think?"

"That would be fine, baby. You always had a good eye for balance."

Kiswana was beginning to relax. There was little she did that attracted her mother's approval. It was like a rare bird, and she had to tread carefully around it lest it fly away.

"Are you going to leave that statue out like that?"

"Why, what's wrong with it? Would it look better somewhere else?"

There was a small wooden reproduction of a Yoruba goddess with large protruding breasts on the coffee table.

"Well," Mrs. Browne was beginning to blush, "it's just that it's a bit suggestive, don't you think? Since you live alone now, and I know you'll be having male friends stop by, you wouldn't want to be giving them any ideas. I mean, uh, you know, there's no point in putting yourself in any unpleasant situations because they may get the wrong impressions and uh, you know, I mean, well . . ." Mrs. Browne stammered on miserably.

Kiswana loved it when her mother tried to talk about sex. It was the only time she was at a loss for words.

"Don't worry, Mama." Kiswana smiled. "That wouldn't bother the type of men I date. Now maybe if it had big feet . . ." And she got hysterical, thinking of Abshu.

Her mother looked at her sharply. "What sort of gibberish is that about feet? I'm being serious, Melanie."

"I'm sorry, Mama." She sobered up. "I'll put it away in the closet," she said, knowing that she wouldn't.

"Good," Mrs. Browne said, knowing that she wouldn't either. "I guess you think I'm too picky, but we worry about you over here. And you refuse to put in a phone so we can call and see about you.''

''I haven't refused, Mama. They want seventy-five dollars for a deposit, and I can't swing that right now.''

''Melanie, I can give you the money.''

''I don't want you to be giving me money—I've told you that before. Please, let me make it by myself.''

''Well, let me lend it to you, then.''

''No!''

''Oh, so you can borrow money from your brother, but not from me.''

Kiswana turned her head from the hurt in her mother's eyes. ''Mama, when I borrow from Willie, he makes me pay him back. You never let me pay you back,'' she said into her hands.

''I don't care. I still think it's downright selfish of you to be sitting over here with no phone, and sometimes we don't hear from you in two weeks—anything could happen—especially living among these people.''

Kiswana snapped her head up. ''What do you mean, *these people.* They're my people and yours, too, Mama—we're all black. But maybe you've forgotten that over in Linden Hills.''

''That's not what I'm talking about, and you know it. These streets—this building—it's so shabby and rundown. Honey, you don't have to live like this.''

''Well, this is how poor people live.''

''Melanie, you're not poor.''

''No, Mama, *you're* not poor. And what you have and I have are two totally different things. I don't have a husband in real estate with a five-figure income and a home in Linden Hills—*you* do. What I have is a weekly unemployment check and an overdrawn checking account at United Federal. So this studio on Brewster is all I can afford.''

''Well, you could afford a lot better,'' Mrs. Browne snapped, ''if you hadn't dropped out of college and had to resort to these dead-end clerical jobs.''

''Uh-huh, I knew you'd get around to that before long.'' Kiswana could feel the rings of anger begin to tighten around her lower backbone, and they sent her forward onto the couch. ''You'll never understand, will you? Those bourgie schools were counterrevolutionary. My place was in the streets with my people, fighting for equality and a better community.''

''Counterrevolutionary!'' Mrs. Browne was raising her voice. ''Where's your revolution now, Melanie? Where are all those black revolutionaries who were shouting and demonstrating and kicking up a lot of dust with you on that campus? Huh? They're sitting in wood-paneled offices with their degrees in mahogany frames, and they won't even drive their cars past this street because the city doesn't fix potholes in this part of town.''

''Mama,'' she said, shaking her head slowly in disbelief, ''how can you—a black woman—sit there and tell me that what we fought for during the Movement wasn't important just because some people sold out?''

''Melanie, I'm not saying it wasn't important. It was damned important to stand up and say that you were proud of what you were and to get the vote and other social opportunities for every person in this country who had it due. But you kids thought you were going to turn the world upside down, and it just wasn't so. When all the smoke had cleared, you found yourself with a fistful of new federal laws and a country still full of obstacles for black people to fight their way over— just because they're black. There was no revolution, Melanie, and there will be no revolution.''

''So what am I supposed to do, huh? Just throw up my hands and not care about what happens to my people? I'm not supposed to keep fighting to make things better?''

''Of course, you can. But you're going to have to fight within the system, because it and these so-called 'bourgie' schools are going to be here for a long time. And that means that you get smart like a lot of your old friends and get an important job where you can have some influence. You don't have to sell out, as you say, and work for some corporation, but you could become an assemblywoman or a civil liberties lawyer or open a freedom school in this very neighborhood. That way you could really help the community. But what help are you going to be to these people on Brewster while you're living hand-to-mouth on file-clerk jobs waiting for a revolution? You're wasting your talents, child.''

''Well, I don't think they're being wasted. At least I'm here in day-to-day contact with the problems of my people. What good would I be after four or five years of a lot of white brainwashing in some phony, prestige institution, huh? I'd be like you and Daddy and those other educated blacks sitting over there in Linden Hills with a terminal case of middle-class amnesia.''

''You don't have to live in a slum to be concerned about social conditions, Melanie. Your father and I have been charter members of the NAACP for the last twenty-five years.''

''Oh, God!'' Kiswana threw her head back in exaggerated disgust. ''That's being concerned? That middle-of-the-road, Uncle Tom dumping ground for black Republicans!''

''You can sneer all you want, young lady, but the organization has been working for black people since the turn of the century, and it's still working for them. Where are all those radical groups of yours that were going to put a Cadillac in every garage and Dick Gregory in the White House? I'll tell you where.''

I knew you would, Kiswana thought angrily.

"They burned themselves out because they wanted too much too fast. Their goals weren't grounded in reality. And that's always been your problem.''

"What do you mean, my problem? I know exactly what I'm about.''

"No, you don't. You constantly live in a fantasy world—always going to extremes—turning butterflies into eagles, and life isn't about that. It's accepting what is and working from that. Lord, I remember how worried you had me, putting all that lacquered hair spray on your head. I thought you were going to get lung cancer—trying to be what you're not.''

Kiswana jumped up from the couch. "Oh, God, I can't take this anymore. Trying to be something I'm not—trying to be something I'm not, Mama! Trying to be proud of my heritage and the fact that I was of African descent. If that's being what I'm not, then I say fine. But I'd rather be dead than be like you—a white man's nigger who's ashamed of being black!''

Kiswana saw streaks of gold and ebony light follow her mother's flying body out of the chair. She was swung around by the shoulders and made to face the deadly stillness in the angry woman's eyes. She was too stunned to cry out from the pain of the long fingernails that dug into her shoulders, and she was brought so close to her mother's face that she saw her reflection, distorted and wavering, in the tears that stood in the older woman's eyes. And she listened in that stillness to a story she had heard from a child.

"My grandmother,'' Mrs. Browne began slowly in a whisper, "was a full-bloodied Iroquois, and my grandfather a free black from a long line of journeymen who had lived in Connecticut since the establishment of the colonies. And my father was a Bajan who came to this country as a cabin boy on a merchant mariner.''

"I know all that,'' Kiswana said, trying to keep her lips from trembling.

"Then, know this.'' And the nails dug deeper into her flesh. "I am alive because of the blood of proud people who never scraped or begged or apologized for what they were. They lived asking only one thing of this world—to be allowed to be. And I learned through the blood of these people that black isn't beautiful and it isn't ugly—black is! It's not kinky hair and it's not straight hair—it just is.

"It broke my heart when you changed your name. I gave you my grandmother's name, a woman who bore nine children and educated them all, who held off six white men with a shotgun when they tried to drag one of her sons to jail for 'not knowing his place.' Yet you needed to reach into an African dictionary to find a name to make you proud.

"When I brought my babies home from the hospital, my ebony son and my golden daughter, I swore before whatever gods would listen—those of my mother's people or those of my father's people—that I would use everything I had and could ever get to see that my children were prepared to meet this world on its own terms, so that no one could sell them short and make them ashamed of what they were or how they looked—whatever they were or however they looked. And Melanie, that's not being white or red or black—that's being a mother."

Kiswana followed her reflection in the two single tears that moved down her mother's cheeks until it blended with them into the woman's copper skin. There was nothing and then so much that she wanted to say, but her throat kept closing up every time she tried to speak. She kept her head down and her eyes closed, and thought, Oh, God, just let me die. How can I face her now?

Mrs. Browne lifted Kiswana's chin gently. "And the one lesson I wanted you to learn is not to be afraid to face anyone, not even a crafty old lady like me who can outtalk you." And she smiled and winked.

"Oh, Mamma, I . . ." and she hugged the woman tightly.

"Yeah, baby." Mrs. Browne patted her back. "I know."

She kissed Kiswana on the forehead and cleared her throat. "Well, now, I better be moving on. It's getting late, there's dinner to be made, and I have to get off my feet-these new shoes are killing me."

Kiswana looked down at the beige leather pumps. "Those are really classy. They're English, aren't they?"

"Yes, but, Lord, do they cut me right across the instep." She removed the shoe and sat on the couch to massage her foot.

Bright red nail polish glared at Kiswana through the stockings. "Since when do you polish your toenails?" she gasped. "You never did that before."

"Well . . ." Mrs. Browne shrugged her shoulders, "your father sort of talked me into it, and, uh, you know, he likes it and all, so I thought, uh, you know, why not, so . . ." And she gave Kiswana an embarrassed smile.

I'll be damned, the young woman thought, feeling her whole face tingle. Daddy's into feet! And she looked at the blushing woman on her couch and suddenly realized that her mother had trod through the same universe that she herself was now traveling. Kiswana was breaking no new trails and would eventually end up just two feet away on that couch. She stared at the woman she had been and was to become.

"But I'll never be a Republican," she caught herself saying aloud.

"What are you mumbling about, Melanie?" Mrs. Browne slipped on her shoe and got up from the couch.

She went to get her mother's coat. "Nothing, Mama. It's really nice of you to come by. You should do it more often."

"Well, since it's not Sunday, I guess you're allowed at least one lie."

They both laughed.

After Kiswana had closed the door and turned around, she spotted an envelope sticking between the cushions of her couch. She went over and opened it up; there was seventy-five dollars in it.

"Oh, Mama, darn it!" She rushed to the window and started to call to the woman, who had just emerged from the building, but she suddenly changed her mind and sat down in the chair with a long sigh that caught in the upward draft of the autumn wind and disappeared over the top of the building.

● ● ● ● ●

From *The Deity Nodded*

Arthenia J. Bates Millican

A native of Sumter, North Carolina, born in 1920, Arthenia Millican now resides in Baker, Louisiana. She received her B.A. degree in 1941 from Morris College in Sumter, her M.A. degree in 1948 from Atlanta University, and her Ph.D. degree in 1972 from Louisiana State University. She taught English and creative writing in various high schools and colleges throughout the South before retiring from the Baton Rouge campus of Southern University in 1979. Her fiction includes two collections of short stories, *Seeds beneath the Snow* (1969) and *Such Things from the Valley* (1977), and a novel, *The Deity Nodded* (Harlo, 1973), which reflects the religious repression within her own family. Her short stories, vignettes, poetry, and criticism have appeared in *CLA Journal, Black World, The Last Cookie, Negro American Literature Forum, Callaloo,* and *Obsidian*. Although numerous illnesses have curtailed Millican's writing career, she has received many certificates of recognition as a writer and community worker. In 1975 the University of South Carolina established an Arthenia Bates Millican file to preserve her writings, and in 1976 it recognized her as an honorary member of the South Caroliniana Society (an organization established in 1937 to collect and preserve manuscripts of South Carolinians).

Millican was a recent Catholic convert when she began *The Deity Nodded* in 1965. Her youngest sister, Catherine Alia, a Black Muslim convert, inspired her to write the book as a contribution to the black arts movement of the 1960s. Reflecting on Catherine Alia, the real-life counterpart to the novel's protagonist Tisha Dees, Millican has said, "Alia, as a child who would become a physical scientist, never received answers to satisfy her mind when she asked question after question about the mysteries of the Christian religion. Her mother pointed her out as a sinner in the open congregation during a revival meeting that led her to the mourner's bench and on to baptism at 11. Catherine Alia called baptism 'a cool shower' and church attendance 'putting a bandage on deep heart wounds.'" As a teenager, Catherine, like Tisha, defied her mother by leaving home, marrying, and converting to Islam. Accepting Allah gave Catherine "recourse to the benefits that the Messenger outlined in the 'Dedication . . . to My People' in his book, *Message to the Black Man in America:* Justice, Equality, Happiness, Peace of Mind, Contentment, Money, Good Jobs, Decent Homes."[1] Also like Tisha, Catherine became a convert, then a proselyte.

In *The Deity Nodded* the split between mother and daughter is spiritual: the daughter, Tisha Dees, rejects the Christian faith of old Mother McCullum—a kind of godmother to her—and embraces the Muslim faith. For Tisha, Mother McCullum, who as "Mother" of the local church has attained its highest distinction for women, embodies the Christian faith: she has lived according to its tenets, and her life is a testament to such a faith. She says to Tisha, "You see what He's done for me, don't you, child?"; but what Tisha sees is ugliness and impoverishment—a life dedicated to the hereafter, to death. "The old woman was dying," Tisha thinks, "dying as she had done every day of her life. . . . Her ugly life was death." The Muslim faith, she tries to explain to Mother McCullum, "helps us to have heaven right here on earth and that's what I want, for I can enjoy life every day of my life." Tisha is far more comfortable with her choice than either Walker's Meridian or Naylor's Kiswana. She still cherishes certain memories of Mother McCullum and is able to separate the religion she hates from the woman she cares for.

NOTE

1. Arthenia J. Bates Millican, letter to the author, 8 February 1991.

The thick evergreens screened Georgia Ann McCullum's front porch so well that Tisha did not see her sitting in the porch swing until she reached the top step—the eighth—because she had once measured her age by these steps. She had practiced the salutation "Mother" Georgia to pay honor to this distant cousin, who had reached the highest point of distinction for a woman in Chute Bay. She had been made Mother of Chute Bay Memorial Baptist Church which had been built by the people in the Bay on a pay-as-you-go basis during the depression years.

Tisha stood quietly, hugging herself in the full length Natural Emba Autumn Haze mink coat as she waited for the old woman to recognize her. Even though it was a bright day, the temperature held at 23 degrees above zero and a stiff breeze blew in from the north.

The noise of a truck coming down Front Street, jostled the swinger from an apparent reverie. She slipped from the swing and started forward, then recognized Tisha. Their eyes met and held long enough for the old woman to make a good guess. She fumbled in her mind, grunted, then caught by pain, she backed back to the swing to steady herself. The swing moved backward, almost causing her to miss her seat.

Tisha rushed to catch her.

"Don't fall Mother Georgia—please don't fall," she pleaded.

"Don't tell me," Mother Georgia said, "you Flora Dees' baby. Ain't you now?"

"Yes, Mother Georgia," she answered, and relaxed her grip, helping the old woman to seat herself in the swing.

"This here Tisha. Sweet little Tisha. Just as pretty, too. You look good enough to eat. Your Grandpa still call you his little spicy gal?"

"Grandpa hasn't had time to talk to me yet, Mother Georgia."

"I see," she answered. "But thang God. Thang God. Thang God. I talk to Him the other night, 'bout you, and here He done sent you already. I ain't scared of you—just 'cause you gone astray." She cradled Tisha in her arms and muzzled her thin cheeks with a bottom lip packed hard with Railroad Mill snuff. Coins hit the porch and began to roll as they reeled in this odd pantomime of genuine affection. She finally held Tisha away at arm-length and gloating over her, told of the wonders that had come with the title, "Mother" Georgia.

Old white men whose shirts she had ironed until arthritis twisted both of her wrists—who had brought shirts to her even though they opened a one-day service laundry in Crystal Hill, who now brought hand-outs to supplement the $54.00 a month from the "government"— even they used the title of honor "Mother" Georgia when they had for decades, called her "anty."

After this rehearsal, Tisha began to pick up the coins from the floor.

She found several nickels and a dime, but Mother Georgia said that was not all.

"Don't bother yourself," she told Tisha. "Go on in, and make yourself at home. You needn't act like company when this your second home. I'm slow, but I'm coming."

Tisha walked into the front room, a room she knew by heart before she left Chute Bay. She glanced about, noticing that it was the same. She waited for a minute for Mother Georgia, then brushed the bottom of a chair with her fingers to test it for dust. Her finger tips were black with coal dust. She walked to the door to check on the old woman's delay. She did not want to be caught cleaning the chair. She walked to the door and looked out in time to see Mother Georgia crawling about slowly on her knees and fumbling up an down the porch planks with her drawn hands.

"Mother Georgia, can I help?"

"No Sugar, I got all but two pennies. Hope the Lord them two didn't roll off the porch. If it was Mr. Pogue truck, I'd get my coal if I was a few cents short. But this truck want every cent. I don't know who it belongst to."

"Come on in, Mother Georgia," Tisha said, "I'll give you what you need for the coal man." She then went out and helped her up from the floor.

"Sugar, they got them ole engines what pull theirself. If they was still using coal like they used to, I'd be out there up and down them tracks with my bucket, picking me up all the coal I want."

"Yes mam," Tisha replied. "Now tell me how much the coal cost and I'll sit out there and wait for the truck."

"No, Sugar. You so dressed up, he might not stop if he don't see me. You just sit tight and soons he come, I'm going to make up a great big fire in the heater. It ain't cold, is it? I got on plenty clothes and you got on that big fine coat. Don't get hetted up 'cause I got to ask you for myself 'bout that Allie what Flora worried to death 'bout. She worried plumb stiff 'bout that God've yours just like she can't put you back in your place. Humph. I said, send her to me when she come home. I'll get her straight before she go back out yonder."

Tisha patted her feet as Mother Georgia talked because her toes were getting stiff from the cold. A minute later, a truck pulled up and she let Tisha give him $1.25 for a croker sack of coal and a bunch of lightwood splinters. She built a fire in the heater with two splinters and a few lumps of coal. She washed her hands in a basin on the washstand, then sat down to watch Tisha.

"Lord, Sugar, you look good enough to bite on the jaw. The only thing got me bothered is what your Ma told me 'bout that Allie. You know you got her nearly distracted? What's that, anyhow child—talkin 'bout gointa serve Allie? That ain't no God. You know Mother Georgia ain't gonta tell you nothing wrong long's I had my hand on the gospel plough. That was 'fore they spanked your Ma, so you know I'm a soldier. You got no business turning your back on God."

"Allah, Mother Georgia, is the true God. You see, I know He's the right God, because of what He's done for me. Okay?" Tisha started to stand, but the old woman waved her back to her chair. "He helps us to have heaven right here on earth and that's what I want, for I can enjoy life every day of my life."

"What I'm telling you—that is what Mother Georgia, ambassador to Christ, is telling you, is that ain't no God you found up the road. Your Ma learned you 'bout the right God from your cradle and it ought to be good enough to take you to your grave. You see what He's done for me, don't you, child? That Allie you heard tell of way out yonder, is just a make-shift God the crowd harkning after. And I'm trying to tell you better 'cause, you, Flora and every child she got rest close to my heart. We kin as cousins, but I been a mother to her and to y'all before I come a Mother to the church. You better turn to the true and living God 'fore it's a day and hour and eternity too late."

Tisha started to let the argument rest, but she felt that she would be a shameful volunteer for Allah if she let this occasion pass without sharing an idea of his worth.

"I'm serving Allah," she persisted, "and I hope to serve Him better. For the first time, I've learned the truth about Christianity, Mother Georgia. The slave masters gave us that religion. It's not ours."

"I'm going on these knees, little Miss, to the Master I know—who'll open your eyes. Look at me." Mother Georgia hoisted her huge frame from the rocker and fastened her dim brown eyes on Tisha. "I'm seventy-six odd years old. How you reckon I made it without the Lord? You see that sack of coal? The Lord sent it here. Let me tell you, the pastor—I reckon you don't know Reverend Sarks—anyway, he come here faithful as the days is long and brings me ration just like he take it home. And Mr. Dwyer—I guess you forgot him—he sends me all the bones from his store to feed these six dogs I got on the yard for company. Some of them oxtails 'n stuff the dogs don't see, 'cause I make me a pot've soup."

"Well, let's not get excited," Tisha said. "I brought a present for you. Let's look after that." Tisha handed her a small Christmas wrapped package which the old woman shook.

"What these, drawers?" she asked.

Tisha shook her head. "You see," she told Mother Georgia, "we don't have Christmas, but you do."

"You mean Allie don't let ya'll have no Christmas? How do you do when you don't ever have no Christmas? How can you live with no Christmas?"

"Everyday ought to be important in this life." Tisha had lost her ardor.

"Oh, these them pretty head rags!—well, I'm going to wear this cotton one to Prayer meeting and the silk one on Communion Sunday." She rewrapped the gift in the same paper.

"That will be nice." Tisha was pleased with her happiness over the small gift. It was one of the things she always cherished about Mother Georgia.

It was warm enough now for Tisha to remove her coat. The old woman got up to leave for the kitchen, but Tisha tried to persuade her to relax or if she insisted on making coffee, to make it on the heater, but she would not listen.

"You're company now," she maintained, "and a fine lady at that, so I'll treat you like one, no matter if you did used to help me out. You make yourself at home now while I get straight in the kitchen. And you get up and turn that coat insadouter, so's no smoke'll hit it."

"Yes man," she answered.

Tisha sat there remembering the room as she had known it years before. This room was full of furniture. There was an upright grand piano, a three-piece bedroom suite, a washstand, two rocking chairs, a davenport with sugar-starched crocheted pieces on the arm rests. The center table held a large metal oil lamp on the top and a big family Bible on the bottom tier. The old green wool rug was practically eaten from the floor and the wallpaper of unidentified color was smoky and filled with rainwater circles.

There was an array of several pretty vases on the mantle piece of odd shapes and sizes and pictures hung indiscriminately wherever a nail could be placed to hold them. High above the mantle was a picture of cupid asleep with the bow and arrow beside him. Glancing around the wall, she found the pictures of undertakers, ministers, church groups, family members, movie stars and flowers. There was a lone insurance policy hanging above the door sill going to the middle room. She tried to evaluate the holdings of this room in terms of financial worth—the most valuable possessions in the house secured from a lifetime of satisfactory labor. They hardly added up to dollars and cents.

After a while, Mother Georgia came in with a cup of coffee and a plate of cake on a tray.

"I made your coffee on the hot plate. I got 'lectric, you know," and pointed to the bulb hanging on a suspended wire in the center of the room. "I have my lamp lighted half the time, before I remember I can pull that little chain to get some light." She watched Tisha a minute, then encouraged her to eat the five slices of cake because she had baked the cakes herself. They were her specials: raisin, chocolate, pineapple, coconut and strawberry jelly.

"Mother Georgia," she said, "you remember the time I ate a whole plateful of cake when I was a child? Well, that was the best cake I'd ever had in my life at that time. And since then I've found out how to enjoy life the way I enjoyed that first plate of cake you gave me. As long as you enjoy this life, there's nothing to worry about."

"I don't want to spoil your appetite, but you're gone from your raising. You're caught in the web of sin. And you know what that mean. You sitting there all pretty, but you dying, Sugar." The old woman shook her head. Everyone seemed to shake their heads, Tisha thought, in regard to her decision.

Dying! Tisha turned and looked at Georgia Ann McCullum. *She* was dying. The old woman was dying—dying as she had done every day of her life, though she was too good a minstrel man to know it. Her ugly life was death. She no doubt would have a beautiful funeral according to their pattern, with a nice long obituary, good remarks from the deacons, a wailing eulogy from the preacher and honest tears from unknown visitors at the grave; but her life was and always had been an ugly death.

"Thang God you come though, Sugar. Look—put your cake you left in a bag and take it home with you. And when you go back up the road, you'll remember what God has done for me, and you'll forget about that Allie and the Mooselims. They'll run the world off the map if you not careful. You were raised to know that no colored folks can't rule the world by theirself. My folks told me white folks is a mess, but a nigger ain't nothing."

"Yes mam," Tisha said as she put on her coat to leave. She was not going to argue with the old lady because more than anyone else, Mother Georgia had given her the final proof that she had chosen the right path—the path away from the religion of the Cross. God, the God of Mother Georgia, the God of her parents, the God who had let His only Son be crucified by wicked men, was uncaring. Then, as now, she told herself, if He was up there, He was oblivious of all the Georgia Ann McCullums in the universe.

She pulled the mink closer to her ears as she faced the cold crisp air on the walk back to her parents' home down Front Street, happy in the thought that she had learned to praise Allah who cared for His black children enough to help them find heaven on earth.

PART 3

Black Women and the Black Feminist Movement

If I should take a notion to jump into the ocean,
   'Tain't nobody's biz-ness if I do.
If I go to church on Sunday, then just shimmy down on Monday,
   'Tain't nobody's biz-ness if I do.
                                   —Porter Grainger and Everett Robbins
                                   'Tain't Nobody's Biz-ness If I Do

Black Women Search for Sisterhood

• • • • •

"The black movement and the feminist movement, with all their internal currents and tensions, have presided over recent developments in Afro-American women's political and self-consciousness."[1] What is most interesting in Elizabeth Fox-Genovese's statement is the phrase "with all their internal currents and tensions"; in many respects it was the ways in which black women found themselves at odds with both movements that led them to black feminism. Black women were at home in neither the feminist movement, which was dominated by white women, nor the black movement, which was dominated by black men. At the heart of each movement were the concerns of its dominant members. Beyond those concerns black women had in common with white female feminists because of their sex and with male black power advocates because of their skin color, other issues important and particular to them were considered peripheral, were simply not considered at all, or were even considered in conflict with the interests of the movements.

At the turn of the century, when much of the groundwork for the women's suffrage movement was being laid, women's organizations seeking to further the position of women in American society burgeoned. Groups for both white and black women proliferated but remained segregated. The more obvious reason is that black women were simply excluded from most groups founded by white women because of their race. In 1890 Josephine Ruffin, a New Englander of mixed ancestry, attended a convention of the all-white General Federation of women's

Clubs. She was representing the largely white New England Federation of Women's Clubs as well as the all-black New Era Club and presented credentials from both. "When it was discovered that the New Era Club was composed of colored women, the uproar was not confined to verbal exchanges; efforts were made on the convention floor to snatch Mrs. Ruffin's badge."[2] The credentials committee ended up accepting her as a representative of the white clubs but not of the black club. Rebecca Lowe, as president of the General Federation of Women's Clubs, once said of Ruffin that if "she were the cultured lady everyone says she is, she should put her education and her talents to good uses as a colored woman among colored women."[3]

The other, more compelling reason black women organized groups for themselves (or "clubs," as they were then called) was that the circumstances of their lives were far different from those of white women:

> Because they were barred from all but the most menial jobs, they were not concerned with trade unions, nor was suffrage an issue except to a small educated number among them. Even in those sections of the country where Negroes had greater opportunity than in the South, they remained for a long time second-class citizens, dependent largely on themselves for those social benefits which were increasingly a matter of civic responsibility in the white community: care of the sick, homeless and aged, and concern with health and education. The frequent separation of families, often caused by the husband's search for work or for sheer physical safety, brought with it another whole complex of problems, including actual destitution.[4]

Parallels between the climate for black women at the turn of the century and during the 1970s and early 1980s exist. Then, as later, the influence of racism and stark differences in life experience blinded white women to the needs of black women and kept black and white women from working together toward their common goals.

The racism in the modern feminist movement was not as explicit as Rebecca Lowe's in 1900, but nonetheless it existed. As Bell Hooks wrote in 1984, "The ideology of Sisterhood as expressed by contemporary feminist activists indicated *no acknowledgment* that racist discrimination, exploitation, and oppression of multi-ethnic women by white women had made it impossible for the two groups to feel they shared common interests or political concerns. . . . Historically, many black women experienced white women as the white supremacist group who most directly exercised power over them, often in a manner far more brutal and dehumanizing than that of white racist men [italics added]."

Hooks also addresses the effect of their different life experience on black women's view of the feminist movement; many perceived that the "women's liberation movement as outlined by bourgeois white women would serve their interests at the expense of poor and working class women, many of whom were black." This difference in experience also created a disrespect in black women for certain qualities associated with privileged white women. Hooks quotes Toni Morrison: "Black women have been able to envy white women; . . . they could fear them . . . and even love them; . . . but black women have found it impossible to respect white women. . . . White women were ignorant of the facts of life. . . . They were totally dependent on marriage or male support (emotionally and economically). They confronted their sexuality with furtiveness, complete abandon, or repression. Those who could afford it gave over the management of the house and the rearing of children to others."[5] Morrison notes that the two primary focuses of rebellion by the educated middle- and upper-class women who dominated the feminist movement of the late 1960s were dependence on male support and lack of sexual freedom. But the financial, sexual, and psychological liberation of the suburban housewife, as argued for in Betty Friedan's landmark text *The Feminine Mystique* (1963) and popularized in the media, held little interest for most black women.

The disenfranchisement of black women on the black liberation front was rooted in nineteenth-century black activism, continued in the civil rights movement of the late 1950s and early 1960s, and intensified in the black power movement. Michele Wallace, in chronicling her attempts as a young woman to find liberation from sexual and racial oppression, describes her disappointment in what she calls the "Black Movement": "The message of the Black Movement was that I was being watched, on probation as a black woman, that any signs of aggressiveness, intelligence, or independence would mean I'd be denied even the one role still left open to me as 'my man's woman,' keeper of the house." Later, after she had entered college, "young black female friends of mine were dropping out of school because their boyfriends had convinced them that it was 'not correct' and 'counterrevolutionary' to strive to do anything but have babies and clean house."

From the late 1960s until the mid-1980s, black women more than black men have continued a struggle for black liberation that has brought them survival and upward mobility. According to Deborah King, the black woman seems to realize that her "survival depends on her ability to use all the economic, social, and cultural resources available to her from both the larger society and within her community."[6] No longer dependent on the black male activist to enumerate her duties within the black community, the black woman has taken it upon herself to become more goal-oriented, setting her sights on educational and employment opportunities as a means of freeing herself from poverty and oppression. Moreover, black women have earnestly tried to keep the African-American race alive by raising children as single parents at a time when the supply of black males eligible for marriage and procreation has dwindled, a time that seems for black men to be a nadir in the struggle for black liberation.

In the early 1970s black women formed a number of groups to meet their own needs, heralding the beginning of an organized search for sisterhood among black women. They organized the National Black Feminist Organization (NBFO) in 1973 to address issues relating to welfare, unwed mothers, domestic workers, and reproductive freedom.[7] They established the Combahee River Collective in 1974 to address racial, classist, sexual, and heterosexual oppression.[8] They formed satellite groups such as the League of Black Women (Chicago), the National Black Women's Political Leadership Caucus (Detroit), and the Black Women's Organization for Action (San Francisco). They organized the Black Women's Studies Faculty and Curriculum Development Project (1983–85) to assist black women faculty members at traditionally black schools in developing black women's studies courses and making curriculum changes to account for the historic roles of black women in all subject areas.

The black women who joined such groups often found affirmation and support, but they also encountered criticism and setbacks. A primary criticism was that these segregated groups "both endorsed and perpetuated the very 'racism' they were supposedly attacking," and that they "did not provide a critical evaluation of the women's movement and offer to all women a feminist ideology uncorrupted by racism or the opportunistic desires of individual groups."[9] A major setback for black feminists was their failure to appeal to the masses of black women—primarily because, traditionally, black women did not separate their concerns as women from the concerns of the African-American race. "While Black women have fostered and encouraged sisterhood," writes Bonnie Thornton Dill, "we have not used it as an anvil to forge out political identities."[10] Black women in America have always identified themselves first as blacks and second as women. Dorothy Height, president of the National Council of Negro Women, sums up the feelings of black women: "I think that it is not that black women are not interested in the liberation of women, but many people have not recognized that everyone has to work for the liberation of black people—men and women."[11]

Although black feminism during the 1970s and 1980s did not win over the larger share of the black female population, it was an important organized effort to acknowledge and give voice to the experiences and needs of the black woman. Like any powerful movement, it offered something larger than life—greater than the individual—with which black women could identify and from which they could draw sustenance. Crystal Rhodes's play The Trip offers a glimpse of life without the benefit of such meaning. It not only depicts the complex, largely political, essentially idealistic search for sisterhood discussed in the pieces by Hooks and Wallace, but it also portrays the antithesis of such a search. The young black women in the play seem lost, with no strong connection to anything larger than themselves—their friendships, their families, the church, a social or political movement. They are, in a sense, personally disenfranchised, and the play demonstrates the pitfalls of such an existence—by no means an unusual one for the late 1970s and 1980s.

NOTES

1. Fox-Genovese, "My Statue, My Self," 182.
2. Eleanor Flexner, *Century of Struggle: The Woman's Rights Movement in the United States* (New York: Atheneum, 1970), 191.
3. Rayford Logan, *The Betrayal of the Negro* (New York: Macmillan, 1954), 241.
4. Flexner, *Century of Struggle*, 186.
5. Toni Morrison, "What the Black Woman Thinks about Women's Lib" *New York Times Magazine*, 22 August 1971, 15.
6. Deborah K. King, "Multiple Jeopardy, Multiple Consciousness: The Context of a Black Feminist Ideology," in Hine, *Black Women in U.S. History*, 10:338.
7. "Black Feminism: A New Mandate," *Ms.* 2 (May 1974): 97.
8. "A Black Feminist Statement: The Combahee River Collective," in *All the Women Are White, All the Blacks Are Men, But Some of Us Are Brave*, ed. Gloria T. Hull, Patricia Bell Scott, and Barbara Smith (Old Westbury, N.Y.: Feminist Press, 1982), 13–14.
9. Hooks, *Ain't I a Woman*, 154.
10. Bonnie Thornton Dill, "Race, Class, and Gender: Prospects for an All-Inclusive Sisterhood," in Hine, *Black Women in U.S. History*, 9:124.
11. Quoted in Renee Ferguson, "Women's Liberation Has a Different Meaning for Blacks," in *Black Women in White America: A Documentary History*, ed. Gerda Lerner (New York: Random House, 1973), 589–90.

• • • • •

"Sisterhood: Political Solidarity Between Women"

Bell Hooks

A native of Hopkinsville, Kentucky, Bell Hooks was born in 1952 and began writing poetry at 13. The burden of schoolwork, domestic chores, and part-time jobs soon made her realize that she would not be able to make a living as a writer. In college she chose English as a major primarily to steer herself into a profession in which she could use her writing skills. An associate professor of English and women's studies at Oberlin College, Hooks has taught English, creative writing, and women's studies at the University of California at Santa Cruz and at Yale University. Her interest extends beyond the art of writing; she is also concerned about the financial and emotional support that writers, particularly black women writers, need. In her essay "Black Women Writing: Creating More Space" (*Sage*, Spring 1985), Hooks notes that it took her seven years to complete her first major feminist publication, *Ain't I a Woman: Black Women and Feminism* (1981), and that the encouragement of friends and published women writers helped her complete and publish it. Hooks's other books on feminism include *Feminist Theory: From Margin to Center* (1984) and *Talking Back, Thinking Feminist, Thinking Black* (1988).

Hooks says that she wrote "Sisterhood: Political Solidarity between Women" because she wants whites to understand that black women do embrace sisterhood but that their vision of sisterhood differs from that of whites. That difference, she says, is "a conscious sisterhood, one that crosses races, classes, and generations, and not just a sentimental sisterhood which forces relationships based on false premises."[1]

In "Sisterhood: Political Solidarity between Women," an essay originally published in *Feminist Theory* (South End Press), Hooks explores the racism, the classicism, and the conflicting factions within the women's movement. Both racism and classicism, she argues, have fueled sexism by diminishing women of color and working-class women. Hooks dismisses the movement's use of the term *sisterhood:* it falsely assumed a fundamental similarity among women based solely on gender and a common bond based on their oppression and victimization. She calls instead for a genuine, more practicable form of sisterhood that acknowledges the differences among women and focuses more on shared strengths. "Women do not need to eradicate difference to feel solidarity," Hooks suggests. "We do not need to share common

240

oppression to fight equally to end oppression. We do not need anti-male sentiments to bond together, so great is the wealth of experience, culture, and ideas we have to share with one another." Her essay charts the problems and progress of the women's movement into the early 1980s and traces the emergence of the black woman's voice both within and outside the movement.

NOTE

1. Bell Hooks, telephone interview with the author, 11 February 1991.

Women are the group most victimized by sexist oppression. As with other forms of group oppression, sexism is perpetuated by institutional and social structures; by the individuals who dominate, exploit, or oppress; and by the victims themselves who are socialized to behave in ways that make them act in complicity with the status quo. Male supremacist ideology encourages women to believe we are valueless and obtain value only by relating to or bonding with men. We are taught that our relationships with one another diminish rather than enrich our experience. We are taught that women are "natural" enemies, that solidarity will never exist between us because we cannot, should not, and do not bond with one another. We have learned these lessons well. We must unlearn them if we are to build a sustained feminist movement. We must learn to live and work in solidarity. We must learn the true meaning and value of Sisterhood.

Although contemporary feminist movement should have provided a training ground for women to learn about political solidarity, Sisterhood was not viewed as a revolutionary accomplishment women would work and struggle to obtain. The vision of Sisterhood evoked by women's liberationists was based on the idea of common oppression. Needless to say, it was primarily bourgeois white women, both liberal and radical in perspective, who professed belief in the notion of common oppression. The idea of "common oppression" was a false and corrupt platform disguising and mystifying the true nature of women's varied and complex social reality. Women are divided by sexist attitudes, racism, class privilege, and a host of other prejudices. Sustained woman bonding can occur only when these divisions are confronted and the necessary steps are taken to eliminate them. Divisions will not be eliminated by wishful thinking or romantic reverie about common oppression despite the value of highlighting experiences all women share.

In recent years Sisterhood as slogan, motto, rallying cry no longer evokes the spirit of power in unity. Some feminists now seem to feel that unity between women is impossible given our differences. Abandoning the idea of Sisterhood as an expression of political solidarity weakens and diminishes feminist movement. Solidarity strengthens resistance struggle. There can be no mass-based feminist movement to end sexist oppression without a united front—women must take the initiative and demonstrate the power of solidarity. Unless we can show that barriers separating women can be eliminated, that solidarity can exist, we cannot hope to change and transform society as a whole. The shift away from an emphasis on Sisterhood has occurred because many women, angered by the insistence on "common oppression," shared identity, sameness, criticized or dismissed feminist movement altogether. The emphasis on Sisterhood was often seen as the emotional appeal masking the opportunism of manipulative bourgeois white women. It was seen as a cover-up hiding the fact that many women exploit and oppress other women. Black woman activist lawyer Florynce Kennedy wrote an essay, published in the anthology *Sisterhood Is Powerful*, voicing her suspicions about the existence of solidarity between women as early as 1970:

> It is for this reason that I have considerable difficulty with the sisterhood mystique: "We are sisters," "Don't criticize a 'sister' publicly," etc. When a female judge asks my client where the bruises are when she complains about being assaulted by her husband (as did Family Court Judge Sylvia Jaffin Liese), and makes smart remarks about her being overweight, and when another female judge is so hostile that she disqualifies herself but refuses to order a combative husband out of the house (even though he owns property elsewhere with suitable living quarters) these judges are not my sisters.[1]

Women were wise to reject a false Sisterhood based on shallow notions of bonding. We are mistaken if we allow these distortions or the women who created them (many of whom now tell us bonding between women is unimportant) to lead us to devalue Sisterhood.

Women are enriched when we bond with one another but we cannot develop sustaining ties or political solidarity using the model of Sisterhood created by bourgeois women's liberationists. According to their analysis, the basis for bonding was shared victimization, hence the emphasis on common oppression.[2] This concept of bonding directly reflects male supremacist thinking. Sexist ideology teaches women that to be female is to be a victim. Rather than repudiate this equation (which mystifies female experience—in their daily lives most women are not continually passive, helpless, or powerless "victims"), women's liberationists embraced it, making shared victimization the basis for woman bonding. This meant that women had to conceive of themselves as "victims'' in order to feel that feminist movement was relevant to their lives. Bonding as victims created a situation in which assertive, self-affirming women were often seen as having no place in feminist movement. It was this logic that led white women activists (along with black men) to suggest that black women were so ''strong'' they did not need to be active in feminist movement. It was this logic that led many white women activists to abandon feminist movement when they no longer embraced the victim identity. Ironically, the women who were most eager to be seen as ''victims,'' who overwhelmingly stressed the role of victim, were more privileged and powerful than the vast majority of women in our society. An example of this tendency is some writing about violence against women. Women who are exploited and oppressed daily cannot afford to relinquish the belief that they exercise some measure of control, however relative, over their lives. They cannot afford to see themselves solely as ''victims'' because their survival depends on continued exercise of whatever personal powers they possess. It would be psychologically demoralizing for these women to bond with other women on the basis of shared victimization. They bond with other women on the basis of shared strengths and resources. This is the woman bonding feminist movement should encourage. It is this type of bonding that is the essence of Sisterhood.

Bonding as ''victims,'' white women liberationists were not required to assume responsibility for confronting the complexity of their own experience. They were not challenging one another to examine their sexist attitudes towards women unlike themselves or exploring the impact of race and class privilege on their relationships to women outside their race/class groups. Identifying as ''victims,'' they could abdicate responsibility for their role in the maintenance and perpetuation of sexism, racism, and classicism, which they did by insisting that only men were the enemy. They did not acknowledge and confront the enemy within. They were not prepared to forego privilege and do the ''dirty work'' (the struggle and confrontation necessary to build political awareness as well as the many tedious tasks to be accomplished in day-to-day organizing) that is necessary in the development of radical political consciousness. The first task must be an honest critique and evaluation of one's social status, values, political beliefs, etc. These women engaged in a narcissistic self-focus without self-interrogation. Sisterhood became yet another shield against reality, another support system. Their version of Sisterhood was informed by racist and classist assumption about white womanhood, that the white ''lady'' (that is to say bourgeois woman) should be protected from all that might upset or discomfort her and shielded from negative realities that might lead to confrontation. Their version of Sisterhood dictated that sisters were to ''unconditionally'' love one another; that they were to avoid conflict and minimize disagreement; that they were not to criticize one other, especially in public. For a time these mandates created an illusion of unity suppressing the competition, hostility, perpetual disagreement, and abusive criticism (trashing) that was often the norm in feminist groups. Today many splinter groups who share common identities (e.g., Wasp working class; white academic faculty women; anarchist feminists, etc.) use this same model of Sisterhood, but participants in these groups endeavor to support, affirm, and protect one another while demonstrating hostility (usually through excessive trashing) towards women outside the chosen sphere. Bonding between a chosen circle of women who strengthen their ties by excluding and devaluing women outside their group closely resembles the type of personal bonding between women that has always occurred under patriarchy: the one difference being the interest in feminism.

To develop political solidarity between women, feminist activists cannot bond on the terms set by the dominant ideology of the culture. We must define our own terms. Rather than bond on the basis of shared victimization or in response to a false sense of a common enemy, we can bond on the basis of our political commitment to a feminist movement that aims to end sexist oppression. Given such a commitment, our energies would not be concentrated on the issue of equality with men or solely on the struggle to resist male domination. We would no longer accept a simplistic good girls/bad boys account of the structure of sexist oppression. Before we can resist male domination we must break our attachment to sexism; we must work to transform female consciousness. Working together to expose, examine, and eliminate sexist socialization within ourselves, women would strengthen and affirm one another and build a solid foundation for developing political solidarity.

Between women and men, sexism is most often expressed in the form of male domination which leads to discrimination, exploitation, or oppression. Between women, male supremacist values are expressed through suspicious, defensive, competitive behavior. It is sexism that leads women to feel threatened by one another without cause. While sexism teaches women to be sex objects for men, it is also manifest when women who have repudiated this role feel contemptuous and superior in relation to those women who have not. Sexism leads women to devalue parenting work while inflating the value of jobs and careers. Acceptance of sexist ideology is indicated when women teach children that there are only two possible behavior patterns: the role of dominant or submissive being. Sexism teaches women woman-hating, and both consciously and unconsciously we act out this hatred in our daily contact with one another.

Although contemporary feminist activists, especially radical feminists, called attention to women's absorption in sexist ideology, ways

244

that women who are advocates of patriarchy, as well as women who uncritically accept sexist assumptions, could unlearn that socialization were not stressed.[3] It was often assumed that to support feminism was synonymous with repudiation of sexism in all its forms. Taking on the label "feminist" was accepted as a sign of personal transformation; as a consequence, the process by which values were altered was either ignored or could not be spelled out because no fundamental change had occurred. Sometimes consciousness-raising groups provided space for women to explore their sexism. This examination of attitudes towards themselves and other women was often a catalyst for transformation. Describing the function of rap groups in *The Politics of Women's Liberation*, Jo Freeman explains:

> Women come together in small groups to share personal experiences, problems, and feelings. From this public sharing comes the realization that what was thought to be individual is in fact common: that what was thought to be a personal problem has a social cause and a political solution. The rap group attacks the effects of psychological oppression and helps women to put it into a feminist context. Women learn to see how social structures and attitudes have molded them from birth and limited their opportunities. They ascertain the extent to which women have been denigrated in this society and how they have developed prejudices against themselves and other women. They learn to develop self-esteem and to appreciate the value of group solidarity.[4]

As consciousness-raising groups lost their popularity new groups were not formed to fulfill similar functions. Women produced a large quantity of feminist writing but placed little emphasis on ways to unlearn sexism.

Since we live in a society that promotes fadism and temporary superficial adoption of different values, we are easily convinced that changes have occurred in arenas where there has been little or no change. Women's sexist attitudes towards one another are one such arena. All over the United States, women spend hours of their time daily verbally abusing other women, usually through malicious gossip (not to be confused with gossip as positive communication). Television soap operas and nighttime dramas continually portray woman-to-woman relationships as characterized by aggression, contempt, and competitiveness. In feminist circles sexism towards women is expressed by abusive trashing, total disregard and lack of concern or interest in women who have not joined feminist movement. This is especially evident at university campuses where feminist studies is often seen as a discipline or program having no relationship to feminist movement. In her commencement address at Barnard College in May, 1979, black woman writer Toni Morrison told her audience:

> I want not to ask you but to tell you not to participate in the oppression of your sisters. Mothers who abuse their children are women, and

245

another woman, not an agency, has to be willing to stay their hands. Mothers who set fire to school buses are women, and another woman, not an agency, has to tell them to stay their hands. Women who stop the promotion of other women in careers are women, and another woman must come to the victim's aid. Social and welfare workers who humiliate their clients may be women, and other women colleagues have to deflect their anger.

I am alarmed by the violence that women do to each other: professional violence, competitive violence, emotional violence. I am alarmed by the willingness of women to enslave other women. I am alarmed by a growing absence of decency on the killing floor of professional women's worlds.[5]

To build a politicized, mass-based feminist movement, women must work harder to overcome the alienation from one another that exists when sexist socialization has not been unlearned, e.g., homophobia, judging by appearance, conflicts between women with diverse sexual practices. So far, feminist movement has not transformed woman-to-woman relationships, especially between women who are strangers to one another or from different backgrounds, even though it has been the occasion for bonding between individuals and groups of women. We must renew our efforts to help women unlearn sexism if we are to develop affirming personal relationships as well as political unity.

Racism is another barrier to solidarity between women. The ideology of Sisterhood as expressed by contemporary feminist activists indicated no acknowledgment that racist discrimination, exploitation, and oppression of multi-ethnic women by white women had made it impossible for the two groups to feel they shared common interests or political concerns. Also, the existence of totally different cultural backgrounds can make communication difficult. This has been especially true of black and white female relationships. Historically, many black women experienced white women as the white supremacist group who most directly exercised power over them, often in a manner far more brutal and dehumanizing than that of racist white men. Today, despite predominant rule by white supremacist patriarchs, black women often work in situations where the immediate supervisor, boss, or authority figure is a white woman. Conscious of the privileges white men as well as white women gain as a consequence of racial domination, black women were quick to react to the feminist call for Sisterhood by pointing to the contradiction—that we should join with women who exploit us to help liberate them. The call for Sisterhood was heard by many black women as a plea for help and support for a movement that did not address us. As Toni Morrison explains in her article "What the Black Woman Thinks about Women's Lib," many black women do not respect bourgeois white women and could not imagine supporting a cause that would be for their benefit.

Black women have been able to envy white women (their looks, their easy life, the attention they seem to get from their men); they could fear them (for the economic control they have had over black women's lives); and even love them (as mammies and domestic workers can); but black women have found it impossible to respect white women. . . . Black women have no abiding admiration of white women as competent, complete people, whether vying with them for the few professional slots available to women in general, or moving their dirt from one place to another, they regarded them as willful children, pretty children, mean children, but never as real adults capable of handling the real problems of the world.

White women were ignorant of the facts of life—perhaps by choice, perhaps with the assistance of men, but ignorant anyway. They were totally dependent on marriage or male support (emotionally and economically). They confronted their sexuality with furtiveness, complete abandon, or repression. Those who could afford it gave over the management of the house and the rearing of children to others. (It is a source of amusement even now to black women to listen to feminist talk of liberation while somebody's nice black grandmother shoulders the daily responsibility of child rearing and floor mopping, and the liberated one comes home to examine the housekeeping, correct it, and be entertained by the children.) If Women's Lib needs those grandmothers to thrive, it has a serious flaw.[6]

Many perceived that women's liberation movement as outlined by bourgeois white women would serve their interests at the expense of poor and working class women, many of whom are black. Certainly this was not a basis for Sisterhood and black women would have been politically naive had we joined such a movement. However, given the struggles of black women's participation historically and currently in political organizing, the emphasis could have been on the development and clarification of the nature of political solidarity.

White females discriminate against and exploit black women while simultaneously being envious and competitive in their interactions with them. Neither process of interaction creates conditions wherein trust and mutually reciprocal relationships can develop. After constructing feminist theory and praxis in such a way as to omit focus on racism, white women shifted the responsibility for calling attention to race onto others. They did not have to take the initiative in discussions of racism or race privilege but could listen and respond to nonwhite women discussing racism without changing in any way the structure of feminist movement, without losing their hegemonic hold. They could then show their concern with having more women of color in feminist organizations by encouraging greater participation. They were not confronting racism. In more recent years, racism has become an accepted topic in feminist discussions not as a result of black women calling attention to it (this was done at the very onset of the movement), but as a result of white female input validating such discussions, a process which is indicative of how racism works. Commenting on this tendency in her essay "The Incompatible Menage À Trois: Marxism, Feminism, and Racism," Gloria Joseph states: "To date feminists have not concretely demonstrated the potential or capacity to become involved in fighting racism on an equal footing with sexism. Adrienne Rich's recent article on feminism and racism is an exemplary one on this topic. She reiterates much that has been voiced by black female writers, but the acclaim given her article shows again that it takes whiteness to give even Blackness validity."[7]

Focus on racism in feminist circles is usually directed at legitimating the "as is" structure of feminist theory and praxis. Like other affirmative action agendas in white supremacist capitalist patriarchy, lengthy discussions of racism or lip-service to its importance tend to call attention to the "political correctness" of current feminist movement; they are not directed at an overall struggle to resist racist oppression in our society (not just racism in feminist movement). Discussions of racism have been implicitly sexist because of the focus on guilt and personal behavior. Racism is not an issue simply because white women activists are individually racist. They represent a small percentage of women in this society. They could have all been anti-racist from the outset but eliminating racism would still need to be a central feminist issue. Racism is fundamentally a feminist issue because it is so inter-connected with sexist oppression. In the West, the philosophical foundations of racist and sexist ideology are similar. Although ethnocentric white values have led feminist theorists to argue the priority of sexism over racism, they do so in the context of attempting to create an evolutionary notion of culture, which in no way corresponds to our lived experience. In the United States, maintaining white supremacy has always been as great if not a greater priority than maintaining strict sex role divisions. It is no mere coincidence that interest in white women's rights is kindled whenever there is mass-based anti-racist protest. Even the most politically naive person can comprehend that a white supremacist state, asked to respond to the needs of oppressed black people and/or the needs of white women (particularly those from the bourgeois classes), will find it in its interest to respond to whites. Radical movement to end racism (a struggle that may have died to advance) is far more threatening than a women's movement shaped to meet the class needs of upwardly mobile white women.

It does not in any way diminish the value of or the need for feminist movement to recognize the significance of anti-racist struggle. Feminist theory would have much to offer if it showed women ways in which racism and sexism are immutably connected rather than pitting one struggle against the other or blatantly dismissing racism. A central issue for feminist activists has been the struggle to obtain for women the right to control their bodies. The very concept of white supremacy relies on the perpetuation of a white race. It is in the interest of continued white racist domination of the planet for white patriarchy to maintain control over all women's bodies. Any white female activist who works daily to help women gain control over their bodies and is racist negates and undermines her own effort. When white women attack white supremacy they are simultaneously participating in the struggle to end sexist oppression. This is just one example of the intersecting, complementary nature of racist and sexist oppression. There are many others that need to be examined by feminist theorists.

Racism allows white women to construct feminist theory and praxis in such a way that it is far removed from anything resembling radical struggle. Racist socialization teaches bourgeois white women to think they are necessarily more capable of leading masses of women than other groups of women. Time and time again, they have shown that they do not want to be part of feminist movement—they want to lead it. Even though bourgeois white women liberationists probably know less about grassroots organizing than many poor and working class women, they were certain of their leadership ability, as well as confident that theirs should be the dominant role in shaping theory and praxis. Racism teaches an inflated sense of importance and value, especially when coupled with class privilege. Most poor and working class women or even individual bourgeois non-white women would not have assumed that they could launch a feminist movement without first having the support and participation of diverse groups of women. Elizabeth Spelman stresses this impact of racism in her essay, "Theories of Race and Gender: The Erasure of Black Women":

> . . . this is a racist society, and part of what this means is that, generally, the self-esteem of white people is deeply influenced by their difference from and supposed superiority to black people. White people may not think of themselves as racists, because they do not own slaves or hate blacks, but that does not mean that much of what props up white people's sense of self-esteem is not based on the racism which unfairly distributes benefits and burdens to whites and blacks.[8]

One reason white women active in feminist movement were unwilling to confront racism was their arrogant assumption that their call for Sisterhood was a non-racist gesture. Many white women have said to me, "we wanted black women and other non-white women to join the movement," totally unaware of their perception that they somehow "own" the movement, that they are the "hosts" inviting us as "guests."

Despite current focus on eliminating racism in feminist movement, there has been little change in the direction of theory and praxis. While white feminist activists now include writings by women of color on course outlines, or hire one woman of color to teach a class about her ethnic group, or make sure one or more women of color are represented in feminist organizations (even though this contribution of women of color is needed and valuable), more often than not they are attempting to cover up the fact that they are totally unwilling to surrender their hegemonic dominance of theory and praxis, a dominance which they would not have established were this not a white supremacist, capitalist state. Their attempts to manipulate women of color, a component of the process of dehumanization, do not always go unnoticed. In the July 1983 issue of *In These Times,* a letter written by Theresa Funiciello was published on the subject of poor women and the women's movement which shows the nature of racism within feminist movement:

> Prior to a conference some time ago on the Urban Woman sponsored by the New York City chapter of NOW, I received a phone call from a NOW representative (whose name I have forgotten) asking for a welfare speaker with special qualifications. I was asked that she not be white—she might be "too articulate"—(i.e., not me), that she not be black, she might be "too angry." Perhaps she could be Puerto Rican? She should not say anything political or analytical but confine herself to the subject of "what the women's movement has done for me."

Funiciello responded to this situation by organizing a multi-racial women's takeover of the conference. This type of action shows the spirit of Sisterhood.

Another response to racism has been the establishment of unlearning racism workshops, which are often led by white women. These workshops are important, yet they tend to focus primarily on cathartic individual psychological acknowledgment of personal prejudice without stressing the need for corresponding change in political commitment and action. A woman who attends an unlearning racism workshop and learns to acknowledge that she is racist is no less a threat than one who does not. Acknowledgment of racism is significant when it leads to transformation. More research, writing, and practical implementation of findings must be done on ways to unlearn racist socialization. Many white women who daily exercise race privilege lack awareness that they are doing so (which explains the emphasis on confession in unlearning racism workshops). They may not have conscious understanding of the ideology of white supremacy and the extent to which it shapes their behavior and attitudes towards women unlike themselves. Often, white women bond on the basis of shared racial identity without conscious awareness of the significance of their actions. This unconscious maintenance and perpetuation of white supremacy is dangerous because none of us can struggle to change racist attitudes if we do not recognize that they exist. For example, a group of white feminist activists who do not know one another may be present at a meeting to discuss feminist theory. They may feel they are bonded on the basis of shared womanhood, but the atmosphere will noticeably change when a woman of color enters the room. The white women will become tense, no longer relaxed, no longer celebratory. Unconsciously, they felt close to one another because they shared racial identity. The "whiteness" that bonds them together is a racial identity that is directly related to the experience of non-white people as "other" and as a "threat." Often when I speak to white women about racial bonding, they deny that it exists; it is not unlike sexist men denying their sexism. Until white supremacy is understood and attacked by white women there can be no bonding between them and multi-ethnic groups of women.

Women will know that white feminist activists have begun to confront racism in a serious and revolutionary manner when they are not simply acknowledging racism in feminist movement or calling attention to personal prejudice, but are actively struggling to resist racist oppression in our society. Women will know they have made a political commitment to eliminating racism when they help change the direction of feminist movement, when they work to unlearn racist socialization prior to assuming positions of leadership or shaping theory or making contact with women of color so that they will not perpetuate and maintain racial oppression or, unconsciously or consciously, abuse and hurt non-white women. These are the truly radical gestures that create a foundation for the experience of political solidarity between white women and women of color.

White women are not the only group who must confront racism if Sisterhood is to emerge. Women of color must confront our absorption of white supremacist beliefs, "internalized racism," which may lead us to feel self-hate, to vent anger and rage at injustice at one another rather than at oppressive forces, to hurt and abuse one another, or to lead one ethnic group to make no effort to communicate with another. Often women of color from varied ethnic groups have learned to resent and hate one another, or to be competitive with one another. Often Asian, Latina, or Native American Indian groups find they can bond with whites by hating blacks. Black people respond to this by perpetuating racist stereotypes and images of these ethnic groups. It becomes a vicious cycle. Divisions between women of color will not be eliminated until we assume responsibility for uniting (not solely on the basis of resisting racism) to learn about our cultures, to share our knowledge and skills, and to gain strength from our diversity. We need to do more research and writing about the barriers that separate us and the ways we can overcome such separation. Often the men in our ethnic groups have greater contact with one another than we do. Women often assume so many job-related and domestic responsibilities that we lack the time or do not make the time to get to know women outside our group or community. Language differences often prevent us from communicating; we can change this by encouraging one another to learn to speak Spanish, English, Japanese, Chinese, etc.

One factor that makes interaction between multi-ethnic groups of women difficult and sometimes impossible is our failure to recognize that a behavior pattern in one culture may be unacceptable in another, that it may have different signification cross-culturally. Through repeated teaching of a course titled "Third World Women in the United States," I have learned the importance of learning what we called one another's cultural codes.[9] An Asian-American student, of Japanese heritage, explained her reluctance to participate in feminist organizations by calling attention to the tendency among feminist activists to speak rapidly without pause, to be quick on the uptake, always ready with a response. She had been raised to pause and think before speaking, to consider the impact of one's words, a characteristic which she felt was particularly true of Asian-Americans. She expressed feelings of inadequacy on the various occasions she was present in feminist groups. In our class, we learned to allow pauses and appreciate them. By sharing this cultural code, we created an atmosphere in the classroom that allowed for different communication patterns. This particular class was peopled primarily by black women. Several white women students complained that the atmosphere in the class was "too hostile." They cited the noise level and direct confrontations that took place in the room prior to class starting as an example of this hostility. Our response was to explain that what they perceived as hostility and aggression, we considered playful teasing and affectionate expressions of our pleasure at begin together. Our tendency to talk loudly we saw as a consequence of being in a room with many people speaking as well as cultural background: many of us were raised in families where individuals speak loudly. In their upbringing as white, middle class females, the complaining students had been taught to identify loud and direct speech with anger. We explained that we did not identify loud or blunt speech in this way, and encouraged them to switch codes, to think of it as an affirming gesture. Once they switched codes, they not only began to have a more creative, joyful experience in the class, but they also learned that silence and quiet speech can in some cultures indicate hostility and aggression. By learning one another's cultural codes and respecting our differences, we felt a sense of community, of Sisterhood. Respecting diversity does not mean uniformity or sameness.

A crucial concern in these multi-racial classroom settings was recognition and acknowledgement of our differences and the extent to which they determine how we will be perceived by others. We had to continually remind one another to appreciate difference since many of us were raised to fear it. We talked about the need to acknowledge that we all suffer in some way but that we are not all oppressed nor equally oppressed. Many of us feared that our experiences were irrelevant because they were not as oppressive or as exploited as the experience of others. We discovered that we had a greater feeling of unity when people focused truthfully on their own experiences without comparing them with those of others in a competitive way. One student, Isabel Yrigoyei, wrote: "We are not equally oppressed. There is no joy in this. We must speak from within us, our own experiences, our own oppressions—taking someone else's oppression is nothing to feel proud of. We should never speak for that which we have not felt." When we began our communication by focusing on individual experiences, we found them to be varied even among those of us who shared common ethnic backgrounds. We learned that these differences mean we have no monolithic experiences that we can identify as "Chicana experience," "Black experience," etc. A Chicana growing up in a rural environment in a Spanish-speaking home has a life experience that differs from that of a Chicana raised in an English-speaking family in a bourgeois, predominantly white New Jersey suburb. These two women will not automatically feel solidarity. Even though they are from the same ethnic group, they must work to develop Sisterhood. Seeing these types of differences, we also confronted our tendency to value some experiences over others. We might see the Spanish-speaking Chicana as being more "politically correct" than her English-speaking peer. By no longer passively accepting the learned tendency to compare and judge, we could see value in each experience. We could also see that our different experiences often meant that we had different needs, that there was no one strategy or formula for the development of political consciousness. By mapping out various strategies, we affirmed our diversity while working towards solidarity. Women must explore various ways to communicate with one another cross-culturally if we are to develop political solidarity. When women of color strive to learn with and about one another we take responsibility for building Sisterhood. We need not rely on white women to lead the way to solidarity; all too often opportunistic concerns point them in other directions. We can establish unity among ourselves with anti-racist women. We can stand together united in political solidarity, in feminist movement. We can restore to the idea of Sisterhood its true meaning and value.

Cutting across racial lines, class is a serious political division between women. It was often suggested in early feminist literature that class would not be so important if more poor and working class women would join the movement. Such thinking was both a denial of the existence of class privilege gained through exploitation as well as a denial of class struggle. To build Sisterhood, women must criticize and repudiate class exploitation. The bourgeois woman who takes a less privileged "sister" to lunch or dinner at a fancy restaurant may be acknowledging class but she is not repudiating class privilege—she is exercising it. Wearing secondhand clothing and living in low-cost housing in a poor neighborhood while buying stock is not a gesture of solidarity with those who are deprived or under-privileged. As in the case of racism in feminist movement, the emphasis on class has been focused on individual status and change. Until women accept the need for redistribution of wealth and resources in the United States and work towards the achievement of that end, there will be no bonding between women that transcends class.

It is terribly apparent that feminist movement so far has primarily served the class interests of bourgeois white women and men. The great majority of women from middle class situations who recently entered the labor force (an entry encouraged and promoted by feminist movement) helped strengthen the economy of the 1970s. In *The Two-Paycheck Marriage*, Caroline Bird emphasizes the extent to which these women (most of whom are white) helped bolster a waning economy:

> Working wives helped families maintain that standard of living through inflation. The Bureau of Labor Statistics has concluded that between 1973 and 1974 the real purchasing power of single-earner families dropped 3 percent compared with only 1 percent for families in which the wife was working. . . . Women especially will put themselves out to defend a standard of living they see threatened.
>
> Women did more than maintain standards. Working women lifted millions of families into middle class life. Her pay meant the difference between an apartment and a house, or college for the children. . . .
>
> . . . Working wives were beginning to create a new kind of rich— and . . . a new kind of poor.[10]

More than ten years later, it is evident that large numbers of individual white women (especially those from middle class backgrounds) have made economic strides in the wake of feminist movement support of careerism, and affirmative action programs in many professions. However, the masses of women are as poor as ever, or poorer. To the bourgeois "feminist," the million-dollar salary granted newscaster Barbara Walters represents a victory for women. To working class women who make less than the minimum wage and receive few if any benefits, it means continued class exploitation.

Leah Fritz's *Dreamers and Dealers* is a fine example of the liberal woman's attempt to gloss over the fact that class privilege is based on exploitation, that rich women support and condone that exploitation, that the people who suffer most are poor, under-privileged women and children. Fritz attempts to evoke sympathy for all upper class women by stressing their psychological suffering, their victimization at the hands of men. She concludes her chapter "Rich Women" with the statement:

> Feminism belongs as much to the rich woman as to the poor woman. It can help her to understand that her own interests are linked with the advancement of all womankind; that comfort in dependency is a trap; that the golden cage has bars, too; and that, rich and poor, we are all wounded in the service of the patriarchy, although our scars are different. The inner turmoil that sends her to a psychoanalyst can generate energy for the movement which alone may heal her, by setting her free.[11]

Fritz conveniently ignores that domination and exploitation are necessary if there are to be rich women who may experience sexist discrimination or exploitation. She conveniently ignores class struggle.

Women from lower class groups had no difficulty recognizing that the social equality women's liberationists talked about equated careerism and class mobility with liberation. They also knew who would be exploited in the service of this liberation. Daily confronting class exploitation, they cannot conveniently ignore class struggle. In the anthology *Women of Crisis*, Helen, a working class white woman, who works as a maid in the home of a bourgeois white "feminist" expresses her understanding of the contradiction between feminist rhetoric and practice.

> I think the missus is right: everyone should be equal. She keeps on saying that. But then she has me working away in her house, and I'm not equal with her—and she doesn't want to be equal with me; and I don't blame her, because if I was her I'd hold on to my money just like she does. Maybe that's what the men are doing—they're holding on to their money. And it's a big fight, like it always is about money. She should know. She doesn't go throwing big fat pay checks at her "help." She's fair; she keeps on reminding us—but she's not going to "liberate" us, any more than the men are going to "liberate" their wives or their secretaries or the other women working in their companies.[12]

Women's liberationists not only equated psychological pain with material deprivation to de-emphasize class privilege; they often suggested it was the more severe problem. They managed to overlook the fact that many women suffer both psychologically and materially and for that reason alone changing their social status merited greated attention than careerism. Certainly the bourgeois woman who is suffering psychically is more likely to find help than the woman who is suffering material deprivation as well as emotional pain. One of the basic differences in perspective between the bourgeois woman and the working class or poor woman is that the latter know that being discriminated against or exploited because one is female may be painful and dehumanizing, or threatening as being without food or shelter, as starvation, as being deathly ill but unable to obtain medical care. Had poor women set the agenda for feminist movement, they might have decided that class struggle would be a central feminist issue; that poor and privileged women would work to understand class structure and the way it pits women against one another.

Outspoken socialist feminists, most of whom are white women, have emphasized class but they have not been effective in changing attitudes towards class in feminist movement. Despite their support of socialism, their values, behaviors, and lifestyles continue to be shaped by privilege. They have not developed collective strategies to convince bourgeois women who have no radical political perspective that eliminating class oppression is crucial to efforts to end sexist oppression. They have not worked hard to organize with poor and working class women who may not identify as socialists but do identify with the need for redistribution of wealth in the United States. They have not worked to raise the consciousness of women collectively. Much of their energy has been spent addressing the white male left, discussing the connections between marxism and feminism, or explaining to other feminist activists that socialist feminism is the best strategy for revolution. Emphasis on class struggle is often incorrectly deemed the sole domain of socialist feminists. Although I call attention to directions and strategies they have not employed, I wish to emphasize that these issues should be addressed by all activists in feminist movement. When women face the reality of classism and make political commitments to eliminating it, we will no longer experience the class conflicts that have been so apparent in feminist movement. Until we focus on class divisions between women, we will be unable to build political solidarity.

Sexism, racism, and classism divide women from one another. Within feminist movement, divisions and disagreements about strategy and emphasis led to the formation of a number of groups with varied political positions. Splintering into different political factions and special-interest groups has erected unnecessary barriers to Sisterhood that could easily be eliminated. Special interest groups lead women to believe that only socialist feminists should be concerned about class; that only lesbian feminists should be concerned about the oppression of lesbians and gay men; that only black women or other women of color should be concerned about racism. Every woman can stand in political opposition to sexist, racist, heterosexist, and classist oppression. While she may choose to focus her work on a given political issue or a particular cause, if she is firmly opposed to all forms of group oppression, this broad perspective will be manifest in all her work irrespective of its particularity. When feminist activists are anti-racist and against class exploitation, it will not matter if women of color are present or poor women, etc. These issues will be deemed important and will be addressed, although the women most personally affected by particular exploitations will necessarily continue in the forefront of those struggles. Women must learn to accept responsibility for fighting oppressions that may not directly affect us as individuals. Feminist movement, like other radical movements in our society, suffers when individual concerns and priorities are the only reason for participation. When we show our concern for the collective, we strengthen our solidarity.

Solidarity was a word seldom used in contemporary feminist movement. Much greater emphasis was placed on the idea of "support." Support can mean upholding or defending a position one believes is right. It can also mean serving as a prop or a foundation for a weak structure. This latter meaning had greater significance in feminist circles. Its value emerged from the emphasis on shared victimization. Identifying as "victims," women were acknowledging a helplessness and powerlessness as well as a need for support, in this case the support of fellow feminist activists, "sisters." It was closely related to the shallow notion of Sisterhood. Commenting on its usage among feminist activists in her essay "With All Due Respect," Jane Rule explains:

> *Support* is a much used word in the women's movement. For too many people it means giving and receiving unqualified approval. Some women are awfully good at . . . withdrawing it at crucial moments. Too many are convinced they can't function without it. It's a false concept which has produced barriers to understanding and done real emotional damage. Suspension of critical judgement is not necessary for offering real support, which has to do instead with self-respect and respect for other people even at moments of serious disagreement.[13]

Women's legacy of woman-hating, which includes fierce, brutal, verbal tearing apart of one another, has to be eliminated if women are to make critiques and engage in disagreements and arguments that are constructive and caring, with the intention of enriching rather than diminishing. Woman-to-woman negative, aggressive behavior is not unlearned when all critical judgement is suspended. It is unlearned when women accept that we are different, that we will necessarily disagree, but that we can disagree and argue with one another without acting as if we are fighting for our lives, without feeling that we stand to lose all self-esteem by verbally trashing someone else. Verbal disagreements are often the setting where women can demonstrate their engagement with the win-or-lose competitiveness that is most often associated with male interactions, especially in the arena of sports. Women, like men, must learn how to dialogue with one another without competition. Jane Rule suggests that women can disagree without trashing if they realize they do not stand to lose value or self-worth if they are criticized: "No one can discredit my life if it is in my own hands, and therefore I do not have to make anyone carry the false burden of my frightened hostility."[14]

Women need to come together in situations where there will be ideological disagreement and work to change that interaction so communication occurs. This means that when women come together, rather than pretend union, we would acknowledge that we are divided and must develop strategies to overcome fears, prejudices, resentments, competitiveness, etc. The fierce negative disagreements that have taken place in feminist circles have led many feminist activists to shun group or individual interaction where there is likely to be disagreement which leads to confrontation. Safety and support have been redefined to mean hanging out in groups where the participants are alike and share similar values. While no woman wants to enter a situation in which she will be psychically annihilated, women can face one another in hostile confrontation and struggle and move beyond the hostility to understanding. Expression of hostility as an end in itself is a useless activity, but when it is the catalyst pushing us on to greater clarity and understanding, it serves a meaningful function.

Women need to have the experience of working through hostility to arrive at understanding and solidarity if only to free ourselves from the sexist socialization that tells us to avoid confrontation because we will be victimized or destroyed. Time and time again, I have had the experience of making statements at talks that anger a listener and lead to assertive and sometimes hostile verbal confrontation. The situation feels uncomfortable, negative, and unproductive because there are angry voices, tears, etc. and yet I may find later that the experience has led to greater clarity and growth on my part and on the part of the listener. On one occasion, I was invited by a black woman sociologist, a very soft-spoken individual, to speak in a class she was teaching. A young Chicana woman who could pass for white was a student in the class. We had a heated exchange when I made the point that the ability to pass for white gave her a perspective on race totally different from that of someone who is dark-skinned and can never pass. I pointed out that any person meeting her with no knowledge of her ethnic background probably assumes that she is white and relates to her accordingly. At the time the suggestion angered her. She became quite angry and finally stormed out of the class in tears. The teacher and fellow students definitely saw me as the "bad guy" who had failed to support a fellow sister and instead reduced her to tears. They were annoyed that our get-together had not been totally pleasurable, unemotional, dispassionate. I certainly felt miserable in the situation. The student, however, contacted me weeks later to share her feelings that she had gained new insights and awareness as a result of our encounter which aided her personal growth. Incidents like this one, which initially appear to be solely negative because of tension or hostility, can lead to positive growth. If women always seek to avoid confrontation, to always be "safe," we may never experience any revolutionary change, any transformation, individually or collectively.

When women actively struggle in a truly supportive way to understand our differences, to change misguided, distorted perspectives, we lay the foundation for the experience of political solidarity. Solidarity is not the same as support. To experience solidarity, we must have a community of interests, shared beliefs and goals around which to unite, to build Sisterhood. Support can be occasional. It can be given and just as easily withdrawn. Solidarity requires sustained, ongoing commitment. In feminist movement, there is need for diversity, disagreement, and difference if we are to grow. As Grace Lee Boggs and James Boggs emphasize in *Revolution and Evolution in the Twentieth Century:*

> The same appreciation of the reality of contradiction underlies the concept of criticism and self-criticism. Criticism and self-criticism is the way in which individuals who are united by common goals can consciously utilize their differences and their limitations, i.e., the negative, in order to accelerate their positive advance. The popular formulation for this process is "changing a bad thing into a good thing . . ."[15]

Women do not need to eradicate difference to feel solidarity. We do not need to share common oppression to fight equally to end oppression. We do not need anti-male sentiments to bond us together, so great is the wealth of experience, culture, an ideas we have to share with one another. We can be sisters united by shared interests and beliefs, united in our appreciation for diversity, united in our struggle to end sexist oppression, united in political solidarity.

NOTES

1. Florynce Kennedy, "Institutionalized Oppression vs. The Female," in *Sisterhood Is Powerful: An Anthology of Writings from the Women's Liberation Movement,* ed. Robin Morgan (New York: Vintage, 1970), 500.
2. In early contemporary feminist writings (e.g., *Redstockings Manifesto*) the image of woman as victim was evoked. Joan Cassell's study of sisterhood and symbolism in the feminist movement, *A Group Called Women,* examines the ideology of bonding among feminist activists. Contemporary writers like Leah Fritz evoke an image of woman as victim to encourage woman bonding. Barbara Smith discusses this tendency in her introduction to *Home Girls.*

3. At the onset of contemporary feminist movement I (and many other black women) often heard white women in Women's Studies classes, consciousness-raising groups, meetings, etc., respond to questions about the lack of black female participation by stressing that this was not related to problems with the structure of feminist movement but an indication that black women were already liberated. The image of the "strong" black woman is evoked in the writings of a number of white activists (e.g., Sara Evans, *Personal Politics;* Bettina Aptheker, *Woman's Legacy*).

4. Jo Freeman, *The Politics of Women's Liberation: A Case Study of an Emerging Social Movement and Its Relation to the Policy Process* (New York: David McKay, 1975), 118.

5. Toni Morrison, "Cinderella's Stepsisters," *Ms.,* September 1979, 41.

6. Toni Morrison, "What the Black Woman Thinks about Women's Lib," *New York Times Magazine,* 22 August 1971, 15.

7. Gloria Joseph, "The Incompatible Menage À Trois: Marxism, Feminism, and Racism," in *Women and Revolution,* ed. Lydia Sargent (Boston: South End Press, 1981), 105.

8. Elizabeth V. Spelman, "Theories of Race and Gender: The Erasure of Black Women," *Quest: A Feminist Quarterly* 5, no. 4 (1982): 41.

9. My experience teaching "Third World Women in the United States" at San Francisco State has deeply enriched my understanding of women from diverse backgrounds. I am grateful to all the students I taught there, especially Betty and Susan.

10. Caroline Bird. *The Two-Paycheck Marriage* (New York: Rawson, Wade, 1979), 9.

11. Leah Fritz, *Dreamers and Dealers: An Intimate Appraisal of the Women's Movement* (Boston: Beacon Press, 1979), 225–26.

12. Robert Coles and Jane Coles, *Women of Crisis* (New York: Dell, 1978), 266.

13. Jane Rule, "With All Due Respect," *Outlander* (Tallahassee: Naiad, 1981), 177–78.

14. *Ibid.,* 178.

15. Grace Lee Boggs and James Boggs, *Revolution and Evolution in the Twentieth Century* (New York: Monthly Review Press, 1974), 133.

• • • • •

"Anger in Isolation: A Black Feminist's Search for Sisterhood"

Michele Wallace

Born and reared in Harlem, Michele Wallace is the daughter of the artist and writer Faith Ringgold and the musician Robert Earl Wallace. She graduated in 1974 from City College in New York and became a founding member of the National Black Feminist Organization the same year. Five years after her college graduation, Wallace published a much-discussed sociopolitical study entitled *Black Macho and the Myth of the Super-woman* (1979). It is a penetrating analysis of the civil rights and black liberation movements of the 1950s and 1960s and the influences they had on black male-female relations. In the book Wallace contends that the black women falsely perceived as "super-women" were victims of racism and sexism, and that despite the racial gains blacks were making, black males were rejecting black women to validate their manhood through interracial dating. Wallace defines the black "super-woman" as one having "inordinate strength, with the ability for tolerating an unusual amount of misery and heavy, distasteful work." Possessing sexual and life-giving reserves, the super-woman is the archetypal mother, a manifestation of Mother Earth.

Wallace's most recent book, *Invisibility Blues: From Pop to Theory* (1990), examines further the politics of race and gender. Her shorter pieces, including articles, poems, and short stories, can be found in *Esquire*, *Ms.*, and the *Village Voice*.

Black women have bonded—in their blood relationships, sororities, and religious, social, and community improvement associations—since they first came to America. Yet sisterhood was often beyond the grasp of the black women who searched for female companionship in the 1960s to discuss and negotiate issues pertaining to feminism. In her zealous plea for black feminism, Wallace has alienated some critics, including the noted poet June Jordan, who maintains that Wallace was too young in the 1960s to make generalizations based on her personal experience.

"Anger in Isolation: A Black Feminist's Search for Sisterhood" (*Village Voice*, 28 July 1975) is the author's recollection of how and why she became a feminist, and of how difficult it was to become a black feminist in the face of opposition from other black women, as well as black men, and a lack of empathy and common understanding from white feminists. Both personal and candid, Wallace's essay details the

261

hard choices confronting a young black woman intent on finding a place for herself in a world that is largely at odds with her values.

When I was in the third grade I wanted to be president. I can still remember the stricken look on my teacher's face when I announced it in class. By the time I was in the fourth grade I had decided to be the president's wife instead. It never occurred to me that I could be neither because I was black. Growing up in a dreamy state of mind not uncommon to the offspring of the black middle class, I was convinced that hatred was an insubstantial emotion and would certainly vanish before it could affect me. I had the world to choose from in planning a life.

On rainy days my sister and I used to tie the short end of a scarf around our scrawny braids and let the rest of its silken mass trail to our waists. We'd pretend it was hair and that we were some lovely heroine we'd seen in the movies. There was a time when I would have called that wanting to be white, yet the real point of the game was being feminine. Being feminine *meant* being white to us.

One day when I was 13 on my bus ride home from school I caught a brief but enchanting glimpse of a beautiful creature—slender, honey brown, and she wore her hair natural. Very few people did then, which made her that much more striking. *This* was a look that I could imitate with some success. The next day I went to school with my hair in an Afro.

On my way out of my building people stared and some complemented me, but others, the older permanent fixtures in the lobby, gaped at me in horror. Walking the streets of Harlem was even more difficult. The men on the corners, who had been only moderately attentive before, now began to whoop and holler as I came into view. Becoming exasperated after awhile, I asked someone why. "They think you're a whore, sugar." I fixed my hair and was back to normal by the next morning. Letting the world in on the secret of my native naps appealed to my proclivity for rebellion but having people think I was not a "nice girl" was The War already and I was not prepared for it. I pictured myself in a police station trying to explain how I'd been raped. "Come on, baby, you look like you know your way around" sneered an imaginary policeman.

In 1968 when I was 16, and the term "black consciousness" was becoming popular, I started wearing my hair natural again. This time I ignored my "elders." I was too busy reshaping my life. Blackness, I reasoned, meant that I could finally be myself. Besides recognizing my history of slavery and my African roots, I began a general housecleaning. All my old values, gathered from "playing house" in nursery school to *Glamour* magazine's beauty tips, were discarded.

No more makeup, high heels, stockings, garter belts, girdles. I wore

T-shirts and dungarees, or loose African print dresses, sandals on my feet. My dust-covered motto, "Be a nice well-rounded colored girl so that you can get yourself a nice colored doctor husband," I threw out on the grounds that it was another remnant of my once "whitified" self. My mind clear now, I was starting to think about being someone again, not *something*—the presidency was still a dark horse but maybe I could be a writer. I dared not even say it aloud: my life was my own again. I thanked Malcolm and LeRoi—wasn't it their prescription that I was following?

It took me three years to fully understand that Stokely was serious when he said my position in the movement was "prone," three years to understand that the countless speeches that all began "the black man . . ." did not include me.[1] I learned. I mingled more and more with a black crowd, attended the conferences and rallies and parties and talked with some of the most loquacious of my brothers in blackness, and as I pieced together the ideal that was being presented for me to emulate, I discovered my newfound freedoms being stripped from me, one after another. No I wasn't to wear makeup but yes I had to wear long skirts that I could barely walk in. No I wasn't to go to the beauty parlor but yes I was to spend hours controlling my hair. No I wasn't to flirt with or take shit off white men but yes I was to sleep with and take unending shit off black men. No I wasn't to watch television or read *Vogue* or *Ladies' Home Journal* but yes I should keep my mouth shut. I would still have to iron, sew, cook, and have babies.

Only 16, I decided there were a lot of things I didn't know about black male/female relationships. I made an attempt to fill myself in by reading—*Soul on Ice, Native Son,* and *Rage*—and by joining the National Black Theatre. In the theatre's brand of a consciousness-raising session I was told of the awful ways in which black women, me included, had tried to destroy the black man's masculinity; how we had castrated him; worked when he made no money, spent our nights and days in church praying to a jive white boy named Jesus while he collapsed into alcoholism, drug addiction, and various forms of despair; how we'd always been too loud and domineering, too outspoken.

We had much to make up for by being gentle in the face of our own humiliation, by being soft-spoken (ideally to the point where our voices could not be heard at all), by being beautiful (whatever that was), by being submissive—how often that word was shoved at me in poems and in songs as something to strive for.

At the same time, one of the brothers who was a member of the theatre was also a paraprofessional in the school where my mother then taught. My mother asked him what he liked about the theatre. Not knowing that I was her daughter, he answered without hesitation that you could get all the pussy you wanted. NBT was a central institution in the black cultural movement. Much time was spent reaching for the "godlike" in one another, the things beyond the "flesh" and beyond all the "whitewashing." And what it boiled down to was that now the brother could get more pussy. If that was his revolution, what was mine?

So I was again obsessed with my appearance, worried about the rain again—the black woman's nightmare—for fear that my huge, full Afro would shrivel up to my head. (Despite blackness, black men still didn't like short hair.) My age was one thing I had going for me. "Older black women are too hard," my brothers informed me as they looked me up and down.

The message of the Black Movement was that I was being watched, on probation as a black woman, that any signs of aggressiveness, intelligence, or independence would mean I'd be denied even the one role still left open to me as "my man's woman," keeper of house, children, and incense burners. I grew increasingly desperate about slipping up—they, black men, were threatening me with being deserted, with being *alone.* Like any "normal" woman, I eagerly grabbed at my own enslavement.

After all, I'd heard the horror stories of educated black women who had to marry ditchdiggers and get their behinds kicked every night. I had thought the Black Movement would offer me much better. In 1968 I had wanted to become an intelligent human being. I had wanted to be serious and scholarly for the first time in my life, to write and perhaps get the chance Stokely and Baldwin and Imamu Baraka (then LeRoi Jones) had gotten to change the world—that was how I defined not wanting to be white. But by 1969, I simply wanted a man.

When I chose to go to Howard University in 1969, it was because it was all black. I envisioned a super black utopia where for the first time in life I would be completely surrounded by people who totally understood me. The problem in New York had been that there were too many white people.

Thirty pounds overweight, my hair in the ultimate Afro—washed and left to dry without combing—my skin blue-black from a summer in the sun. Howard's students, the future polite society of NAACP cocktail parties, did not exactly greet me with open arms. I sought out a new clique each day and found a home in none. Finally I found a place of revelation, if not of happiness, with other misfits in the girls' dorm on Friday and Saturday nights.

These misfits, all dark without exception, all with Afros that were too nappy, chose to stay in and watch television or listen to records rather than take advantage of the score of one-night stands they could probably achieve before being taunted into running home to their parents as "fallen women." They came to Howard to get husbands; if you slept around or if it got out that you had slept with someone you weren't practically engaged to, then there would be very little possibility of a husband for you at Howard.

Such restrictions are not unique in this world, but at Howard, the scene of student takeovers just the previous year, of riots and much revolutionary talk about casting aside Western values, archaic Victorian morals seemed curiously "unblack." Baffled by my new environment, I did something I've never done before—I spent most of my time with women, often turning down the inevitable humiliation or, worse, boredom of a date (a growing possibility as I shed the extra pounds) even when it was offered to me. Most of the women were from small southern and midwestern communities. They thought me definitely straitjacket material with my well-polished set of "sophisticated" New York views on premarital sex and atheism. I learned to listen more than I spoke.

But no one talked about why we stayed in on Friday and Saturday nights on a campus that was well-known for its parties and nightlife. No one talked about why we drank so much or why our hunger for Big Macs was insatiable. We talked about men—all kinds, black and white, Joe Namath, Richard Roundtree, the class president who earned quite a reputation for driving coeds out on the highway and offering them a quick screw or a long walk home. "But girl, ain't he fine?" We talked about movie stars and singing groups into the wee hours of the morning. Guzzling gin, cheating at poker, choking on cigarettes that dangled precariously from the corners of our mouths, we'd signify. "If we could only be woman (white) enough" was the general feeling of most of us as we trotted off to bed.

Meanwhile the males on the campus had successfully burned the old standards of light, curly haired young men with straight noses. They sported large, unruly Afros, dashikis, and flaring nostrils. Their coal black eyes seemed to say "The nights *and* the days belong to me," as we passed one another on the campus green, a fashionable, thin, colorless little creature always on their arm.

Enough was enough. I left Howard for City College after one term, and the significance of all I'd seen there had not entirely escaped me, because I remember becoming a feminist about then. No one had been doing very well when I left New York but now it seemed even worse—the "new blackness" was fast becoming the new slavery for sisters.

I discovered my voice and when brothers talked to me, I talked back. This had its hazards. Almost got my eye blackened several times. My social life was like guerilla warfare. Here was the logic behind our grandmothers' old saying, "a nigga man ain't shit." It was shorthand for "the black man has learned to hate himself and to hate you even more. Be careful. He will hurt you."

I am reminded of a conversation I had with a brother up at City College one mild spring day. We were standing on a corner in front of the South Campus gates and he was telling me what the role of the black woman was. When a pause came in his monologue, I asked him what the role of the black man was. He mumbled something about, "Simply to be a man." When I suggested that might not be enough, he went completely ape. He turned purple. He started screaming, "The black man doesn't have to do anything. He's a man he's a man he's a man."

Whenever I raised the question of a black woman's humanity in conversation with a black man, I got a similar reaction. Black men, at least the ones I knew, seemed totally confounded when it came to treating black women like people. Trying to be what we were told to be by the brothers of the "nation"—sweet and smiling—a young black woman I knew had warmly greeted a brother in passing on Riverside Drive. He responded by raping her. When she asked the brothers what she should do, they told her not to go to the police and to have the baby though she was only seventeen.

Young black female friends of mine were dropping out of school because their boyfriends had convinced them that it was "not correct" and "counterrevolutionary" to strive to do anything but have babies and clean house. "Help the brother get his thing together," they were told. Other black women submitted to polygamous situations where sometimes they were called upon to sleep with the friends of their "husband." This latter duty was explained to me once by a "priest" of the New York Yoruban Temple. "If your brother has to go to the bathroom and there is no toilet in his house then wouldn't you let him use your toilet?" For toilet read black woman.

The sisters got along by keeping their mouths shut, by refusing to see what was daily growing more difficult to ignore—a lot of brothers were doing double time, uptown with the sisters and downtown with the white women whom they always vigorously claimed to hate. Some of the bolder brothers were quite frank about it. "The white woman lets me be a man."

The most popular justification black women had for not becoming feminists was their hatred for white women. They often repeated this for approving black male ears. (Obviously the brother had an interest in keeping black and white women apart—"Women will chatter.") But what I figured out was that the same black man who trembled with hatred for white men found the white woman irresistible because she was not a human being but a possession in his eyes—the higher-priced spread of woman he saw on television. "I know that the white man made the white woman the symbol of freedom and the black woman the symbol of slavery" (*Soul on Ice*, Eldridge Cleaver).

When I first became a feminist my black friends used to cast pitying eyes upon me and say, "That's whitey's thing." I used to laugh it off, thinking, yes there are some slight problems, a few things white women don't completely understand but we can work them out. In *Ebony, Jet,* and *Encore,* and even in the *New York Times,* various black writers cautioned black women to be wary of smiling white feminists. The Women's Movement enlists the support of black women only to lend credibility to an essentially middle-class, irrelevant movement, they asserted. Time has shown that there was more truth to these claims than their shrillness indicated. Today when many white feminists think of black women, they too often think of faceless masses of welfare mothers and rape victims to flesh out their statistical studies of woman's plight.

One unusually awkward moment for me as a black feminist was when I found out that white feminists often don't view black men as men but as fellow victims. I've got no pressing quarrel with the notion that white men have been the worst offenders but that isn't very helpful for a black woman from day to day. White women don't check out a white man's bank account or stockholdings before they accuse him of being sexist—they confront white men with and without jobs, with and without membership in a male consciousness-raising group. Yet when it comes to the black man, it's hands off.

A black friend of mine was fired by a black news service because she was pregnant. When she proposed doing an article on this for *Ms.,* an editor there turned down the proposal with these words: "We got a special policy for the black man." For a while I thought that was just the conservative feminist position until I overheard a certified radical feminist explaining why she dated only black men and other nonwhite men. "They're less of a threat to women, they're less oppressive."

Being a black woman means frequent spells of impotent, self-consuming rage. Such a spell came upon me when I recently attended a panel discussion at a women artists' conference. One of the panel members, a museum director and a white feminist, had come with a young black man in sweatshirt, Pro-Keds, and rag tied around the kind of gigantic Afro you don't see much anymore. When asked about her commitment to black women artists, she responded with, "Well what about Puerto Rican women artists, and Mexican women artists, and Indian women artists? . . ." But she doesn't exhibit Hispanic women any more than she does black women—do I have to say anything about Indian women?—which is seldom indeed, though her museum is located in an area that is predominantly black and Puerto Rican. Yet she was confident in the position she took because the living proof of her liberalism and good intentions sat in the front row, black and unsmiling, six foot some-thing and militant-*looking*.

In the spring of 1973, Doris Wright, a black feminist writer, called a meeting to discuss "Black Women and Their Relationship to the Women's Movement." The result was the National Black Feminist Organization, and I was fully delighted until, true to Women's Movement form, we got bogged down in an array of ideological disputes, the primary one being lesbianism versus heterosexuality. Dominated by the myths and facts of what white feminists had done and not done before us, it was nearly impossible to come to any agreement about our position on anything; and action was unthinkable.

Many of the prime movers in the organization seemed to be representing other interest groups, and whatever commitment they might have had to black women's issues appeared to take a back-seat to that. Women who had initiative and spirit usually attended one meeting, and were turned off by the hopelessness of ever getting anything accomplished, and never returned again. Each meeting brought almost all new faces. Overhearing an aspiring political candidate say only half-jokingly at NBFO's first conference, "I'm gonna get me some votes out of these niggas," convinced me that black feminists were not ready to form a movement in which I could, with clear conscience, participate.

It is very possible that NBFO was not meant to happen when it did, that the time was not yet ripe for such an organization.

I started a black women's consciousness-raising group around the same time. When I heard one of my friends, whom I considered the closest thing to a feminist in the room, saying at one of our sessions, "I feel sorry for any woman who tries to take my husband away from me because she's just going to have a man who has to pay alimony and child support," even though she was not married to the man in question, I felt a great sinking somewhere in the chest area. Here was a woman who had insisted (at least to me) upon her right to bear a child outside of marriage, trying to convince a few black women that she was really married, unlike they, who were mostly single and very worried about it. In fact, one of the first women to leave the group was a recent graduate of Sarah Lawrence, her excuse being, "I want to place myself in situations where I will meet more men." The group eventually disintegrated. We had no strength to give to one another. Is that possible? At any rate, that's the way it seemed, and perhaps it was the same on a larger scale with NBFO.

Despite a sizable number of black feminists who have contributed much to the leadership of the Women's Movement, there is still no Black Women's Movement, and it appears there won't be for some time to come. It is conceivable that the level of consciousness feminism would demand in black women wouldn't lead to any sort of separatist movement anyway—despite our very separate problems. Perhaps a multicultural women's movement is somewhere in the future.

But for now, black feminists, of necessity it seems, exist as individuals—some well-known, like Eleanor Holmes Norton, Florynce Kennedy, Faith Ringgold, Shirley Chisholm, Alice Walker, and some unknown like me. We exist as women who are black who are feminists, each stranded for the moment, working independently because there is not yet an environment in this society remotely congenial to our struggle—because, being on the bottom, we would have to do what no one else has done: we would have to fight the world. . . .

NOTE

1. Wallace is referring to Stokely Carmichael's response in 1964 to Ruby Doris Smith Robinson, who confronted the male leadership of SNCC with a position paper on the sexist roles of women in the organization.

• • • • •

The Trip

Crystal V. Rhodes

Crystal V. Rhodes, born in Indianapolis, Indiana, in 1948, has published numerous newspaper and magazine articles, written for stage, screen, and radio, and produced 11 full-length plays. Her first play, *The Trip*, was produced by the Black Repertory Group Theater in Berkeley, California, in 1979. Among her other theatrical works are the comedies *Mama's Man*, *The Loot*, and *Who Killed Black Pride;* the dramas *Queen of the Niger*, *Please Don't Bury Me before I Die*, *Crystal Palaces*, *Too Tough*, and *The Waiting Room;* and the musical comedies *Blue Jazz Cabaret* and *Country Girl Suite.*

   The Trip (published in Eileen Joyce Ostrow, ed., *Centerstage: An Anthology of Twenty-one Contemporary Black American Plays* [Sea Urchin Press, 1982]) grew out of a cross-country vacation that Rhodes took in the mid-1970s with some friends. That trip, she has said, "led to some strenuous moments and some hilarious ones." The play explores the theme of black women searching for sisterhood. The characters, four black women who have been friends since high school and are now nearly 30, are variously plagued by problematic relationships with men, unresolved relationships with parents, and difficulty in supporting themselves. During a long-planned cross-country trip, the strains of travel bring out petty jealousies and grievances that threaten the shaky underpinnings of their friendships, which seem to have been forged by pressure from parents and the desire to confer or receive status. "There are boundaries in friendship which should not be crossed—unspoken words better left unsaid, opinions better left unexpressed," writes Rhodes.[1]

On one level, Rhodes's play is simply about a much-awaited trip gone awry: the travelers get lost, are forced to stay in sleazy motels, become bored and edgy because their rental car does not have a radio, and grate on one another's nerves. On another level, however, the play can be seen as the dark side of any genuine search for sisterhood, where women talk at one another instead of with one another, are quick to attack others and defend themselves, and are willing to sacrifice their friendship—their sisterhood—rather than acknowledge their own shortcomings and others' points of view.

NOTE

1. Crystal V. Rhodes, letter to the author, 6 January 1991.

CAST

NIKKI: *An introverted personality, she wants to be more dominant but must develop her assertiveness. She has been dominated all of her life by personalities much stronger than her own. In situations of crisis, however, she displays leadership abilities unrecognized by her peers.*

VICTORIA: *Fairly assertive at times and is often the mediator when disagreements arise between her companions. She displays leadership abilities and is not easily dominated by others.*

JO ANNE: *A chronic complainer, she is a totally negative personality. She is argumentative, aggressive to a fault, demanding, and self-centered. She is basically an insecure individual and harbors feelings of jealousy towards her companions.*

GINNY: *A leader, she is aggressive, sure of herself, and assertive. She serves as the dominant personality among her companions. She rejects feelings of defeat, but displays a lack of self-confidence when faced with a crisis situation.*

SETTING

The interior of a car. Four chairs sit in the center of the stage facing the audience. Two chairs sit side by side; two chairs sit behind them, positioned so that the occupants can be seen by the audience. The chairs are occupied by the young women. Each one is dressed casually in blue jeans and T-shirt. Luggage is stacked up behind the women in the back two chairs.

A PLAY IN ONE ACT

Scene 1

(The three passengers are waving goodbye to the city of Chicago as they head toward a California vacation. GINNY *is driving;* NIKKI *sits beside her;* JO ANNE *sits behind* NIKKI, *and* VICTORIA *sits behind* GINNY*)*

WOMEN: *(Unison)* Goodbye Chicago. Goodbye . . . Goodbye.

NIKKI: Goodbye State Street!

VICTORIA: Goodbye Lake Michigan!

JO ANNE: Good Riddance!

GINNY: California sunshine here we come!!

VICT: Hallelujah!!

NIKKI: I can't wait!

GINNY: I don't know, I'm going to miss the Windy City for these two weeks.

JO ANNE: Sure Ginny, you're a swinging single in the big city. I'm an old married woman. My thrills are few and far between.

VICT: Old married woman! Jo Anne, you and Charles have been married for eighteen months. Don't tell me it's over already??

JO ANNE: Believe me Victoria, if I hadn't been looking forward to this trip for so long, I'd be in bed right now, and I wouldn't be by myself.

GINNY: Well alright!

(Everyone laughs)

VICT: I still can't believe we're going. Fifteen years ago we said we were going to do this and now, look at us, we're actually on our way.

NIKKI: A lot of time's passed. We'll all be thirty years old this year. It took a long time, but we got ourselves together. Good lord, today I feel like that fourteen-year-old freshman that Ginny took pity on and befriended.

GINNY: Aw girl, be for real.

VICT: Don't feel bad Nikki, at least your mother didn't force your friendship on the three of you like mine did. I've never been so embarrassed in my life. She just pushed me on poor Ginny. I thought Ginny's mother would change telephone numbers, Mama called her so much.

JO ANNE: Your mother's a social climber. She wanted you to rub elbows with the idle rich.

NIKKI: Who's rich?

JO ANNE: You and Ginny.

GINNY: Girl, you know we're not rich!

JO ANNE: Come on Ginny, the Hyde Park area of Chicago is a long way from the State Street housing projects where Victoria and I came from.

VICT: Aw, that's water under the bridge. I sure don't want to remember those days. We've come a long way since then.

JO ANNE: Thank God! Sometimes I sit in our apartment and look over the lake and I just want to drop down on my knees and say thank you . . . thank you Lord for taking me out of the projects!

VICT: I heard that! Mama almost killed herself trying to move us out of those projects. I will always be grateful.

GINNY: Hey, stop it now! We said we weren't going to look back. We've been planning this trip for months and we're finally on our way. This is our first vacation together since we've known each other; let's talk about good things. (*Turns to* NIKKI) How many hours to St. Louis?

(NIKKI *looks at the map carefully, tracing the distance as she does so*)

NIKKI: We're here . . . this far from Chicago. We've got about an hour . . . maybe an hour and a half to go.

JO ANNE: (*Groans*) We should have started earlier. It'll be ten o'clock at night before we get there. I told you Ginny, we should have left sooner.

VICT: O.K. Jo Anne, I know what you're thinking. Go on, blame me. It's my fault we started late. We shouldn't have stopped by my mama's house.

JO ANNE: You've got to admit, your mother can talk.

VICT: If I hadn't stopped by and seen that woman, she would have made my life hell when I got back to Chicago!

GINNY: Don't worry about it Vic, we're just a little behind schedule. No big deal. Do the three of you want to stop and get something to eat before we reach St. Louis or should we eat when we get there? (*There is no response*) Well? What do you want to do?

NIKKI: I don't know.

VICT: Whatever the group decides.

JO ANNE: We should have brought some food with us. I told you that, Ginny. It wouldn't be a problem if you had listened to me.

GINNY: (*Agitated*) Well we didn't bring anything, Jo Anne, except some junk food, so what do you want to do? (*Once more there is no response. Disgusted*) Nikki, look in my purse and give me a stick of gum.

(NIKKI *opens the purse on the seat next to* GINNY, *takes a piece of gum out, unwraps it and hands it to* GINNY. GINNY *sticks the gum into her mouth*)

GINNY: Anybody else want some?

(*The response is negative.* VICTORIA *reaches into the back of the car and gets a bag of potato chips. Sitting back in her seat, she opens the bag*)

VICT: I'm glad you rented a station wagon, Nikki, we need the room for all this junk we brought. Especially you, Jo Anne. We told you to pack lightly and bring one suitcase. Look at all of this stuff, and your suitcase must weigh a ton!

JO ANNE: Well I just have a lot of stuff, that's all. I can't help it.

VICT: Well we're not helping you carry that junk.

JO ANNE: I won't ask you to. (*Reaches for the potato chip bag*) Give me some of those. I hope I don't starve to death before we reach St. Louis.

(GINNY *makes a face at this last statement and begins to smack on her gum loudly. There is a period of silence in the car as the other women become aware of the noise* GINNY *is making.* JO ANNE *looks at* GINNY *and frowns; she exchanges glances with* VICTORIA *who gives* GINNY *a puzzled look.* NIKKI *gives* GINNY *a quick sideward glance, while* GINNY *remains unaware of the looks of disapproval her companions are giving her*)

VICT: Nikki, turn the radio on; let's see if we can still get Chicago or something . . . anything.

(NIKKI *fiddles with the radio knobs. There is no sound. She continues to fumble with the knobs. The others look concerned.* JO ANNE, *annoyed with the lack of results, leans across the seat, crowding* GINNY, *to fumble with the radio herself*)

GINNY: Jo Anne!!

JO ANNE: (*Ignoring* GINNY) You're not doing it right, Nikki; let me try it.

JO ANNE: (*Fumbles with the knobs. Again there is no sound*) What's wrong with this thing?

VICT: Must be broken.

(JO ANNE *bangs on the radio in frustration*)

GINNY: Obviously it's broken, Jo Anne; that's not going to do any good.

JO ANNE: (*Leans back in her seat in disgust*) I don't believe it! I just don't believe it!! Nikki, didn't you check the radio when you picked the car up? How can we drive all the way across the country with no radio?

NIKKI: I . . . I didn't know. I . . .

JO ANNE: This is ridiculous. How far are we from Chicago? Let's take this car back! Now!!

VICT: Be for real, Jo Anne! You're the one complaining about us leaving late. If we go back now, we'll really be behind schedule. We can get it taken care of in L.A.

JO ANNE: Well I'd rather get to California one day later than have to drive across half the wheat fields in America with no music!! Who's for turning back?

GINNY: No way!

VICT: Not hardly!

NIKKI: I'm sorry about the radio, Jo Anne, but it seems like a waste of gas and time to turn back.

(JO ANNE *slumps in her seat, muttering to herself. She reaches into the potato chip bag, grabs a handful, stuffs them into her mouth and munches them ferociously.* GINNY'S *gum smacking has subsided, and the silence is now interrupted by* JO ANNE *as she begins to suck her teeth.* GINNY *notices it first and frowns as she looks at* JO ANNE *through the rear view mirror.* NIKKI *then* VICTORIA *begin to notice the sound. Each looks annoyed. The lights dim denoting a passage of time. When the lights come back up. The four women are sitting quietly in their seats)*

VICT: St. Louis, fifteen miles. Thank Goodness! (*Glances at her watch*) We made pretty good time. How you doing up there, Ginny?

GINNY: Fine, I can make it. Nikki, do you remember which route to take to the motel?

NIKKI: Yeah, just stay on this highway. You can see the sign from the road. It's going to seem funny going back there again. That's where Norman and I stayed when we were here for a conference of his. We were happy then. Who could have guessed we'd ever separate.

JO ANNE: Honey, you're better off without that turkey. He's been a turd since high school.

VICT: Jo Anne!!

JO ANNE: Well it's true! Nikki knows it's true! Norman was a player in high school, and he just kept right on playing when he graduated and they got married.

NIKKI: I didn't find out about his playing around until later. I loved Norman. He was the only boyfriend I ever had.

GINNY: Norman's a nice guy. He's just got his ways, that's all . . . strange ways, but they're his ways.

NIKKI: Nobody really understands Norman. He's always been ambitious. He's obsessed with the idea of success. He has a hang-up because he had such a hard time as a kid, and he felt that my parents thought he wasn't good enough for me. They never did care for him, especially my father.

GINNY: He almost had a heart attack when you dropped out of college to help put Norman through. He begged me to talk to you. I really felt sorry for him.

NIKKI: I know. Mama said he used to pray that I'd leave Norman. I guess his prayers were answered . . . it took ten years, but, it looks like we're heading for a divorce.

VICT: Well, take it from me, separation is hard enough, but that divorce can be a killer. I thought I would die if I didn't get my freedom from Harry, but when it happened I was depressed for months. I still don't know why. I didn't even love Harry by the time we busted up. I guess I was just use to having him around.

JO ANNE: I don't believe that! You treated that man terrible . . . throwin' his stuff out in the snow . . . changin' the locks on the door.

VICT: I did him a favor. I probably saved his life 'cause I was mad enough to kill him when he acted a fool with me.

GINNY: That's cold, Victoria. Anyway, you didn't love Harry the way Nikki loves Norman, and you know it. You were only married to him a year.

VICT: The roughest year of my life.

NIKKI: I don't love Norman anymore.

JO ANNE: Sure Nikki, and it don't snow in Chicago in the winter time. You always were a fool for that man. You put him through school, obeyed his every order. He treated you like a slave. Hell, I would've eliminated him a long time ago . . . no loss at all.

GINNY: Jo Anne, you oughta quit it. How do you know Charles is not another Norman? I'm sure he's not perfect.

JO ANNE: Honey, I have Charley in line; believe me, he's no Norman. I don't play that.

(Her companions look skeptical)

NIKKI: Hey, that's the motel! There's the sign, The Wayward Inn, over there. Take the next exit, Ginny.

(GINNY *turns the wheel toward the exit. Parking the car, she turns it off, and the four of them sit stunned as they stare upward at the motel)*

JO ANNE: This is it?

VICT: This crummy joint?

GINNY: I'm scared to get outta the car.

NIKKI: This can't be . . . it looks like it . . . it has the same name . . . but . . .

JO ANNE: How long ago was it when you were here, Nikki?

NIKKI: Five years . . . but . . . I didn't think it would have changed this much.

VICT: I don't want to go in there.

JO ANNE: Me either!

GINNY: We really don't have a choice. The town is booked solid because of the big convention, remember.

JO ANNE: Well I can understand why this one's not full. Those dudes in the lobby look like Alcatraz rejects.

GINNY: *(Swallows hard)* Well, let's go in. If we can make it through the lobby without getting raped or robbed, maybe we'll luck up and make it to our room alive.

VICT: I hope the door has a lock.

JO ANNE: I hope the room has a door.

(*The four women open their car doors slowly as they look around suspiciously. Closing the doors, they walk back to the back of the car and take their suitcases out.* JO ANNE *struggles with hers. Huddled together, they inch across the stage as they look around from side to side fearfully. They exit. Lights out*)

Scene 2

(*As the lights go up,* JO ANNE *is driving.* GINNY *sits beside her.* NIKKI *sits behind the driver and* VICTORIA *sits beside* NIKKI. GINNY *is reading the map*)

JO ANNE: Thank God that motel last night in Denver wasn't as raunchy as the one in St. Louis. At least I didn't have to sit up all night in fear for my life.

NIKKI: I said I was sorry about that motel, Jo Anne.

GINNY: It's not your fault, Nikki, you didn't build the motel.

VICT: Yeah, anyway, it wasn't that bad, sleeping in shifts, I mean. We got plenty of sleep in that stretch between St. Louis and Denver.

GINNY: I'll say, that was the most boring ride I've had in my life. Reminded me of the time we drove to that stupid camp in Indiana.

NIKKI: Oh no! I'd forgotten all about that! How old were we? Sixteen? We had the nerve to call ourselves counselors. I almost died trapped in those woods for three months.

VICT: I could stand the weeds and bushes, but the kids almost drove me crazy. They must've pulled every trick in the book on me.

NIKKI: At least they did have some respect for us. They used to call me Miss Nicole. I've always liked being called Nicole. I always asked you . . .

JO ANNE: Aw girl, you don't look like a Nicole, you look like a Nikki!

GINNY: What possessed us to take those jobs anyway? We must've been crazy!

VICT: I took it for the money.

JO ANNE: That's for sure. If it hadn't been for the money, I would've packed up and left a week after we got there.

VICT: After that summer I decided to be childless forever.

GINNY: You're not by yourself.

NIKKI: Oh, I don't know. I don't think the kids were that bad. I always wanted children, but Norman . . .

JO ANNE: Forget Norman! I wish Charles would tell me I couldn't have any kids. Why didn't Norman get a vasectomy? Why did you have to get your tubes tied? Now you're up a creek without a paddle, and he's laying around Chicago overpopulating.

NIKKI: I never thought Norman and I would split up. I really thought we'd be together until death us do part. I really did.

GINNY: That's what we were led to believe with all of those fairy tales that were read to us when we were kids. The only reality in life is that everything must change and we've got to accept those changes. That's why I change boyfriends every two years. Two years . . . three . . . that's tops! If no commitment is made by then it's over jack; hit the road. I'm getting ready to get rid of Bill as soon as I get back home.

VICT: Get rid of him! That fine hunk of man. The two of you have been living together for three years! Didn't he just get a promotion to the executive suite? I wouldn't let all that money slip through my fingers for nothing. If you don't want him, I'll take him!!

(The others laugh)

GINNY: Well you can have him. I'm tired of the changes he's been putting me through. Bill's so snobbish now it's pitiful. He used to be a real down-to-earth person, but now he's a walking status symbol. I sent him out for some beer the other night, and he came back with a six-pack of Perrier water. Water! I've got my lips set for some beer, and the man brings home water!!! Hell, I had water in the faucet. Here he comes talking about "we're going to get some class in this place." The man's got to go.

VICT: Well Bill is used to nice things. He is a doctor's son.

GINNY: Well he'll need the good doctor when I get through with him.

JO ANNE: I'm glad my Charles is different. He's nothing like Norman or Harry or Bill. He's just about perfect.

VICT: Humph. I never made the mistake of thinking that Harry was perfect. He was an ass when I met him and a bigger ass when I threw him out.

GINNY: Why did you marry him anyway? I never understood it. Here you are the first woman manager of the Windy City Loan Company and here he is a little nobody. You always were smarter than him.

VICT: I married Harry to get out of my mother's house. I would've married King Kong to get away from her . . . come to think of it, I did marry him. Anyway Ginny, I didn't exactly have men falling all over me like you did. After they met my mother, they usually didn't come back. He did. I should have known something was wrong when he got along with her. If I hadn't been such a coward and let Mama scare me so bad about living alone, I would have moved out by myself, then I wouldn't have taken such a desperate step as marriage. Lord knows my apartment is as expensive as hell and it's a struggle to keep going, but I'm not falling for her tricks anymore if I can help it. She's doing everything she can to get me back home now.

NIKKI: Well I'm determined not to go back home. My father is giving me a hard time, but I've made it so far in these four months by myself and I'm holding out.

JO ANNE: I don't blame you. Your father's a tyrant. He always did scare me. Norman's just like him too, bossy as hell. I dare Charles to try and boss me around the way Norman bossed you.

NIKKI: Well Norman means well, he just . . .

VICT: They all mean well, Nikki, but anybody will take advantage of you and say anything they want to you if you let them. You have to learn to speak up for yourself.

GINNY: I agree with Vic. You have to speak up for yourself sometimes, Nikki. How could you become the District Manager for the largest chain of boutiques in Chicago without speaking up?

JO ANNE: Some people are good in business, but losers in their personal lives. Take me, for instance. The three of you thought I was crazy when I took that job as a secretary after I graduated from college. But I knew what I was doing. I worked my way up to a position as an executive legal secretary and made as much money as the rest of you and then landed a well-to-do lawyer to boot. I turned this potential loser into a winner. Some people know how, others don't

GINNY: (*Teasing*) Congratulations, Jo Anne; let me commend you on your fortitude. I think I'll write your life story and see if I can get backing for a production. It could be a movie of the week, prime time. I'm sure the nation is interested in your story. It'll get great ratings.

VICT: Yeah Jo Anne, maybe Ginny can get you a spot on her talk show. You'll be a star then, an even bigger success story than you are now.

JO ANNE: Very funny, you two are really a riot. (*Pause*) Hey Ginny, check the map. Are you sure we're on the right road? I don't see any other cars around, and this road is beginning to look awfully rough.
(*Everyone looks out of their window in concern.* GINNY *checks the map and traces the route with her finger*)

NIKKI: This road is narrow too, and I don't see any guard rails.

VICT: How high up are we? It sure looks like a long way down. Look at the tops of those trees. Look . . . snow . . . a mountain stream . . . wow!

GINNY: We're on the right route. This is the fastest route to Highway 80. This connects Denver to Salt Lake City. I guess we could have taken State Road 25 to 80, but this is supposed to be a state highway too.

JO ANNE: Look at this road! This is primitive. We're on the top of a mountain. Here's a sign coming up. How high are we?
(*They each strain to see the upcoming sign*)

VICT: Eleven . . . eleven thousand feet.

JO ANNE: Eleven thousand feet!! Oh damn!! I'm turning this baby around. We're too high up.

GINNY: Turning around! Are you crazy!!! Where the hell are you going to turn the car around? The mountain's on one side and there's an eleven thousand–foot drop on the other! You better drive this sucker and drive it like you've never driven before!

JO ANNE: (*Hysterical*) Drive it? Drive? I've never driven on the highway before in my life! Oh my god! We're climbing higher! Look at that sign, eleven thousand three hundred feet! Oh my god!

VICT: (*Shouts*) Never driven on the highway before!! What do you mean you've never driven on the highway? Why didn't you say something before we left Chicago or while we were planning the trip??!!

GINNY: I bet you better drive this car, Jo Anne, and stop acting like a fool!

JO ANNE: I can't! I can't! (*Whines*) You drive, Ginny. I'll stop and you drive.

VICT: Don't stop! Don't stop! Look how far up we are and still climbing. If we fall off the road they'll never find us in all those trees. Oh Lord!

GINNY: There's no place to stop! Drive this car!

NIKKI: (*Leans forward and begins to talk to* JO ANNE *calmly*) Jo Anne, you can do it. Don't think you can't. You know how determined you can be when you really want something, so I know that you're not going to let a little mountain stop you now. Just stay calm and check the gears. Are you in low? If you're not, then put it in low.

GINNY: Twelve thousand feet!! Oh Shit!!

(JO ANNE *grips the wheel tightly, in terror, but she does as she is instructed.* VICTORIA *looks out of the window, her eyes wide with fear*)

VICT: Don't get too close, Jo Anne, you're too close to the edge, move over . . . move over!

GINNY: (*Equally as fearful as her companions, begins to pray loudly*) Oh Lord, I swear I'll go to church for four weeks straight if you get us out of this!

NIKKI: Just steer straight and don't let anything or anyone bother you. You're doing great.

VICT: Fourteen thousand feet! Fourteen thousand feet! We're up here with the angels!!!

GINNY: (*Louder*) Six weeks, Lord . . . six weeks. I swear this sinner will spend six solid Sundays in Church!!!

NIKKI: You're doing great, Jo Anne, just beautifully. Keep it up.

JO ANNE: There's a scenic view sign! The scenic view is only one mile away! I'm turning off! I'm turning off! Somebody else take the wheel!

VICT: O.K. turn off, but don't get close to the edge. We're still high up.

(JO ANNE *turns the car off the road. The four women slump back in their seats simultaneously. They give sighs of relief*)

GINNY: Thank you, Lord.

VICT: Amen.

JO ANNE: Who in the hell drew this route? Who in the hell tried to kill me?

NIKKI: Triple A drew the route.

JO ANNE: Well they'll get a piece of my mind when I get back home.

GINNY: Come on, let's get off this mountain. Whose turn is it to drive?

VICT: Mine.

JO ANNE: Well come on, let's go. (JO ANNE *hurries from the driver's seat and rushes around the car to the back where* VICTORIA *is sitting.* VICTORIA *gets out of the car reluctantly*) Hurry up!

VICT: I'm hurrying! I'm hurrying!

(JO ANNE *jumps into the car while* VICTORIA *walks around car to the driver's side and slides in behind the wheel*)

NIKKI: Victoria, I'll take your turn if you want me to.

VICT: No . . . no I'll do it, just hand me a cigarette out of my purse. I'm gonna need a drag of something for this. From the looks of that road, it's straight down all the way.

(NIKKI *hands* VICTORIA *her purse from the back.* VICTORIA *digs into it, withdraws a cigarette, and lights it shakily. She takes a long, slow draw and exhales.* GINNY *coughs and glances at* VICTORIA *in disgust. All three passengers roll their windows down and glare at* VICTORIA. *Unaware of their discomfort, she takes another puff and starts the car. She pulls the car onto the road as the others hang out of their windows and wave the smoke out of the car*)

NIKKI: (*Coughing*) Remember, Vic, take the car out of second going downhill and don't ride the brake.

(VICTORIA *nods, changes gears, then putting her foot down on the gas pedal hard, she leans forward on the wheel as if imitating a race car driver as she races down the mountain*)

GINNY: Slow down Vic! Slow down!

JO ANNE: Step on the brake! Step on the brake!

NIKKI: No! Don't ride the brake! Don't ride the brake!

VICT: Shut up, everybody! We're getting down this mountain, *today!!!* (*The lights dim denoting a passage of time. The lights come back up.* VICTORIA *is still driving. She is calm now. Her companions, however, sit huddled in their respective places against the car doors, still shaken*)

JO ANNE: I'm glad I'm alive to tell my grandchildren how I flew down a mountain.

VICT: I got you down, didn't I?

GINNY: Thanks a lot, Victoria. I almost had a heart attack.

VICT: Well why didn't you drive the car then? I didn't hear you volunteering, just praying.

GINNY: Don't knock it if you haven't tried it.

JO ANNE: You know you haven't been to church in years. Ginny. How many weeks did you promise?

GINNY: Six.

NIKKI: Oh oh, I'll have to see this for myself.

GINNY: I'm going to go! I really am! I just didn't say when I was going to start.

NIKKI: Girl, you better not play with God like that.

JO ANNE: Especially when you've got to go through this damn desert for Lord knows how long, and without a radio I might add.

GINNY: Jo Anne, would you please lay off of the radio. I'm tired of hearing about it.

JO ANNE: Well excuse me. Can I help it if I enjoy some form of entertainment when I'm stuck out in the middle of nowhere.

GINNY: Well why don't you just hum.

JO ANNE: My . . . my, aren't we testy. (*She reaches into the back of the car and brings out a box of cookies. She pops one in her mouth, eats it and begins to suck her teeth. The others tense up*) I sure hope this car makes it through the desert. Do we have enough gas? Did the man at the gas station check the water and oil?

VICT: Will you stop being so negative. This is a brand new station wagon. It only had three thousand miles on it when we got it.

JO ANNE: Well there's more than three thousand miles on it now. Climbing that mountain might have hurt it.

GINNY: Oh be quiet, Jo Anne; the car's O.K. Hand me my purse, will you? I need some gum.

(*The others look dismayed as* JO ANNE *reaches for the purse. She glances at* GINNY, *who is looking out of her window and reaches into* GINNY's *purse.* VICTORIA *observes* JO ANNE *through the rear view mirror as* JO ANNE *takes the gum out of the purse and puts it into her pocket. She hands the purse to* GINNY. GINNY *digs in her purse frantically looking for the gum*)

GINNY: Where is that gum. I was sure I had two sticks of gum left. I'm positive about it. Where the hell is it?

(*As she continues to go through her purse,* NIKKI, JO ANNE, *and* VICTORIA *stifle their giggles*)

VICT: Maybe you lost the gum back at the filling station when you went in your purse.

GINNY: I guess I did. It's not in here. Anybody else have any? (*Her companions respond in the negative, smiling gratefully*) Oh well, I'll get some when we stop again.

(*The others groan. There is a moment of silence which is interrupted by* JO ANNE *who begins to suck her teeth*)

VICT: You know, Jo Anne, in all these years I've known you I never noticed that you sucked your teeth.

JO ANNE: (*Surprised*) I do?? Hmmm, I never noticed it either. I forgot to bring my dental floss. I must be doing it unconsciously. I hate that little goop that gets there in between your teeth. (*Demonstrates*) You know, those little pieces of food that get stuck up there and just drive you crazy. You know what I mean?

GINNY: Yeah, we know. Why don't you buy some floss when we stop in the next big town and do us all a big favor.

JO ANNE: I'll do that, Ginny, if you'll do me a favor and . . .

NIKKI: Jo Anne! Ginny! Please, stop fussing!

VICT: Yeah, why don't you look on the map, Jo Anne, and see where we are.

JO ANNE: (Snatches the map up and studies it) We're a couple of miles outside of Wendover, Utah in the middle of nowhere, without a radio. For all we know, we might be the only people left on earth.

GINNY: Well we don't have a radio, Jo Anne, so why don't you shut up about it! I'm tired of hearing your mouth.

JO ANNE: I'm not choked up about hearing your mouth either, Ginny. Everytime you open it another order comes out. You always did act like you knew everything.

GINNY: (Turning to JO ANNE) I beg your pardon.

JO ANNE: You've always been bossy. Ever since we were kids you've had to have your way about everything. Quite frankly, I never did like that superior attitude of yours.

GINNY: It's not hard to feel superior to you, Jo Anne. If it hadn't been for me you never would have made it through high school, you never were heavy in the smarts department, and everybody knows how you got through college.

JO ANNE: And exactly what do you mean by that?

NIKKI: Hey, come on. Cut it out. We've got almost a week and a half to be together, come on now.

JO ANNE: No, she's got something to say, let her say it.

VICT: Oh the hell, I don't feel like hearing all this crap. We've got five miles to go until we reach the next town, and I'm tired. The two of you can fuss later, right now look for a vacancy sign on a motel so we can all get some rest.

(JO ANNE and GINNY glare at each other, their anger festering)

JO ANNE: I've got to pee.

VICT: Ah, can't you hold it until we get to Wendover? It'll just be a few minutes more.

JO ANNE: No I cannot. Now stop this car Victoria, and let me out near some bushes or something!

GINNY: You must have kidney failure, Jo Anne. You've left piss every ten miles from Illinois to Utah.

JO ANNE: Stop this car, Victoria!!!

(VICTORIA pulls off of the highway angrily. JO ANNE jumps out of the car, slamming the door behind her)

NIKKI: There's some bushes over there, Jo Anne.

GINNY: And hurry up.

(JO ANNE *exits. The others sit in the car waiting*)

VICT: I hope the sun cooks her butt.

(*Her companions giggle. Offstage a scream is heard, and* JO ANNE *rushes back onto the stage, carrying one shoe and limping. The others look concerned*)

NIKKI: What happened, Jo Anne?

JO ANNE: I stepped in it!! I stepped in some cow shit!! Right over there . . . right by those bushes! (*The three women in the car begin to laugh hysterically while* JO ANNE *cleans off her shoe then gets back into the car.* VICTORIA *pulls back onto the road*)

JO ANNE: I don't think it's funny. I ruined a good pair of shoes.

NIKKI: Oh Jo Anne, where's your sense of humor?

GINNY: How do you know it was cow shit?

JO ANNE: As big as it was it had to be. I know cow shit when I see it.

GINNY: Oh? I thought you'd be more familiar with bullshit.

JO ANNE: Ginny, if you say . . .

VICT: Ginny! Jo Anne! Pleassssseee!

NIKKI: Thank goodness, we're in Wendover. There's a vacancy sign, over there to your right, Vic.

VICT: O.K., I see it.

JO ANNE: You're not going in there are you? It's a dump.

VICT: It won't be the first dump we've slept in, or have you forgotten St. Louis?

JO ANNE: I tried to.

(VICTORIA *pulls the car into the parking lot and turns off the ignition*)

JO ANNE: If we are going to go in *there*, I'd prefer that we get two separate rooms, and I don't want Ginny as my roommate.

GINNY: Listen, honey, the feeling is mutual. I'd rather sleep in the car than in the same room with you.

VICT: (*Impatient*) If you two want to get separate rooms, go right ahead. I've been through hell today and I'm tired, and I plan on sleeping in a bed, in a room, in that motel, tonight.

NIKKI: Right on!

(NIKKI *and* VICTORIA *get out of the car and exit.* JO ANNE *and* GINNY *continue to sit, eyeing each other on occasion with hostility. A few moments later* NIKKI *and* VICTORIA *return to the car.* NIKKI *goes to* GINNY's *window and knocks on it.* GINNY *rolls the window down*)

NIKKI: We're in room 2-A on the first floor, straight through the lobby. (*Neither woman replies.* NIKKI *looks at* VICTORIA, *who shrugs, and both of them exit.* GINNY *and* JO ANNE *continue to sit in silence. Then* GINNY *slowly opens the car door and gets out of the car. She slams the door behind her, glares once again at* JO ANNE, *goes back to the back of the car and gets her suitcase. And with one last defiant exchange of gestures between* GINNY *and* JO ANNE, GINNY *exits. Lights out*)

Scene 3

(*As the lights go up,* NIKKI *is driving.* JO ANNE *sits beside her in the front seat.* VICTORIA *sits behind* JO ANNE, *and* GINNY *sits behind* NIKKI. *The tension is at its height, and their attitudes reflect this*)

JO ANNE: Whose idea was it to wear halters and shorts in San Francisco?

NIKKI: (*Defensive*) How did I know it wasn't hot in San Francisco!!

JO ANNE: I just know I'm gonna catch pneumonia. I've never been so cold in my life. I would have dropped dead if I had to climb one more hill!

GINNY: (*Mutters*) In that case, maybe we should have stayed longer.

JO ANNE: (*Turns to* GINNY *angrily*) Ginny . . .

VICT: (*Shouts*) I can't stand it! I just can't stand it! Will you two stop it; both of you are getting on my nerves. I just started my period and I don't need this aggravation!

(VICTORIA *takes a cigarette out of her purse and lights it shakily. Taking a long draw, she exhales. Her companions roll their windows down simultaneously.* JO ANNE *waves the smoke out of the car, then begins to suck on her teeth.* GINNY *smacks on her gum.* NIKKI *becomes irritated*)

NIKKI: How far is it to L.A., Jo Anne?

JO ANNE: (*Checks the map*) We just left Santa Barbara . . . now we're about one hundred miles from L.A. We'll be there soon.

NIKKI: It won't be soon enough for me. I can't wait.

JO ANNE: So that's the reason that you're driving so fast. Why don't you slow down and save a life, mine.

VICT: It's her ticket if she gets caught, not yours, Jo Anne; she's comfortable, so let her alone.

JO ANNE: Since you brought the subject of comfort up, Victoria, don't you think it's about time that you had some consideration for the rest of us and lay off of those cigarettes so we can all breathe a little?

VICT: Really?? I didn't know you felt that way about my smoking. But yours is the only voice I seem to hear objecting. Nikki? Ginny? (*Neither of the women respond as they shift in their seats uncomfortably*) Ginny, is my smoking bothering you?

GINNY: (*Hesitant*) Well Vic, you know I never did smoke . . .

VICT: (*Interrupts*) Nikki? Do you feel the same way?

NIKKI: Uh huh.

VICT: (*Puts her cigarette out angrily*) You'd think that my best friends would have said something to me about this sooner. If my smoking bothered you, all you had to do was tell me.

GINNY: Aw Victoria, don't sound so hurt. It's just that closed up in this car on such a long trip . . . well, it's kind of hard to take . . . you know.

VICT: Yeah, I know, Ginny, just like your gum chewing; Smack, Smack,

Smack, Chomp, Chomp, Chomp. I can identify with your feelings very well.

(JO ANNE *and* NIKKI *laugh.* GINNY *bristles*)

GINNY: I see . . . yes . . . I see. So that's why my gum has been disappearing so mysteriously in the last few days. Yeah, I understand now. Nobody had the nerve to ask me politely not to chew the gum. Instead, somebody . . . (*Eyes* VICTORIA, *then* JO ANNE) steals my gum, like a child would and hides it. Very clever . . . immature, but clever.

JO ANNE: Ah calm down, Ginny. Hell, you could've busted our eardrums with that noise. Between choking to death on Vic's smoke and going deaf behind your gum chewing, I'm surprised we've made it this far.

GINNY: Humph, you've done your little bit to add to the symphony of sound, Jo Anne. (*She begins to suck her teeth*) Does that sound familiar?

(JO ANNE *says nothing as she stares out of the window, furious. The situation is potentially explosive as* NIKKI *increases her speed, stepping harder on the gas pedal.* JO ANNE *turns to* NIKKI *nervously*)

JO ANNE: Nikki, will you slow this crate down, for God's sake!!!

NIKKI: Fuck you, Jo Anne.

(*There is a collective gasp as her companions sit stunned*)

JO ANNE: What did you say?

NIKKI: You heard what I said.

VICT: I don't believe it! I just don't believe it!! Miss Take Anything finally speaks up. After all these years, she finally speaks up!!

JO ANNE: (*Amused*) Nikki, Little Miss Perfect . . . Miss Goody Two Shoes curses. She actually curses. I knew the truth would come out. I knew you weren't as perfect as you always pretended to be.

NIKKI: I never pretended to be perfect, Jo Anne. The simple fact of the matter is that you were always such a bitch that you made everybody around you look good.

(GINNY *and* VICTORIA *convulse in laughter*)

JO ANNE: (*Angry*) If I made you look good Nikki, then I was doing you a favor.

GINNY: (*Snickering*) Jo Anne, why don't you . . .

NIKKI: Be quiet, Ginny; I can handle this. For once in your life stop taking up for me. Stop butting in. I'm capable of taking care of myself.

GINNY: (*Hurt*) Well I just wanted to help.

NIKKI: I know you wanted to help, but sometimes you go too far. You're always defending me against somebody, then you turn right around and boss me around yourself. I'm tired of it. Stop butting into my life.

VICT: That's really gratitude for you. Ginny always was there for you, Nikki. You never had the guts to stand up for yourself . . . always creeping around like some ghost, scared of your own shadow. You're afraid of your father, afraid of Norman . . . afraid of everybody. You wouldn't even have the job you have now if it hadn't been for Ginny talking you into taking those promotions. There you were ready and willing to live in Norman's shadow and continuing to be a dumb Miss Nobody.

NIKKI: Listen who's talking about being afraid, Miss Mama's Baby of 1902! You won't even go to the toilet unless she tells you to. You're always bragging about how you threw Harold out! You know damn well your mother picked him out for you and told you when to get rid of him. The poor man probably was more than happy to leave. Between you and your mother, his life must've been hell!

JO ANNE: (To NIKKI) I'm certain living with Victoria had to be hell for poor Harry, especially with a mother like hers.

VICT: (Controlled fury) I could respect your observations about my private life, Nikki, if they didn't come from a woman who was stupid enough to let the biggest woman chaser in Chicago talk her into getting her tubes tied. As for your two cents worth, Jo Anne, I do not appreciate you talking about my mother, and there is no way that I would ever listen to a thing you would have to say anyway. Everybody who went to college with you knows where your brains lie . . . and it's not between your ears.

(JO ANNE whirls completely around in her seat, enraged, as she faces VICTORIA. NIKKI leans forward in her seat, stepping on the gas even harder as she vents her anger)

JO ANNE: I oughta kick your ass.

VICT: Then you'd better go get some help 'cause I don't think you're woman enough to handle the job.

NIKKI: Victoria, you're a liar!!! Norman didn't make me do a thing I didn't want to do. Tell her, Ginny!!

GINNY: Me? . . . You want me to butt in . . . are you kidding? And you, Jo Anne, I don't know why you're acting so indignant. You know Victoria's telling the truth. You screwed your way from State Street to Lake Shore Drive, nonstop.

JO ANNE: (Turns to GINNY) You're not exactly a virgin yourself, Ginny. You know something, you've been on my case since we left Chicago, and I'm sick of it. As a matter of fact, I'm sick of you. Big bad, Ginny . . . cute Ginny . . . smart Ginny . . . popular Ginny. People always made me feel like I should have gotten down on my knees and kissed your feet 'cause you took this poor little girl from the projects into your precious inner circle of silly friends. I always knew you felt that you were better than me, and I swore to myself that I'd make it in this life even if I had to use you or anybody else to do it. Now I have made it . . . living right there on Lake Shore Drive where I swore I would be . . . right there with you and your struck up little Billy boy, and you . . . (*Points to* GINNY) you can't stand it. It eats you up inside.

GINNY: Frankly, my dear, I don't give a damn. I'm sure lots of whores live on Lake Shore Drive.

(JO ANNE *tries to leap into the back seat, going for* GINNY's *throat. She bumps against* NIKKI, *who fights to control the wheel of the car.* VICTORIA *attempts to break up the ensuing fight as squeals and obscenities fill the air*)

NIKKI: Damn it, stop! Stop it! You trying to kill us??

(NIKKI *pulls the car off of the road, cuts off the ignition, and helps* VICTORIA *pull the two women apart. She pulls a crumpled* JO ANNE *back into the front seat, while a frazzled* VICTORIA *holds* GINNY, *equally rumpled, in the back seat.* JO ANNE *jerks loose from* NIKKI's *grip on her*)

JO ANNE: Let go of me.

NIKKI: (*Shouts*) We are now in the Los Angeles city limits. We've got two choices. Either we complete this trip in peace or we turn this car around and go back home, *now!*

GINNY: Are you kidding! Do you think I would go another mile with that . . . (*Points to* JO ANNE)

JO ANNE: The feeling's mutual, baby!!!

VICTORIA: I've got a better idea. Hand me that L.A. map, Nikki, I'm gonna find a route to the airport and you can drop me off there. I can't stand another minute of this madness.

GINNY: Sounds good to me, I'm going with you.

JO ANNE: Oh, no you don't. I'm not getting stuck here with her. (*Indicates* NIKKI)

NIKKI: Well you can get the hell out of the car now for all I care!!

JO ANNE: The hell I will; I helped pay for this car and I plan on staying in it as long as everybody else!

NIKKI: That won't be long!!! (*Starts the car*) The map won't be necessary, Victoria. I've already studied it and I know how to get to the airport. I'm not as *dumb* as all of you seem to think I am. (*She pulls into traffic so suddenly that the others are tossed around in the car*)

JO ANNE: Hey watch it, what are you trying to do, kill me!!??

NIKKI: Don't tempt me.

(NIKKI *drives with a vengeance as each woman keeps a look out for the airport exit*)

GINNY: There's the sign, three more miles, over there!

NIKKI: I can read, Ginny, thank you.

VICT: This really amazes me, after all of these years of growing up with someone, sharing secrets, sharing experiences, practically sharing your life, you think you know your friends and you don't really know them at all. Life can pull some cruel jokes.

JO ANNE: Yeah, and our so-called friendship is the cruelest joke of them all. Here's TWA, you can let me off here. (*Pause*) Hey, you're passing it!

NIKKI: I fly United!!

GINNY: You? Fly? What about the car? It's in your name.

NIKKI: Hertz will take care of it.

(NIKKI *pulls the car over and stops. Taking the key out of the ignition, she bolts from the car, followed by* JO ANNE. *As* VICTORIA *opens her car door, it hits* JO ANNE *who falls back stunned*)

JO ANNE: You hit me with that car door on purpose!!!

(VICTORIA *ignores her as she and* JO ANNE *join* GINNY *and* NIKKI *at the back of the car.* NIKKI *pitches the luggage to the ground as she gets her own bag*)

GINNY: Watch it, Nikki!! That's my stuff you're throwing around.

(VICTORIA *and* JO ANNE *go into the back of the car for their things at the same time, bumping and elbowing each other viciously. Grabbing the same bag, they grapple over it*)

VICT: That's my bag!! Let go!

(JO ANNE *lets go as* VICTORIA *is tugging, and* VICTORIA *loses her balance.* JO ANNE *chuckles in triumph as she reaches for her own suitcases.* VICTORIA *swings her bag at* JO ANNE, *who dodges it successfully. As this is happening,* NIKKI *starts to exit, then turns back toward the others before she leaves the stage*)

NIKKI: One more thing, for fifteen years I've begged the three of you to call me Nicole. Well I'm not begging anymore. My name is Nicole and don't you call me Nikki again, *ever!!!* (*She exits*)

VICT: (*Calls after her*) Don't worry, I won't call you period! Come on, Ginny, let's walk down to American Airlines.

GINNY: All right. I wouldn't ride United or TWA if someone paid me! (*The two women start toward the exit*)

JO ANNE: Thank God, I won't have to ride on the same plane. I'm going to call Charley, I can't wait to get home.

(GINNY *and* VICTORIA *stop, grin at each other, and turn back to* JO ANNE)

GINNY: Oh, Jo Anne, when you get back to Chicago you'd better take a cab to 4305 Smith Street, apartment 11-A. Charley will probably be sleeping there tonight . . . that is if United Airlines is faster than TWA.

(GINNY *and* VICTORIA *exit laughing loudly.* JO ANNE *stands rooted for a minute, looking puzzled and muttering to herself*)

JO ANNE: 4305 Smith Street . . . 4305 Smith Street . . . (*She gasps*) 4305 Smith Street . . . that's Nikki's place!!!! (*Laden with her overweight luggage, she rushes toward the exit which* NIKKI *has taken*) Nikki! You bitch!!!   (*She exits*)

(*Lights out*)

Black Women Define Themselves

• • • • •

The selections in this book address the African-American woman's struggle with a legacy of racism and sexism. But just beneath the surface all of them also address an idea that is central to liberation from both forms of oppression—self-definition. To a great degree, the African-American woman's struggle to free herself from the burdens of racism and sexism can be viewed as the struggle to free herself from others' definitions of who she is. The ex-slaves writing letters to the federal government for help during the Depression were struggling to free themselves from the country's view of them as nonentities, as noncitizens with no entitlement to assistance. Ann Petry's Lutie Johnson struggles to free herself from the entrapment of two men, Junto and Boots, who see her as a whore simply because she is young, attractive, black, poor, and therefore vulnerable. Alice Walker's Meridian struggles to free herself from her mother's definition of black womanhood, which includes marriage, children, and a sense of community with other black women, but not freedom to test the boundaries of that community—to fight for civil rights, attain higher education, achieve professional success.

Much in the canon of writing by and about black women represents an effort to confront and disassemble others' definitions of who they are: where they should live, how they should behave, how they should earn a living, how they should look. The relatively few early slave narratives by African-American women were intended to make known not only the conditions of slavery in order to help eliminate them but the true circumstances of the female slave's life in order to dispel the myth that she was subhuman and immoral. Harriet Jacobs, a former slave who took a lover at 15 to thwart the sexual advances of her owner, explains that she wrote the narrative *Incidents in the Life of a Slave Girl* "to arouse the women of the North to a realizing sense of the condition of two millions of women at the South, still in bondage, suffering what I suffered, and most of them far worse."[1] Conscious of the Victorian standard of female chasteness espoused by most of her intended audience, Jacobs takes great pains to make her situation comprehensible to them and to invoke their sympathy. On her decision to take a lover, she comments, "It seems less degrading to give one's self than to submit to compulsion. There is something akin to freedom in having a lover who has no control over you, except that which he gains by kindness and attachment. . . . In looking back calmly, on the events of my life, I feel that the slave woman ought not to be judged by the same standard as others."[2] In stating that her choice was the "*less* degrading" one, Jacobs acknowledges that she nonetheless did feel degraded in having to make it. She tries to make her reader understand that the conditions of slavery elicited from black women behaviors they would not otherwise have exhibited. Jacobs was aware that the female slave's vulnerability to sexual exploitation at a very early age was interpreted by the white population as a moral failing, not an infliction of abuse.

In 1925, in "On Being Young—a Woman—and Colored," Marita Bonner wrote of how difficult it was for her to live in a world that could not reconcile her being "young," "a woman," and "colored" with also being intelligent, educated, and middle-class: "Why do they see a colored woman only as a gross collection of desires, all uncontrolled, reaching out for their Appollos and the Quasimodos with avid indiscrimination? Why unless you talk in staccato squawks—brittle as seashells—unless you "champ" gum—unless you cover two yards square when you laugh—unless your taste runs to violent colors—impossible perfumes and more impossible clothes—are you a feminine Caliban craving to pass for Ariel?"[3] Gwendolyn Brooks's *Maud Martha* is about a plain-looking black woman struggling toward independence. Mary Helen Washington quotes Maud's reference to those "usual representatives of womanly beauty, pale and pompadoured" and concludes that, "casual and parenthetical as that reference appears, it tells us something about Maud's rejection of what black American society values in women; it is a criticism of the standards of womanhood set by all patriarchal institutions in the black world."[4]

During the 125 years that have passed since the days of slavery, the black American woman's desirability has been judged by Western standards of beauty, her giftedness as a writer or artist defined by white male standards of what is interesting and significant, and her power as a wage earner degraded by the assumption of the prevailing culture that in being black and female she is, literally, worth less. But just as beauty is in the eye of the beholder, the victim is in the eye of the oppressor. The selections that follow continue the tradition, starting with the earliest slave narratives of black women, not the white, male culture, interpreting the lives of black women; written on the heels of the feminist and black power movements of the 1960s and 1970s, however, these selections go even further.

Alice Walker, in her essay "Beyond the Peacock: The Reconstruction of Flannery O'Connor," describes a journey back to the poor home of her birth, now entirely run-down and abandoned, and to the large, comfortable home of the writer Flannery O'Connor, which is well maintained even though no one lives there any longer. As Walker knocked on the door of O'Connor's house, she was filled with anger at the disparity between the condition of her home and O'Connor's, seeing it as a symbol of her own "disinheritance" and of the enormous difference that rights of birth can make in people's lives. "I think," she writes, "it all comes back to houses. To how people live. There are rich people who own houses to live in and poor people who do not. And this is wrong." Walker recalls that while no one remembers where in Mississippi Richard Wright lived, William Faulkner's home, like O'Connor's, has been carefully preserved. "What comes close to being unbearable," Walker concludes, "is that I know how damaging to my own psyche such injustice is. In an unjust society the soul of the sensitive person is in danger of deformity from just such weights as this. For a long time I will feel Faulkner's house, O'Connor's house, crushing me. *To fight back will require a certain amount of energy, energy better used doing something else* [italics added]."[5]

The black American women of the 1970s and 1980s who enjoyed the benefits won by the civil rights, feminist, and black power movements were freer to put their energy into "doing something else" than their foremothers were. However much as these movements were problematic for African-American women and failed to accomplish fully the changes they sought, they did deal with some of the most tangible consequences of racism and sexism. These accomplishments, combined with the more subtle, creative, psychological work done by their foremothers, made black American women of the 1970s and 1980s freer to direct their energies into discovering who they would become and what they would do, and into celebrating who they had been all along, as do Gwendolyn Brooks and Maya Angelou in their poems "To Those of My Sisters Who Kept Their Naturals" and "Phenomenal Woman."

Carolyn Rodgers's poem "I Have Been Hungry," like those by

Brooks and Angelou, explores her sense of physicality. Where Brooks and Angelou are self-affirming, however—prizing in the appearance of black women what has traditionally been denigrated—Rodgers is tentative and questions the depth and staying power of the notion that black is suddenly beautiful. She does not feel transformed:

> and how could you think that i
> after being empty for so long
> could fill up on fancy fierce platitudes. . . .
>
> am i—really—so beautiful
> as i sweat and am black and oh so
> greasy in the noonday sun

Civil rights activist Ruby Doris Smith Robinson "hated white women for a period of years when she realized that they represented a cultural ideal of beauty and femininity which by inference defined black women as ugly and unwomanly."[6] Together, the poems by Brooks, Angelou, and Rodgers speak both to the spirit of joy that accompanies the long-awaited release from such oppression and to the painful and complex feelings of the aftermath as a new way of seeing oneself—figuratively and literally—evolves.

Frances Beal's "Double Jeopardy: To Be Black and Female" also expresses seemingly contradictory sentiments in delineating the social and political position of black American women as the 1960s drew to a close. Her anger with the forces that have undermined black women's economic and social standing in America's capitalist society is irrepressible, yet no more so than her hopefulness about the possibilities for reshaping that society in the interest of black women. "The black community and black women especially must begin raising questions about the kind of society we wish to see established," she concludes. "We must note the ways in which capitalism oppresses us and then move to create institutions that will eliminate these destructive influences." The enormity of the goal Beal sets for herself and her readers reflects the extraordinary youthfulness of the times and the widespread belief in the potential for both personal and social change.

The contributions by Faith Ringgold and Margaret Walker address in personal terms several of the issues raised by Beal: how to be a mother and an artist simultaneously in a culture that offers few rewards to either, and how to nurture creativity and maintain integrity in a culture that places such a high value on commercial success. Both women are committed to establishing and living by their own priorities and values.

Ringgold and Walker give personal testament to the struggle for self-definition as creative women; Deborah McDowell chronicles the ongoing effort of black feminist scholars and critics to define the literary outpouring of such women. Black feminist critics emerged in the 1970s to claim the literary tradition of black women. They investigated forgotten writers, examined and revised distortions about black women's contributions to the American literary tradition, and practiced sociopolitical analysis. Black feminist criticism developed, as McDowell explains in "New Directions for Black Feminist Criticism," "because of the recognition among black female critics and writers that white women, white men, and Black men consider their experiences as normative and black women's as deviant."

The search for identity in black feminist criticism has produced many literary anthologies and writings that attempt to reconstruct a literature of and by black American women. Among those published during the 1970s and early 1980s were Mary Helen Washington's *Black-Eyed Susans: Classic Stories by and about Black Women* (1975) and *Midnight Birds: Stories by Contemporary Black Women Writers* (1980); Barbara Smith's "Toward a Black Feminist Criticism" (1977); Erlene Stetson's *Black Sister: Poetry by Black Women Writers, 1974–1980* (1980); Barbara Christian's *Black Women Novelists: The Development of a Tradition, 1892–1976* (1980); Gloria T. Hull, Patricia Bell Scott, and Barbara Smith's *All the Women Are White, All the Blacks Are Men, But Some of Us Are Brave* (1982); Claudia Tate's *Black Women Writers at Work* (1983); and Marjorie Pryse and Hortense J. Spillers's *Conjuring: Black Women, Fiction, and Literary Tradition* (1985).

NOTES

1. Harriet Jacobs, *Incidents in the Life of a Slave Girl: Written by Herself* (Boston: 1861), 6.
2. Quoted in Mary Helen Washington, "Introduction: Meditations on History: The Slave Woman's Voice," in her *Invented Lives: Narratives of Black Women 1860–1960* (New York: Doubleday, 1987), 6.
3. Marita Bonner, "On Being Young—a Woman—and Colored," in Washington, *Invented Lives*, 170–71.
4. Gwendolyn Brooks, *Maud Martha* (New York, Harper and Row, Washington, *Invented Lives*, 401. 1953) 27.
5. Alice Walker, "Beyond the Peacock: The Reconstruction of Flannery O'Connor," in *In Search of Our Mothers' Gardens*, 58.
6. Sara Evans, *Personal Politics*, 88.

● ● ● ● ●

"To Those of My Sisters Who Kept Their Naturals"

Gwendolyn Brooks

Gwendolyn Brooks has encountered tremendous changes in blacks' social attitudes from the time she published *Maud Martha* in 1953 until 1980 when she published "To Those of My Sisters Who Kept Their Naturals." "I who have 'gone the gamut' from an almost angry rejection of my dark skin by some of my brainwashed brothers and sisters to a surprised queenhood in the new black sun—am qualified to enter at least the kindergarten of new consciousness now." Brooks had always felt that being black is good, but her new consciousness embraces blackness as natural and celebrates the black woman for what she is. Brooks confides, "It frightens me to realize that, if I had died before the age of fifty, I would have died a 'Negro' fraction."[1]

The spirit of "To Those of My Sisters Who Kept Their Naturals" (written in 1980 and published in *Blacks* [1987]), is in direct contrast to that of *Maud Martha*, written 27 years earlier; above all the poem is celebratory. Brooks praises black women in their "natural" state, accepting the full range of their emotion—"stern, kind./ . . . loud soft, with crying and with smiles"—and connecting them with the universal. In synchrony, black women "withhold," "extend," "Step out," "go back"; Brooks calls up images of the tides, the changes in season, the cycles of birth and death. The sense of alienation and separateness in a white, male-oriented world that is felt so acutely by Maud Martha when she attends a nightclub dance with her husband is replaced here by a keen sense of connection to and place in the wider natural world. Likewise, the "pale and pompadoured" beauty prized in Maud Martha's time has given way to women who have "not bought Blondine./ . . . have not hailed the hot-comb recently." In this poem, having a *natural*—hair in the Afro style natural to African-Americans—is emblematic of being true to one's nature, of exercising the "natural Respect of Self."

NOTE

1. Brooks, *Report from Part One*, 21.

Black Women Define Themselves

Never to look
a hot comb in the teeth.

Sisters!
I love you.
Because you love you.
Because you are erect.
Because you are also bent.
In season, stern, kind.
Crisp, soft—in season.
And you withhold.
And you extend.
And you Step out.
And you go back.
And you extend again.
Your eyes, loud-soft, with crying and
    with smiles,
are older than a million years.
And they are young.
You reach, in season.
You subside, in season.
And All
below the richrough righttime of your hair.

You have not bought Blondine.
You have not hailed the hot-comb recently.
You never worshipped Marilyn Monroe.
You say: Farrah's hair is hers.
You have not wanted to be white.
Nor have you testified to adoration of that
    state
with the advertisement of imitation
(*never* successful because the hot-comb is
    laughing too.)

But oh the rough dark Other music!
the Real,
the Right.
The natural Respect of Self and Seal!
    Sisters!
Your hair is Celebration in the world!

● ● ● ● ●

"Phenomenal Woman"

Maya Angelou

The passage of time and affectionate encounters with others certainly contributed not only to Maya Angelou's maturation but also to her ability to recover from the damage done to her sense of self as a child. Enabling her to make a positive declaration of self, however, was the advice of her mother: "Since you are black, you have to hope for the best. Be prepared for the worst and always know that anything can happen."[1] Maya Angelou articulates what is best in herself.

In "Phenomenal Woman" (from *And Still I Rise* [Random House, 1978]), as she states in the poem, she is not "cute or built to suit a fashion model's size"; rather, she is tall, large-boned, physically imposing. Like Brooks in "To Those of My Sisters Who Kept Their Naturals," Angelou rejects the white male culture's standard of female beauty. But her poem is a far more personal statement; in expressing the unabashed pleasure she takes in being herself, it is a marker for both her personal growth and the tenor of the times. Her evolution from the sometimes painfully silent, self-effacing girl of the 1930s and 1940s she describes in *I Know Why the Caged Bird Sings* signifies the greater possibility over the past fifty years for such self-acceptance among black women. Her simple celebration of herself as a woman is offered up as a call to other black women to celebrate themselves as well.

NOTE

1. Maya Angelou, *The Heart of a Woman* (New York: Bantam, 1981), 52.

Pretty women wonder where my secret lies.
I'm not cute or built to suit a fashion model's size
But when I start to tell them,
They think I'm telling lies.
I say,
It's in the reach of my arms,
The span of my hips,
The stride of my step,
The curl of my lips.

I'm a woman
Phenomenally.
Phenomenal woman,
That's me.

I walk into a room
Just as cool as you please,
And to a man,
The fellows stand or
Fall down on their knees.
Then they swarm around me,
A hive of honey bees.
I say,
It's the fire in my eyes,
And the flash of my teeth,
The swing in my waist,
And the joy in my feet.
I'm a woman
Phenomenally.
Phenomenal woman,
That's me.

Men themselves have wondered
What they see in me.
They try so much
But they can't touch
My inner mystery.
When I try to show them
They say they still can't see.
I say,
It's in the arch of my back,
The sun of my smile,
The ride of my breasts,
The grace of my style.
I'm a woman
Phenomenally.
Phenomenal woman,
That's me.

Now you understand
Just why my head's not bowed.
I don't shout or jump about
Or have to talk real loud.
When you see me passing
It ought to make you proud.

I say,
It's in the click of my heels,
The bend of my hair,
the palm of my hand,
The need for my care.
'Cause I'm a woman
Phenomenally.
Phenomenal woman,
That's me.

●　●　●　●　●

"I Have Been Hungry"

Carolyn Rodgers

Chicago bred and reared, Carolyn Rodgers, born in 1945, was one of the "new black poets" in the 1960s who participated in the Writers' Workshop of the Chicago Organization of Black American Culture. She began writing "quasi seriously" during her first year at the University of Illinois; by the time she graduated with a B.A. degree from Chicago's Roosevelt University in 1965, she was a committed and serious participant in the very productive black arts movement, which encourage black poetry to speak directly to the black community and to manifest its own symbolism and iconography. Combining art and polemics, Rodgers's poetry explores a wide range of themes, including racial identity, religious experience, and intricacies of black womanhood, survival, and black male-female love. Her poetry volumes are *Paper Soul* (1968), *2 Love Raps* (1969) (both of these collections were criticized for their obscenities and lengthy, proselike lines), *Song of a Black Bird* (1969), *How I Got Ovah* (1976), *The Heart Is Ever Green* (1978), and *Translation* (1980). Rodgers has also published several poetic broadsides and contributed to numerous anthologies. Her awards and honors include the Conrad Kent Rivers Writing Award (1969), the National Endowment for the Arts Award (1970), the Society of Midland Authors Poet Laureate Award (1970), and several PEN awards.

Rodgers's 1960s poetry was rooted in the black arts movement, but a decade later she said, "I have no distinct and defined political stance." In the 1970s her poems spoke to the African-American community, especially to black women, whose "life, love, eternity, pain, and joy" she focused on in order to characterize them more clearly and honestly in their oppressive environment.[1]

"I Have Been Hungry" (from *How I Got Ovah* [Doubleday, 1975]) is a poem of self-definition: the poet is determined not to conform to others' expectations and in her conclusion simply declares who she is. Rodgers rejects overtures of sisterhood from white women, whom she neither identifies with nor trusts, and she rejects the belief that what has become politically correct thinking—that all women are sisters, that all blacks are beautiful—has genuine personal meaning. She also rejects the idea of certain strains of feminist thinking that it is wrong to need a man. What, then, does Rodgers accept? Ultimately, she defines herself, in the simplest human terms, according to her need for love, her hunger for it. Rodgers strips away the politics that in the 1960s and 1970s was given the power to define so much of the psychological and social life of an entire generation and reveals her small, individual self—"a saved / sighing / singular thing, a woman. . . .

NOTE

1. Quoted in Mari Evans, *Black Women Writers (1950–1980): A Critical Evaluation* (New York: Anchor, 1984), 373.

Preface: This poem was written because I was asked to contribute to an anthology of black and white women, and the title of the anthology was *I Had Been Hungry All My Years*.

1

and you white girl
shall i call you sister now?
can we share any secrets of sameness,
any singularity of goals. . . .
you, white girls with the head that
perpetually tosses over-rated curls
while i religiously toss my over-rated behind
you white girl
i am yet suspicious of /
for deep inside of me
there is the still belief that
i am
a road

you would travel
to my man.

2

   and how could you, any of you
think that a few loud words and years
could erase the tears
blot out the nightmares and knowledge,
smother the breeded mistrust
and how could any of you think that i
after being empty for so long
could fill up on fancy fierce platitudes. . . .

      some new/old knowledge has risen in me like yeast
   but still old doubts deflate

am i—really—so beautiful
as i sweat and am black and oh so
greasy in the noonday sun

the most beauty that i am i am inside
and so few deign to touch
i am a forest of expectation.
the beauty that i will be is yet
to be defined

   what i can be even i can not know.

3

   and what does a woman want?
what does any woman want
but a soft man to hold her hard
a sensitive man to help her fight off
the insensitive pangs of living.
and what is living to a woman
without the weight of some man
pulling her down/puffing her out

   do not tell me
liberated tales of woman/woeman
who seek only to satisfy them selves

with them selves, all, by them selves
i will not believe you
i will call you a dry canyon
them, a wilderness
of wearying and failures
a fearing of hungerings from
and deep into
the wonderment of loneliness
and what makes any woman so.

4

as for me—
i am simple
a simple foolish woman.
all that i have ever wanted
i have not had
and much of what i have had
i have not wanted.

   my father never wanted three girls
and only one son, one sun. . . .
God, how he wished his seeds
had transformed themselves into
three boys and only one girl—
for heaven's sake, only one good for nothing
wanting needing love and approval seeking bleeding
girl.
and so, i have spent my days
so many of my days seeking the approval
which was never there
craving the love
i never got
and what am i now,
no longer a simple girl
bringing lemonade and cookies
begging favor
   and what am i now
no longer a world-torn woman
showering my ''luck'' in a
cold bottle of cold duck

and—who—am i now
but a

saved
sighing
singular thing, a woman. . . .
ah, here i am
and
here have i been
i say,
i
have been hungry,
ravenously hungry,
all
my
years

•　•　•　•　•

"Double Jeopardy: To Be Black and Female"

Frances Beal

Frances Beal, a civil rights activist and feminist, worked in the 1960s with the national staff of the Student Nonviolent Coordinating Committee and served as New York coordinator of SNCC's Black Women's Liberation Committee. She is now a journalist who writes about black history and politics. Her articles and essays have appeared in *Ms.*, *Black Times*, and the *Black Scholar*, for which she has served as associate editor.

"Double Jeopardy: To Be Black and Female" (first published in Robin Morgan, ed., *Sisterhood Is Powerful: An Anthology of Writings from the Women's Liberation Movement* [Random House, 1970]) appears in many anthologies of women's literature and is perhaps Beal's best-known work. It is widely anthologized because it is one of the few essays written in the early 1970s that addresses the issue of black women's race and sex oppression in America and tells black women how to avoid that oppression. It is a manifesto for the revolutionary of the early 1970s whose aim was to eliminate all forms of racist and sexist oppression. The essay is both an attack on the role that capitalism has played in determining the economic, psychological, and social lives of African-Americans—African-American women in particular—and a call for radical change: "A revolutionary has the responsibility of not only toppling those who are now in a position of power but creating new institutions that will eliminate all forms of oppression." Beal criticizes every faction of American culture that would impede its complete transformation: all women who accept the traditional, white, middle-class role of homemaker and who remain submissive to men; black men who deny black women equal standing in the struggle for black liberation; and white women committed to their own liberation who do not speak to the elimination of racism. If black women are to redefine their personal, economic, and social standing on their own terms, Beal argues, they must redefine the source of their oppression—the very society they live in.

In attempting to analyze the situation of the black woman in America, one crashes abruptly into a solid wall of grave misconceptions, outright distortions of fact, and defensive attitudes on the part of many. The System of capitalism (and its afterbirth—racism) under which we all live, has attempted by many devious ways and means to destroy the humanity of all people, and particularly the humanity of black people. This has meant an outrageous assault on every black man, woman, and child who resides in the United States.

In keeping with its goal of destroying the black race's will to resist its subjugation, capitalism found it necessary to create a situation where the black man found it impossible to find meaningful or productive employment. More often than not, he couldn't find work of any kind. And the black woman, likewise, was manipulated by the System, economically exploited and physically assaulted. She could often find work in the white man's kitchen, however, and sometimes became the sole breadwinner of the family. This predicament has led to many psychological problems on the part of both man and woman and has contributed to the turmoil in the black family structure.

Unfortunately, neither the black man nor the black woman understood the true nature of the forces working upon them. Many black women tended to accept the capitalist evaluation of manhood and womanhood and believed, in fact, that black men were shiftless and lazy; otherwise they would get a job and support their families as they ought to. Personal relationships between black men and women were thus torn asunder and one result has been the separation of man from wife, mother from child, etc.

America has defined the roles to which each individual should subscribe. It has defined "manhood" in terms of its own interests and "femininity" likewise. Therefore, an individual who has a good job, makes a lot of money, and drives a Cadillac is a real "man," and conversely, an individual who is lacking in these "qualities" is less of a man. The advertising media in this country continuously informs the American male of his need for indispensable signs of his virility—the brand of cigarettes that cowboys prefer, the whisky that has a masculine tang, or the label of the jock strap that athletes wear.

The ideal model that is projected for a woman is to be surrounded by hypocritical homage and estranged from all real work, spending idle hours primping and preening, obsessed with conspicuous consumption, and limiting life's functions to simply a sex role. We unqualitatively reject these respective models. A woman who stays at home, caring for children and the house, leads an extremely sterile existence. She must lead her entire life as a satellite to her mate. He goes out into society and brings back a little piece of the world for her. His interests and his understanding of the world become her own and she cannot develop herself as an individual, having been reduced to only a biological function. This kind of woman leads a parasitic existence that can aptly be described as "legalized prostitution."

Furthermore, it is idle dreaming to think of black women simply caring for their homes and children like the middle-class white model. Most black women have to work to help house, feed, and clothe their families. Black women make up a substantial percentage of the black working force and this is true for the poorest black family as well as the so-called "middle-class" family.

Black women were never afforded any such phony luxuries. Though we have been browbeaten with this white image, the reality of the degrading and dehumanizing jobs that were relegated to us quickly dissipated this mirage of womanhood. The following excerpts from a speech that Sojourner Truth made at a Women's Rights Convention in the nineteenth century show us how misleading and incomplete a life this model represents for us:

> . . . Well, children whar dar is so much racket dar must be something out o'kilter. I tink dat 'twixt de niggers of de Souf and de women at de Norf all a talkin' 'bout rights, de white men will be in a fix pretty soon. But what's all dis here talkin' 'bout? Dat man ober dar say dat women needs to be helped into carriages, and lifted ober ditches, and to have de best place every whar. Nobody ever help me into carriages, or ober mud puddles, or gives me any best places . . . and ar'nt I a woman? Look at me! Look at my arm! . . . I have plowed, and planted, and gathered into barns, and no man could head me—and ar'nt I a woman? I could work as much as a man (when I could get it), and bear de lash as well—and ar'nt I a woman? I have borne five chilern

and I seen 'em mos' all sold off into slavery, and when I cried out with
a mother's grief, none but Jesus heard—and ar'nt I a woman?

Unfortunately, there seems to be some confusion in the Movement
today as to who has been oppressing whom. Since the advent of Black
Power, the black male has exerted a more prominent leadership role in
our struggle for justice in this country. He sees the System for what it
really is, for the most part, but where he rejects its values and mores on
many issues, when it comes to women, he seems to take his guidelines
from the pages of the *Ladies' Home Journal.* Certain black men are maintaining that they have been castrated by society but that black women
somehow escaped this persecution and even contributed to this emascu-
lation.

Let me state here and now that the black woman in America can
justly be described as a "slave of a slave." When the black man in America was reduced to such an abject state, the black woman had no protector and was used and is still being used in some cases as the scapegoat
for the evils that this horrendous System has perpetrated on black men.
Her physical image has been maliciously maligned; she has been sexually
assaulted and abused by the white colonizer; she has suffered the worst
kind of economic exploitation, having been forced to serve as the white
woman's maid and wet nurse for white offspring while her own children were starving and neglected. It is the depth of degradation to be
socially manipulated, physically raped, used to undermine your own
household—and to be powerless to reverse this syndrome.

It is true that our husbands, fathers, brothers, and sons have been
emasculated, lynched, and brutalized. They have suffered from the
cruellest assault of mankind that the world has ever known. However,
it is a gross distortion of fact to state that black women have oppressed
black men. The capitalist System found it expedient to oppress them
and proceeded to do so without consultation or the signing of any agree-
ments with black women.

It must also be pointed out at this time, that black women are not
resentful of the rise to power of black men. We welcome it. We see in
it the eventual liberation of all black people from this oppressive System
of capitalism. Nevertheless, this does not mean that you have to negate
one for the other. This kind of thinking is a product of miseducation;
that it's either X or it's Y. It is fallacious reasoning that in order for the
black man to be strong, the black woman has to be weak.

Those who are exerting their "manhood" by telling black women
to step back into a submissive role are assuming a counterrevolutionary
position. Black women likewise have been abused by the System and
we must begin talking about the elimination of all kinds of oppression.

If we are talking about building a strong nation, capable of throwing off the yoke of capitalist oppression, then we are talking about the total involvement of every man, woman, and child, each with a highly developed political consciousness. We need our whole army out there dealing with the enemy, and not half an army.

There are also some black women who feel that there is no more productive role in life than having and raising children. This attitude often reflects the conditioning of the society in which we live and is adopted from a bourgeois white model. Some young sisters who have never had to maintain a household and accept the confining role which this entails, tend to romanticize (along with the help of a number of brothers) this role of housewife and mother. Black women who have had to endure this kind of function are less apt to have these utopian visions. Those who project in an intellectual manner how great and rewarding this role will be and who feel that the most important thing that they can contribute to the black nation is children, are doing themselves a great injustice. This line of reasoning completely negates the contributions that black women have historically made to our struggle for liberation. These black women include Sojourner Truth, Harriet Tubman, Mary McLeod Bethune, and Fannie Lou Hamer, to name but a few.

We live in a highly industrialized society and every member of the black nation must be as academically and technologically developed as possible. To wage a revolution, we need competent teachers, doctors, nurses, electronics experts, chemists, biologists, physicists, political scientists, and so on and so forth. Black women sitting at home reading bedtime stories to their children are just not going to make it.

Economic Exploitation of Black Women

The economic System of capitalism finds it expedient to reduce women to a state of enslavement. They oftentimes serve as a scapegoat for the evils of this system. Much in the same way that the poor white cracker of the South, who is equally victimized, looks down upon blacks and contributes to the oppression of blacks—so, by giving to men a false feeling of superiority (at least in their own home or in their relationships with women)—the oppression of women acts as an escape valve for capitalism. Men may be cruelly exploited and subjected to all sorts of dehumanizing tactics on the part of the ruling class, but they have someone who is below them—at least they're not women.

Women also represent a surplus labor supply, the control of which is absolutely necessary to the profitable functioning of capitalism. Women are consistently exploited by the System. They are often paid less for the same work that men do and jobs that are specifically rele-gated to women are lowpaying and without the possibility of advance-ment. Statistics from the Women's Bureau of the United States Depart-ment of Labor show that in 1967, the wage scale for white women was even below that of black men; and the wage scale for nonwhite women was the lowest of all:

White Males	$6704
Non-White Males	4277
White Females	3991
Non-White Females	2861

Those industries that employ mainly black women are the most ex-ploitative in the country. The hospital workers are a good example of this oppression; the garment workers in New York City provide us with another view of this economic slavery. The International Ladies Gar-ment Workers Union (ILGWU), whose overwhelming membership con-sists of black and Puerto Rican women, has a leadership that is nearly all lily-white and male. This leadership has been working in collusion with the ruling class and has completely sold its soul to the corporate structure.

To add insult to injury, ILGWU has invested heavily in business enterprises in racist, apartheid South Africa—with union funds. Not only does this bought-off leadership contribute to our continued exploi-tation in this country by not truly representing the best interests of its membership, but it audaciously uses funds that black and Puerto Rican women have provided to support the economy of a vicious government that is engaged in the exploitation and murder of our black brothers and sisters in our motherland, Africa.

The entire labor movement in the United States has suffered as a result of the superexploitation of black workers and women. The unions have historically been racist and male chauvinistic. They have upheld racism in this country and have failed to fight the white-skin privileges of white workers. They have failed to struggle against inequities in the hiring and pay of women workers. There has been virtually no struggle against either the racism of the white worker or the economic exploita-tion of the working woman, two factors which have consistently im-peded the advancement of the real struggle against the ruling class.

The racist, chauvinistic, and manipulative use of black workers and women, especially black women, has been a severe cancer on the Ameri-can labor scene. It therefore becomes essential for those who under-stand the workings of capitalism and imperialism to realize that the ex-ploitation of black people and women works to everyone's disadvantage and that the liberation of these two minority groups is a stepping stone

307

to the liberation of all oppressed people in this country and around the world.

Bedroom Politics

I have briefly discussed the economic and psychological manipulation of black women, but perhaps the most outlandish act of oppression in modern times is the current campaign to promote sterilization of nonwhite women, in an attempt to maintain the population and power imbalance between the white "haves" and the non-white "have nots."

These tactics are but another example of the many devious schemes that the ruling class elite attempts to perpetrate on the black population in order to keep itself in control. It has recently come to our attention that a massive campaign for so-called "birth control" is presently being prompted not only in the underdeveloped non-white areas of the world, but also in black communities here in the United States. However, what the authorities in charge of these programs refer to as "birth control" is in fact nothing but a method of outright surgical genocide.

The United States has been sponsoring sterilization clinics in nonwhite countries, especially in India where already some three million young men and boys in and around New Delhi have been sterilized in makeshift operating rooms set up by the American Peace Corps workers. Under these circumstances, it is understandable why certain countries view the Peace Corps not as a benevolent project, not as evidence of America's concern for underdeveloped areas, but rather as a threat to their very existence. This program could more aptly be named the "Death Corps."

The vasectomy, which is performed on males and takes only six or seven minutes, is a relatively simple operation. The sterilization of a woman, on the other hand, is admittedly major surgery. This operation (salpingectomy) must be performed in a hospital under general anesthesia.[1] This method of "birth control" is a common procedure in Puerto Rico. Puerto Rico has long been used by the colonialist exploiter, the United States, as a huge experimental laboratory for medical research before allowing certain practices to be imported and used here. When the birth-control pill was first being perfected, it was tried out on Puerto Rican women and selected black women (poor), as if they were guinea pigs to see what its effect would be and how efficient the Pill was.

The salpingectomy has now become the commonest operation in Puerto Rico, commoner than an appendectomy or a tonsilectomy. It is so widespread that it is referred to simply as *la operación. On the Island, 20 percent of the women between the ages of fifteen and forty-five have already been sterilized.*

And now, as previously occurred with the Pill, this method has been imported into the United States. These sterilization clinics are cropping up around the country in the black and Puerto Rican communities. These so-called "Maternity Clinics," specifically outfitted to purge black women or men of their reproductive possibilities, are appearing more and more in hospitals and clinics across the country.

A number of organizations have recently been formed to popularize the idea of sterilization, such as The Association for Voluntary Sterilization, and the Human Betterment (!!!?) Association for Voluntary Sterilization, Inc., which has its headquarters in New York City. Front Royal, Virginia, has one such "Maternity Clinic" in Warren Memorial Hospital. The tactics used in the clinic in Fauquier County, Virginia, where poor and helpless black mothers and young girls are pressured into undergoing sterilization, are certainly not confined to that clinic alone.

Threatened with the cut-off of relief funds, some black welfare women have been forced to undergo this sterilization procedure in exchange for a continuation of welfare benefits. Mt. Sinai Hospital in New York City performs these operations on its ward patients whenever it can convince the women to undergo this surgery. Mississippi and some of the other Southern states are notorious for this act. Black women are often afraid to permit any kind of necessary surgery because they know from bitter experience that they are more likely than not to come out without their insides. (Both salpingectomies and hysterectomies are performed.)

We condemn this use of the black woman as a medical testing ground for the white middle class. Reports of the ill effects, including deaths, from the use of the birth-control pill only started to come to light when the white privileged class began to be affected. These outrageous Nazi-like procedures on the part of medical researchers are but another manifestation of the totally amoral and brutal behavior that the capitalist System perpetrates on black women. The sterilization experiments carried on in concentration camps some twenty-five years ago have been denounced the world over, but no one seems to get upset by the repetition of these same racist practices today in the United States of America—the land of the free and home of the brave.

The rigid laws concerning abortions in this country are another means of subjugation and, indirectly, of outright murder. Rich white women somehow manage to obtain these operations with little or no difficulty. It is the poor black and Puerto Rican woman who is at the mercy of the local butcher. Statistics show us that the non-white death rate at the hands of the unqualified abortionist is substantially higher than for white women. Nearly half of the child-bearing deaths in New York City are attributed to abortion alone and out of these, 79 percent are among non-whites and Puerto Rican women.

We are not saying that black women should not practice birth control. Black women have the right and the responsibility to determine when it is in *the interest of the struggle to have children or not to have them and this right must not be relinquished to anyone.* It is also her right and responsibility to determine when it is in *her own best interests* to have children, how many she will have, and how far apart. The lack of the availability of safe birth-control methods, the forced sterilization practices, and the inability to obtain legal abortions are all symptoms of a sick society that jeopardizes the health of black women (and thereby the entire black race) in its attempt to control the very life processes of human beings. This is a symptom of a society that is attempting to bring economic and political factors into the privacy of the bedchamber. The elimination of these horrendous conditions will free black women for full participation in the revolution, and thereafter in the building of the new society.

Relationship to White Movement

Much has been written recently about the white women's liberation movement in the United States and the question arises whether there are any parallels between this struggle and the movement on the part of black women for total emancipation. While there are certain comparisons that one can make because we both live under the same exploitative System, there are certain differences, some of which are quite basic.

The white woman's movement is far from being monolithic. Any white woman's group that does not have an anti-imperialist and antiracist ideology has absolutely nothing in common with the black woman's struggle. In fact, some groups come to the incorrect conclusion that their oppression is due simply to male chauvinism. They therefore have an extremely antimale tone to their dissertations. Black people are engaged in a life-and-death struggle and the main emphasis of black women must be to combat the capitalist, racist exploitation of black people. While it is true that male chauvinism has become institutionalized in American society, one must always look for the main enemy—the fundamental cause of the female condition.

Another major differentiation is that the white woman's movement is basically middle class. Very few of these women suffer the extreme economic exploitation that most black women are subjected to day by day. This is the factor that is most crucial for us. It is not an intellectual persecution alone; it is not an intellectual outburst for us; it is quite real. We as black women have got to deal with the problems that the black masses deal with, for our problems in reality are one and the same.

If the white groups do not realize that they are in fact fighting capitalism and racism, we do not have common bonds. If they do not realize that the reasons for their condition lie in the System and not simply that men get a vicarious pleasure out of "consuming their bodies for exploitative reasons" (this kind of reasoning seems to be quite prevalent in certain white women's groups), then we cannot unite with them around common grievances or even discuss these groups in a serious manner because they're completely irrelevant to the black struggle.

The New World

The black community and black women especially must begin raising questions about the kind of society we wish to see established. We must note the ways in which capitalism oppresses us and then move to create institutions that will eliminate these destructive influences.

The new world that we are attempting to create must destroy oppression of any type. The value of this new system will be determined by the status of the person who was low man on the totem pole. Unless women in any enslaved nation are completely liberated, the change cannot really be called a revolution. If the black woman has to retreat to the position she occupied before the armed struggle, the whole movement and the whole struggle will have retreated in terms of truly freeing the colonized population.

A people's revolution that engages the participation of every member of the community, including man, woman, and child, brings about a certain transformation in the participants as a result of this participation. Once you have caught a glimpse of freedom or experienced a bit of self-determination, you can't go back to old routines that were established under the racist, capitalist regime. We must begin to understand that a revolution entails not only the willingness to lay our lives on the firing line and get killed. In some ways, this is an easy commitment to make. To die for the revolution is a one-shot deal; to live for the revolution means taking on the more difficult commitment of changing our day-to-day life patterns.

This will mean changing the routines that we have established as a result of living in a totally corrupting society. It means changing how you relate to your wife, your husband, your parents, and your co-workers. If we are going to liberate ourselves as a people, it must be recognized that black women have very specific problems that have to be spoken to. We must be liberated along with the rest of the population. We cannot wait to start working on those problems until that great day in the future when the revolution, somehow, miraculously, is accomplished.

To assign women the role of housekeeper and mother while men go forth into battle is a highly questionable doctrine for a revolutionary to maintain. Each individual must develop a high political consciousness in order to understand how this System enslaves us all and what actions we must take to bring about its total destruction. Those who consider themselves revolutionary must begin to deal with other revolutionaries as equals. And, so far as I know, revolutionaries are not determined by sex.

Old people, young people, men, and women must take part in the struggle. To relegate women to purely supportive roles or purely cultural consideration is dangerous doctrine to project. Unless black men who are preparing themselves for armed struggle understand that the society which we are trying to create is one in which the oppression of *all* members of that society is eliminated, then the revolution will have failed in its avowed purpose.

Given the mutual commitment of black men and black women alike to the liberation of our people and other oppressed peoples around the world, the total involvement of each individual is necessary. A revolutionary has the responsibility of not only toppling those who are now in a position of power, but creating new institutions that will eliminate all forms of oppression. We must begin to rewrite our understanding of traditional personal relationships between man and woman.

All the resources that the black community can muster up must be channeled into the struggle. Black women must take an active part in bringing about the kind of society where our children, our loved ones, and each citizen can grow up and live as decent human beings, free from the pressures of racism and capitalist exploitation.

NOTE

1. Salpingectomy: through an abdominal incision, the surgeon cuts both fallopian tubes and ties off the separated ends, after which there is no way for the egg to pass from the ovary to the womb.

● ● ● ● ●

From "Being My Own Woman"
Faith Ringgold

A painter, mixed-media sculptor, performance artist, and writer, Faith Ringgold was born in Harlem in 1930 to Willi Posey Jones (a fashion designer) and Andrew Louis Jones, Sr. She received her B.A. and M.A. degrees in fine arts, as well as an honorary doctorate (May 1991) from City College of New York. A resident of New York City and professor of art at the University of California at San Diego, Ringgold jets from coast to coast frequently. She is represented by the Bernice Steinbaum Gallery in New York City and is best known for her political paintings of the 1960s, her mixed-media masks and sculpture of the 1970s, and her painted story-quilts of the 1980s. The *American People Series* (1962), *Slave Rape Series* (1970), and *Echoes of Harlem* (1980) represent her work from each of these periods. *Faith Ringgold: Twenty-five Years of Painting, Sculpture, and Performance*, a retrospective exhibition curated by the Fine Arts Museum of Long Island, opened a three-year national tour of museums in the United States in 1990. Ringgold has written an unpublished autobiography, "Being My Own Woman" (1983), and has written and illustrated a children's book, *Tar Beach* (1991). She has two daughters—Michele Wallace, a writer whose essay "Anger in Isolation: A Black Feminist's Search for Sisterhood" appears in this volume, and Barbara Faith Wallace, a sociolinguist and teacher.

Ringgold has been simultaneously concerned about her own development as an artist and about black family unity and its importance to the black community's political power. Her concern for family is evident in this selection from her autobiography, in which she describes her struggle to balance her responsibilities to her daughters with her own need to devote time and attention to her painting. In the course of this struggle she is forced to reexamine and reject others' views of what it means to be a mother and a woman and to test the durability of the new ways in which she has defined herself.

I found myself longing to paint come the summer of 1969. I had developed a new light in my painting, which I called Black Light, a way of looking at us that came out of our new "black is beautiful" sense of ourselves. My palette was all dark colors. Placed on a white ground they appeared to be only black. But next to each other the dark tones of reds, greens, blues, browns, and grays came alive, no matter how subtle the nuance. It was magic. Ad Rinehardt had done it but I could not find out what method he had used. And, furthermore, he did *abstract* black

313

paintings. Mine were black paintings of black people. I had trouble with the glazes. They produced too much glare, or they made the surface quality of the paint too fragile. I needed time to experiment. My second one-woman show was scheduled for January 1970. The summer would be my only real chance to paint. I had a lot of ideas for new paintings. The subjects taunted me: mask faces, dancing figures of black life, a dark flag with the letters D-I-E in the stars and the letters N-I-G-G-E-R in the stripes. But there was no telling what the summer would produce with two trouble-some teenagers stalking my every move. I had to solve that problem first.

The girls, aged sixteen and seventeen, were into rebellion by then. People who didn't have children thought the youth of the day would be our salvation.

"The young people's rebellion is revolutionary," they would say. Revolutionary was a word they used for defiant, youthful, modern, anything for which you could be condemned as too old if you didn't agree with it. Revolutionary could mean practically anything but *a revolution*. They were just doing their thing was another popular explanation for youthful rebellion. That one was more like it. But whose thing was it really?

What made me so upset was that my girls seemed more like they were into doing someone else's thing. They were more the doees than the doers. And as their mother and an older woman in her thirties, I was the target for all the rage they felt for giving up so much for so little. It was as if their brains froze over at the mere sight of a man.

Stokely Carmichael echoed the sentiments they seemed to embrace: "The only position of women . . . is prone."

"But how do you feel about this?" I asked them, trying not to reveal to them the horror I felt that they could repeat this statement without feeling some of the rage they just normally aimed at me. Michele was objective about her feelings: this was his point of view; it had nothing to do with how she felt. Barbara had not been present at the theater group when Stokely spoke so she couldn't really comment.

"Please don't allow yourselves to be used by anyone, male or female," I said. "If you lay your heart out there, it is sure that some creep will come along and step on it. Don't just let life happen to you. Defy *his* ideas as you do mine. Don't just let life happen to you."

But Michele had a super crush on Stokely Carmichael, and Barbara was excited just to hear that she had met him.

"What's he like?" she asked. It was obvious no one heard a word I said.

They had already been told by all the movements that Mother is the undisputed enemy of all revolutionary ideas. Contradictions didn't matter.

"Have a baby for the Revolution!"

Would they then be revolutionary mothers or just more of the old breed, mere women with the added burden of a child to bring up, possibly alone?

Birdie, my husband, was very expressive on the baby issue.

"We don't want a baby, Barbara and Michele. If we did we could have one ourselves. Your mother and I are not as old as we seem. Hold those boys off. The Revolution my ass! All they want to do is fuck and run."

"But, Daddy," said Barbara, "you don't know the boys of today. They are honest. We're not into the lies of your generation."

"We who? You better speak for yourself. You don't know what those little motherfucas are into!"

The young were in a hurry. They rationalized that Vietnam had given them a sense of urgency. Life was cheap, the death toll a regular feature on the nightly news. Some were even saying that school was a waste of time.

"Drop out!" was high "revolutionary rhetoric." And money was "dirt." Anybody who had it felt guilty and those who didn't were angry, as I was the day I tried to explain to Barbara and Michele our financial situation:

"Even though you girls have had many advantages in life, you must understand we are not rich people like many of your classmates at New Lincoln. We are poor people struggling to see that you . . ."

Michele interrupted me: "The only one who has ever been poor here is you."

Drugs, however, were the pill I could not swallow. There were parents at their school who smoked pot with their children to share the experience. Michele was the friend of a white girl whose mother had a black boyfriend, a jazz musician, and they all got high together. My kids thought that was great—family unity.

"You're too emotional on the subject. Everybody who uses drugs is not a drug addict," they informed me.

I was outraged. Earl and Andrew flashed in my mind. Their deaths were all I could see. The girls standing before me, mere children of thirteen and fourteen at that time, were just a blur. Birdie came between us.

"Don't talk anymore, leave 'em alone. They're just trying to taunt you," he said. "They're young and crazy. They don't understand."

But back to the summer of 1969. I got an idea for a vacation they would like: summer study abroad at the University of Mexico in Mexico City. Barbara could study her favorite subjects, Spanish and Portuguese, and Michele could study hers, art and literature. They could live in a student house where they could be on their own with other young

315

people. A sense of freedom was apparently what they yearned for. Maybe that was just what they needed, an opportunity to show how mature they really were. The trip would be a good test at any rate. They could no longer say that I had babied them and never allowed them to make decisions on their own. The trip would also be a high school graduation present for Michele, and an introduction to college life. She was due to go to Howard University in the fall. Though Barbara was only in her senior year in high school, she was in her fourth year in both French and Spanish at school. Languages were something she "ate up."

Though Mother disapproved of my allowing the girls to go to Mexico by themselves, she admitted that they really had enjoyed studying French at the Alliance Française when she had taken them to Paris in the summer of 1967. It was what saved the trip from total disaster, because they had presented quite a discipline problem to Mother. That summer was a great success for me. Back in New York I had painted my three murals: *The Flag Is Bleeding, U.S. Postage Stamp Commemorating the Advent of Black Power,* and my riot mural, *Die.* Had it not been for Mother taking the girls to Europe *that* summer, I would not have been able to complete those paintings for my first one-woman show.

Birdie and I had been separated since then, since 1967. We had had to have some time away from each other. There was just too much going on: the girls, the art, teaching, and then the house. That was why I walked out the summer Mother took the girls to Europe. I didn't want to spend my summer cleaning the house and cooking, so I moved into Mother's apartment and spent my days at the gallery painting till well into the night. At the end of the summer when the girls and Mother came home from Europe, Birdie had left. Who could blame him? So we had been living apart since then. I needed him, but I needed my freedom too. Maybe later we could get back together again, after things calmed down and we could have some time for ourselves. But if I called him now he would just say, "Don't let those girls go away alone. Keep them with you. Give up the art. Postpone the show. They'll be back at school in a few months anyhow." But then so would I.

They left for Mexico after a thorough briefing: remember to lock your door; be careful when you meet strangers; stay together; and most of all look out for each other. Michele was the oldest by eleven months. She was responsible for Barbara. Kelly, the man I was seeing then, was fluent in Spanish and he knew Mexico City. He contributed to the planning of the trip and he took the girls to the airport to see them off, while I finished my last days of teaching for the year. Right away I began to assemble my canvasses and paints and set about perfecting the glaze formulas I needed to prevent glare on my Black Light paintings. For the first day or two I did nothing but work. Kelly was busy too, catching up with the time he had lost in editing his magazine with helping the girls to get ready to go to Mexico. We talked on the phone and the girls called. They were in Mexico and starting school the next day. Everything was perfect.

Thereafter Kelly came evenings for dinner, and remained with me well into the early morning. I had to stop painting at 4 P.M. to shop and cook in preparation for his nightly visits. He was taking too much time from my work. He argued that I had the summer, but I worried about "the best laid plans" and the "mice" and the girls, not to mention "the men." I told him so. He began to bring the food each night and cook it himself.

The very next evening after our conversation, Kelly arrived early with a package of groceries. I greeted him and returned to my studio. Soon after he called me to eat. But I was right in the middle of a breakthrough, the attainment of a gorgeous metallic blackness. What glazes had I mixed? I was in heaven. My paintings were talking to me. I wanted to share this with Kelly as he had shared with me his writing and his other successes.

"Kelly, let's eat in the studio so I can show you my painting," I said. "I've got something interesting to show you here."

He appeared at the door of my studio wearing my ruffled apron over his shirt, tie, and the pants of his three-piece suit. Kelly was a very serious, highly intelligent man with not much of a sense of humor. I could rarely look at him without wanting to laugh. For one thing he had an afro that was more than twice the size it should have been, and for another he wore horn-rimmed glasses. They were just exactly the sort of glasses that someone would wear who had far more brains than brawn. I wasn't laughing this time though.

"See," I said to his impassive face, "you have to look at it from the side. There is a kind of metallic sheen on this black here and it is because I've mixed certain glazes, and I am trying to find out what the underpainting is . . ."

His eyes remained expressionless, two beads in the center of huge horn rims. I tried to go on, "The underpainting is . . ."

He sucked his teeth.

". . . the paint that . . ."

He sucked his teeth again and turned to leave the studio.

"Come outside and eat," he commanded. "Your food is getting cold."

Two A.M. on a hot July morning, Barbara was on the phone. She was in New York at Kennedy Airport on her way uptown in a taxi.

"Be downstairs to pay the taxi driver. I'm all out of money," she said and hung up.

Kelly was with me. He was excellent to be with at times like this. He could even be humorous about it. We waited together in front of the building for Barbara. I was facing another hard moment of truth in my life. Kelly was making small talk with the doorman saying something about the long hot summer some dude had predicted from his air-conditioned limousine. I was far away, out of my mind with worry, and talking to myself as if there was no one around.

"Barbara home . . . barely two weeks . . . Where's Michele? Out of money . . . Oh, God, Oh, maybe . . ."

Kelly paid the driver and I embraced Barbara. She looked so young and adorable, my baby, acting so grown up in a new white dress with Mexican embroidery on it. I wanted to hold her and kiss her again and again but she wasn't for it. She was cool, mater of fact, in a hurry to get the greetings over with. She had on her cut-the-kid-stuff, I'm-a-woman-now mask face.

Finally Barbara got down to the story. She and Michele had met some "Mexican revolutionary students" the first day of classes and decided to go live with them at their commune in the suburbs of Mexico City. There were three men and two women in their middle to late twenties, except for the leader of the commune who was thirty-two. Michele would not be coming home. She had fallen in love with one of the "revolutionaries," a South American, and had "joined the movement." They would live on at the commune and be happy forever after. I was to send consent for Michele to marry if that would make me feel any better. Otherwise they would just live together. Ramos, a white Mexican and a Jew, the leader of the commune, would take care of everything. Michele had turned over all of their money to him. Barbara came home because she didn't fit in. As for the nature of their "revolutionary activities," the story was vague. They were doing some takes for a movie, in the nude. Otherwise they smoked a lot of pot. The "girls" did housework, though there was a maid, and the men each worked one day a week in town.

I called Michele immediately, ordering her to come home. She was cool too. I could feel her mask through the phone. As far as she was concerned, "I am home," she told me. If I'd feel any better about it I could send permission so that she could get married. That was all she had to say. Ramos, the head of the commune, was there to speak to me if I didn't understand.

Our conversation was hot. He said that I was a reactionary individualist artist, a domineering self-serving woman, a pawn of the capitalist system who had to be destroyed. I was a menace. My children should and must leave me for I was a dangerous negative influence. People like me were beyond hope.

I reached back to my native Harlem street language for what I had

318

to say. That language which used to make me gasp when I heard it spoken. It was now all I knew how to say. A lifetime of careful speech and whitified rhetoric went right through the window. Racial epithets and cultural slurs came on like a river.

"Me? You motherfuck . . . bastard, son of a honky bitch. You have taken advantage of my child. You fucked up pervert. Whoever said a white racist full of shit creep like you . . ."

He was very upset, his hot breath coming through the phone. I could almost feel it.

"Mrs. Ringgold," he said. His Mexican accent was heavier now and his voice was out of control, almost cracking, ". . . your daughter has left you . . ."

"Let me warn you," I screamed. "You're not fucking with a fool. I am a black woman. Your honky ass will be hotter than hell if . . ."

"Mrs. Ringgold," he interrupted me again, "there is nothing you can do. Michele is . . ."

"Listen, you murky, white cracker junkie half-ass revolutionary pimp motherfucker, what have you given her? Some of your dope? My daughter Barbara tells me you have a fucking drugstore there. Well, you dopey freaked-out sack of shit, you better not take me lightly. This "black capitalist bitch" will cause you more trouble than it is worth. What kind of revolutionary are you? You freak. You haven't seen no revolution! The best you can do, you motherfucking drug addict bastard is send my daughter home or . . ."

"Good day Mrs. Ringgold."

On the other end, Michele told me later, Ramos was beet red and trembling uncontrollably. She had never seen a man, a white man so afraid before or since. On my end, I had never been so angry. If words could kill? But Ramos was still alive and Michele was still in Mexico.

I called the American Embassy in Mexico. The ambassador was conveniently out of town. His assistant spoke with me. I told him the story, and that I was rescinding permission for Michele to be in Mexico. I was waving a copy of my letter of consent in my hand. He attempted to explain to me that it would not be possible to make Michele leave Mexico unless she was doing something unlawful.

"Unlawful?" I screamed. "What do you think they are doing over there? Watching the sun set?"

"I don't know Mrs. Ringgold," came the disinterested voice of the assistant.

"And you don't care either, do you? Well, if you know what's good for you, you'll get your ass over there and see what they . . ."

Suddenly I realized I was raving to a dial tone. The assistant had hung up on me.

I had to get a grip on myself. I called the State Department in Washington, D.C. Calmer still, I called the White House and tried to get through to the President, which was, would you believe, Richard Nixon. Then I sent the following telegram to all the appropriate officials.

". . . my daughter is a minor being held in a Mexican commune *against my will*. I am her mother and a black woman, an American citizen, a registered voter, and a taxpayer, and I demand immediate action or any harm that comes to her is the responsibility of all of you who do not assist me in bringing her home immediately. She has a return flight ticket. I expect her in America by sundown tomorrow . . ."

Now the assistant to the ambassador was calling me. He was at the commune. And he wanted to know what Michele looked like.

"She's black!" I bellowed. "Can't you see? Now what are you going to do?"

"Well," he said, "everything looks all right to me here."

"Save your comments," I said. "I'll be there in the morning. At that time you can say that to the proper authorities. You can be my witness, since you are there and see what is going on."

He hesitated. His voice softened, "Well, what do you want me to do?"

"Take her out of there *now*. Put her in a hotel where she will be safe for the night. And tomorrow put her on the first flight home. That is all. Don't leave her there. She is only seventeen, in a strange land alone with strange people, and she does not know what she is doing or whom she is with. She is too young to make such decisions. She does not even speak their language. Can't you see they are adults, taking advantage of a young girl, a young black girl?"

The assistant to the ambassador did as I instructed. One car from the Embassy remained at the commune to see that Michele did not return there. The day Michele boarded the flight to America, she had no ticket, no identification or papers of any kind, and no money. But none were necessary. All she needed was her name and she was given the go ahead. In New York the same was true. She gave her name and she did not have to go through Customs but was sent immediately through a little gate to the side and hustled into a taxi at Kennedy Airport.

Michele arrived without notice. She looked as pretty as Barbara had, in a little Mexican dress that seemed to be made for her. She was a little thinner but healthy looking. Her skin and hair glowed. She was hostile, admitting nothing about the drugs: my sore spot. As far as she was concerned I had destroyed her chance for happiness. And like Barbara, she had nothing but contempt for me. As soon as her friends from Mexico came, she would be off again to the commune.

I was most fearful of a drug addiction. Barbara and Michele had been raised on a program of drug prevention. Both Birdie and I had shared with them the accounts of the many friends we both knew who had passed on by the needle. We kept no skeletons in the closet for them to stumble over. Experimenting with drugs was a no-no. Their Uncle Andrew, my brother, and Earl, their father, had done that two decades before them. They were both fatalities, Andrew in 1961 while we were in Rome, and their father in 1966. There was no need to repeat the experiment. It didn't work.

I wanted them both examined for drugs, health—mental and physical. It was as if Earl had come back to haunt us, to take us with him. However, I knew he would have been so disappointed to see what we were going through. He was a very moral man, a musician. Compulsive but not evil. He never wanted to spread his misery around. He didn't need that kind of company.

I searched the Yellow Pages for a community service, someone to talk to who knew more than I did. I found a familiar name, dialed the number. A friendly voice answered in the name of the agency.

"I'd like to talk to someone. I have trouble with my daughters. They, well, have just come from Mexico where they joined a commune and I don't know where to . . . what . . . or if. . . .''

There was an accommodating silence on the other end. Embarrassed, I rambled on, "I don't know why my daughters did this . . . I thought we . . . all knew . . . our struggle was, and what we should be . . . I thought communes were for . . . I didn't think young black people had time for . . . We have so many other important . . .''

She cut me off. "Mrs. Ringgold, please come down to see us. We will talk.''

From the way she cut me off, I knew she was a black woman and I could feel that she understood what I was going through.

"But can you tell me why this is happening? Is this not out of character for . . .''

"Please Mrs. Ringgold," she interrupted me again. "Just come in and bring Michele and Barbara the first thing Monday morning.''

The conversation ended. The wait through the night began. A quiet desperation crept over me. What would become of us?

Back in Mexico at that very time hundreds of young white Americans were being arrested on marijuana charges, many of whom were forced into heroin addiction in the Mexican penal system, their parents forced to pay thousands of American dollars each year to maintain their board and the habits forced upon them by unscrupulous prison personnel. A large group of them were released in 1979 in exchange for Mexican prisoners serving time in American jails. So I was lucky although I didn't realize it then.

I never saw the black woman I spoke to on the phone. At the social service agency I was greeted by a real cold, pale white, young woman from the old school of social workers. She established my ability to pay and then fell into a dead silence. She had us all figured out before she ever saw us. But I knew enough about the world of social service to know it. Social service organizations and their social workers and psychologists don't have any answers for black girls in trouble. They only have services and only a few of those. And Michele at seventeen was actually too old for what they did have. Little black girls of seventeen are ready for jail. That is the hard truth of the matter. They want us to fit the case study in their book, be the research study they did or the statistic they feel comfortable with. She didn't know the first thing about us. In spite of what she saw and heard, she advised us to go home and wait for all hell to break out then she would feel more comfortable, more in character talking to the police caseworker, or the hospital caseworker, or placing Barbara or Michele with a member of the family while I did time for hurting them or they did time for hurting me.

I was through with talk. I needed help. Michele had to be placed somewhere. She couldn't stay with me anymore. And there was no one else who could keep her. She was, as far as I could tell, determined to turn her life over to the Mexicans, and I was determined that she know full well what she was doing when and if she did that. I would not go through this again. She was going to Howard University in September. If she wanted to leave from there and go back to the commune, so be it. I wouldn't even know when she left. But I wanted her to be somewhere for now. I could not caretake her. I was too potentially violent. I wanted to strike her, to make her feel some of the pain I was feeling.

More than pain, I felt anger for the waste of our energy, time, and resources. It is the ghetto in us that drives so many young women, no matter how richly endowed and carefully brought up, to seek out The Enemy and give themselves over to him. And he is always right there waiting, expecting us to do just that. Can't we disappoint the bastard, leave him standing there as we sashay on by?

At my request, Michele was put in a Catholic girls' home. She had to remain there until it was time for her to go to college in the fall. That would be in five weeks. If she promised not to run away with the Mexicans, she could come home and we would try again. She refused.

It was time for the system to deal with her. It would be either now or later. Somehow she had to learn what it is like to be a black woman in America. Like a doe surrounded by lions, she was fair game and nobody thinks twice about her destruction. She is just another statistic. In fact, they are more prepared to deal with her as a victim, because then they can remand, rehabilitate, hospitalize, or otherwise service her. But to protect, prevent, promote, and prepare her for a good life is the job of her family and those who love her. But who can protect a willing victim?

● ● ● ● ●

"On Being Female, Black, and Free"

Margaret Walker

A native of Birmingham, Alabama, Margaret Walker (Alexander) received her B.A. degree (1935) from Northwestern University and her M.A. (1940) and Ph.D. (1965) degrees from the University of Iowa. Her first volume of poetry, *For My People* (1942), won the Yale Award for Younger Poets (1942). Her other poetry volumes are *Prophets for a New Day* (1970), *October Journey* (1973), and *Poems for Parish Street* (1986). Her only novel, *Jubilee* (1966), was her doctoral dissertation and received the Houghton Mifflin Literary Fellowship Award. Her pamphlet "How I Wrote *Jubilee*" (1972) details the history, research, and inspiration behind the novel, which is about her maternal great-grandmother. Walker's most recent work is her biography of Richard Wright, *Richard Wright: Daemonic Genius* (1988). During her career as a writer Walker taught English at Jackson State University, where she founded the Institute for the Study of the History, Life, and Culture of Black People, which she directed from its inception in 1968 until her retirement in 1979. Her works have been translated into several languages, and she has received numerous awards, citations, and certificates of honor, including a proclamation from Mississippi governor William Winter of a Margaret Walker Alexander Day.

In lectures given in the late 1970s at Purdue University in Lafayette, Indiana, and at Texas Southern University in Houston, Walker deplored others' definitions of the black woman:

"The image of black women in American literature has rarely been a positive and constructive one. White American literature has portrayed the black woman as she is seen in society, exploited because of her sex, her race, and her poverty. The black male writer has largely imitated his white counterparts, seeing all black characters and particularly females as lowest on the socioeconomic scale: as slaves or servants, as menial, marginal persons, evil, disreputable and powerless. The status of women throughout the world is probably higher now than ever before in the history of civilization. Black women have as much status in this regard as white women (who really don't have much either)."[1]

Walker's concern about the status of black women is reflected in her positive portrayal of black women characters in her own writings.
Written in 1980 when Walker was 63, "On Being Female, Black,

and Free'' (published in Janet Sternburg, ed., *The Writer and Her Work* [W.W. Norton, 1980]) is the work of an independent thinker who has come to know herself well. Walker begins with a simple description of herself as black, female, and free—the conditions of her birth that, as a grown woman, she has learned both to strongly identify with and to understand as anything but simple. Her expressions of pride in her black heritage, of pleasure in being a woman, and of commitment to creative freedom are complemented by thorough examinations of the difficulties attending each. The three characteristics that defined her at birth very much define Walker's sense of herself; yet they also signify her great determination to make her own conscious choice of how to identify with them. "Always I am determined to overcome adversity, determined to be me, myself at my best, always female, always black, always everlastingly free. I think this is who the woman writer wants to be, herself, inviolable, and whole.''

NOTE

1. Quoted in Tate, *Black Women Writers at Work*, 202.

My birth certificate reads female, Negro, date of birth and place. Call it fate or circumstance, this is my human condition. I have no wish to change it from being female, black, and free. I like being a woman. I have a proud black heritage, and I have learned from the difficult exigencies of life that freedom is a philosophical state of mind and existence. The mind is the only place where I can exist and feel free. In my mind I am absolutely free.

My entire career of writing, teaching, lecturing, yes, and raising a family is determined by these immutable facts of my human condition. As a daughter, a sister, a sweetheart, a wife, a mother, and now a grandmother, my sex or gender is preeminent, important, and almost entirely deterministic. Maybe my glands have something to do with my occupation as a creative person. About this, I am none too sure, but I think the cycle of life has much to do with the creative impulse and the biorhythms of life must certainly affect everything we do.

Creativity cannot exist without the feminine principle, and I am sure God is not merely male or female but He-She—our Father-Mother God. All nature reflects this rhythmic and creative principle of feminism and femininity: the sea, the earth, the air, fire, and all life whether plant or animal. Even as they die, are born, grow, reproduce, and grow old in their cyclic time, so do we in lunar, solar, planetary cycles of meaning and change.

Ever since I was a little girl I have wanted to write and I have been writing. My father told my mother it was only a puberty urge and would not last, but he encouraged my early attempts at rhyming verses just the same, and he gave me the notebook or daybook in which to keep my poems together. When I was eighteen and had ended my junior year in college, my father laughingly agreed it was probably more than a puberty urge. I had filled the 365 pages with poems.

Writing has always been a means of expression for me and for other black Americans who are just like me, who feel, too, the need for freedom in this "home of the brave, and land of the free." From the first, writing meant learning the craft and developing the art. Going to school had one major goal, to learn to be a writer. As early as my eighth year I had the desire, at ten I was trying, at eleven and twelve I was learning, and at fourteen and fifteen I was seeing my first things printed in local school and community papers. I have a copy of a poem published in 1930 and an article with the caption, "What Is to Become of Us?" which appeared in 1931 or 1932. All of this happened before I went to Northwestern.

I spent fifteen years becoming a poet before my first book appeared in 1942. I was learning my craft, finding my voice, seeking discipline as life imposes and superimposes that discipline upon the artist. Perhaps my home environment was most important in the early stages—hearing my mother's music, my sister and brother playing the piano, reading my father's books, hearing his sermons, and trying every day to write a poem. Meanwhile, I found I would have to start all over again and learn how to write prose fiction in order to write the novel I was determined to create to the best of my ability and thus fulfill my promise to my grandmother. A novel is not written exactly the same way as a poem, especially a long novel and a short poem. The creative process may be basically the same—that is, the thinking or conceptualization— but the techniques, elements, and form or craft are decidedly and distinctively different.

It has always been my feeing that writing must come out of living, and the writer is no more than his personality endures in the crucible of his times. As a woman, I have come through the fires of hell because I am a black woman, because I am poor, because I live in America, and because I am determined to be both a creative artist and maintain my inner integrity and my instinctive need to be free.

I don't think I noticed the extreme discrimination against women while I was growing up in the South. The economic struggle to exist and the racial dilemma occupied all my thinking until I was more than an adult woman. My mother had undergone all kinds of discrimination in academia because of her sex; so have my sisters. Only after I went back to school and earned a doctorate did I begin to notice discrimination against me as a woman. It seems the higher you try to climb, the more rarefied the air, the more obstacles appear. I realize I had been naïve, that the issues had not been obvious and that as early as my first employment I felt the sting of discrimination because I am female.

I think it took the women's movement to call my attention to cases of overt discrimination that hark back to my WPA days on the Writers' Project. It did not occur to me that Richard Wright as a supervisor on the project made $125 per month and that he claimed no formal education, but that I had just graduated from Northwestern University and I was a junior writer making $85 per month. I had no ambitions to be an administrator; I was too glad to have a job; I did not think about it. Now I remember the intense antagonism on the project toward the hiring of a black woman as a supervisor, none other than the famous Katherine Dunham, the dancer, but it never occurred to me then that she was undergoing double discrimination.

When I first went to Iowa and received my master's degree that year there were at least five or six women teaching English in the university. When I returned to study for the doctorate, not a single woman was in the department. At Northwestern my only woman teacher had taught personal hygiene. I did not expect to find women at Yale, but it slowly dawned on me that black women in black colleges were more numerous than white women in coed white universities.

And then I began looking through the pages of books of American and English literature that I was teaching, trying in vain to find the works of many women writers. I have read so many of those great women writers of the world—poets, novelists, and playwrights: Sigrid Undset and Selma Lagerlof, Jane Austen, George Sand, George Eliot, and Colette. All through the ages women have been writing and publishing, black and white women in America and all over the world. A few women stand out as geniuses of their times, but those are all too few. Even the women who survive and are printed, published, taught and studied in the classroom fall victim to negative male literary criticism. Black women suffer damages at the hands of every male literary critic, whether he is black or white. Occasionally a man grudgingly admits that some woman writes well, but only rarely.

Despite severe illness and painful poverty, and despite jobs that always discriminated against me as a woman—never paying me equal money for equal work, always threatening or replacing me with a man or men who were neither as well educated nor experienced but just men—despite all these examples of discrimination I have managed to work toward being a self-fulfilling, re-creating, reproducing woman, raising a family, writing poetry, cooking food, doing all the creative things I know how to do and enjoy. But my problems have not been simple; they have been manifold. Being female, black, and poor in America means I was born with three strikes against me. I am considered at the bottom of the social class-caste system in these United States, born low on the totem pole. If "a black man has no rights that a white man is bound to respect," what about a black woman?

Racism is so extreme and so pervasive in our American society that no black individual lives in an atmosphere of freedom. The world of physical phenomena is dominated by fear and greed. It consists of pitting the vicious and the avaricious against the naïve, the hunted, the innocent, and the victimized. Power belongs to the strong, and the strong are BIG in more ways than one. No one is more victimized in this white male American society than the black female.

There are additional barriers for the black woman in publishing, in literary criticism, and in promotion of her literary wares. It is an insidious fact of racism that the most highly intellectualized, sensitized white person is not always perceptive about the average black mind and feeling, much less the creativity of any black genius. Racism forces white humanity to underestimate the intelligence, emotion, and creativity of black humanity. Very few white Americans are conscious of the myth about race that includes the racial stigmas of inferiority and superiority. They do not understand its true economic and political meaning and therefore fail to understand its social purpose. A black, female person's life as a writer is fraught with conflict, competitive drives, professional rivalries, even danger, and deep frustrations. Only when she escapes to a spiritual world can she find peace, quiet, and hope of freedom. To choose the life of a writer, a black female must arm herself with a fool's courage, foolhardiness, and serious purpose and dedication to the art of writing, strength of will and integrity, because the odds are always against her. The cards are stacked. Once the die is cast, however, there is no turning back.

In the first place, the world of imagination in which the writer must live is constantly being invaded by the enemy, the mundane world. Even as the worker in the fires of imagination finds that the world around her is inimical to intellectual activity, to the creative impulse, and to the kind of world in which she must daily exist and also thrive and produce, so, too, she discovers that she must meet that mundane world head-on every day on its own terms. She must either conquer or be conquered.

A writer needs certain conditions in which to work and create art. She needs a piece of time; a peace of mind; a quiet place; and a private life.

Early in my life I discovered I had to earn my living and I would not be able to eke out the barest existence as a writer. Nobody writes while hungry, sick, tired, and worried. Maybe you can manage with one of these but not all four at one time. Keeping the wolf from the door has been my full-time job for more than forty years. Thirty-six of those years I have spent in the college classroom, and nobody writes to full capacity on a full-time teaching job. My life has been public, active, and busy to the point of constant turmoil, tumult, and trauma. Sometimes the only quiet and private place where I could write a sonnet was in the bathroom, because that was the only room where the door could be locked and no one would intrude. I have written mostly at night in my adult life and especially since I have been married, because I was determined not to neglect any members of my family; so I cooked every meal daily, washed dishes and dirty clothes, and nursed sick babies.

I have struggled against dirt and disease as much as I have against sin, which, with my Protestant and Calvinistic background, was always to be abhorred. Every day I have lived, however, I have discovered that the value system with which I was raised is of no value in the society in which I must live. This clash of my ideal with the real, of my dream world with the practical, and the mystical inner life with the sordid and ugly world outside—this clash keeps me on a battlefield, at war, and struggling, even tilting windmills. Always I am determined to overcome adversity, determined to win, determined to be me, myself at my best, always female, always black, and everlastingly free. I think this is always what the woman writer wants to be, herself, inviolate, and whole. Shirley Chisholm, who is also black and female, says she is unbossed and unbought. So am I, and I intend to remain that way. Nobody can tell me what to write because nobody owns me and nobody pulls my strings. I have not been writing to make money or earn my living. I have taught school as my vocation. Writing is my life, but it is an avocation nobody can buy. In this respect I believe I am a free agent, stupid perhaps, but *me* and still free.

When I was younger I considered myself an emancipated woman, freed from the shackles of mind and body that typified the Victorian woman, but never would I call myself the liberated woman in today's vernacular; never the bohemian; never the completely free spirit living in free love; never the lesbian sister; always believing in moderation and nothing to excess; never defying convention, never radical enough to defy tradition; not wanting to be called conservative but never moving beyond the bounds of what I consider the greatest liberty within law, the greatest means of freedom within control. I have lived out my female destiny within the bonds of married love. For me, it could not have been otherwise. In the same way I refuse to judge others, for if tolerance is worth anything, love is worth everything. Everyone should dare to love.

I am therefore fundamentally and contradictorily three things. I am religious almost to the point of orthodoxy—I go to church, I pray, I believe in the stern dogma and duty of Protestant Christianity; I am radical but I wish to see neither the extreme radical left nor the radical right in control. And I am like the astrological description of a crab, a cancer—quick to retreat into my shell when hurt or attacked. I will wobble around circuitously to find another way out when the way I have chosen has been closed to me. I believe absolutely in the power of my black mind to create, to write, to speak, to witness truth, and to be heard.

Enough for a time about being female and black. What about freedom? The question of freedom is an essential subject for any writer. Without freedom, personal and social, to write as one pleases and to express the will of the people, the writer is in bondage. This bondage may seem to be to others outside oneself but closely related by blood or kinship in some human fashion; or this bondage may appear to be to the inimical forces of the society that so impress or repress that individual.

For the past twenty years or longer I have constantly come into contact with women writers of many different races, classes, nationalities, and degrees. I look back on more than forty years of such associations. Whether at a cocktail party for Muriel Rukeyser at *Poetry* magazine or at Yaddo where Carson MacCullers, Jean Stafford, Karen Blixen, Caroline Slade, and Katherine Anne Porter were guests; or meeting Adrienne Rich and Erica Jong in Massachusetts at Amherst, or having some twenty-five of my black sister-poets at a Phillis Wheatley poetry festival here in Mississippi, including many of the young and brilliant geniuses of this generation; or here in Mississippi where I have come to know Eudora Welty and Ellen Douglas, or having women from foreign countries journey to Jackson to see me, women like Rosey Pool from Amsterdam and a young woman writer a few weeks ago from Turkey or Bessie Head from South Africa—all these experiences have made me know and understand the problems of women writers and our search for freedom.

For the nonwhite woman writer, whether in Africa, Asia, Latin America, the islands of the Caribbean, or the United States, her destiny as a writer has always seemed bleak. Women in Africa and Asia speak of hunger and famine and lack of clean water at the same time that their countries are riddled with warfare. Arab women and Jewish women think of their children in a world that has no hope of peace. Irish women, Protestant and Catholic, speak of the constant threat of bombs and being blown to bits. The women of southern Africa talk of their lives apart from their husbands and their lives in exile from their homelands because of the racial strife in their countries. A Turkish woman speaks of the daily terrorism in her country, of combing the news each evening to see if there are names known on the list of the murdered.

I have read the works of scores of these women. I saw Zora Neale Hurston when I was a child and I know what a hard life she had. I read the works of a dozen black women in the Harlem Renaissance, who despite their genius received only a small success. Langston Hughes translated Gabriela Mistral, and I read her before she won the Nobel

329

Prize for Literature. Hualing Nieh Engle tells of her native China, and my friends in Mexico speak of the unbelievable poverty of their people. Each of these internationally known women writers is my sister in search of an island of freedom. Each is part of me and I am part of her.

Writing is a singularly individual matter. At least it has historically been so. Only the creative, original individual working alone has been considered the artist working with the fire of imagination. Today, this appears no longer to be the case. In America, our affluent, electronic, and materialistic society does not respect the imaginative writer regardless of sex, race, color, or creed. It never thought highly of the female worker, whether an Emily Dickinson or Amy Lowell, Phillis Wheatley, or Ellen Glasgow. Our American society has no respect for the literary values of intellectual honesty nor for originality and creativity in the sensitive individual. Books today are managed, being written by a committee and promoted by the conglomerate, corporate structures. Best sellers are designed as commodities to sell in the marketplace before a single word is written. Plastic people who are phony writers pretending to take us into a more humanistic century are quickly designated the paper heroes who are promoted with super-HYPE. Do I sound bitter? A Black Woman Writer who is free? Free to do what? To publish? To be promoted? Of what value is freedom in a money-mad society? What does freedom mean to the racially biased and those bigots who have deep religious prejudices? What is my hope as a woman writer?

I am a black woman living in a male-oriented and male-dominated white world. Moreover, I live in an American Empire where the financial tentacles of the American Octopus in the business-banking world extend around the globe, with the multinationals and international conglomerates encircling everybody and impinging on the lives of every single soul. What then are my problems? They are the pressures of a sexist, racist, violent, and most materialistic society. In such a society life is cheap and expendable; honor is a rag to be scorned; and justice is violated. Vice and money control business, the judicial system, government, sports, entertainment, publishing, education, and the church. Every other arm of this hydra-headed monster must render lip service and yeoman support to extend, uphold, and perpetuate the syndicated world-system. The entire world of the press, whether broadcast or print journalism, must acquiesce and render service or be eliminated. And what have I to do with this? How do I operate? How long can I live under fear before I too am blown to bits and must crumble into anonymous dust and nonentity?

Now I am sixty-three. I wish I could live the years all over. I am sure I would make the same mistakes and do all the things again exactly the same way. But perhaps I might succeed a little more; and wistfully I hope, too, I might have written more books.

What are the critical decisions I must make as a woman, as a writer? They are questions of compromise, and of guilt. They are the answers to the meaning and purpose of all life; questions of the value of life lived half in fear and half in faith, cringing under the whip of tyranny or dying, too, for what one dares to believe and dying with dignity and without fear. I must believe there is more wisdom in a righteous path that leads to death than an ignominious path of living shame; that the writer is still in the avant-garde for Truth and Justice, for Freedom, Peace, and Human Dignity. I must believe that women are still in that humanistic tradition and I must cast my lot with them.

Across the world humanity seems in ferment, in war, fighting over land and the control of people's lives; people who are hungry, sick, and suffering, most of all fearful. The traditional and historic role of womankind is ever the role of the healing and annealing hand, whether the outworn modes of nurse, and mother, cook, and sweetheart. As a writer these are still her concerns. These are still the stuff about which she writes, the human condition, the human potential, the human destiny. Her place, let us be reminded, is anywhere she chooses to be, doing what she has to do, creating, healing, and always being herself. Female, Black, and Free, this is what I always want to be.

● ● ● ● ●

"New Directions for Black Feminist Criticism"

Deborah E. McDowell

Deborah E. McDowell was born in 1951 in Birmingham, Alabama. An associate professor in the English department at the University of Virginia, McDowell has published numerous articles and reviews and has lectured widely on African-American literature. She is the general editor of the Black Women Writers Series at Beacon Press, which has reissued such out-of-print works as Ann Petry's *The Street* (1946), Alice Childress's *Like One in the Family* (1956), and Frances E. W. Harper's

Iola Leroy: Shadows Uplifted (1892). McDowell served from 1985 to 1989 on the advisory board of *PMLA (Publications of the Modern Language Association)* and has served on the board of editors for the Black Periodical Fiction Project at Yale University since 1984 and on the MLA Commission on the Status of Women in the Profession, which she cochaired in 1983–84. McDowell received her B.A. degree (1972) from Tuskegee Institute and her M.A. (1974) and Ph.D. (1979) degrees from Purdue University.

McDowell emerged in the 1980s as a significant critic of black women's works. She approaches a black woman's work with respect for the different perspective and experience it presents, and she has urged others—especially male critics, both black and white—to rid their commentaries of propaganda. She notes that "the recognition and use of difference is one of the more salient features of black women's literature, and it calls urgently for methods and modes of critical evaluation that both recognize and permit difference, that resist the impulse to homogenize these writers to the point that they become indistinguishable from each other. That so late in this century, criticism of Afro-American literature is still rehearsing the same questions that are reducible to a conflict between art and propaganda is regrettable."[1] That McDowell has to make this plea five years after the publication of "New Directions in Black Feminist Criticism" is a telling commetary on how some critics still view black women's works.

Published in *Black American Literature Forum* (Winter 1980), this essay delineates much of the work that still needs to be done to define the creative literary endeavors of black women. The author asks that the works of black women writers be viewed on their own terms, that they be subjected to rigorous critical analysis but not to judgments based on largely male norms and perceptions.

NOTE

1. Deborah E. McDowell, "Criticism in Arrest," review of Evans, *Black Women Writers, in Callaloo: A Black South Journal of Arts and Letters* 8 (Spring-Summer 1985): 497.

"What is commonly called literary history," writes Louise Bernikow, "is actually a record of choices. Which writers have survived their times and which have not depends upon who noticed them and chose to record their notice."[1] Women writers have fallen victim to arbitrary selection. Their writings have been "patronized, slighted, and misunderstood by a cultural establishment operating according to male norms out of male perceptions."[2] Both literary history's "sins of omissions" and literary criticism's inaccurate and partisan judgments of women writers have come under attack since the early 1970s by feminist critics.[3] To date, no one has formulated a precise or complete definition of feminist criticism, but since its inception, its theorists and practitioners have agreed that it is a "corrective, unmasking—omissions and distortions of the past—the errors of a literary critical tradition that arise from and reflect a culture created, perpetuated, and dominated by men."[4]

These early theorists and practitioners of feminist literary criticism were largely white females who, wittingly or not, perpetrated against the Black woman writer the same exclusive practices they so vehemently decried in white male scholars. Seeing the experiences of white women, particularly white middle-class women, as normative, white female scholars proceeded blindly to exclude the work of Black women writers from literary anthologies and critical studies. Among the most flagrant examples of this chauvinism is Patricia Meyer Spacks's *The Female Imagination*. In a weak defense of her book's exclusive focus on women in the Anglo-American literary tradition, Spacks quotes Phyllis Chesler (a white female psychologist): "I have no theory to offer of Third World female psychology in America. . . . As a white woman, I'm reluctant and unable to construct theories about experiences I haven't had."[5] But, as Alice Walker observes, "Spacks never lived in 19th century Yorkshire, so why theorize about the Brontës?"[6]

Not only have Black women writers been "disenfranchised" from critical works by white women scholars on the "female tradition," but they have also been frequently excised from those on the Afro-American literary tradition by Black scholars, most of whom are males. For example, Robert Stepto's *From Behind the Veil: A Study of Afro-American Narrative* purports to be "a history . . . of the historical consciousness of an Afro-American art form—namely, the Afro-American written narrative."[7] Yet, Black women writers are conspicuously absent from the table of contents. Though Stepto does have a token two-page discussion of Zora Neale Hurston's *Their Eyes Were Watching God* in which he refers to it as a "seminal narrative in Afro-American letters."[8] he did not feel that the novel merited its own chapter or the thorough analysis accorded the other works he discusses.

When Black women writers are neither ignored altogether nor given honorable mention, they are critically misunderstood and summarily dismissed. In *The Negro Novel*, for example, Robert Bone's reading of Jessie Fauset's novels is both partisan and superficial and might explain the reasons Fauset remains obscure. Bone argues that Fauset is the foremost member of the "Rear Guard" or writers "who lagged behind," clinging to established literary traditions. The "Rear Guard" drew their source material from the Negro middle class in their efforts "to orient Negro art toward white opinion," and "to apprise educated whites of the existence of respectable Negroes." Bone adds that Fauset's emphasis on the Black middle class results in novels that are "uniformly sophomoric, trivial and dull."[9]

While David Littlejohn praises Black fiction since 1940, he denigrates the work of Fauset and Nella Larsen. He maintains that "the newer writers are obviously writing as men, for men," and are avoiding the "very close and steamy" writing that is the result of "any subculture's taking itself too seriously, defining the world and its values exclusively in the terms of its own restrictive norms and concerns."[10] This "phallic criticism,"[11] to use Mary Ellman's term, is based on masculine-centered values and definitions. It has dominated the criticism on Black women writers and has done much to guarantee that most would be, in Alice Walker's words, "casually pilloried and consigned to a sneering oblivion."[12]

Suffice it to say that the critical community has not favored Black woman writers. The recognition among Black female critics and writers that white women, white men, and Black men consider their experiences as normative, and Black women's experiences as deviant has given rise to Black feminist criticism. Much like white feminist criticism, the critical postulates of Black women's literature are only skeletally defined. Although there is no concrete definition of Black feminist criticism, a handful of Black female scholars have begun the necessary enterprise of resurrecting forgotten Black women writers and revising misinformed critical opinions of them. Justifiably enraged by the critical establishment's neglect and mishandling of Black women writers, these critics are calling for "nonhostile and perceptive analysis of works written by persons outside the 'mainstream' of white/male cultural rule."[13]

Despite the urgency and timeliness of the enterprise, however, no substantial body of Black feminist criticism—either in theory or practice—exists, a fact which might be explained partially by our limited access to and control of the media.[14] Another explanation for the paucity of Black feminist criticism, notes Barbara Smith in "Toward a Black Feminist Criticism," is the lack of a "developed body of Black feminist political theory whose assumptions could be used in the study of Black women's art."

Despite the strained circumstances under which Black feminist critics labor, a few committed Black female scholars have broken necessary ground. For the remainder of this paper I would like to focus on selected writings of Black feminist critics, discussing their strengths and weaknesses and suggesting new directions toward which the criticism might move and pitfalls that it might avoid.

Unfortunately, Black feminist scholarship has been decidedly more practical than theoretical, and the theories developed thus far have often lacked sophistication and have been marred by slogans, rhetoric, and idealism. The articles that attempt to apply these theoretical tenets often lack precision and detail. These limitations are not without reason. As Dorin Schumacher observes, "The feminist critic has few philosophical shelters, pillars, or guideposts," and thus "feminist criticism is fraught with intellectual and professional risks, offering more opportunity for creativity, yet greater possibility of errors."[15]

The earliest theoretical statement on Black feminist criticism is Barbara Smith's "Toward a Black Feminist Criticism." Though its importance as a ground-breaking piece of scholarship cannot be denied, it suffers from lack of precision and detail. In justifying the need for a Black feminist aesthetic, Smith argues that a "Black feminist approach to literature that embodies the realization that the politics of sex as well as the politics of race and class are crucially interlocking factors in the works of Black women writers is an absolute necessity." Until such an approach exists, she continues, "we will not ever know what these writers mean."[16]

Smith points out that "thematically, stylistically, aesthetically, and conceptually, Black women writers manifest common approaches to the art of creating literature as a direct result of the specific political, social and economic experience they have been obliged to share" (p. 32). She offers, as an example, the incorporation of rootworking, herbal medicine, conjury and midwifery in the stories of Zora Neale Hurston, Margaret Walker, Toni Morrison, and Alice Walker. While these folk elements certainly do appear in the work of these writers, they also appear in the works of certain Black male writers, a fact that Smith omits. If Black women writers use these elements differently from Black male writers, such a distinction must be made before one can effectively articulate the basis of a Black feminist aesthetic.

Smith maintains further that Zora Neale Hurston, Margaret Walker, Toni Morrison, and Alice Walker use a "specifically black female language to express their own and their characters' thoughts" (p. 32), but she fails to describe or to provide examples of this unique language. Of course we have come recently to acknowledge that "many of our habits of language usage are sex-derived, sex-associated, and/or sex-distinctive," that "the ways in which men and women internalize and manipulate language" are undeniably sex-related.[17] But this realization in itself simply paves the way for further investigation that can begin by exploring some critical questions. For example, is there a monolithic Black female language? Do Black female high school drop-outs, welfare mothers, college graduates and Ph.D.s share a common language? Are there regional variations on this common language? Further, some Black male critics have tried to describe the uniquely "Black linguistic elegance"[18] that characterizes Black poetry. Are there noticeable differences between the languages of Black females and Black males? These and other

335

questions must be addressed with precision if current feminist terminology is to function beyond mere critical jargon.

Smith turns from her discussion of the commonalities between Black women writers to describe the nature of her critical enterprise. "Black feminist criticism would by definition be highly innovative," she maintains. "Applied to a particular work [it] can overturn previous assumptions about [the work] and expose for the first time its actual dimensions" (p. 32). Smith then proceeds to demonstrate this critical postulate by interpreting Toni Morrison's *Sula* as a lesbian novel, an interpretation she believes is maintained in "the emotions expressed, in the definition of female character and in the way that the politics of heterosexuality are portrayed" (p. 39). Smith vacillates between arguing forthrightly for the validity of her interpretation and recanting or overqualifying it in a way that undercuts her own credibility.

According to Smith, "If in a woman writer's work a sentence refuses to do what it is supposed to do, if there are strong images of women and if there is a refusal to be linear, the result is innately lesbian literature" (p. 33). She adds, "Because of Morrison's consistently critical stance towards the heterosexual institutions of male/female relationships, marriage, and the family" (p. 33), *Sula* works as a lesbian novel. This definition of lesbianism is vague and imprecise; it subsumes far more Black women writers, particularly contemporary ones, than not into the canon of Lesbian writers. For example, Jessie Fauset, Nella Larsen, and Zora Neale Hurston all criticize major socializing institutions as do Gwendolyn Brooks, Alice Walker, and Toni Cade Bambara. Further, if we apply Smith's definition of lesbianism, there are probably a few Black male writers who qualify as well. All of this is to say that Smith has simultaneously oversimplified and obscured the issue of lesbianism. Obviously aware of the delicacy of her position, she interjects that "the very meaning of lesbianism is being expanded in literature" (p. 39). Unfortunately, her qualification does not strengthen her argument. One of the major tasks ahead of Black feminist critics who write from a lesbian perspective, then, is to define lesbianism and lesbian literature precisely. Until they can offer a definition which is not vacuous, their attempts to distinguish Black lesbian writers from those who are not will be hindered.[19]

Even as I call for firmer definitions of lesbianism and lesbian literature, I question whether or not a lesbian aesthetic is finally a reductive approach to the study of Black women's literature which possibly ignores other equally important aspects of the literature. For example, reading *Sula* solely from a lesbian perspective overlooks the novel's density and complexity, its skillful blend of folklore, omens, and dreams, its metaphorical and symbolic richness. Although I do not quarrel with Smith's appeal for fresher, more innovative approaches to Black woman's literature, I suspect that "innovative" analysis is pressed to the service of an individual political persuasion. One's personal and political presuppositions enter into one's critical judgments. Nevertheless, we should heed Annette Kolodny's warning for feminist critics to "be wary of reading literature as though it were polemic. . . . If when using literary materials to make what is essentially a political point, we find ourselves virtually rewriting a text, ignoring certain aspects of plot or characterization, or over-simplifying the action to fit our 'political' thesis, then we are neither practicing an honest criticism nor saying anything useful about the nature of art (or about the art of political persuasion, for that matter)."[20] Alerting feminist critics to the dangers of political ideology yoked with aesthetic judgment is not synonymous with denying that feminist criticism is a valid and necessary cultural and political enterprise. Indeed, it is both possible and useful to translate ideological positions into aesthetic ones, but if the criticism is to be responsible, the two must be balanced.

Because it is a cultural and political enterprise, feminist critics, in the main, believe that their criticism can affect social change. Smith certainly argues for socially relevant criticism in her conclusion that "Black feminist criticism would owe its existence to a Black feminist movement while at the same time contributing ideas that women in the movement could use" (p. 33). This is an exciting idea in itself, but we should ask: What ideas, specifically, would Black feminist criticism contribute to the movement? Further, even though the proposition of a fruitful relationship between political activism and the academy is an interesting (and necessary) one, I doubt its feasibility. I am not sure that either in theory or in practice Black feminist criticism will be able to alter significantly circumstances that have led to the oppression of Black women. Moreover, as Lillian Robinson pointedly remarks, there is no assurance that feminist aesthetics "will be productive of a vision of art or of social relations that is of the slightest use to the masses of women, or even one that acknowledges the existence and struggle of such women."[21] I agree with Robinson that "ideological criticism must take place in the context of a political movement that can put it to work. The revolution is simply not going to be made by literary journals."[22] I should say that I am not arguing a defeatist position with respect to the social and political uses to which feminist criticism can be put. Just as it is both possible and useful to translate ideological positions into aesthetic ones, it must likewise be possible and useful to translate aesthetic positions into the machinery for social change.

Despite the shortcomings of Smith's article, she raises critical issues on which Black feminist critics can build. There are many tasks ahead of these critics, not the least of which is to attempt to formulate some clear definitions of what Black feminist criticism is. I use the term in this paper simply to refer to Black female critics who analyze the works of Black female writers from a feminist or political perspective. But the term can also apply to any criticism written by a Black woman regardless of her subject or perspective—a book written by a male from a feminist or political perspective, a book written by a Black woman or about Black women authors in general, or any writings by women.[23]

In addition to defining the methodology, Black feminist critics need to determine the extent to which their criticism intersects with that of white feminist critics. Barbara Smith and others have rightfully challenged white women scholars to become more accountable to Black and Third World women writers, but will that require white women to use a different set of critical tools when studying Black woman writers? Are white women's theories predicated upon culturally specific values and assumptions? Andrea Benton Rushing has attempted to answer these questions in her series of articles on images of Black women in literature. She maintains, for example, that critical categories of women, based on analyses of white women characters, are Euro-American in derivation and hence inappropriate to a consideration of Black women characters.[24] Such distinctions are necessary and, if held uniformly, can materially alter the shape of Black feminist scholarship.

Regardless of which theoretical framework Black feminist critics choose, they must have an informed handle on Black literature and Black culture in general. Such a grounding can give this scholarship more texture and completeness and perhaps prevent some of the problems that have had a vitiating effect on the criticism.

This footing in Black history and culture serves as a basis for the study of the literature. Termed "contextual" by theoreticians, this approach is often frowned upon if not dismissed entirely by critics who insist exclusively upon textual and linguistic analysis. Its limitations notwithstanding, I firmly believe that the contextual approach to Black women's literature exposes the conditions under which literature is produced, published, and reviewed. This approach is not only useful but necessary to Black feminist critics.

To those working with Black women writers prior to 1940, the contextual approach is especially useful. In researching Jessie Fauset, Nella Larsen, and Zora Neale Hurston, for example, it is useful to determine what the prevalent attitudes about Black women were during the time that they wrote. There is much information in the Black "little" magazines published during the Harlem Renaissance. An examination of *The Messenger*, for instance, reveals that the dominant social attitudes about Black women were strikingly consistent with traditional middle class expectations of women. *The Messenger* ran a monthly symposium for some time entitled "Negro Womanhood's Greatest Needs." While a few female contributors stressed the importance of women being equal to men socially, professionally, and economically, the majority emphasized that a woman's place was in the home. It was her duty "to cling to the home [since] great men and women evolve from the environment of the hearthstone."[25]

One of the most startling entries came from a woman who wrote:

> The New Negro Woman, with her head erect and spirit undaunted is resolutely marching forward, ever conscious of her historic and noble mission of doing her bit toward the liberation of her people in particular and the human race in general. Upon her shoulders rests the big task to create and keep alive, in the breast of black men, a holy and consuming passion to break with the slave traditions of the past; to spurn and overcome the fatal, insidious inferiority complex of the present, which . . . bobs up ever and anon, to arrest the progress of the New Negro Manhood Movement; and to fight with increasing vigor, with dauntless courage, unrelenting zeal and intelligent vision for the attainment of the stature of a full man, a free race and a new world.[26]

Not only does the contributor charge Black women with a formidable task, but she also sees her solely in relation to Black men.

This information enhances our understanding of what Fauset, Larsen, and Hurston confronted in attempting to offer alternative images of Black women. Moreover, it helps to clarify certain textual problems and ambiguities of their work. Though Fauset and Hurston, for example, explored feminist concerns, they leaned toward ambivalence. Fauset is especially alternately forthright and cagey, radical and traditional, on issues which confront women. Her first novel, *There is Confusion* (1924), is flawed by an unanticipated and abrupt reversal in characterization that brings the central female character more in line with a feminine norm. Similarly, in her last novel, *Seraph on the Swanee* (1948), Zora Neale Hurston depicts a female character who shows promise for growth and change, for a departure from the conventional expectations of womanhood, but who, in the end, apotheosizes marriage, motherhood, and domestic servitude.

These two examples alone clearly capture the tension between social pressure and artistic integrity which is felt, to some extent, by all women writers. As Tillie Olsen points out, the fear of reprisal from the publishing and critical arenas is a looming obstacle to the woman writer's coming into her own authentic voice. "Fear—the need to please, to be safe—in the literary realm too. Founded fear. Power is still in the hands of men. Power of validation, publication, approval, reputation. . . ."[27]

While insisting on the validity, usefulness, and necessity of contextual approaches to Black women's literature, the Black feminist critic must not ignore the importance of rigorous textual analysis. I am aware of many feminist critics' stubborn resistance to the critical methodology handed down by white men. Although the resistance is certainly politically consistent and logical, I agree with Annette Kolodny that feminist criticism would be "shortsighted if it summarily rejected all the inherited tools of critical analysis simply because they are male and western." We should, rather, salvage what we find useful in past methodologies, reject what we do not, and, where necessary, move toward "inventing new methods of analysis."[28] Particularly useful is Lillian Robinson's suggestion that "A radical kind of textual criticism . . . could usefully study the way the texture of sentences, choice of metaphors, patterns of exposition and narrative relate to [feminist] ideology."[29]

This rigorous textual analysis involves, as Barbara Smith recommends, isolating as many thematic, stylistic, and linguistic commonalities among Black women writers as possible. Among contemporary Black female novelists, the thematic parallels are legion. In Alice Walker and Toni Morrison, for example, the theme of the thwarted female artist figures prominently.[30] Pauline Breedlove in Morrison's *The Bluest Eye,* for example, is obsessed with ordering things: "Jars on shelves at canning, peach pits on the step, sticks, stones, leaves. . . . Whatever portable plurality she found, she organized into neat lines, according to their size, shape or gradations of color. . . . She missed without knowing what she missed—paints and crayons."[31] Similarly, Eva Peace in *Sula* is forever ordering the pleats in her dress. And Sula's strange and destructive behavior is explained as "the consequence of an idle imagination." "Had she paints, clay, or knew the discipline of the dance, or strings; had she anything to engage her tremendous curiosity and her gift for metaphor, she might have exchanged the restlessness and preoccupation with whim for an activity that provided her with all she yearned for. And like any artist with no form, she became dangerous."[32] Likewise, Meridian's mother in Alice Walker's novel, *Meridian,* makes artificial flowers and prayer pillows too small for kneeling.

The use of "clothing as iconography"[33] is central to writings by Black women. For example, in one of Jessie Fauset's early short stories, "The Sleeper Wakes" (1920), Amy, the protagonist, is associated with pink clothing (suggesting innocence and immaturity) while she is blinded by fairy-tale notions of love and marriage. However, after she declares her independence from her racist and sexist husband, Amy no longer wears pink. The imagery of clothing is abundant in Zora Neale Hurston's *Their Eyes Were Watching God* (1937). Janie's apron, her silks and satins, her head scarves, and finally her overalls all symbolize various stages of her journey from captivity to liberation. Finally, in Alice Walker's *Meridian,* Meridian's railroad cap and dungarees are emblems of her rejection of conventional images and expectations of womanhood.

A final theme that recurs in the novels of Black women writers is the motif of the journey. Though one can also find this same motif in the works of Black male writers, they do not use it in the same way as do Black female writers.[34] For example, the journey of the Black male character in works by Black men takes him underground. It is a "descent into the underworld,"[35] and is primarily political and social in its implications. Ralph Ellison's *Invisible Man*, Imamu Amiri Baraka's *The System of Dante's Hell*, and Richard Wright's "The Man Who Lived Underground" exemplify this quest. The Black female's journey, on the other hand, though at times touching the political and social, is basically a personal and psychological journey. The female character in the works of Black women is in a state of becoming "part of an evolutionary spiral, moving from victimization to consciousness."[36] The heroines in Zora Neale Hurston's *Their Eyes Were Watching God*, in Alice Walker's *Meridian*, and in Toni Cade Bambara's *The Salt Eaters* are emblematic of this distinction.

Even though isolating such thematic and imagistic commonalities should continue to be one of the Black feminist critic's most urgent tasks, she should beware of generalizing on the basis of too few examples. If one argues authoritatively for the existence of a Black female "consciousness" or "vision" or "literary tradition," one must be sure that the parallels found recur with enough consistency to support these generalizations. Further, Black feminist critics should not become obsessed in searching for common themes and images in Black women's works. As I pointed out earlier, investigating the question of "female" language is critical and may well be among the most challenging jobs awaiting the Black feminist critic. The growing body of research on gender-specific uses of language might aid these critics. In fact wherever possible, feminist critics should draw on the scholarship of feminists in other disciplines.

An equally challenging and necessary task ahead of the Black feminist critic is a thoroughgoing examination of the works of Black male writers. In her introduction to *Midnight Birds*, Mary Helen Washington argues for the importance of giving Black women writers their due first. She writes: "Black women are searching for a specific language, specific symbols, specific images with which to record their lives, and, even though they can claim a rightful place in the Afro-American tradition and the feminist tradition of women writers, it is also clear that, for purposes of liberation, black women writers will first insist on their own name, their own space."[37] I likewise believe that the immediate concern of Black feminist critics must be to develop a fuller understanding of Black women writers who have not received the critical attention Black male writers have. Yet, I cannot advocate indefinitely such a separatist position, for the countless thematic, stylistic and imagistic parallels between Black male and female writers must be examined. Black feminist critics should explore these parallels in an effort to determine the ways in which these commonalities are manifested differently in Black women's writing and the ways in which they coincide with writings by Black men.

Of course, there are feminist critics who are already examining Black male writers, but much of the scholarship has been limited to discussions of the negative images of Black women found in the works of these authors.[38] Although this scholarship served an important function in pioneering Black feminist critics, it has virtually run its course. Feminist critics run the risk of plunging their work into cliche and triviality if they continue merely to focus on how Black men treat Black women in literature. Hortense Spillers offers a more sophisticated approach to this issue in her discussion of the power of language and myth in female relations in James Baldwin's *If Beale Street Could Talk*. One of Spillers's most cogent points is that "woman-freedom or its negation, is tied to the assertions of myth, or ways of saying things."[39]

Black feminist criticism is a knotty issue, and while I have attempted to describe it, to call for clearer definitions of its methodology, to offer warnings of its limitations, I await the day when Black feminist criticism will expand to embrace other modes of critical inquiry. In other words, I am philosophically opposed to what Annis Pratt calls "methodolatry." Wole Soyinka has offered one of the most cogent defenses against critical absolutism. He explains: "The danger which a literary ideology poses is the act of consecration—and of course excommunication. Thanks to the tendency of the modern consumer-mind to facilitate digestion by putting in strict categories what are essentially fluid operations of the creative mind upon social and natural phenomena, the formulation of a literary ideology tends to congeal sooner or later into instant capsules which, administered also to the writer, may end by asphixiating the creative process."[40]

Whether or not Black feminist criticism will or should remain a separatist enterprise is a debatable point. Black feminist critics ought to move from this issue to consider the specific language of Black women's literature, to describe the ways Black women writers employ literary devices in a distinct way, and to compare the way Black women writers create their own mythic structures. If they focus on these and other pertinent issues, Black feminist critics will have laid the cornerstone for a sound, thorough articulation of the Black feminist aesthetic.

NOTES

1. Louise Bernikow, *The World Split Open: Four Centuries of Women Poets in England and America, 1552–1950* (New York: Vintage Books, 1974), p. 3.

2. William Morgan, "Feminism and Literary Study: A Reply to Annette Kolodny," *Critical Inquiry*, 2 (Summer 1976), B11.

3. The year 1970 was the beginning of the Modern Language Association's Commission on the Status of Women that offered panels and workshops that were feminist in approach.

4. Statement by Barbara Desmarais quoted in Annis Pratt, "The New Feminist Criticisms: Exploring the History of the New Space," in *Beyond Intellectual Sexism: A New Woman, A New Reality*, ed. Joan I. Roberts (New York: David McKay, 1976), p. 176.

5. Patricia Meyer Spacks, *The Female Imagination* (New York: Avon Books, 1972), p. 5. Ellen Moers, *Literary Women: The Great Writers* (Garden City, NY: Anchor Books, 1977) is another example of what Alice Walker terms "white female chauvinism."

6. Alice Walker, "One Child of One's Own—An Essay on Creativity," *Ms.*, August 1979, p. 50.

7. Robert Stepto, *From behind the Veil: A Study of Afro-American Narrative* (Urbana: University of Illinois Press, 1979), p. x. Other sexist critical works include *Five Black Writers*, ed. Donald B. Gibson (New York: New York University Press, 1970), a collection of essays on Wright, Ellison, Baldwin, Hughes, and Leroi Jones, and Jean Wagner, *Black Poets of the United States: From Paul Lawrence Dunbar to Langston Hughes*, trans. Kenneth Douglas (Urbana: University of Illinois Press, 1973).

8. Stepto, p. 166.

9. Robert Bone, *The Negro Novel in America* (1958; rpt. New Haven: Yale University Press, 1972), pp. 97, 101

10. David Littlejohn, *Black on White: A Critical Survey of Writing by American Negroes* (New York: The Viking Press, 1966), pp. 48-49.

11. Ellman's concept of "phallic criticism" is discussed in a chapter of the same name in her *Thinking about Women* (New York: Harcourt Brace Jovanovich, 1968), pp. 28-54.

12. Introduction to *Zora Neale Hurston: A Literary Biography* by Robert Hemenway (Urbana: University of Illinois Press, 1976), p. xiv. Although Walker makes this observation specifically about Hurston, it is one that can apply to a number of Black women writers.

13. Barbara Smith, "Toward a Black Feminist Criticism," *Conditions: Two*, 1 (October 1977), 27.

14. See Evelyn Hammonds, "Toward a Black Feminist Aesthetic," *Sojourner*, October 1980, p. 7, for a discussion of the limitations on Black feminist critics. She correctly points out that Black feminist critics "have no newspapers, no mass marketed magazines or journals that are explicitly oriented toward the involvement of women of color in the feminist movement."

15. Dorin Schumacher, "Subjectivities: A Theory of the Critical Process," in *Feminist Literary Criticism: Exploitations in Theory*, ed. Josephine Donovan (Lexington: The University Press of Kentucky, 1975), p. 34.

16. Smith, pp. 27-28. Subsequent references to the article will be indicated by page numbers in parentheses in the text.

17. Annette Kolodny, "Critical Response: The Feminist as Literary Critic," *Critical Inquiry*, 2 (Summer 1976), 824-25. See also Cheris Kramer, Barrie

Thorne, and Nancy Henley, "Perspectives on Language and Communication," *Signs*, 3 (Summer 1978) and Nelly Furman, "The Study of Women and Language: Comment on Vol. 3, no. 3," *Signs*, 4 (Autumn 1978).

18. Stephen Henderson, *Understanding the New Black Poetry: Black Speech and Black Music as Poetic References* (New York: William Morrow, 1973), pp. 31–46.

19. Some attempts have been made to define or at least discuss lesbianism. See Adrienne Rich's two essays, "It Is the Lesbian in Us . . ." and "The Meaning of Our Love for Woman Is What We Have," in her *On Lies, Secrets and Silence* (New York: W. W. Norton, 1979), pp. 199–202 and 223–30, respectively. See also Bertha Harris's "Notes toward Defining the Nature of Lesbian Literature," *Heresies*, 1 (Fall 1977), and Blanche Cook's "'Women Alone Stir My Imagination': Lesbianism and the Cultural Tradition," *Signs*, 4 (Summer 1979), 728–39. Also, at least one bibliography of Black lesbian writers has been compiled. See Ann Allen Shockley's "The Black Lesbian in American Literature: An Overview," *Conditions: Five*, 2 (Autumn 1979), 133–42.

20. Annette Kolodny, "Some Notes on Defining a 'Feminist Literary Criticism,'" *Critical Inquiry*, 2 (Autumn 1975), 90.

21. Lillian Robinson, "Working Women Writing," in *Sex, Class, and Culture* (Bloomington: Indiana University Press, 1978), p. 226.

22. Robinson, "The Critical Task," in *Sex, Class, and Culture*, p. 52.

23. I am borrowing here from Kolodny who makes similar statements in "Some Notes," p. 75.

24. Andrea Benton Rushing, "Images of Black Women in Afro-American Poetry," in *The Afro-American Woman: Struggles and Images*, ed. Sharon Harley and Rosalyn Terborg-Penn (Port Washington, NY: Kennikat Press, 1978), pp. 74–84. She argues that few of the stereotypic traits which Mary Ellman describes in *Thinking about Women* "seem appropriate to Afro-American images of black women," See also her "Images of Black Women in Modern African Poetry: An Overview," in *Sturdy Black Bridges: Visions of Black Women in Literature* (New York: Anchor Press-Doubleday, 1979), pp. 18–24. Rushing argues similarly that Mary Ann Ferguson's categories of women (the submissive wife, the mother angel or "mom," the woman on a pedestal, for example) cannot be applied to Black women characters whose cultural imperatives are different from white women's.

25. *The Messenger*, 9 (April 1927), 109.

26. *The Messenger*, 5 (July 1923), 757.

27. Tillie Olsen, *Silences* (New York: Delacorte Press, 1978), p. 257.

28. Kolodny, "Some Notes," p. 89.

29. Robinson, "Dwelling in Decencies: Radical Criticism and the Feminist Perspectives," in *Feminist Criticism*, ed. Cheryl Brown and Karen Alsex (New Jersey: The Scarcrow Press, 1978), p. 34.

30. For a discussion of Toni Morrison's frustrated female artists see Renita Weems, "Artists without Art Form: A Look at One Black Woman's World of Unrevered Black Women," *Conditions: Five*, 2 (Autumn 1979), 48–58. See also Alice Walker's classic essay, "In Search of Our Mothers' Gardens," *Ms.*, May 1974, for a discussion of Black women's creativity in general.

31. Toni Morrison, *The Bluest Eye* (New York: Pocket Books-Simon and Schuster, 1970), pp. 88–89.

32. Toni Morrison, *Sula* (New York: Bantam Books, 1980), p. 105.

33. Kolodny, "Some Notes," p. 86.

34. In an NEH Summer Seminar at Yale University, Summer 1980, Carolyn Naylor of Santa Clara University suggested this to me.

35. For a discussion of this idea see Michael G. Cooke, "The Descent into the Underworld and Modern Black Fiction," *Iowa Review,* 5 (Fall 1974), 72–90.

36. Mary Helen Washington, *Midnight Birds* (Garden City, NY: Anchor Press-Doubleday, 1980), p. 43.

37. Washington, p. xvii.

38. See Saundra Towns, "The Black Woman as Whore: Genesis of the Myth," *The Black Position,* 3 (1973), 39–59, and Sylvia Keady, "Richard Wright's Women Characters and Inequality," *Black American Literature Forum,* 10 (1976), 124–28, for example.

39. "The Politics of Intimacy: A Discussion," in *Sturdy Black Bridges,* p. 88.

40. Wole Soyinka, *Myth, Literature and the African World* (London: Cambridge University Press, 1976), p. 61.

Black Women Demand
Accountability

• • • • •

The writings in this last section of the book address the personal and political emergence of black women in the 1970s and 1980s as reflected in the black feminist movement, which developed from the growing acknowledgment among black women that they had to pay attention to their own particular needs and concerns. These pieces also address three areas traditionally of great concern to black women but over which they have had little control: abortion rights, the role of women in the church, and heterosexism. As black women have sought to gain control over these areas, they have held patriarchal interests, whether enforced by males or other females, accountable for subsuming or flatly denying the genuine interests of black women.

Of primary concern to black women is the issue of abortion rights. Historically, black women, like white women, have been hurt by criminal abortion statutes that make inducing a miscarriage in a woman, unless it is necessary to save her life, punishable by imprisonment. Such laws have seriously affected poor black women and teenagers who were ill equipped economically and/or psychologically to care for the children they conceived. Some black slave women aborted their own fetuses or killed their children because they did not want them to experience the miserable condition of slavery. The fugitive slave Margaret Garner, for instance, killed her own daughter and then boasted, "Now, she would never know what a woman suffers as a slave."[1] During and after slavery many women perpetuated a family cycle of involuntary motherhood; others became targets for illegal abortionists, who often left them infertile and otherwise permanently injured.

Although legislation guaranteeing women's right to abortion was in the interest of black women, relatively few joined white feminists in the fight for its passage during the early 1970s. Some associated abortions with sterilization as a racist form of birth control; they regarded the legalization of abortion as the white establishment's attempt to keep black population growth in check. Traditionally, the birth control movement had targeted poor women, especially poor black women, for involuntary sterilization as a means of decreasing the welfare rolls. In June 1972 the Montgomery (Alabama) Community Action Agency, which operated a federally supported family planning clinic, illegally sterilized two black girls, 14-year-old Mary Alice Relf and her 12-year-old sister Minnie Lee, because "boys were hanging around" the public housing project in which they lived. Their mother, an illiterate welfare recipient with four children and a husband, had marked an X on a paper authorizing her children to receive immunization shots. Another black woman, 20-year-old Nial Ruth Cox of New Bern, North Carolina, discovered in 1972 that she had been illegally sterilized in 1964 after she was told that the procedure was temporary and that if she did not submit to it, her family would no longer receive welfare benefits. Forced sterilization of persons who receive medical assistance from the federal government was and still is prohibited by the federal government, yet eugenics commissions and state legislatures, particularly those in the South, used punitive sterilization measures to control the poor black population. Before 1973, 65 percent of the women illegally sterilized in North Carolina were black, and 35 percent were white.[2]

Fear of sterilization within the black community has not been unfounded, but it is misguided to connect illegal sterilization practices with the legalization of abortion. That black women do favor abortion rights can be gleaned from the fact that in the 1970s, after New York decriminalized abortions, black and Puerto Rican women received almost half of the total abortions in that state.[3]

In "Facing the Abortion Question," Shirley Chisholm, a former congresswoman from New York and president of the National Association for the Repeal of Abortion Laws (NARAL), attributes to "male rhetoric" the belief in the black community that family planning and legal abortion programs are genocidal in intent; Chisholm "does not know any black . . . *women* who feel that way." In explaining why abortion rights are so crucial to black women, she cites a sobering statistic from a 1960–62 study: for 49 percent of pregnant black women who died in the United States, abortion was the cause of death. In 1988 only 35 black women nationwide were reported to have died from an aborted pregnancy.[4] Advocating an end to compulsory pregnancy, Chisholm argues that the old laws, which forced poor black women to seek illegal and sometimes fatal abortions, were ultimately more harmful to the black community than the new laws, which give women greater choice in family planning and safer abortions when they choose to have them.

Chisholm was among the vanguard lobbying for abortion rights and finally claiming victory in 1973 with the Supreme Court cases of *Roe v. Wade* and *Doe v. Bolton.* Jane Roe,[5] a single pregnant woman unable to obtain an abortion in Texas, challenged the constitutionality of Texas criminal abortion laws in the Supreme Court after losing her case in the District Court of Texas. John and Mary Doe, a married Georgia couple, filed a companion complaint to Roe's in the Supreme Court after unsuccessfully challenging the unconstitutionality of Georgia's abortion statutes. Mrs. Doe, who was not pregnant at the time of the Supreme Court hearing, asserted that she had a "neural-chemical" disorder and that should she become pregnant she would wish to abort the fetus with the aid of a competent physician. In both cases the Supreme Court ruled that a woman's right to individual privacy implied her right to choose whether or not to obtain an abortion.[6]

Although "pro-choice" advocates won these landmark cases almost two decades ago, Louisiana still bans abortions except in cases of rape and incest and to save a woman's life. Nineteen states have passed enforceable laws restricting a minor's right to abortion by requiring her to notify one or both parents, obtain parental consent, or secure a judge's approval. Only Hawaii, American Samoa, Puerto Rico, and U.S. Virgin Islands have no laws governing abortions.[7] A decided setback came in October 1989 when Pres. George Bush vetoed legislation that would have made federal funds for abortions available to poor women who are victims of rape and incest.

Black feminists have also demanded accountability from the black church. During slavery, the operation of the church and the services and duties that arose from it were the domain of black men. Freedman churches rallied around the male preacher, fought against slavery, participated in war relief, and started schools. After Reconstruction, when banks, stores, and other white institutions turned blacks away, the black church headed by black men took on social and economic functions in addition to its religious tasks. The conservative sex bias of the nineteenth century is evident in the case of Jarena Lee, the first woman preacher of the African Methodist Episcopal (AME) Church; her preaching career was delayed eight years by Richard Allen, founder of the

AME Church, for no other reason than that she was a woman. Lee reports in her journal that in response to her request to preach, Allen said, "As to women preaching . . . our Discipline knew nothing at all about it—that it did not call for women preachers."[8]

Although women compose more than 70 percent of the membership in the black church, black women are seldom represented in the pulpit. They made up only 25 percent of the clergy in black churches in 1990, a 20 percent increase since 1979.[9] Except in the area of religious education, women who have become influential church leaders have done so in spite of tremendous obstacles. Black female ministers who have come up through the ranks have complained that male ministers anticipate and delight in their errors, that male parishioners have relinquished their memberships in churches where women have been invited to preach, and that both men and women have walked out of church when a woman began to preach because they did not want to hear a woman's voice.[10]

Black liberation theology, which came into vogue in the 1960s to eradicate racism in the church, did little to eliminate sexism. Jacquelyn Grant, in her essay "Black Theology and the Black Woman," asserts that "if the church does not share in the liberation struggle of Black women, its liberation struggle is not authentic." She charges that "black men have accepted without question the patriarchal structures of the white society as normative for the black community," with the consequence that black women have been confined to a subservient role in the church hierarchy. Grant asks black theologians to acknowledge the sexism of their views and behavior and to address the liberation of *all* black people.

Since the late 1970s black women have assumed more responsible roles in the black church. They have served as assistant bishops and pastors and have been ordained priests. In 1976 the Episcopal church ordained Pauli Murray as the first black woman priest, and in 1989 Barbara Clementine Harris, a civil rights activist, became the first woman consecrated as an Episcopalian bishop. Still other women have founded their own churches: for example, Charleszetta "Mother" Waddles, an ordained minister of the First Pentecostal Church, founded the Perpetual Mission for Saving Souls of All Nations, Inc. in downtown Detroit.

In yet another area, black lesbians have demanded accountability for the heterosexist orientation of our culture. Heterosexism within a culture subjugates all women through every institution, including the family, the church, the school, and the workplace, and it severely oppresses black women. As we have seen in parts 1 and 2 of this book, since slavery black women have been relegated to certain subclasses (female, black, poor) in a society where the power resides ultimately in the hands of capitalistic white males. As a subgroup, black lesbians are denigrated even more than straight women because they have rejected the heterosexual female role by assuming a sexual or affectional preference for other women. Derisively called "bulldagger" in the black folk culture, the lesbian was believed to be "a creature of enormous power to those who were terrorized by the tales of her knife-toting ways, her smooth charm, her exceptional and extraordinary sexual parts—her clitoris was called 'a hammer' or 'a pertongue' (or pearl tongue). It was thought to be elongated, a very different organ between her legs that could hook onto a woman's libido and enslave her heart or ruin her health."[11]

Nevertheless, lesbianism has been an alternative sexuality since slavery for black women who wish to practice "social masculinity." Mary Fields, an ex-slave who went west in the 1880s to drive a stagecoach on a U.S. mail route, wore men's clothes (except for an apron and a skirt), smoked cigars, drank hard liquor, carried a .38 Smith and Wesson, and fought gun duels with men.[12] Annie Lee Grant wrapped her large breasts and passed as "James McHarris" from the 1930s until her discovery in 1954 when she was arrested in Kosciusko, Mississippi, for driving a car with improper lights. When the white male superintendent advised her upon her release from jail, "Girl, you get you a dress now and do the things a woman ought to do," she defiantly answered, "I don't see it like that"; she intended to remain a "man" in what was considered a man's world.[13]

Many black lesbians who had not gone public did so from the late 1960s until the early 1980s, during the height of the feminist movement. They subscribed to the general belief of lesbian feminists that "*no females will ever be free to choose to be anything until we are also free to choose to be lesbians, because the domination of heterosexuality is a mainstay of male supremacy.*"[14] Lesbianism has been a threat to patriarchy both in society and in the civil rights and feminist movements. In his famous barb of 1965, Stokely Carmichael distinguished between women and lesbians when he said, "The only position of women in SNCC is prone—with the exception of women who either dress or look like men."[15] At a feminist coalition meeting attended by both lesbian and straight women, one black woman advised a group, "I don't know if we should be working with them because they're gay."[16]

Heterosexual bias, more often called homophobia, has always been present in the black community, but it became more visible as lesbians and homosexual men came out of the closet in the 1970s and early 1980s. In her essay "I Am Your Sister," Audre Lorde addresses the issue of heterosexism and how it breeds homophobia and prevents people who are similarly oppressed by sexism from working together to solve common issues. Lorde advises black women to forget about lesbian stereotypes and charges them to "not waste each other's resources . . . [to] recognize each sister on her own terms so that we may better work together toward our mutual survival."

In the 1970s and 1980s black lesbians increasingly demanded their right to a believable cultural context and social and cultural visibility. They have tried to make society more aware of their existence.[17] They have published works that counteract the stereotype of the "marginal and forbidden" lesbian character; they have established lesbian magazines (*Azalea, Black Light,* and *Salsa Soul Gayzette*); and in 1983 Barbara Smith and others founded Kitchen Table: Women of Color Press, the first publishing house of its kind in America. Black lesbians have also set up their own organizations to address issues that directly affect them: the Combahee River Collective in Boston (1974), Sapphire Sapphos in Washington, D.C. (1975), and the Study Group on Black Lesbians in New York (1977).

Whether taking control over their bodies, gaining prominent roles in the church, or affirming their lesbianism, black women have had to overcome tremendous obstacles. Assuming an equal place in society has often meant holding others accountable for their oppression and sometimes severing communication even with those facing the same gender and racial discrimination. Even as they forged ahead during the 1970s and 1980s, at a time when women nationwide were fighting to achieve equality, black women did not forget the pains of their foremothers, who had struggled against the odds and prevailed.

NOTES

1. Quoted in Davis, *Women, Race, and Class,* 205.
2. Jack Slater, "Sterilization: Newest Threat to the Poor," *Ebony* 38 (October 1973): 150, 152.
3. Davis, *Women, Race, and Class,* 204.
4. *Vital Statistics of the United States,* vol. 2 (Hyattsville, Md.: U.S. Department of Health and Human Services, 1990), 190.
5. Jane Roe and Mary Doe are pseudonyms. In both cases, district attorneys served as the defendants.
6. *Supreme Court Reporter* (St. Paul, Minn.: West Publishing CO., 1972), 93:705–63.
7. The states restricting access to abortion are Alabama, California, Florida, Georgia, Illinois, Indiana, Maine, Massachusetts, Minnesota, Mississippi, Missouri, North Dakota, Ohio, Rhode Island, South Carolina, Utah, West Virginia, Wisconsin, and Wyoming. See "List of Laws, State by State," *USA Today,* 10 July 1990, 8A.

8. Jarena Lee, *Religious Experience and Journal of Mrs. Jarena Lee, Giving an Account of Her Call to Preach the Gospel* (Philadelphia: 1849), 11.

9. Rev. Madelene Beard (minister of Galatians United Christian Church in Suffolk, Virginia), interview with the author, 3 May 1991. In 1985 Reverend Beard was the first female to join the Interdenominational Ministerial Alliance of Suffolk, Virginia.

10. *Ibid.*

11. SDiane A. Bogus, "The Myth and Tradition of the Black Bulldagger," *Black Lace* 1 (Spring 1991): 25.

12. Gary Cooper, "Stagecoach Mary," *Ebony* 32 (October 1977): 96–98, 100–102.

13. "The Woman Who Lived as a Man for Fifteen Years," *Ebony* 10 (November 1954): 98.

14. Charlotte Bunch, "Lesbian Feminist Theory (1978)," in *Women and the Politics of Culture*, ed. Michele Wender Zak and Patricia A. Moots (New York: Longman, 1983), 416.

15. Quoted in Evans, *Personal Politics*, 239.

16. Tania Abdulahad et al., "Black Lesbian/Feminist Organizing: A Conversation (1983)," in *Home Girls: A Black Feminist Anthology*, ed. Barbara Smith (New York: Kitchen Table: Women of Color Press, 1983), 314.

17. According to Cheryl Clarke (telephone interview, 24 April 1991), there are approximately 125,000 black lesbians in the United States.

● ● ● ● ●

"Facing the Abortion Question" [from *Unbought and Unbossed*]

Shirley Chisholm

One of four daughters of West Indian parents, Shirley Chisholm was born in Brooklyn, New York, in 1924. She attended Brooklyn College, where she founded Ipothia (In Pursuit Of The Highest In All), an all-black sorority. She developed political interests while in college and worked for the Urban League, joined the Seventeenth Assembly Democratic Club, and participated in question-and-answer periods following the speeches of local politicians. In 1953 she campaigned to elect Lewis S. Flagg, Jr., to be Brooklyn's first black judge. In 1964 she was elected herself to the New York State Assembly, and in 1968 she became the first black American woman to be elected to the U.S. Congress. Part of her campaign slogan became the title of her autobiography, *Unbought and Unbossed* (Houghton Mifflin, 1970), which chronicles her life from childhood to her rise in politics. In 1972 Chisholm became the first black woman to run for president of the United States, and her second book, *The Good Fight* (1973), gives an account of that presidential campaign. She has also written many letters, essays, newspaper articles, and speeches.

While a delegate to the New York State Assembly, Chisholm "continually introduced legislation that reflected her concern for women, children, and the disadvantaged."[1] As a congresswoman she also worked on issues pertinent to women and minorities; one such issue was abortion. Her appointment in 1969 as president of the National Association for the Repeal of Abortion Laws gave her the opportunity to study the effect of abortion laws on poor women.

In this excerpt from her autobiography, Chisholm makes a compelling case for the repeal of the restrictive abortion laws in existence before the 1970s, arguing that they harmed poor black women by subjecting them to potentially lethal illegal abortions. Chisholm traces the evolution of her personal opinion on abortion and of her political involvement with the issue. As she explains, openly advocating the repeal of abortion laws was fraught with risk for a politician in the 1960s and 1970s; even more so than now, it was a highly charged, controversial issue with great potential for alienating constituents. Chisholm's willingness to take a strong, visible position on this issue reflects both the intensity of her conviction that the laws were harmful to women and her political courage.

NOTE

1. Susan Duffy, *Shirley Chisholm: A Bibliography of Writings by and about Her* (Metuchen, N.J.: Scarecrow, 1988), v.

In August of 1969 I started to get phone calls from NARAL, the National Association for the Repeal of Abortion Laws, a new organization based in New York City that was looking for a national president. In the New York State Assembly I had supported abortion reform bills introduced by Assemblyman Albert Blumenthal, and this had apparently led NARAL to believe I would sympathize with its goal: complete repeal of all laws restricting abortion. As a matter of fact, when I was in the Assembly I had not been in favor of repealing all abortion laws, a step that would leave the question of having or not having the operation entirely up to a woman and her doctor. The bills I had tried to help pass in Albany would only have made it somewhat easier for women to get therapeutic abortions in New York State, by providing additional legal grounds and simplifying the procedure for getting approval. But since that time I had been compelled to do some heavy thinking on the subject, mainly because of the experiences of several young women I knew. All had suffered permanent injuries at the hands of illegal abortionists. Some will never have children as a result. One will have to go to a hospital periodically for treatment for the rest of her life.

It had begun to seem to me that the question was not whether the law should allow abortions. Experience shows that pregnant women who feel they have compelling reasons for not having a baby, or another baby, will break the law and, even worse, risk injury and death if they must to get one. Abortions will not be stopped. It may even be that the number performed is not being greatly reduced by laws making an abortion a "criminal operation." If that is true, the question becomes simply that of what kind of abortions society wants women to have—clean, competent ones performed by licensed physicians or septic, dangerous ones done by incompetent practitioners.

So when NARAL asked me to lead its campaign, I gave it serious thought. For me to take the lead in abortion repeal would be an even more serious step than for a white politician to do so, because there is a deep and angry suspicion among many blacks that even birth control clinics are a plot by the white power structure to keep down the numbers of blacks, and this opinion is even more strongly held by some in regard to legalizing abortions. But I do not know any black or Puerto Rican *women* who feel that way. To label family planning and legal abortion programs "genocide" is male rhetoric, for male ears. It falls flat to female listeners, and to thoughtful male ones. Women know, and so do many men, that two or three children who are wanted, prepared for, reared amid love and stability, and educated to the limit of their ability will mean more for the future of the black and brown races from which they come than any number of neglected, hungry, ill-housed and ill-clothed youngsters. Pride in one's race, as well as simple humanity, supports this view. Poor women of every race feel as I do, I believe. There is objective evidence of it in a study by Dr. Charles F. Westhoff of the Princeton Office of Population Research. He questioned 5600 married persons and found that 22 percent of their children were unwanted. But among persons who earn less than $4,000 a year, 42 percent of the children were unwanted. The poor are more anxious about family planning than any other group.

Why then do the poor keep on having large families? It is not because they are stupid or immoral. One must understand how many resources their poverty has deprived them of, and that chief among these is medical care and advice. The poor do not go to doctors or clinics except when they absolutely must; their medical ignorance is very great, even when compared to the low level of medical knowledge most persons have. This includes naturally, information about contraceptives and how to get them. In some of the largest cities, clinics are now attacking this problem; they are nowhere near to solving it. In smaller cities and in most of the countryside, hardly anything is being done.

Another point is this: not only do the poor have large families, but also large families tend to be poor. More than one fourth of all the families with four children live in poverty, according to the federal government's excessively narrow definition; by humane standards of poverty, the number would be much larger. The figures range from 9 percent of one-child families that have incomes below the official poverty line, up to 42 percent of the families with six children or more. Sinking into poverty, large families tend to stay there because of the educational and social handicaps that being poor imposes. It is the fear of such a future for their children that drives many women, of every color and social stratum, except perhaps the highest, to seek abortions when contraception has failed.

Botched abortions are the largest single cause of death of pregnant women in the United States, particularly among nonwhite women. In 1964, the president of the New York County Medical Society, Dr. Carl Goldmark, estimated that 80 percent of the deaths of gravid women in Manhattan were from this cause.

Another study by Edwin M. Gold, covering 1960 through 1962, gave lower percentages but supplied evidence that women from minority groups suffer most. Gold said abortion was the cause of death in 25 percent of the white cases, 49 percent of the black ones, and 65 percent of the Puerto Rican ones.

Even when a poor woman needs an abortion for the most impeccable medical reasons, acceptable under most states' laws, she is not likely to succeed in getting one. The public hospitals to which she must go are far more reluctant to approve abortions than are private, voluntary hospitals. It's in the records: private hospitals in New York City perform 3.9 abortions for every 1,000 babies they deliver, public hospitals only 1 per 1,000. Another relevant figure is that 90 percent of the therapeutic abortions in the city are performed on white women. Such statistics convinced me that my instinctive feeling was right: a black woman legislator, far from avoiding the abortion question, was compelled to face it and deal with it.

But my time did not permit me to be an active president of NARAL, so I asked to be made an honorary president. My appearances on television in September 1969, when the association's formation was announced, touched off one of the heaviest flows of mail to my Washington office that I have experienced. What surprised me was that it was overwhelmingly in favor of repeal. Most of the letters that disagreed with me were from Catholics, and most of them were temperate and reasoned. We sent those writers a reply that said in part, "No one should be forced to have an abortion or to use birth control methods which for religious or personal reasons they oppose. But neither should others who have different views be forced to abide by what they do not and cannot believe in." Some of the mail was from desperate women who thought I could help them. "I am forty-five years old," one wrote, "and have raised a family already. Now I find that I am pregnant and I need help. Please send me all the information." A girl wrote that she was pregnant and did not dare tell her mother and stepfather: "Please send me the name of a doctor or hospital that would help. You said if my doctor wouldn't do it to write to you. Where can I turn?" We sent the writers of these letters a list of the names and addresses of the chapters of the Clergy Consultation Service on Abortion and suggested that they find a local family planning or birth control clinic.

The reaction of a number of my fellow members of Congress seemed to me a little strange. Several said to me, "This abortion business . . . my God, what are you doing? That's not politically wise." It was the same old story; they were not thinking in terms of right or wrong, they were considering only whether taking a side of the issue would help them stay in office—or in this case, whether taking a stand would help me get reelected. They concluded that it would not help me, so it was a bad position for me to take. My advisers were, of course, all men. So I decided to shake them up a little with a feminist line of counterattack. "Who told you I shouldn't do this?" I asked them. "Women are dying every day, did you know that? They're being butchered and maimed. No matter what men think, abortion is a fact of life. Women will have them; they always have and always will. Are they going to have good ones or bad ones? Will the good ones be reserved for the rich while poor women have to go to quacks? Why don't we talk about real problems instead of phony ones?"

One member asked the question that was on the minds of all the others: "How many Catholics do you have in your district?" "Look," I told him, "I can't worry about that. That's not the problem." Persons who do not deal with politicians are often baffled by the peculiarly simple workings of their minds. Scientists and scholars in particular are bewildered by the political approach. When a member of Congress makes a statement, the scholar's first thought is "Is what he said true? Is he right or wrong?" The falseness or validity of an officeholder's statement is almost never discussed in Washington, or anyplace where politics sets the tone of discourse. The question political people ask is seldom "Is he right?" but "Why did he say that?" Or they ask, "Where does he expect that to get him?" or "Who put him up to that?"

But returning to abortion, the problem that faced me was what action I should take in my role as a legislator, if any; naturally, I intended to be as active as possible as an advocate and publicist for the cause, but was there any chance of getting a meaningful bill through Congress? Some NARAL officials wanted me to introduce an abortion repeal bill as a gesture. This is very common; probably a majority of the bills introduced in all legislative bodies are put in for the sake of effect, to give their sponsor something to talk about on the stump. That was never my style in Albany, and I have not adopted it in Washington. When I introduce legislation, I try to draft it carefully and then look for meaningful support from people who have the power to help move the bill.

So I looked for House members, in both parties and of all shades of conservatism and liberalism, who might get together on abortion repeal regardless of party. I wrote letters to a number of the more influential House members. It would have been easy to get three or four, or even ten or twelve, liberal Democrats to join me in introducing a bill, but nothing would have happened. A majority of House members would have said, "Oh, that bunch again," and dismissed us. But just a few conservative Republican co-sponsors, or conservative Democratic ones, would change all that. The approach I took was eminently sound, but it didn't work. A few members replied that they would support my bill if it ever got to the floor, but could not come out for it publicly before then or work for it. I did not doubt their sincerity, but it was a safe thing to say because the chances of a bill's reaching the floor seemed slim. Several others answered with longish letters admiring my bold position and expressing sympathy, but not agreement. "I am not ready to assume such a position," one letter said. Another said, in almost these words, "This kind of trouble I don't need." So I put my roughly drafted bill in a drawer and decided to wait. There is no point in introducing it until congressmen can be persuaded to vote for it, and only one thing will persuade them. If a congressman feels he is in danger of losing his job, he will change his mind—and then try to make it look as though he had been leading the way. The approach to Congress has to be through the arousal and organization of public opinion.

The question will remain "Is abortion *right?*" and it is a question that each of us must answer for himself. My beliefs and my experience have led me to conclude that the wisest public policy is to place the responsibility for that decision on the individual. The rightness or wrongness of an abortion depends on the individual case, and it seems to me clearly wrong to pass laws regulating all cases. But there is more to it than that. First, it is my view, and I think the majority's view, that abortion should always remain a last resort, never a primary method of limiting families. Contraceptive devices are the first choice: *devices,* because of their established safety compared to the controversial oral contraceptives. The weight of responsible medical opinion, by which I mean the opinions of qualified persons who have never been in the pay of the drug industry, seems to be that the question of the Pill's safety is not proven and that there are clear warnings that much more study is needed. So Pill research should continue, and meanwhile the emphasis—particularly in a publicly supported family planning program—should be on proven safe and effective methods. Beyond that, still from the standpoint of public policy, there must be far more stress on providing a full range of family planning services to persons of all economic levels. At present, the full gamut of services, from expert medical advice to, as a last resort, safe "legal" abortions, is available for the rich. Any woman who has the money and the sophistication about how things are done in our society can get an abortion within the law. If she is from a social stratum where such advice is available, she will be sent to a sympathetic psychiatrist and he will be well paid to believe her when she says she is ready to kill herself if she doesn't get rid of her pregnancy. But unless a woman has the $700 to $1,000 minimum it takes to travel this route, her only safe course in most states is to have the child.

This means that, whether it was so intended, public policy as expressed in American abortion laws (excepting the handful of states where the repeal effort has succeeded) is to maximize illegitimacy. Illegitimate children have always been born and for the foreseeable future they will continue to be. Their handicap is not some legal blot on their ancestry; few intelligent persons give any thought to that today. The trouble is that illegitimate children are usually the most unwanted of the unwanted. Society has forced a woman to have a child in order to punish her. Our laws were based on the Puritan reaction of "You've had your pleasure—now pay for it." But who pays? First, it is the helpless woman, who may be a girl in her early teens forced to assume the responsibility of an adult; young, confused, partially educated, she is likely to be condemned to society's trash heap as a result. But the child is often a worse loser. If his mother keeps him, she may marry or not (unmarried mothers are even less likely to marry than widows or divorcées). If she does not, she will have to neglect him and work at undesirable jobs to feed him, more often than not. His homelife will almost certainly be abnormal; he may survive it and even thrive, depending on his mother's personal qualities, but the odds have to be against him.

Of course, there should be no unwanted children. Whether they are legitimate or illegitimate is not of the first importance. But we will not even approach the ideal of having every child wanted, planned for, and cherished, until our methods of contraception are fully reliable and completely safe, and readily available to everyone. Until then, unwanted pregnancies will happen, in marriage and out of it. What is our public policy to be toward them? There are very few more important questions for society to face; this question is one that government has always avoided because it did not dare intrude on the sanctity of the home and marriage. But the catastrophic perils that follow in the train of overpopulation were not well known in the past and those perils were not imminent, so the question could be ducked. It cannot be any longer.

For all Americans, and especially for the poor, we must put an end to compulsory pregnancy. The well-off have only one problem when an unwanted pregnancy occurs; they must decide what they want to do and what they believe is right. For the poor, there is no such freedom. They started with too little knowledge about contraception, often with none except street lore and other misinformation. When trapped by pregnancy, they have only two choices, both bad—a cheap abortion or an unwanted child to plunge them deeper into poverty. Remember the statistics that show which choice is often taken: 49 percent of the deaths of pregnant black women and 65 percent of those of Puerto Rican women . . . due to criminal, amateur abortions.

Which is more like genocide, I have asked some of my black brothers—this, the way things are, or the conditions I am fighting for in which the full range of family planning services is freely available to women of all classes and colors, starting with effective contraception and extending to safe, legal termination of undesired pregnancies, at a price they can afford?

● ● ● ● ●

"Black Theology and the Black Woman"

Jacquelyn Grant

Born in Georgetown, South Carolina, in 1948, Jacquelyn Grant received her B.A. degree in 1970 from Bennett College in Greensboro, North Carolina, her M.Div. degree in 1973 from Turner Theological Seminary at the Interdenominational Theological Center in Atlanta, Georgia, and her M.Phil. (1980) and Ph.D. (1985) degrees from Union Theological Seminary in New York. She has lectured and taught at Harvard Divinity School, Emory University, and Princeton Theology Seminary. She is currently an associate professor of systematic theology at the Interdenominational Theological Center, where she is founder and director of Black Women in Church and Society, a program that develops the leadership and participation of black women in the church. An ordained elder in the African Methodist Episcopal Church in Atlanta, she also serves as associate minister at Atlanta's Flipper Temple AME Church. Her essay "Black Theology and the Black Woman" was first published in Gayraud S. Wilmore and James H. Cone's anthology, *Black Theology: A Documentary History, 1966–1979* (Orbis, 1979). Her other essays include "Tasks of a Prophetic Church" (in Cornell West, ed., *Theology in the Americas* [1982]) and "A Black Response to Feminist Theology" (in Janet Kalven and Mary Buckley, eds., *Women's Spirit Bonding* [1984]). Her most recent feminist work is the book *White Women's Christ and Black Women's Jesus: Feminist Christology and Womanist Response* (1989).

The daughter of an AME minister, Grant was a frequent church-goer as a child and made an early commitment to Jesus. At that time she was aware neither of sexism within the church nor of the limitations of a male savior. After growing up, however, "I was able to see the issues in my life—my studies and my ministry. For in my adult-hood, not only did I recognize the sexual politics in theology in a patriarchal society, but also the racial politics in theology in a racist society."[1]

In "Black Theology and the Black Woman," Grant addresses the problem of sexism in the church and the need for women to be recognized not only as members of the flock but as its potential leaders. She argues that the tendency of black churchmen to be highly sensitive to racism but ignorant of their own sexism is mirrored in the black community. "There is usually a direct relationship between what goes on in the Black church and the Black secular community." She believes that a black liberation theology that is designed to free black men from a traditionally racist interpretation of the gospel but does not free black women from a sexist interpretation as well, is not a *liberation* theology at all.

NOTE

1. Jacquelyn Grant, *White Women's Christ and Black Women's Jesus: Feminist Christology and Womanist Response* (Atlanta: Scholars Press, 1989), ix–x.

Liberation theologies have arisen out of the contexts of the liberation struggles of Black Americans, Latin Americans, American women, Black South Africans and Asians. These theologies represent a departure from traditional Christian theology. As a collective critique, liberation theologies raise serious questions about the normative use of Scripture, tradition and experience in Christian theology. Liberation theologians assert that the reigning theologies of the West have been used to legitimate the established order. Those to whom the church has entrusted the task of interpreting the meaning of God's activity in the world have been too content to represent the ruling classes. For this reason, say the liberation theologians, theology has generally not spoken to those who are opposed by the political establishment.

Ironically, the criticism that liberation theology makes against classical theology has been turned against liberation theology itself. Just as most European and American theologians have acquiesced in the oppression of the West, for which they have been taken to task by liberation theologians, some liberation theologians have acquiesced in one or more oppressive aspects of the liberation struggle itself. Where racism is rejected, sexism has been embraced. Where classism is called into question, racism and sexism have been tolerated. And where sexism is repudiated racism and classism are often ignored.

Although there is a certain validity to the argument that any one analysis—race, class or sex—is not sufficiently universal to embrace the needs of all oppressed peoples, these particular analyses, nonetheless, have all been well presented and are crucial for a comprehensive and authentic liberation theology. In order for liberation theology to be faithful to itself it must hear the critique coming to it from the perspective of the Black woman—perhaps the most oppressed of all the oppressed.

I am concerned in this essay with how the experience of the Black woman calls into question certain assumptions in Liberation Theology in general, and Black Theology in particular. In the Latin American context this has already been done by women such as Beatriz Melano Couch and Consuelo Urquiza. A few Latin American theologians have begun to respond. Beatriz Couch, for example, accepts the starting point of Latin American theologians, but criticizes them for their exclusivism with respect to race and sex. She says:

> . . . we in Latin America stress the importance of the starting point, the praxis, and the use of social science to analyze our political, historical situation. In this I am in full agreement with my male colleagues . . . with one qualitative difference. I stress the need to give importance to the different cultural forms that express oppression; to the ideology that divides people not only according to class, but to race to sex. Racism and sexism are oppressive ideologies which deserve a specific treatment in the theology of liberation.[1]

More recently, Consuelo Urquiza called for the unification of Hispanic-American women in struggling against their oppression in the church and society. In commenting on the contradiction in the Pauline Epistles which undergird the oppression of the Hispanic-American woman, Urquiza said: "At the present time all Christians will agree with Paul in the first part of [Galatians 3:28] about freedom and slavery that there should not be slaves. . . . However, the next part of this verse . . . has been ignored and the equality between man and woman is not accepted. They would rather skip that line and go to the epistle to Timothy [2:9–15]."[2] Women theologians of Latin background are beginning to do theology and to sensitize other women to the necessity of participating in decisions which affect their lives and the life of their communities. Latin American theology will gain from these inputs which women are making to the theological process.

Third World and Black women[3] in the United States will soon collaborate in an attack on another aspect of Liberation Theology—Feminist Theology. Black and Third World women have begun to articulate their differences and similarities with the Feminist Movement, which is dominated by White American women who until now have been the chief authors of Feminist Theology. It is my contention that the theological perspectives of Black and Third World women should reflect these differences and similarities with Feminist Theology. It is my purpose, however, to look critically at Black Theology as a Black woman in an effort to determine how adequate is its conception of liberation for the total Black community. Pauli Murray and Theressa Hoover have in their own ways challenged Black Theology. Because their articles appear in this section (Documents 39 and 37), it is unnecessary for me to explain their point of view. They have spoken for themselves.

I want to begin with the question: "Where are Black women in Black Theology?" They are, in fact, invisible in Black Theology and we need to know why this is the case. Because the Black church experience and Black experience in general are important sources for doing Black Theology, we need to look at the Black woman in relation to both in order to understand the way Black Theology has applied its conception of liberation. Finally, in view of the status of the Black Woman vis-à-vis Black Theology, the Black Church and the Black experience, a challenge needs to be presented to Black Theology. This is how I propose to discuss this important question.

The Invisibility of Black Women in Black Theology

In examining Black Theology it is necessary to make one of two assumptions: (1) either Black women have no place in the enterprise, or (2) Black men are capable of speaking for us. Both of these assumptions are false and need to be discarded. They arise out of a male-dominated culture which restricts women to certain areas of the society. In such a culture, men are given the warrant to speak for women on all matters of significance. It is no accident that all of the recognized Black theologians are men. This is what might be expected given the status and power accorded the discipline of theology. Professional theology is done by those who are highly trained. It requires, moreover, mastery of that power most accepted in the definition of manhood, the power or ability to "reason." This is supposedly what opens the door to participation in logical, philosophical debates and discussions presupposing rigorous intellectual training, for most of history, outside the "woman's sphere." Whereas the nature of men has been defined in terms of reason and the intellect, that of women has to do with intuition and emotionalism. Women were limited to matters related to the home while men carried out the more important work, involving use of the rational faculties.[4] These distinctions were not as clear in the slave community.[5] Slaves and women were thought to share the characteristics of emotionality and irrationality. As we move further away from the slave culture, however, a dualism between Black men and women increasingly emerges. This means that Black males have gradually increased their power and participation in the male-dominated society, while Black females have continued to endure the stereotypes and oppressions of an earlier period.

When sexual dualism has fully run its course in the Black community (and I believe that it has), it will not be difficult to see why Black women are invisible in Black Theology. Just as White women formerly had no place in White Theology—except as the receptors of White men's theological interpretations—Black women have had no place in the development of Black Theology. By self-appointment, or by the sinecure of a male-dominated society, Black men have deemed it proper to speak for the entire Black community, male and female.

In a sense, Black men's acceptance of the patriarchal model is logical and to be expected. Black male slaves were unable to reap the benefits of patriarchy. Before emancipation they were not given the opportunity to serve as protector and provider for Black women and children, as White men were able to do for their women and children. Much of what was considered "manhood" had to do with how well one could perform these functions. It seems only natural that the post-emancipation Black men would view as of primary importance the reclaiming of their property—their women and their children. Moreover, it is natural that Black men would claim their "natural" right to the "man's world." But it should be emphasized that this is logical and natural only if one has accepted without question the terms and values of patriarchy—the concept of male control and supremacy.

Black men must ask themselves a difficult question. How can a White society characterized by Black enslavement, colonialism, and imperialism provide the normative conception of women for Black society? How can the sphere of the woman, as defined by White men, be free from the evils and oppressions that are found in the White society? The important point is that in matters relative to the relationship between the sexes, Black men have accepted without question the patriarchal structures of the White society as normative for the Black community. How can a Black minister preach in a way which advocates St. Paul's dictum concerning women while ignoring or repudiating his dictum concerning slaves? Many Black women are enraged as they listen to "liberated" Black men speak about the "place of women" in words and phrases similar to those of the very White oppressors they condemn.

Black women have been invisible in theology because theological scholarship has not been a part of the woman's sphere. The first of the above two assumptions results, therefore, from the historical orientation of the dominant culture. The second follows from the first. If women have no place in theology it becomes the natural prerogative of men to monopolize theological concerns, including those relating specifically to women. Inasmuch as Black men have accepted the sexual dualisms of the dominant culture they presume to speak for Black women.

Before finally dismissing the two assumptions a pertinent question should be raised. Does the absence of Black women in the circles producing Black Theology necessarily mean that the resultant theology cannot be in the best interest of Black women? The answer is obvious. Feminist theologians during the past few years have shown how theology done by men in male-dominated cultures has served to undergird patriarchal structures in society.[6] If Black men have accepted those structures, is there any reason to believe that the theology written by Black men would be any more liberating of Black women than White Theology was for White women? It would seem that in view of the oppression that Black people have suffered Black men would be particularly sensitive to the oppression of others.[7]

James Cone has stated that the task of Black Theology "is to analyze the nature of the gospel of Jesus Christ in the light of oppressed Black people so they will see the gospel as inseparable from their humiliated condition, bestowing on them the necessary power to break the chains of oppression. This means that it is a theology of and for the Black community, seeking to interpret the religious dimensions of the forces of liberation in that community."[8] What are the forces of liberation in the Black community and the Black Church? Are they to be exclusively defined by the struggle against racism? My answer to that question is No. There are oppressive realities in the Black community which are related to, but independent of, the fact of racism. Sexism is one such reality. Black men seek to liberate themselves from racial stereotypes and the conditions of oppression without giving due attention to the stereotypes and oppressions against women which parallel those against Blacks. Blacks fight to be free of the stereotype that all Blacks are dirty and ugly, or that Black represents evil and darkness.[9] The slogan "Black is Beautiful" was a counterattack on these stereotypes. The parallel for women is the history of women as "unclean" especially during menstruation and after childbirth. Because the model of beauty in the White male-dominated society is the "long-haired blonde," with all that goes along with that mystique, Black women have an additional problem with the Western idea of "ugliness," particularly as they encounter Black men who have adopted this White model of beauty. Similarly, the Christian teaching that woman is responsible for the fall of *mankind* and is, therefore, the source of evil has had a detrimental effect in the experience of Black women.

Like all oppressed peoples the self-image of Blacks has suffered damage. In addition they have not been in control of their own destiny. It is the goal of the Black liberation struggle to change radically the socio-economic and political conditions of Black people by inculcating self-love, self-control, self-reliance and political power. The concepts of self-love, self-control, self-reliance and political participation certainly have broad significance for Black women, even though they were taught that, by virtue of their sex, they had to be completely dependent on *man;* yet while their historical situation reflected the need for dependence, the powerlessness of Black men made it necessary for them to seek those values for themselves.

Racism and sexism are interrelated just as all forms of oppression are interrelated. Sexism, however, has a reality and significance of its own because it represents that peculiar form of oppression suffered by Black women at the hands of Black men. It is important to examine this reality of sexism as it operated in both the Black community and the Black Church. We will consider first the Black Church and secondly the Black community to determine to what extent Black Theology has measured up to its defined task with respect to the liberation of Black women.[10]

The Black Church and the Black Woman

I can agree with Karl Barth as he describes the peculiar function of theology as the church's "subjecting herself to a self-test." "She [the church] faces herself with the question of truth, i.e., she measures her action, her language about God, against her existence as a Church."[11]

On the one hand, Black Theology must continue to criticize classical theology and the White Church. But on the other hand, Black Theology must subject the Black Church to a "self-test." The task of the church, according to James Cone, is threefold: (1) "It proclaims the reality of divine liberation. . . . It is not possible to receive the good news of freedom and also keep it to ourselves; it must be told to the whole world. . . ." (2) "It actively shares in the liberation struggle." (3) It "is a visible manifestation that the gospel is a reality. . . . If it [the church] lives according to the old order (as it usually has), then no one will believe its message."[12] It is clear that Black Theology must ask whether or not the Black Church is faithful to this task. Moreover, the language of the Black Church about God must be consistent with its action.[13] These requirements of the church's faithfulness in the struggle for liberation have not been met as far as the issue of women is concerned.

If the liberation of women is not proclaimed, the church's proclamation cannot be about divine liberation. If the church does not share in the liberation struggle of Black women, its liberation struggle is not authentic. If women are oppressed, the church cannot possibly be "a visible manifestation that the gospel is a reality"—for the gospel cannot be real in that context. One can see the contradictions between the church's language or proclamation of liberation and its action by looking both at the status of Black women in the church as laity and Black women in the ordained ministry of the church.

It is often said that women are the "backbone" of the church. On the surface this may appear to be a compliment, especially when one considers the function of the backbone in the human anatomy. Theressa Hoover prefers to use the term "glue" to describe the function of women in the Black Church. In any case, the telling portion of the word backbone is "back." It has become apparent to me that most of the ministers who use this term have reference to location rather than function. What they really mean is that women are in the "background" and should be kept there. They are merely support workers. This is borne out by my observation that in many churches women are consistently given responsibilities in the kitchen, while men are elected or appointed to the important boards and leadership positions. While decisions and policies may be discussed in the kitchen, they are certainly not made there. Recently I conducted a study in one conference of the African Methodist Episcopal Church which indicated that women are accorded greater participation on the decision-making boards of smaller rather than larger churches.[14] This political maneuver helps to keep women "in their place" in the denomination as well as in the local congregations. The conspiracy to keep women relegated to the background is also aided by the continuous psychological and political strategizing that keeps women from realizing their own potential power in the church. Not only are they rewarded for performance in "backbone" or supportive positions, but they are penalized for trying to move from the backbone to the head position—the leadership of the church. It is by considering the distinction between prescribed support positions and the policy-making, leadership positions that the oppression of Black women in the Black Church can be seen more clearly.

For the most part, men have monopolized the ministry as a profession. The ministry of women as fully ordained clergypersons has always been controversial. The Black church fathers were unable to see the injustices of their own practices, even when they paralleled the injustices in the White Church against which they rebelled.

In the early nineteenth century, the Rev. Richard Allen perceived that it was unjust for Blacks, free and slaves, to be relegated to the balcony and restricted to a special time to pray and kneel at the communion table; for this he should be praised. Yet because of his acceptance of the patriarchal system Allen was unable to see the injustice in relegating women to one area of the church—the pews—by withholding ordination from women as he did in the case of Mrs. Jarena Lee.[15] Lee recorded Allen's response when she informed him of her call to "go preach the Gospel":

> He replied by asking in what sphere I wished to move in? I said, among the Methodists. He then replied, that a Mrs. Cook, a Methodist lady, had also some time before requested the same privilege; who it was believed, had done much good in the way of *exhortation*, and holding prayer meetings; and who had been permitted to do so by the *verbal license* of the preacher in charge at the time. But as to women preaching, he said that our Discipline knew nothing at all about it—that *it did not call* for women preachers.[16]

Because of this response Jarena Lee's preaching ministry was delayed for eight years. She was not unaware of the sexist injustice in Allen's response. "Oh how careful ought we be, lest through our by-laws of church government and discipline, we bring into disrepute even the word of life. For as unseemly as it may appear nowadays for a woman to preach, it should be remembered that nothing is impossible with God. And why should it be thought impossible, heterodox, or improper for a woman to preach, seeing the Saviour died for the woman as well as the man?"[17]

Another "colored minister of the gospel," Elizabeth, was greatly troubled over her call to preach, or more accurately, over the response of men to her call to preach. She said: "I often felt that I was unfit to assemble with the congregation with whom I had gathered. . . . I felt that I was despised on account of this gracious calling, and was looked upon as a speckled bird by the ministers to whom I looked for instruction . . . some [of the ministers] would cry out, 'you are an enthusiast,' and others said, 'the Discipline did not allow of any such division of work.'"[18] Sometime later when questioned about her authority to preach against slavery and her ordination status, she responded that she preached "not by the commission of men's hands: if the Lord had ordained me, I needed nothing better."[19] With this commitment to God rather than to a male-dominated church structure she led a fruitful ministry.

Mrs. Amanda Berry Smith, like Mrs. Jarena Lee, had to conduct her ministry outside the structure of the A.M.E. Church. Smith described herself as a "plain Christian woman" with "no money" and "no prominence."[20] But she was intrigued with the idea of attending the General Conference of 1872 in Nashville, Tennessee. Her inquiry into the cost of going to Nashville brought the following comments from some of the A.M.E. brethren:

> "I tell you, Sister, it will cost money to go down there; and if you ain't got plenty of it, it's no use to go"; . . . another said:
> "What does she want to go for?"
> "Woman preacher; they want to be ordained," was the reply.
> "I mean to fight that thing," said the other.
> "Yes, indeed, so will I," said another.[21]

The oppression of women in the ministry took many forms. In addition to not being granted ordination, the authenticity of "the call" of women was frequently put to the test. Lee, Elizabeth, and Smith spoke of the many souls they had brought to Christ through their preaching and singing in local Black congregations, as well as in White and mixed congregations. It was not until Bishop Richard Allen heard Jarena Lee preach that he was convinced that she was of the Spirit. He, however, still refused to ordain her. The "brethren," including some bishops of the 1872 General Conference of the A.M.E. Church, were convinced that Amanda Berry Smith was blessed with the Spirit of God after hearing her sing at a session held at Fisk University. Smith tells us that ". . . the Spirit of the Lord seemed to fall on all the people. The preachers got happy. . . ." This experience brought invitations for her to preach at several churches, but it did not bring an appointment to a local congregation as pastor or the right of ordination. She summed up the experience in this way: ". . . after that many of my brethren believed in me, especially as the question of ordination of women never was mooted in the Conference."[22]

Several Black denominations have since begun to ordain women.[23] But this matter of women preachers having the extra burden of proving their call to an extent not required of men still prevails in the Black Church today. A study in which I participated at Union Theological Seminary in New York City bears this out. Interviews with Black ministers of different denominations revealed that their prejudices against women, and especially women in the ministry, resulted in unfair expectations and unjust treatment of women ministers whom they encountered.[24]

It is the unfair expectations placed upon women and blatant discrimination that keeps them "in the pew" and "out of the pulpit." This matter of keeping women in the pew has been carried to ridiculous extremes. At the 1971 Annual Convocation of the National Conference of Black Churchmen,[25] held at the Liberty Baptist Church in Chicago, I was slightly amused when, as I approached the pulpit to place my cassette tape recorder near the speaker, Walter Fauntroy, as several brothers had already done, I was stopped by a man who informed me that I could not enter the pulpit area. When I asked why not, he directed me to the pastor who told me that women were not permitted in the pulpit, but that he would have a man place the recorder there for me. Although I could not believe that explanation a serious one, I agreed to have a man place it on the pulpit for me and returned to my seat in the sanctuary for the continuation of the convocation. The seriousness of the pastor's statement became clear to me later at that meeting when Mary Jane Patterson, a Presbyterian Church executive, was refused the right to speak from the pulpit.[26] This was clearly a case of sex discrimination in a Black church—keeping women "in the pew" and "out of the pulpit."

As far as the issue of women is concerned it is obvious that the Black Church described by C. Eric Lincoln has not fared much better than the Negro Church of E. Franklin Frazier.[27] The failure of the Black Church and Black Theology to proclaim explicitly the liberation of Black women indicates that they cannot claim to be agents of divine liberation. If the theology, like the church, has no word for Black women, its conception of liberation is inauthentic.

The Black Experience and the Black Woman

For the most part, Black churchmen have not dealt with the oppression of Black women in either the Black Church or the Black community. Frederick Douglass was one notable exception in the 19th century. His active advocacy for women's rights was a demonstration against the contradiction between preaching "justice for all" and practicing the continued oppression of women. He, therefore, "dared not claim a right [for himself] which he would not concede to women."[28] These words describe the convictions of a man who was active both in the church and in the larger Black community. This is significant because there is usually a direct relationship between what goes on in the Black Church and the Black secular community.

The status of Black women in the community parallels that of Black women in the church. Black Theology considers the Black experience to be the context out of which its questions about God and human existence are formulated. This is assumed to be the context in which God's revelation is received and interpreted. Only from the perspective of the poor and the oppressed can theology be adequately done. Arising out of the Black Power Movement of the 1960s, Black Theology purports to take seriously the experience of the larger community's struggle for liberation. But if this is, indeed, the case, Black Theology must function in the secular community in the same way as it should function in the church community. It must serve as a "self-test" to see whether the rhetoric or proclamation of the Black community's struggle for liberation is consistent with its practices. How does the "self-test" principle operate among the poor and the oppressed? Certainly Black Theology has spoken to some of the forms of oppression which exist within the community of the oppressed. Many of the injustices it has attacked are the same as those which gave rise to the prophets of the Old Testament. But the fact that Black Theology does not include sexism specifically as one of those injustices is all too evident. It suggests that the theologians do not understand sexism to be one of the oppressive realities of the Black community. Silence on this specific issue can only mean conformity with the status quo. The most prominent Black theologian, James Cone, has recently broken this silence. "The Black church, like all other churches, is a male dominated church. The difficulty that Black male ministers have in supporting the equality of women in the church and society stems partly from the lack of a clear liberation-criterion rooted in the gospel and in the present struggles of oppressed peoples. . . . It is truly amazing that many black male ministers, young and old, can hear the message of liberation in the gospel when related to racism but remain deaf to a similar message in the context of sexism. . . ."[29] It is difficult to understand how Black men manage to exclude the liberation of Black women from their interpretation of the liberating gospel. Any correct analysis of the poor and oppressed would reveal some interesting and inescapable facts about the situation of women within oppressed groups. Without succumbing to the long and fruitless debate of "who is more oppressed than whom?" I want to make some pointed suggestions to Black male theologians.

It would not be very difficult to argue that since Black women are the poorest of the poor, the most oppressed of the oppressed, their experience provides a most fruitful context for doing Black Theology. The research of Jacquelyne Jackson attests to the extreme deprivation of Black women. Jackson supports her claim with statistical data that "in comparison with black males and white males and females, black women yet constitute the most disadvantaged group in the U.S., as evidenced especially by their largely unenviable educational, occupational, employment and income levels, and availability of marital partners."[30] In other words, in spite of the "quite insignificant" educational advantage that Black women have over Black men, they have "had the greatest access to the worst jobs at the lowest earnings."[31] It is important to emphasize this fact in order to elevate to its rightful level of concern the condition of Black women, not only in the world at large, but in the Black community and the Black Church. It is my contention that if Black Theology speaks of the Black community as if the special problems of Black women do not exist, it is no different from the White Theology it claims to reject precisely because of its inability to take account of the existence of Black people in its theological formulations.

It is instructive to note that the experience of Black women working in the Black Power Movement further accented the problem of the oppression of women in the Black community. Because of their invisibility in the leadership of the movement they, like women of the church, provided the "support" segment of the movement. They filled the streets when numbers were needed for demonstrations. They stuffed the envelopes in the offices and performed other menial tasks. Kathleen Cleaver, in a *Black Scholar* interview, revealed some of the problems in the movement which caused her to become involved in women's liberation issues. While underscoring the crucial role played by women as Black Power activists, Kathleen Cleaver, nonetheless, acknowledged the presence of sex discrimination.

> I viewed myself as assisting everything that was done. . . . The form of assistance that women give in political movements to men is just as crucial as the leadership that men give to those movements. And this is something that is never recognized and never dealt with. *Because women are always relegated to assistance* and this is where I became interested in the liberation of women. Conflicts, constant conflicts came up, conflicts that would rise as a result of the fact that I was married to a member of the Central Committee and I was also an officer in the Party. Things that I would have suggested myself would be implemented. But if I suggested them the suggestion might be rejected. If they were suggested by a man the suggestion would be implemented.
>
> It seemed throughout the history of my working with the Party,

I always had to struggle with this. The suggestion itself was never viewed objectively. *The fact that the suggestion came from a woman gave it some lesser value.* And it seemed that it had something to do with the egos of the men involved. I know that the first demonstration that we had at the courthouse for Huey Newton I was very instrumental in organizing; the first time we went out on the soundtrucks, I was on the soundtrucks; the first leaflet we put out, I wrote; the first demonstration, I made up the pamphlets. And the members of that demonstration for the most part were women. I've noticed that throughout my dealings in the black movement in the United States, that the *most anxious, the most eager, the most active, the most quick to understand the problem and quick to move are women.*[32]

Cleaver exposed the fact that even when leadership was given to women, sexism lurked in the wings. As executive secretary of the Student Nonviolent Coordinating Committee (SNCC), Ruby Doris Robinson was described as the "heart beat of SNCC." Yet there were "the constant conflicts, the constant struggles that she was subjected to because she was a woman."[33]

Notwithstanding all the evidence to the contrary, some might want to argue that the central problem of Black women is related to their race and not their sex. Such an argument then presumes that the problem cannot be resolved apart from the Black struggle. I contend that as long as the Black struggle refuses to recognize and deal with its sexism, the idea that women will receive justice from that struggle alone will never work. It will not work because Black women will no longer allow Black men to ignore their unique problems and needs in the name of some distorted view of the "liberation of the total community." I would bring to the minds of the proponents of this argument the words of President Sekou Toure as he wrote about the role of African women in the revolution. He said, "If African women cannot possibly conduct their struggle in isolation from the struggle that our people wage for African liberation, African freedom, conversely, is not effective unless it brings about the liberation of African women."[34] Black men who have an investment in the patriarchal structure of White America and who intend to do Christian theology have yet to realize that if Jesus is liberator of the oppressed, all of the oppressed must be liberated. Perhaps the proponents of the argument that the cause of Black women must be subsumed under a larger cause should look to South African theologians Sabelo Ntwasa and Basil Moore. They affirm that "Black theology, as it struggles to formulate a theology of liberation relevant to South Africa, cannot afford to perpetuate any form of domination, not even male domination. If its liberation is not human enough to include the liberation of women, it will not be liberation."[35]

A Challenge to Black Theology

My central argument is this: Black Theology cannot continue to treat Black women as if they were invisible creatures who are on the outside looking into the Black experience, the Black Church, and the Black theological enterprise. It will have to deal with the community of believers in all aspects as integral parts of the whole community. Black Theology, therefore, must speak to the bishops who hide behind the statement, "Women don't want women pastors." It must speak to the pastors who say, "My church isn't ready for women preachers yet." It must teach the seminarians who feel that "women have no place in seminary." It must address the women in the church and community who are content and complacent with their oppression. It must challenge the educators who would reeducate the people on every issue except the issue of the dignity and equality of women.

Black women represent more than 50 percent of the Black community and more than 70 percent of the Black Church. How then can an authentic theology of liberation arise out of these communities without specifically addressing the liberation of the women in both places? Does the fact that certain questions are raised by Black women make them any less Black concerns? If, as I contend, the liberation of Black men and women is inseparable, then a radical split cannot be made between racism and sexism. Black women are oppressed by racism *and* sexism. It is therefore necessary that Black men and women be actively involved in combating both evils.

Only as Black women in greater numbers make their way from the background to the forefront will the true strength of the Black community be fully realized. There is already a heritage of strong Black women and men upon which a stronger nation can be built. There is a tradition which declares that God is at work in the experience of the Black woman. This tradition, in the context of the total Black experience, can provide data for the development of a wholistic Black Theology. Such a theology will repudiate the God of classical theology who is presented as an absolute Patriarch, a deserting father who created Black men and women and then "walked out" in the face of responsibility. Such a theology will look at the meaning of the total Jesus Christ Event; it will consider not only how God through Jesus Christ is related to the oppressed men, but to women as well. Such a theology will "allow" God through the Holy Spirit to work through persons without regard to race, sex, or class. This theology will exercise its prophetic function, and serve as a "self-test" in a church characterized by the sins of racism, sexism, and other forms of oppression. Until Black women theologians are fully participating in the theological enterprise, it is important to keep Black male theologians and Black leaders cognizant of their dereliction. They must be made aware of the fact that Black women are needed not only as Christian educators, but as theologians and church leaders. It is only when Black women and men share jointly the leadership in theology and in the church and community that the Black nation will become strong and liberated. Only then will there be the possibility that Black Theology can become a theology of divine liberation.

One final word for those who argue that the issues of racism and sexism are too complicated and should not be confused. I agree that the issues should not be "confused." But the elimination of both racism and sexism is so crucial for the liberation of Black persons that we cannot shrink from facing them together. Sojourner Truth tells us why this is so. In 1867 she spoke out on the issue of suffrage and what she said at that time is still relevant to us as we deal with the liberation of Black women today.

> I feel that if I have to answer for the deeds done in my body just as much as a man, I have a right to have just as much as a man. There is a great stir about colored men getting their rights, but not a word about the colored women; and if colored men get their rights, and not colored women theirs, you see the colored men will be masters over the women, and it will be just as bad as it was before. So I am for keeping the thing going while things are stirring: because if we wait till it is still, it will take a great while to get it going again. . . . [36]

Black women have to keep the issue of sexism "going" in the Black community, in the Black Church, and in Black Theology until it has been eliminated. To do otherwise means that they will be pushed aside until eternity. Therefore, with Sojourner Truth, I'm for "keeping things going while things are stirring. . . ."

NOTES

1. Beatriz Melano Couch, remarks on the feminist panel of Theology in the Americas Conference in Detroit in August 1975, printed in *Theology in the Americas,* ed. Sergio Torres and John Eagleson (Maryknoll, N.Y.: Orbis Books, 1976), p. 375.

2. Consuelo Urquiza, "A Message from a Hispanic-American Woman," *The Fifth Commission: A Monitor for Third World Concerns* IV (June-July 1978), insert. The Fifth Commission is a commission of the National Council of the Churches of Christ in the USA (NCC), 475 Riverside Drive, New York, N.Y.

3. I agree with the Fifth Commission that "the Third World is not a geographical entity, but rather the world of oppressed peoples in their struggle for liberation." In this sense, Black women are included in the term "Third World." However, in order to accent the peculiar identity,

problems, and needs of Black women in the First World or the Third
World contexts, I choose to make the distinction between Black and other
Third World women.

4. For a discussion of sexual dualisms in our society, see Rosemary Ruether,
   New Woman/New Earth (New York: Seabury Press, 1975), chap. 1; and
   Liberation Theology (New York: Paulist Press, 1972), pp. 16ff. Also for a
   discussion of sexual (social) dualisms as related to the brain hemispheres,
   see Sheila Collins, *A Different Heaven and Earth* (Valley Forge: Judson
   Press, 1974), pp. 169–70.

5. Angela Davis, "Reflections on the Black Woman's Role in the
   Community of Slaves," *The Black Scholar*, vol. 4, no. 3 (December 1971),
   pp. 3–15. I do take issue with Davis's point, however. The Black
   community may have experienced "equality in inequality," but this was
   forced on them from the dominant or enslaving community. She does not
   deal with the inequality within the community itself.

6. See Sheila Collins, op. cit., Rosemary Ruether, op. cit., Letty Russell,
   Human Liberation in the Feminist Perspective (Philadelphia: Westminster
   Press, 1974), and Mary Daly, *Beyond God and Father* (Boston: Beacon Press,
   1973).

7. Surely the factor of race would be absent, but one would have to do an
   in-depth analysis to determine the possible effect on the status of Black
   women.

8. James Cone, *A Black Theology of Liberation* (Philadelphia: J. B. Lippincott,
   1970), p. 23.

9. Eulalio Baltazar discusses color symbolism (white is good; black is evil) as
   a reflection of racism in the White Theology which perpetuates it. *The
   Dark Center: A Process Theology of Blackness* (New York: Paulist Press, 1973).

10. One may want to argue that Black Theology is not concerned with sexism
    but with racism. I will argue in this essay that such a theology could
    speak only half the truth, if truth at all.

11. Karl Barth, *Church Dogmatics*, vol. 1, part 1, p. 2.

12. Cone, op. cit., pp. 230–32.

13. James Cone and Albert Cleage do make this observation of the
    contemporary Black Church and its response to the struggles against
    racism. See Cleage, *The Black Messiah* (New York: Sheed and Ward, 1969),
    passim; and Cone, op. cit., passim.

14. A study that I conducted in the Philadelphia Conference of the African
    Methodist Episcopal Church, May 1976. It also included sporadic
    samplings of churches in other conferences in the First Episcopal District.
    As for example, a church of 1,660 members (500 men and 1,160 women)
    had a trustee board of 8 men and 1 woman and a steward board of 13
    men and 6 women. A church of 100 members (35 men and 65 women)
    had a trustee board of 5 men and 4 women and a steward board of 5 men
    and 4 women.

15. Jarena Lee, *The Life and Religious Experiences of Jarena Lee: A Colored Lady
    Giving an Account of Her Call to Preach the Gospel* (Philadelphia, 1836),
    printed in Dorothy Porter, ed., *Early Negro. Writing 1760–1837* (Boston:
    Beacon Press, 1971), pp. 494–514.

16. Ibid., p. 503 (italics added). Carol George in *Segregated Sabbaths* (New
    York: Oxford University Press, 1973) presents a very positive picture of

the relationship between Jarena Lee and Bishop Richard Allen. She feels that by the time Lee approached Allen, he had "modified his views on woman's rights" (p. 129). She contends that since Allen was free from the Methodist Church he was able to "determine his own policy" with respect to women under the auspices of the A.M.E. Church. It should be noted that Bishop Allen accepted the Rev. Jarena Lee as a woman preacher and not as an ordained preacher with full rights and privileges thereof. Even Carol George admitted that Lee traveled with Bishop Allen only "as an unofficial member of their delegation to conference sessions in New York and Baltimore," "to attend," not to participate in them. I agree that this does represent progress in Bishop Allen's view as compared to Lee's first approach; on the second approach, he was at least encouraging. Then he began "to promote her interests" (p. 129)— But he did not ordain her.

17. Ibid.

18. "Elizabeth: A Colored Minister of the Gospel," printed in Bert James Loewenberg and Ruth Bogin, eds., *Black Women in Nineteenth-Century American Life* (University Park, Pa.: The Pennsylvania State University Press, 1976), p. 132. The denomination of Elizabeth is not known to this writer. Her parents were Methodists, but she was separated from her parents at the age of eleven. However, the master from which she gained her freedom was Presbyterian. Her autobiography was published by the Philadelphia Quakers.

19. Ibid., p. 133.

20. Amanda Berry Smith, *An Autobiography: The Story of the Lord's Dealings with Mrs. Amanda Berry Smith, the Colored Evangelist* (Chicago, 1893), printed in Loewenberg and Bogin, op. cit., p. 157.

21. Ibid.

22. Ibid., p. 159.

23. The African Methodist Episcopal Church started ordaining women in 1948, according to the Rev. William P. Foley of Bridgestreet A.M.E. Church in Brooklyn, New York. The first ordained woman was Martha J. Keys.

   The African Methodist Episcopal Zion Church ordained women as early as 1884. At that time, Mrs. Julia A. Foote was ordained Deacon in the New York Annual Conference. In 1894 Mrs. Mary J. Small was ordained Deacon and in 1898, she was ordained Elder. See David Henry Bradley, Sr., *A History of the A.M.E. Zion Church*, vol. (part) II, 1872–1968 (Nashville: The Parthenon Press, 1970), pp. 384, 393.

   The Christian Methodist Episcopal Church enacted legislation to ordain women in the 1970 General Conference. Since then approximately 75 women have been ordained. See the Rev. N. Charles Thomas, general secretary of the C.M.E. Church and director of the Department of Ministry, Memphis, Tennessee.

   Many Baptist churches still do not ordain women. Some churches in the Pentecostal tradition do not ordain women. However, in some other Pentecostal churches, women are founders, pastors, elders, and bishops.

   In the case of the A.M.E.Z. Church, where women were ordained as early as 1884, the important question would be, what happened to the women who were ordained? In addition, all of these churches (except for those which do give leadership to women) should answer the following questions: Have women been assigned to pastor "class A" churches? Have women been appointed as presiding elders? (There is currently one woman presiding elder in the A.M.E. Church.) Have women been elected to serve as bishop of any of these churches? Have women served as presidents of conventions?

24. Yolande Herron, Jacquelyn Grant, Gwendolyn Johnson, and Samuel Roberts, "Black Women and the Field Education Experience at Union Theological Seminary: Problems and Prospects" (New York: Union Theological Seminary, May 1978).

25. This organization continues to call itself the National Conference of Black Churchmen despite the protests of women members.

26. NCBC has since made the decision to examine the policies of its host institutions (churches) to avoid the recurrence of such incidents.

27. E. Franklin Frazier, *The Negro Church in America*; C. Eric Lincoln, *The Black Church since Frazier* (New York: Schocken Books, 1974), passim.

28. Printed in Philip S. Foner, eds., *Frederick Douglass on Women's Rights* (Westport, Conn.: Greenwood Press), p. 51.

29. Cone, "Black Ecumenism and the Liberation Struggle," delivered at Yale University, February 16–17, 1978, and Quinn Chapel A.M.E. Church, May 22, 1978. In two other recent papers he has voiced concern on women's issues, relating them to the larger question of liberation. These papers are: "New Roles in the Ministry: A Theological Appraisal" and "Black Theology and the Black Church: Where Do We Go from Here?" Both papers appear in this volume.

30. Jacquelyne Jackson, "But Where Are the Men?" *The Black Scholar*, op. cit., p. 30.

31. Ibid., p. 32.

32. Kathleen Cleaver was interviewed by Sister Julia Herve. Ibid., pp. 55–56.

33. Ibid., p. 55.

34. Sedkou Toure, "The Role of Women in the Revolution," *The Black Scholar*, vol. 6, no. 6 (March 1975), p. 32.

35. Sabelo Ntwasa and Basil Moore, "The Concept of God in Black Theology," in *The Challenge of Black Theology in South Africa*, ed. Basil Moore (Atlanta, Ga.: John Knox Press, 1974), pp. 25–26.

36. Sojourner Truth, "Keeping the Things Going While Things Are Stirring," printed in Miriam Schneir, ed., *Feminism: The Essential Historical Writings* (New York: Random House, 1972), pp. 129–30.

● ● ● ● ●

"I Am Your Sister: Black Women Organizing Across Sexualities"

Audre Lorde

A teacher, librarian, feminist, and avowed lesbian, Audre Lorde was born in 1934 in New York City to West Indian immigrants. She attended St. Catherine's School, received a B.A. degree in 1959 from Hunter College and the M.L.S. degree in 1961 from Columbia University. As a child she was an avid reader; she would forge notes that permitted her to read public library books on the "closed shelf." An accomplished poet, Lorde's poetry collections include *The First Cities* (1968), *Cables to Rage* (1970), *From a Land Where Other People Live* (1973) (nominated in 1974 for the National Book Award), *New York Head Shop and Museum* (1975), *Coal* (1976), *Between Ourselves* (1976), *The Black Unicorn* (1978), *Chosen Poems: Old and New* (1982), and *Our Dead behind Us* (1986). Among her prose writings are the pamphlet "Uses of the Erotic: The Erotic as Power" (1978); *The Cancer Journals* (1980), which describes her battle with breast cancer and won the 1981 book award from the American Library Association Gay Caucus; an autobiography, *Zami: A New Spelling of My Name* (1982); a collection of essays and speeches, *Sister Outsider* (1984); and a collection of essays, *A Burst of Light* (1988). Most of these works address the issues of eroticism, homophobia, and heterosexism.

Audre Lorde admits that "being an open lesbian in the black community is not easy, although being closeted is even harder." She is particularly concerned about black women, some of whom refer to themselves as feminists, who shun her. Feminists have organized themselves to fight patriarchy, yet some of them ostracize other women, particularly lesbians, who do not adhere to the sexual preferences prescribed by an oppressive heterosexual society. Denying the erotic "on the part of some of our best minds, our most creative and analytical women, is disturbing and destructive," asserts Lorde. "Because we cannot fight old power in old power terms only, the only way we can do it is by creating another whole structure that touches every aspect of our existence, at the same time as we are resisting."[1]

In "I Am Your Sister: Black Women Organizing Across Sexualities," published in *A Burst of Light* (Firebrand, 1988), Lorde identifies heterosexism as one of the old powers to be resisted; it misleads straight women into thinking that lesbians are abnormal. Lorde appeals to straight black women to accept the lesbian as their sister so that they can combine their strengths to fight the oppressive hold that heterosexism has on them and focus their energies on the urgent problems in the community, such as "the destruction of our Black children and the theft of young Black minds."

NOTE

1. Audre Lorde, *Sister Outsider: Essays and Speeches* (Trumansburg, N.Y.: Crossing Press, 1984), 99, 102–3.

Whenever I come to Medgar Evers College I always feel a thrill of antici-pation and delight because it feels like coming home, like talking to fam-ily, having a chance to speak about things that are very important to me with people who matter the most. And this is particularly true when-ever I talk at the Women's Center. But, as with all families, we some-times find it difficult to deal constructively with the genuine differences between us and to recognize that unity does not require that we be iden-tical to each other. Black women are not one great vat of homogenized chocolate milk. We have many different faces, and we do not have to become each other in order to work together.

It is not easy for me to speak here with you as a Black Lesbian femi-nist, recognizing that some of the ways in which I identify myself make it difficult for you to hear me. But meeting across difference always re-quires mutual stretching, and until you *can* hear me as a Black Lesbian feminist, our strengths will not be truly available to each other as Black women.

Because I feel it is urgent that we not waste each other's resources, that we recognize each sister on her own terms so that we may better work together toward our mutual survival, I speak here about hetero-sexism and homophobia, two grave barriers to organizing among Black women. And so that we have a common language between us, I would like to define some of the terms I use: *Heterosexism*—a belief in the inher-ent superiority of one form of loving over all others and thereby the right to dominance; *Homophobia*—a terror surrounding feelings of love for members of the same sex and thereby a hatred of those feelings in others.

In the 1960s, when liberal white people decided that they didn't want to appear racist, they wore dashikis, and danced Black, and ate Black, and even married Black, but they did not want to feel Black or think Black, so they never even questioned the textures of their daily living (why should flesh-colored bandaids always be pink?) and then they wondered, "Why are those Black folks always taking offense so easily at the least little thing? Some of our best friends are Black. . . ."

Well, it is not necessary for some of your best friends to be Lesbian, although some of them probably are, no doubt. But it is necessary for you to stop oppressing me through false judgment. I do not want you to ignore my identity, nor do I want you to make it an insurmountable barrier between our sharing of strengths.

When I say I am a Black feminist, I mean I recognize that my power as well as my primary oppressions come as a result of my Blackness as well as my womanness, and therefore my struggles on both these fronts are inseparable.

When I say I am a Black Lesbian, I mean I am a woman whose primary focus of loving, physical as well as emotional, is directed to women. It does not mean I hate men. Far from it. The harshest attacks I have ever heard against Black men come from those women who are intimately bound to them and cannot free themselves from a subservient and silent position. I would never presume to speak about Black men the way I have heard some of my straight sisters talk about the men they are attached to. And of course that concerns me, because it reflects a situation of noncommunication in the heterosexual Black community that is far more truly threatening than the existence of Black Lesbians.

What does this have to do with Black women organizing?

I have heard it said—usually behind my back—that Black Lesbians are not normal. But what is normal in this deranged society by which we are all trapped? I remember, and so do many of you, when being Black was considered *not normal*, when they talked about us in whispers, tried to paint us, lynch us, bleach us, ignore us, pretend we did not exist. We called that racism.

I have heard it said that Black Lesbians are a threat to the Black family. But when 50 percent of children born to Black women are born out of wedlock, and 30 percent of all Black families are headed by women without husbands, we need to broaden and redefine what we mean by *family*.

I have heard it said that Black Lesbians will mean the death of the race. Yet Black Lesbians bear children in exactly the same way other women bear children, and a Lesbian household is simply another kind of family. Ask my son and daughter.

The terror of Black Lesbians is buried in that deep inner place where we have been taught to fear all difference—to kill it or ignore it. Be assured: loving women is not a communicable disease. You don't catch it like the common cold. Yet the one accusation that seems to render even the most vocal straight Black woman totally silent and ineffective is the suggestion that she might be a Black Lesbian.

If someone says you're Russian and you know you're not, you don't collapse into stunned silence. Even if someone calls you a bigamist, or a childbeater, and you know you're not, you don't crumple into bits. You say it's not true and keep on printing the posters. But let anyone, particularly a Black man, accuse a straight Black woman of being a Black *Lesbian*, and right away that sister becomes immobilized, as if that is the most horrible thing she could be, and must at all costs be proven false. That is homophobia. It is a waste of woman energy, and it puts a terrible weapon into the hands of your enemies to be used against you to silence you, to keep you docile and in line. It also serves to keep us isolated and apart.

I have heard it said that Black Lesbians are not political, that we have not been and are not involved in the struggles of Black people. But when I taught Black and Puerto Rican students writing at City College in the SEEK program in the sixties I was a Black Lesbian. I was a Black Lesbian when I helped organize and fight for the Black Studies Department of John Jay College. And because I was fifteen years younger then and less sure of myself, at one crucial moment I yielded to pressures that said I should step back for a Black man even though I knew him to be a serious error of choice, and I did, and he was. But I was a Black Lesbian then.

When my girlfriends and I went out in the car one July 4th night after fireworks with cans of white spray paint and our kids asleep in the back seat, one of us staying behind to keep the motor running and watch the kids while the other two worked our way down the suburban New Jersey street, spraying white paint over the black jockey statues, and their little red jackets, too, we were Black Lesbians.

When I drove through the Mississippi delta to Jackson in 1968 with a group of Black students from Tougaloo, another car full of redneck kids trying to bump us off the road all the way back into town, I was a Black Lesbian.

When I weaned my daughter in 1963 to go to Washington in August to work in the coffee tents along with Lena Horne, making coffee for the marshalls because that was what most Black women did in the 1963 March on Washington, I was a Black Lesbian.

When I taught a poetry workshop at Tougaloo, a small Black college in Mississippi, where white rowdies shot up the edge of campus every night, and I felt the joy of seeing young Black poets find their voices and power through words in our mutual growth, I was a Black Lesbian. And there are strong Black poets today who date their growth and awareness from those workshops.

When Yoli and I cooked curried chicken and beans and rice and took our extra blankets and pillows up the hill to the striking students occupying buildings at City College in 1969, demanding open admissions and the right to an education, I was a Black Lesbian. When I walked through the midnight hallways of Lehman College that same year, carrying Midol and Kotex pads for the young Black radical women taking part in the action, and we tried to persuade them that their place in the revolution was not ten paces behind Black men, that spreading their legs to the guys on the tables in the cafeteria was not a revolutionary act no matter what the brothers said, I was a Black Lesbian. When I picketed for Welfare Mothers' Rights, and against the enforced sterilization of young Black girls, when I fought institutionalized racism in the New York City schools, I was a Black Lesbian.

But you did not know it because we did not identify ourselves, so now you can say that Black Lesbians and Gay men have nothing to do with the struggles of the Black Nation.

And I am not alone.

When you read the words of Langston Hughes you are reading the words of a Black Gay man. When you read the words of Alice Dunbar-Nelson and Angelina Weld Grimké, poets of the Harlem Renaissance, you are reading the words of Black Lesbians. When you listen to the life-affirming voices of Bessie Smith and Ma Rainey, you are hearing Black Lesbian women. When you see the plays and read the words of Lorraine Hansberry, you are reading the words of a woman who loved women deeply.

Today, Lesbians and Gay men are some of the most active and engaged members of Art Against Apartheid, a group which is making visible and immediate our cultural responsibilities against the tragedy of South Africa. We have organizations such as the National Coalition of Black Lesbians and Gays, Dykes Against Racism Everywhere, and Men of All Colors Together, all of which are committed to and engaged in antiracist activity.

Homophobia and heterosexism mean you allow yourselves to be robbed of the sisterhood and strength of Black Lesbian women because you are afraid of being called a Lesbian yourself. Yet we share so many concerns as Black women, so much work to be done. The urgency of the destruction of our Black children and the theft of young Black minds are joint urgencies. Black children shot down or doped up on the streets of our cities are priorities for all of us. The fact of Black women's blood flowing with grim regularity in the streets and living rooms of Black communities is not a Black Lesbian rumor. It is sad statistical truth. The fact that there is widening and dangerous lack of communication around our differences between Black women and men is not a Black Lesbian plot. It is a reality that is starkly clarified as we see our young people becoming more and more uncaring of each other. Young Black boys believing that they can define their manhood between a sixth grade girl's legs, growing up believing that Black women and girls are the fitting target for their justifiable furies rather than the racist structures grinding us all into dust, these are not Black Lesbian myths. These are sad realities of Black communities today and of immediate concern to us all. We cannot afford to waste each other's energies in our common battles.

What does homophobia mean? It means that high-powered Black women are told it is not safe to attend a Conference on the Status of Women in Nairobi simply because we are Lesbians. It means that in a political action, you rob yourselves of the vital insight and energies of political women such as Betty Powell and Barbara Smith and Gwendolyn Rogers and Raymina Mays and Robin Christian and Yvonne Flowers.[1] It means another instance of the divide-and-conquer routine.

How do we organize around our differences, neither denying them nor blowing them up out of proportion?

The first step is an effort of will on your part. Try to remember to keep certain facts in mind. Black Lesbians are not apolitical. We have been a part of every freedom struggle within this country. Black Lesbians are not a threat to the Black family. Many of us have families of our own. We are not white, and we are not a disease. We are women who love women. This does not mean we are going to assault your daughters in an alley on Nostrand Avenue. It does not mean we are about to attack you if we pay you a compliment on your dress. It does not mean we only think about sex, any more than you only think about sex.

Even if you *do* believe any of these stereotypes about Black Lesbians, begin to practice *acting* like you don't believe them. Just as racist stereotypes are the problem of the white people who believe them, so also are homophobic stereotypes the problem of the heterosexuals who believe them. In other words, those stereotypes are yours to solve, not mine, and they are a terrible and wasteful barrier to our working together. I am not your enemy. We do not have to become each other's unique experiences and insights in order to share what we have learned through our particular battles for survival as Black women. . . .

There was a poster in the 1960s that was very popular: HE'S NOT BLACK, HE'S MY BROTHER! It used to infuriate me because it implied that the two were mutually exclusive—*he* couldn't be both brother and Black. Well, I do not want to be tolerated, nor misnamed. I want to be recognized.

I am a Black Lesbian, and I *am* your sister.

NOTE

1. Betty Powell is a black lesbian writer and activist and was a delegate to the International Women's Year Conference held in Houston, Texas, in 1977. Barbara Smith, a black lesbian feminist, is the founder of Kitchen Table: Women of Color Press, editor of *Home Girls: A Black Feminist Anthology* (1983), and coeditor of

Conditions: Five: The Black Woman's Issue and *All the Women Are White, All the Blacks Are Men, But Some of Us Are Brave* (1981). Gwendolyn Rogers, an Afro-Caribbean writer, was the national coordinator of the Lesbian and Gay Focus of the People's Anti-War Mobilization. She recently left the lesbian community. Raymina Mays is a black lesbian short-story writer who resides in North Carolina. Robin Christian is a lesbian poet and author of the self-published novel, *Lady, These Are for You* (1978). Yvonne Flowers, currently known as Maua Flowers, was a member of the now defunct Jemima Writers' Collective, a black lesbian writers' group in Bronx, New York, and a contributor, with Robin Christian and others, to *Jemima from the Heart* (1977), the collective's first published poetry volume.

Bibliography

"The Angela Davis Case." *Newsweek*, 26 October 1970, 18–22, 24.

Angelou, Maya. *I Know Why the Caged Bird Sings*. New York: Random House, 1969.

——. "Phenomenal Woman." In *And Still I Rise*, 8–10. New York: Random House, 1978.

——. *The Heart of a Woman*. New York: Bantam, 1981.

Aptheker, Bettina. *Woman's Legacy*. Amherst: University of Massachusetts Press, 1982.

Aptheker, Herbert. *Abolitionism: A Revolutionary Movement*. Boston: Twayne, 1989.

Bates, Daisy. *The Long Shadow of Little Rock*. New York: David McKay Co., 1962.

Beal, Frances. "Double Jeopardy: To Be Black and Female." In *Sisterhood Is Powerful: An Anthology of Writings from the Women's Liberation Movement*, ed. Robin Morgan, 382–96. New York: Random House/Vintage, 1970.

"Black Feminism: A New Mandate." *Ms.* 2 (May 1974): 97–100.

"A Black Feminist Statement: The Combahee River Collective." In *All the Women Are White, All the Men Are Black, But Some of Us Are Brave*, ed. Gloria T. Hull, et al., 13–22. Old Westbury, N.Y.: Feminist Press, 1982.

Blumberg, Rhoda Lois. *Civil Rights: The 1960s Freedom Struggle*. Boston: Twayne, 1984.

Bonner, Marita. "Patch Quilt." *The Crisis* 47 (March 1940): 71–72, 92.

Bracey, John H., Jr., ed. *Black Nationalism in America*. New York: Bobbs-Merrill, 1970.

Brisbane, Robert H. *Black Activism: Racial Revolution in the United States 1954–1970*. Valley Forge, N.Y.: Judson Press, 1974.

Bibliography

Brooks, Gwendolyn. *Maud Martha*. New York: Harper, 1953. Reprinted in Gwendolyn Brooks, *Blacks*. Chicago: David Co., 1987. 221–30.

——. *Report from Part One*. Detroit: Broadside Press, 1972.

——. "To Those of My Sisters Who Kept Their Naturals." Chicago: Brooks Press, 1980. Reprinted in Brooks, *Blacks*, 459–60.

Burns, Stewart. *Social Movements of the 1960s: Searching for Democracy*. Boston: Twayne, 1990.

Cairnes, John E. *The Slave Power: Its Character, Career, and Probable Designs*, 2d ed. New York: Augustus M. Kelly, 1968.

Carby, Hazel. *Reconstructing Womanhood: The Emergence of the Afro-American Woman Novelist*. New York: Oxford University Press, 1987.

Carmichael, Stokely, and Charles V. Hamilton. *Black Power: The Politics of Liberation in America*. New York: Vintage, 1967.

Chafe, William Henry. *The American Woman: Her Changing Social, Economic, and Political Roles, 1920–1970*. New York: Oxford University Press, 1972.

Chisholm, Shirley. "Facing the Abortion Question." From *Unbought and Unbossed*, 113–22. Boston: Houghton Mifflin, 1970.

Christian, Barbara. *Black Women Novelists: The Development of a Tradition, 1892–1976*. Westport, Conn.: Greenwood Press, 1980.

Clark, Septima Poinsette. *Echo in My Soul*. New York: E. P. Dutton, 1962.

Cooper, Gary. "Stagecoach Mary." *Ebony* 32 (October 1977): 96–98, 100–102.

Dandridge, Rita B. "The Motherhood Myth: Black Women and Christianity in *The Deity Nodded*," *MELUS* 12 (Fall 1985): 13–22.

——. *Ann Allen Shockley: An Annotated Primary and Secondary Bibliography*. Westport, Conn.: Greenwood Press, 1987.

Davis, Angela. *Angela Davis: An Autobiography*. New York: Random House, 1974.

——. *Women, Race, and Class*. New York: Random House, 1981.

Davis, John P. *The American Negro Reference Book*, 2 vols. Yonkers, N.Y.: Educational Heritage, 1966.

Drake, St. Clair. *Black Metropolis: A Study of Life in a Northern City*. New York: Harcourt, Brace, 1945.

Evans, Mari. *Black Women Writers (1950–1980): A Critical Evaluation*. New York: Anchor, 1984.

Evans, Sara. *Personal Politics: The Roots of Women's Liberation in the Civil Rights Movement and the New Left*. New York: Vintage, 1980.

Flexner, Eleanor. *Century of Struggle: The Woman's Rights Movement in the United States*. New York: Atheneum, 1970.

Gates, Henry Louis, Jr., ed. *Reading Black, Reading Feminist: A Critical Anthology*. New York: Meridian, 1990.

Grant, Jacquelyn. "Black Theology and the Black Woman." In *Black Theology: A Documentary History, 1966–1979*, ed. Gayraud S. Wilmore and James H. Cone, 418–33. Maryknoll, N.Y.: Orbis, 1979.

Hemenway, Robert. *Zora Neale Hurston: A Literary Biography*. Urbana: University of Illinois Press, 1976.

Hernton, Calvin C. *Sex and Racism in America*. New York: Grove Press, 1965.

Hine, Darlene Clark, ed. *Black Women in United States History*, 16 vols. Brooklyn, N.Y.: Carlson, 1990.

Hodge, John L., et al. *Cultural Bases of Racism and Group Oppression*. Berkeley, Calif.: Two Riders Press, 1975.

Holiday, Billie, with William Duffy. *Lady Sings the Blues*. 1956. Reprint. New York: Penguin, 1984.

Hooks, Bell. *Ain't I a Woman: Black Women and Feminism*. Boston: South End Press, 1981.

———. "Sisterhood: Political Solidarity between Women." in *Feminist Theory from Margin to Center*, 43–65. Boston: South End Press, 1984.

Hull, Gloria T., Patricia Bell Scott, and Barbara Smith, eds. *All the Women Are White, All the Blacks Are Men, But Some of Us Are Brave*. Old Westbury, N.Y.: Feminist Press, 1982.

Hurston, Zora Neale. *Their Eyes Were Watching God*. 1937. Reprint. Urbana: University of Illinois Press, 1978.

Jordan, Winthrop D. *White over Black: American Attitudes toward the Negro*. Chapel Hill: University of North Carolina Press, 1968.

Joseph, Gloria I. "Black Mothers and Daughters: Traditional and New Populations." *Sage* 1 (Fall 1984): 17–21.

Kanowitz, Leo. *Women and the Law: The Unfinished Revolution*. Albuquerque: University of New Mexico Press, 1969.

Katz, Maud White. "The Negro Woman and the Law." *Freedomways* 2 (Summer 1962): 278–86.

Keckley, Elizabeth. *Behind the Scenes: Thirty Years a Slave and Four Years in the White House*. 1868. Reprint. Salem, N.H.: Ayer, 1985.

King, Martin Luther, Jr. *Stride toward Freedom: The Montgomery Story*. New York: Harper & Row, 1958.

Koppelman, Susan, ed. *Between Mothers and Daughters: Stories across a Generation*. New York: Feminist Press, 1985.

Kovel, Joel. *White Racism: A Psychohistory*. New York: Pantheon, 1970.

Laws, Janice S., and Joyce Strickland. "Black Mothers and Daughters: A Clarification of the Relationship as an Impetus for Black Power," *Black Books Bulletin* 6 (1980): 26–29, 33.

Lee, Jarena. *Religious Experience and Journal of Mrs. Jarena Lee, Giving an Account of Her Call to Preach the Gospel*. Philadelphia: 1849.

Lerner, Gerda, ed. *Black Women in White America: A Documentary History*. New York: Random House, 1973.

Lewis, David Levering. *King: A Critical Biography*. New York: Praeger, 1970.

Lightfoot, Sara Lawrence. *Balm in Gilead: Journey of a Healer*. Radcliffe Biography Series. Reading, Mass.: Addison-Wesley, 1989.

Lincoln, C. Eric. *The Black Muslims in America*. Boston: Beacon Press, 1961.

Lorde, Audre. "I Am Your Sister: Black Women Organizing across Sexualities." In *A Burst of Light*, 19–26. Ithaca, N.Y.: Firebrand Books, 1988.

McDowell, Deborah E. "New Directions for Black Feminist Criticism." *Black American Literature Forum* 14 (Winter 1980): 153–59.

Millican, Arthenia J. Bates. *The Deity Nodded*. Detroit: Harlo, 1973.

Milner, Richard B., and Christina Milner. *Black Players*. Boston: Little, Brown and Co., 1972.

Minus, Marian. "Girl, Colored." *The Crisis* 47 (September 1940): 284, 297, 301.

Moody, Anne. *Coming of Age in Mississippi*. New York: Doubleday, 1969.

Morrison, Toni. *The Bluest Eye*. New York: Henry Holt and Co., 1970.

Moses, Wilson Jeremiah. *The Golden Age of Black Nationalism: 1850–1925*. Hamden, Conn.: Archon Books, 1978.

Naylor, Gloria. *The Women of Brewster Place,* New York: Viking Penguin, 1983.

Petry, Ann. *The Street*. Boston: Houghton Mifflin, 1946.

Quarles, Benjamin. *The Negro in the Making of America*. New York: Macmillan, 1969.

Rhodes, Crystal V. *The Trip*. In *Centerstage: An Anthology of Twenty-one Contemporary Black American Plays,* ed. Eileen Joyce Ostrow, 208–17. Oakland, Calif.: Sea Urchin Press, 1982.

Ringgold, Faith. "Being My Own Woman." In *Confirmation: An Anthology of African American Women,* ed. Amiri Baraka and Amina Baraka, 300–11. New York: Quill, 1983.

Rodgers, Carolyn. "I Have Been Hungry." In *How I Got Ovah,* 49–52. New York: Doubleday, 1975.

Roses, Lorraine Elena, and Ruth Elizabeth Randolph. *Harlem Renaissance and Beyond: Literary Biographies of One Hundred Black Women Writers 1900–1945*. Boston: G. K. Hall, 1990.

Sanchez, Sonia. *Uh, Uh; But How Do It Free Us?* In *The New Lafayette Theater Presents,* ed. Ed Bullins, 165–215. New York: Anchor, 1974.

Shakur, Assata. *Assata: An Autobiography*. Westport, Conn.: Lawrence Hill, 1987.

Shockley, Ann Allen. "To Be a Man." *Negro Digest* 18 (July 1969): 54–65.

———. "Is She Relevant?" *Black World* 2 (January 1971): 58–65.

———, ed. *Afro-American Women Writers 1746–1933: An Anthology and Critical Guide*. Boston: G. K. Hall, 1988.

Slater, Jack. "Sterilization: Newest Threat to the Poor." *Ebony* 38 (October 1973): 150–52, 154, 156.

Smith, Barbara. "Toward a Black Feminist Criticism." *Conditions: Two* 1 (October 1977).

———, ed. *Home Girls: A Black Feminist Anthology*. New York: Kitchen Table: Women of Color Press, 1983.

Smith, Bob. *They Closed Their Schools: Prince Edward County, Virginia, 1951–1964*. Chapel Hill: University of North Carolina Press, 1965.

Starobin, Robert S. *Industrial Slavery in the Old South*. New York: Oxford University Press, 1970.

Tate, Claudia, ed. *Black Women Writers at Work*. New York: Continuum, 1983.

Towns, Saundra. "The Black Woman as Whore: Genesis of the Myth." *Black Position* 3 (1973): 39–59.

Walker, Alice. "The Revenge of Hannah Kemhuff," In *In Love and Trouble: Stories of Black Women,* 60–80. New York: Harcourt Brace Jovanovich, 1973.

———. *Meridian*. New York: Harcourt Brace Jovanovich, 1976.

———. *In Search of Our Mothers' Gardens and Other Essays*. New York: Harcourt Brace Jovanovich, 1983.

Walker, Margaret. "On Being Female, Black and Free." In *The Writer and Her Work,* ed. Janet Sternburg, 95–106. New York: W. W. Norton, 1980.

Wallace, Michele. "Anger in Isolation: A Black Feminist's Search for Sisterhood." *Village Voice,* 28 July 1975, 6–7.

———. *Black Macho and the Myth of the Super-Woman.* New York: Warner, 1979.

Warner, William Lloyd, et al. *Color and Human Nature: Negro Personality Development in a Northern City.* Washington, D.C.: American Council on Education, 1941.

Washington, Mary Helen, ed. *Black-Eyed Susans: Classic Stories by and about Black Women.* New York: Anchor Books, 1975.

———. "Teaching *Black-Eyed Susans:* An Approach to the Study of Black Woman Writers." *Black American Literature Forum* 11 (Spring 1977): 22–24.

———, ed. *Midnight Birds: Stories by Contemporary Black Women Writers.* Garden City, N.Y.: Anchor/Doubleday, 1980.

———. *Invented Lives: Narratives of Black Women 1860–1960.* New York: Doubleday, 1987.

———, ed. *Black-Eyed Susans, Midnight Birds: Stories by and about Black Women.* New York: Doubleday, 1990.

West, Dorothy. "Mammy." *Opportunity* 18 (October 1940): 298–302.

White, Joseph L. *The Psychology of Blacks: An Afro-American Perspective.* Englewood Cliffs, N.J.: Prentice-Hall, 1984.

"The Woman Who Lived as a Man for Fifteen Years." *Ebony* 10 (November 1954): 93–98.

Works Progress Administration Collection. Box 119-6, folders 87–91. Manuscript Division, Moorland-Spingarn Research Center, Howard University, Washington, D.C.

Zak, Michele Wender, and Patricia A. Moots, eds. *Women and the Politics of Culture.* New York: Longman, 1983.

Index